GRAND CANYON
NATIONAL PARK

JENNIFER DENNISTON

AMY MARR

DAVID LUKAS

LONELY PLANET PUBLICATIONS
Melbourne · Oakland · London · Paris

Grand Canyon National Park
1st edition – March 2004

Published by
Lonely Planet Publications Pty Ltd ABN 36 005 607 983
90 Maribyrnong St, Footscray, Victoria 3011, Australia

Lonely Planet Offices
Australia Locked Bag 1, Footscray, Victoria 3011
USA 150 Linden St, Oakland, CA 94607
UK 72–82 Rosebery Ave, Clerkenwell, London EC1R 4RW
France 1 rue du Dahomey, 75011 Paris

Photographs
Many of the images in this guide are available for licensing from
Lonely Planet Images.
W www.lonelyplanetimages.com

Front cover photograph
Overlooking the canyon, Grand Canyon National Park
(Mark Newman/Lonely Planet Images)
Back cover photograph
Hopi pottery, Museum of Northern Arizona in Flagstaff
(Lee Foster/Lonely Planet Images)

ISBN 1 74059 561 0

GRAND CANYON
CONTENTS

THE AUTHORS

Jennifer Denniston

Born and raised in Chicago, by age 21 Jennifer had traveled independently across five continents. After college in upstate New York, she moved to sunny New Mexico and used her time there to explore the Southwest. In 1995, Jennifer returned to the Midwest, where she earned a master's degree in American Studies, with a focus on the American West and visual culture, and taught writing at the University of Iowa. She has written for Lonely Planet's *USA, Southwest* and *Arizona* books. She focuses her time writing on the Southwest and raising her children. She and her husband, Rhawn, live with their kids Anna Salinas and Harper Averett, and their dog, Cyril, in a small Iowa college town.

Amy Marr

Boston-bred Amy's first foray to the Grand Canyon was at age five, having already tackled Yellowstone at age two and Yosemite at age four. Since then, she has hoofed and pedaled through virtually every national park and all over the world. She worked as a business writer and PR director, led biking and hiking trips, then in 1998 moved to Santa Fe, where she managed *Outside Online*. Now a writer for magazines and a publisher of food books, she is firmly rooted in Marin County, California, but she still exhibits signs of restlessness. For Lonely Planet, she co-authored *Yosemite National Park* and contributed to *Yellowstone & Grand Teton National Parks*.

David Lukas

David has been an avid student of the natural world since he started memorizing field guides at age five. This same love took him around the world for 10 years to study animals and ecosystems in Borneo, the Amazon Basin, and Central America. Now working as a professional naturalist, David leads natural history tours, conducts biological surveys, and writes about natural history. His articles have appeared in *Audubon*, the *Los Angeles Times*, *Orion*, *Sunset*, and elsewhere. His most recent book is *Wild Birds of California*, and he just finished revising *Sierra Nevada Natural History*. David also contributed to Lonely Planet's *Yosemite National Park*, *Yellowstone & Grand Teton National Parks* and *Banff, Jasper & Glacier National Parks*.

Contributing Author

Kimberley O'Neil wrote the 'Rafting the Colorado' section of Experiencing the Grand Canyon, and the Bright Angel backcountry hike. Kimberley enjoys cycling, hiking, backpacking and rafting rivers around the globe. She coauthored (with her husband, John Mock) Lonely Planet's *Hiking in the Sierra Nevada*, winner of the 2002 National Outdoor Book Award , and *Trekking in the Karakoram & Hindukush*. She contributed to Lonely Planet's *Hiking in the USA, Rocky Mountains* and *Pakistan*.

From the Authors

Jennifer Denniston Thank you to Kathleen Munnelly. I appreciate your strong vision, your patience, your flexibility and your kindness. Thanks to Lonely Planet author Rob Rachowiecki, who showed me the ropes and continues to offer guidance. Thank you to editor David Lauterborn and to my talented and inspiring coauthors, Amy Marr, David Lukas and Kimberley O'Neil. I owe thanks to countless rangers and volunteers at Grand Canyon National Park. In particular, thanks to Madelyn Toland, the concierge at El Tovar, Susan Eubank at the Grand Canyon Library and Michael Quinn at the Grand Canyon Archives. Thanks also to Joy and Rudy Rasin for your support and for taking care of Cyril, to Steven Rasin for watching the girls while I wrote, and to Jamie Rasin. Finally, thanks to Anna, always the trooper on our travels; to Harper, who spent most of her first six months on the road without complaint; and especially to Rhawn. Without your help, I wouldn't have been able to write this book. I love you.

Amy Marr Thanks to all who offered information, trail tips, research company over a beer, and much positive encouragement during some very long and hot hiking days (and thankfully moonlit nights). At Lonely Planet, thanks to Kathleen Munnelly, Pete Wheelan, Todd Sotkiewicz, Jennifer Denniston, Kurt Wolff, and Graham Neale. In and around the park, Mike Hobbs, Tom Pettinger, Bette Anne Domilici, Pat Weber, Darren Brune, Tom Miller, Brian Park, Becky Douglas, Natalie Jenson and Mona Mesereau offered invaluable support, advice, regional insights and answers to my litany of questions. A special thanks to Maverick in Grand Canyon Village – I hope I'm still the spry hiker you are at age 77. *Grazie* to my all-star home posse and my *vado pazzo* cohorts in New Mexico. And lastly, thank you to my parents for their unrelenting support, and love and for my early, impressionable introduction to the national parks and outdoor adventure.

David Lukas Special thanks to Burnett and Mimi Miller for their generous hospitality and friendly company while I was researching and writing these chapters, and to Brett Hall Jones of the Squaw Valley Community of Writers for her unstinting support. Elaine Leslie of Grand Canyon National Park provided invaluable feedback and suggestions on the text, and Simone Whitecloud helped me understand and interpret the Grand Canyon's fascinating ecology.

Kimberly O'Neil My heartfelt gratitude goes to George Wendt for inviting me down the Colorado River. Thanks also to the guides, who made it a memorable journey – Bruce Helin for a great run through Lava and all the biggest rapids; his wife, Nancy, for her passion and grace; and Scott Stevens. A warm thanks also to Henny and Anna Marie Kruizinga for thier hospitality, and to Richard and Judith Montgomery.

THIS BOOK

The first edition of *Grand Canyon National Park* was researched and written by Jennifer Denniston, Amy Marr, David Lukas and Kim O'Neil. Coordinating author Jennifer Denniston researched and wrote the Introduction, Itineraries, Planning, Around the Grand Canyon and History chapters, as well as the majority of the Experiencing the Grand Canyon chapter. Amy Marr wrote the Activities chapter, as well as most of the hiking coverage in Experiencing the Grand Canyon. Kim O'Neil wrote the 'Rafting the Colorado' section of the Experiencing the Grand Canyon chapter, as well as the Bright Angel Trail backcountry hike. David Lukas wrote the Geology and Ecosystem chapters.

Credits

Grand Canyon National Park was produced in Lonely Planet's Oakland office under the leadership of US regional publishing manager, Maria Donohoe. The title was commissioned, developed and project managed by Kathleen Munnelly. Design manager Candice Jacobus designed the cover, color pages and the template for the series and the title. She oversaw layout by Emily Douglas and Shelley Firth, and chipped in on layout as well. David Lauterborn edited the book, and Wendy Taylor proofed, with the help of Alex Hershey, Wendy Smith and Suki Gear. Cartographer Bart Wright created the maps. Hayden Foell drew the illustrations. Ken DellaPenta compiled the index.

ACKNOWLEDGEMENTS

Grateful acknowledgement is made to Grand Canyon National Park for the use of their historic photos, and especially to Michael Quinn, of the Grand Canyon National Park Museum, for all of his help.

THE LONELY PLANET STORY

The story begins with a classic travel adventure: Tony and Maureen Wheeler's 1972 journey across Europe and Asia to Australia. There was no useful information about the overland trail then, so Tony and Maureen published the first Lonely Planet guidebook to meet a growing need.

From a kitchen table, Lonely Planet has grown to become the largest independent travel publisher in the world, with offices in Melbourne (Australia), Oakland (USA), London (UK) and Paris (France).

Today Lonely Planet guidebooks cover the globe. There is an ever-growing list of books and information in a variety of media. Some things haven't changed. The main aim is still to make it possible for adventurous travelers to get out there – to explore and better understand the world.

At Lonely Planet we believe travelers can make a positive contribution to the countries they visit – if they respect their host communities and spend their money wisely. Since 1986 a percentage of the income from each book has been donated to aid projects and human rights campaigns, and, more recently, to wildlife conservation.

SEND US YOUR FEEDBACK

We love to hear from travelers – your comments keep us on our toes and help make our books better. Our well-traveled team reads every word on what you loved or loathed about this book. Although we cannot reply individually to postal submissions, we always guarantee that your feedback goes straight to the appropriate authors, in time for the next edition. Each person who sends us information is thanked in the next edition – and the most useful submissions are rewarded with a free book.

To send us your updates – and find out about LP events, newsletters and travel news – visit our award-winning website: **www.lonelyplanet.com**.

Note: We may edit, reproduce and incorporate your comments in Lonely Planet products such as guidebooks, websites and digital products, so let us know if you don't want your comments reproduced or your name acknowledged. For a copy of our privacy policy, email privacy@lonelyplanet.com.au.

INTRODUCTION

A trip to Grand Canyon National Park is an iconic American experience. Initially dismissed as little more than an obstacle to exploration, the canyon first drew 19th century miners bent on exploiting its rich natural resources. Native American resistance and the lack of water slowed development, but by the time Frederick Jackson Turner declared the end of the American frontier in 1893, entrepreneurs had transformed the canyon into one of the country's most celebrated destinations. At the dawn of the industrial revolution, people flocked to the canyon in search of the romanticized wilderness ideal and embraced its sublime beauty. They still do – today, the park attracts five million visitors each year from around the world.

Perhaps the most obvious draw is the spectacular landscape. The Grand Canyon's dramatic scenery enthralls even the most jaded visitors and leaves all who witness it somehow changed.

Its dimensions are mind-blowing. The Grand Canyon is a mile deep and averages 10 miles wide. Snaking along its floor are 277 miles of the Colorado River, which has carved the canyon over the past six million years, exposing rocks up to two billion years old – half of Earth's total life span. Anyone with even a passing interest in geology will find this a fascinating natural classroom. Viewpoints on both rims point out the various gelological features, and rangers talks attract experts and novices alike.

The two rims of the Grand Canyon offer quite different experiences, and as they lie more than 200 miles apart by road, they are rarely visited on the same trip. Most visitors choose the South Rim, which boasts easy access, the bulk of services and the panoramic vistas for which the park is famous. The quieter North Rim has its own charms; at 8200ft elevation (1000ft higher than the South Rim), its cooler temperatures support wildflower meadows and tall, thick stands of aspen and spruce.

Hiking and rafting lure outdoor enthusiasts to the Grand Canyon year-round. With literally hundreds of miles of trails, including everything from moderate ambles through shaded woodland on the North Rim to treacherous scrambles on hot, inner-canyon trails, the park has something for hikers of every ability.

Trails from both rims descend into the canyon, and if you've got at least two days, you can hike from rim to rim. If you'd like to visit the inner canyon without hiking, take a mule trip, departing daily from both rims. Or consider a rafting trip. Each year more than 22,000 people raft the Colorado, and they're not all hardcore thrill-seekers; you'll find people of all ages, experience levels and capabilities on the river.

The canyon is also rich in human and cultural history. After an intensive survey of just 3% of the park, researchers have uncovered more than 4000 archeological resources, some stretching back nearly 10,000 years. Visitors can drive to such ancient sites as the Walhalla ruins on the North Rim or the Tusayan Ruins & Museum on the South Rim. Backcountry hikers can access other sites, including petroglyphs (etched images) and pictographs (painted images) along the canyon walls.

Despite the Grand Canyon's many riches, most visitors only spend a few hours in the park. It is possible to appreciate the canyon though a short stroll along the Rim Trail or an afternoon drive from viewpoint to viewpoint. But stay longer if you can. The more time you have, the more you'll discover its subtle nuances and quiet charm – a fairyland of moss deep in the canyon, a teasing creek cascading over rocks, echoes of history at ancient Pueblo Indian sites, and a silence and stillness that seem to engulf you. Even a short hike beneath the rim forms an intimate connection to the land that adds to the grandeur. Take your time, and let the Grand Canyon reveal its secrets.

Using This Guidebook

The heart of this book is the Experiencing the Grand Canyon chapter, which covers sights and activities on both the South and North Rims. Subsequent chapters on Places to Stay and Places to Eat list a host of accommodations and dining options in and around the park.

Not sure where to begin? The Highlights chapter offers a colorful introduction to the canyon's don't-miss sights, while the Itineraries chapter suggests several timetables, whether you're simply driving through or planning a two-week expedition to both rims. Planning the Trip is filled with such practical advice as when to go, how to get there, what to bring and how to arrange accommodations – even at the last minute. We've also included tips on how to avoid the summer crowds. You'll find lots of options for outdoor fun in Activities, including the best activities and programs for children.

If you have more time, consider exploring the areas described in Around the Grand Canyon, including Lake Mead National Recreation Area, the Havasupai Reservation and Lake Powell National Recreation Area. Cities like Flagstaff and Sedona are good spots to visit on your way to or from the park and provide visitors with additional accommodation and dining options.

The History, Geology and Ecosystem chapters present thorough, engaging details that will enhance any trip to the park. The book also offers detailed maps of the park and surrounding areas, making it easy to locate restaurants, hotels and sights. Finally, the Appendix neatly summarizes important websites and phone numbers.

ITINERARIES

Encompassing 1,217,403 acres (more than 1900 sq miles), the Grand Canyon is a huge park. With so much to see, it's hard to know where to begin. The following itineraries suggest how best to spend your time, including everything from drive-by glimpses of the canyon to extended two-week adventures. With the exception of a one-day visit by rail from Flagstaff, these itineraries require you to rent a car (or bring your own).

South Rim

If you have time to stop at only one overlook along Desert View Drive, make it **Lipan Point** (p89).

DRIVE-BY

- Visit the viewpoints along **Desert View Drive** (p88) – enter the park via the South Entrance, drive east along the rim and exit at the East Entrance, or vice versa.

FOUR HOURS

- Enter the park through the quieter East Entrance.
- Climb **The Watchtower** (p90).
- Continue west along **Desert View Drive** (p88), stopping at the **Tusayan Ruins & Museum** and **Lipan Point**.
- Enjoy lunch at **El Tovar** (p169).

ONE DAY

By Rail
- Board the **Grand Canyon Railway** (p184) in Williams at 10am to arrive at the park at 12:15pm.
- Visit the rim, then head to **El Tovar** (p169) for lunch.

- Walk west along the rim, stopping at the history room in **Bright Angel Lodge** (p91), then **Lookout Studio** and **Kolb Studio** (p93).
- Take the red Hermits Rest Route shuttle to **Pima Point** (p87) and stroll east along the **Rim Trail** (p95) for a few minutes.
- Catch another westbound shuttle to **Hermits Rest** (p87) and take in the sights.
- Return to **Grand Canyon Village** on an eastbound shuttle, walk the rim back to El Tovar, and return to the depot for the train back to Williams.
- In Williams, enjoy a steak dinner at **Rod's Steak House** (p187) or people-watch over a Mexican meal on the outdoor patio at **Pancho McGillicuddy's** (p186).

By Car

- Enter the park through the quieter East Entrance and climb **The Watchtower** (p90), then head west along **Desert View Drive** (p88). Stop en route at the **Tusayan Ruins & Museum** and **Lipan Point**.
- Drive to the unmarked dirt parking lot 6.3 miles west of Grandview Point, and walk the mile-long dirt road out to **Shoshone Point** (p95).
- Continue west to the village and lunch at **El Tovar** (p169).
- Shop for Native American crafts at **Hopi House** (p92).
- After lunch, take in an afternoon **ranger program** (check *The Guide* for a current schedule).
- Walk along the rim to the history room at **Bright Angel Lodge** (p91), then **Lookout Studio** and **Kolb Studio** (p93).
- Head into the canyon on the **South Kaibab Trail** to **Cedar Ridge** (p98; 2.8 miles round-trip).
- Dine at the Arizona Room in **Bright Angel Lodge** (p169).
- Take the red Hermits Rest Route shuttle to **Pima Point** (p87) or **Hopi Point** (p87) for the sunset.
- Exit via the South Entrance.

TWO DAYS

Day One

- Enter the park via the East Entrance and climb **The Watchtower** (p90).
- Buy picnic supplies at the general store (better yet, bring a cooler of supplies into the park).
- Head west along **Desert View Drive** (p88), making sure to stop at **Lipan Point** (p89) and the **Tusayan Ruins & Museum** (p89).
- Continue to the village and stop at **Canyon View Information Plaza** (p81). Browse the exhibits, peruse the bookstore, and stop at the information kiosks. Decide which **ranger program** you'd like to attend, and be sure to note the sunset time.
- Hike along the **Rim Trail** (p95) from Mather Point to Pipe Creek Vista or until you find the perfect picnic spot.

- In the afternoon, attend a **ranger program**.
- Visit **Yavapai Observation Deck** (p91), the history museum at **Bright Angel Lodge** (p91) and **Kolb Studio** (p93).
- Take the blue Village Route shuttle or walk along the **Rim Trail** (p95) as far as time and energy allow.
- Catch the red Hermits Rest Route shuttle to **Pima Point** (p87) for sunset.
- People-watch over hors d'oeuvres and a prickly-pear margarita on the back porch at **El Tovar** (p169), then dine inside.
- Spend the night in a **rim-view cabin** at Bright Angel Lodge or El Tovar.

Day Two

- Breakfast at El Tovar, then pick up a picnic lunch from the **Deli at Marketplace** (p168).
- Descend into the canyon via the **Bright Angel Trail** (p96). A 4.6-mile one-way hike will take you to Indian Garden, where you'll find picnic tables, water and restrooms. Alternatively, hike only as far as the Mile-and-a-Half Resthouse or Three-Mile Resthouse. More ambitious hikers should consider a day hike down the lovely **Grandview Trail** (p99).
- Ride the red Hermits Rest Route shuttle to viewpoints along **Hermit Road** (p86).
- Have an early dinner at the **Arizona Room** (p169) in Bright Angel Lodge before leaving the park.

FOUR DAYS

With four days, you can see some things outside the park. This itinerary starts in Flagstaff.

Day One

- After breakfast at **La Bellavia** (p194) in Flagstaff, head north on Hwy 89 toward Cameron.
- Hike along a lava flow at **Sunset Crater Volcano National Monument** (p190) and visit the ancient Pueblo ruins at **Wupatki National Monument** (p190).
- Stop at **Cameron Trading Post** (p163) to shop for Native American Crafts and lunch on Navajo cuisine.
- Take in the views and browse the craft stalls at **Little Colorado River Gorge Navajo Tribal Park** (p163), 10 miles west of Cameron.
- Enter the park through the **East Entrance** and climb **The Watchtower** (p90).
- Continue west to the village (hold off on the viewpoints till you have more time) and check into your lodge.
- Have a drink on the back porch at **El Tovar** (p169), followed by dinner.

Day Two

- Descend into the canyon on a full-day **mule trip** (p103) – be sure to eat a good breakfast at one of the cafeterias before you leave.
- Dine in the **Arizona Room** (p169) at Bright Angel Lodge.

Day Three

- Check *The Guide* over breakfast for that day's **ranger programs**. Plan your day accordingly.
- Walk along the **Rim Trail** (p95), stopping at the history room in **Bright Angel Lodge** (p91), **Hopi House** (p92), **Lookout Studio** (p93), **Kolb Studio** (p93), **Verkamp's Curios** (p93) and the **Yavapai Observation Deck** (p91).
- Finish at **Mather Point** (p88), then head to the bookstore and visitors center at **Canyon View Information Plaza** (p81).
- Pick up hot dogs or other picnic fare from **Canyon Village Marketplace** (p167) and visit **Apache Stables** (p175) for a campfire saunter or wagon ride into Kaibab National Forest.

Day Four

- Breakfast at El Tovar, then catch the red Hermits Rest Route shuttle to **Hermits Rest** (p87).
- Stop at viewpoints along this **driving tour** (p86).
- If you have the energy, hike between some points and ride the shuttle the rest of the way.
- Return to the village for lunch, then head east on **Desert View Drive** (p88).
- Stop at the unmarked parking area 1.2 miles east of Yaki Point, then hike the mile-long dirt road out to **Shoshone Point** (p95).
- Visit a few more viewpoints and the **Tusayan Ruins & Museum** (p89) before exiting the park via the East Entrance.

ONE WEEK

A week allows you a full day enjoying the sights on your way to the park. As this itinerary begins and ends in Flagstaff, it's best to fly directly into Flagstaff. Otherwise, it's just over two hours to Flagstaff from Phoenix.

Day One

- Spend the day in Flagstaff. A morning visit to the **Museum of Northern Arizona** (p189) and the **Pioneer Museum** (p189) will prepare you for a canyon visit.
- Pick up a picnic lunch at **New Frontiers Natural Food & Deli** (p197) and take it to the **Arboretum** (p189).
- After lunch, take a tour of the arts and crafts mansion at **Riordan Mansion Historic State Park** (p188), and drive to the **Arizona Snowbowl** (p191) for a scenic chairlift ride.
- Enjoy a tasty Mexican meal at **Café Olé** (p196), or Italian fare at **Pasto** (p196).
- Spend the night at the **Monte Vista** (p193) and catch live music at **Charly's** (p197).

Day Two

- After breakfast at **Café Espress** (p195), head toward the canyon.
- Before entering the park, stop at the **IMAX Theater** (p94).
- Park in the El Tovar parking lot and walk out to the rim.

Grand Canyon National Park

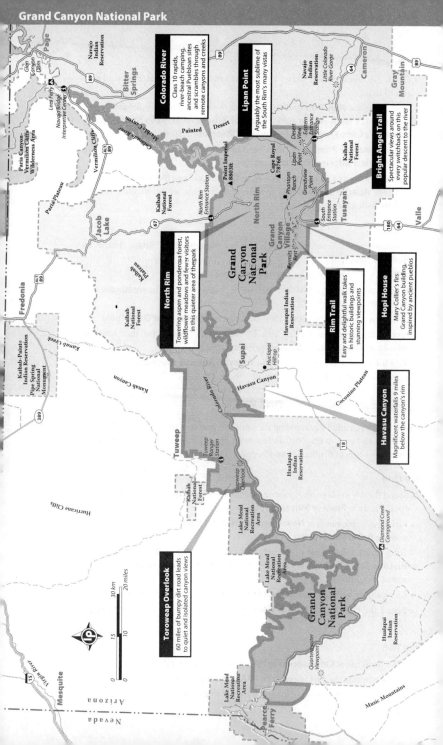

Colorado River
Class 10 rapids, river-beach camping, ancestral Puebloan sites and scrambles through remote canyons and creeks

Lipan Point
Arguably the most sublime of the South Rim's many vistas

Bright Angel Trail
Spectacular views around every switchback on this popular descent to the river

North Rim
Towering aspen and ponderosa forest, wildflower meadows and fewer visitors in this quieter area of the park

Hopi House
Mary Colter's first Grand Canyon building, inspired by ancient pueblos

Rim Trail
Easy and delightful walk takes in historic buildings and stunning viewpoints

Havasu Canyon
Magnificent waterfalls 9 miles below the canyon's rim

Toroweap Overlook
60 miles of bumpy dirt road leads to quiet and isolated canyon views

The magnificence of the Grand Canyon is difficult to express. Even grasping its sheer size is a visceral experience; words cannot prepare you for your first glimpse.

CURTIS MARTIN

GRAND CANYON **HIGHLIGHTS**

Photographs, too, can only capture images. They can't show you the butterscotch smell of the ponderosa pine or the feel of the dry, hot wind on your face. They can't show you the caw of the canyon raven or the sunset howl of the coyote. No matter how many photos of the canyon you admire, and how many you take yourself, the park's awesome drama ultimately cannot be understood through photos alone. You need to hike its dusty trails, breathe its air, listen to its silence. Until you do, however, these images offer teasing hints of the splendors you'll find.

THE WATCHTOWER Inspired by ancient pueblo towers, Mary Colter's 1932 building is the South Rim's highest overlook.

HOPI ART Reproductions of Native American paintings line the walls of the Watchtower.

MULE RIDES Saddle up for a bumpy and breathtaking ride down Bright Angel Trail.

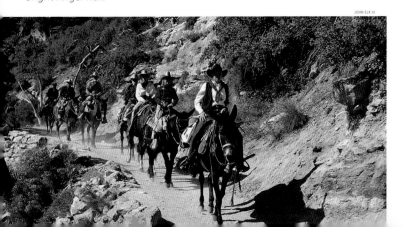

GRAND CANYON The canyon seems infinite beneath a bright blue Arizona sky.

COYOTE Unafraid of humans, coyotes are a common sight.

WILDFLOWERS A dazzling variety of wildflowers, like these Mojave Desert Stars, bloom inside the canyon.

BRIGHT ANGEL CREEK Backcountry campers enjoy a creekside site.

PIMA POINT Peer deep into the canyon from this former tourist hub.

RIBBON FALLS The lush oasis at Ribbon Falls is a recommended detour from the North Kaibab Trail.

NAVAJO ART Distinctive patterns decorate a traditional blanket.

TOROWEEP LOOKOUT A sunrise view of the Colorado River 3000 feet below.

HERMIT'S REST Take a break at Mary Colter's beautiful stone and wood shelter, designed to look like a hermit's den.

KAIBAB TRAIL One of the park's most popular trails, the Kaibab stretches from one rim to the other.

WUKOKI PUEBLO Abandoned mysteriously, the ruins of this pueblo lie within the Wupatki National Monument.

MOONEY FALLS Hikers descend a steep trail to a blue-green swimming hole at the bottom of these falls on the Havasupai Indian Reservation.

Barn Owl One of six owl species found in the Grand Canyon, barn owls use their excellent hearing to hunt rodents.

MARK NEWMAN

MICHAEL AW

Havasu Falls These lovely falls drop 100 feet into a sparkling pool surrounded by cotton-woods in the Havasupai Indian Reservation.

AROUND GRAND CANYON

Cathedral Rock Enjoy a sunset view of Cathedral Rock, near Sedona.

EMILY RIDDELL

MICHAEL AW

POWELL MEMORIAL POINT Grand Canyon National Park was officially dedicated at this spot in 1920.

CAROL POLICH

ANTELOPE CANYON This spectacularly scenic slot canyon is located on the Navajo Reservation.

LAKE POWELL Created by the Glen Canyon Dam, this huge man-made lake is now part of the Glen Canyon National Recreation Area.

MICHAEL AW

- Shop at **Hopi House** (p92) and **Verkamp's Curios** (p93) before heading to **El Tovar** (p169) for lunch.
- After lunch, stroll the **Rim Trail** (p95) to **Mather Point**, stopping at **Yavapai Observation Deck** (p91).
- Head over to **Canyon View Information Plaza** (p81) to check out the kiosks, visit the bookstore and decide which **ranger programs** you'd like to attend.
- Hike east 1.3 miles from Mather to **Pipe Creek Vista**, then take the green **Kaibab Trail Route** shuttle back to Canyon View Information Plaza.
- Ride back to your car on the blue Grand Canyon Village Route shuttle and check into your hotel.
- Ride the red Hermits Rest Route shuttle to **Pima Point** (p87) or **Hopi Point** (p87) for the sunset.
- Dine at one of the cafeterias and attend an evening **ranger program**.

Day Three

- Enroll in a one-day class through **Grand Canyon Field Institute** (p52) – you must arrange this in advance and plan your trip around it.

Day Four

- Wake early, grab coffee and a pastry from **Bright Angel Restaurant** (p168) and drive out to **Lipan Point** (p89) for sunrise.
- Return to the village, pick up picnic supplies from **Canyon Village Marketplace** (p167).
- Hike along the **Rim Trail** (p95) to **Hermits Rest**. If you run out of energy, hop aboard the shuttle.
- Picnic at **Hermits Rest** (p87) or somewhere en route, then hop the shuttle back to the village.
- Attend an afternoon **ranger program** and drive back to Flagstaff.

Day Five

- Hike into the canyon on the **Bright Angel Trail** (p125) and spend the night at **Phantom Ranch** (p128).

Day Six

- Hike out of the canyon on the **South Kaibab Trail** (p127).
- In the evening, relax with a prickly-pear margarita on the back porch of **El Tovar** (p169).
- Dine at El Tovar and spend the sixth night in Grand Canyon Village.

Day Seven

- In the morning stop by **Kolb Studio** (p93), the history museum at **Bright Angel Lodge** (p91) and **Lookout Studio** (p93).
- Take **Desert View Drive** (p88) out of the park, stopping to hike the mile-long dirt road to **Shoshone Point** (p95), visit the **Tusayan Ruins & Museum** (p89) and climb **The Watchtower** (p90).

This itinerary requires you to fly into Phoenix and out of Las Vegas. If you'd rather fly in and out of the same city, you can do so from Las Vegas but you will have to retrace your steps and you'll have less time to enjoy Flagstaff. It's 240 highway miles (four-and-a-half hours) from Las Vegas to Flagstaff, and 135 highway miles (two-and-a-half hours) from Phoenix to Flagstaff.

Week One

- Fly into Phoenix and drive to Flagstaff. Follow the One Week itinerary, above, adapting the first day according to your schedule.

Week Two

- Consider a **rafting trip** (p133) down the Colorado.

or

- Spend the seventh night at **Cameron Trading Post** (p163) and enjoy one week exploring the canyon and other sites outside the park like so:

Day Eight

- From Cameron, drive south on Hwy 89 toward Flagstaff, stopping to tour the Pueblo ruins at **Wupatki National Monument** (p190) and hike the lava flow at **Sunset Crater National Monument** (p190).
- After lunch, take a stroll through historic downtown in Flagstaff.
- Drive to Sedona and spend the night at **Sky Ranch Lodge** (p202) or **Briar Patch Inn** (p202), depending on your budget.
- If you didn't have time for some activities in Flagstaff on Day One, you'll have time this afternoon before driving to Sedona.

Day Nine

- Take a **horseback ride** (p201) through Oak Creek Canyon.
- Enjoy lunch at **Shugrue's Hillside Grill** (p204).
- After lunch, hike through red rock country.

Day Ten

- Browse through Sedona's shops and drive to Peach Springs.
- Spend the night at **Hualapai Lodge** (p181).

Day Eleven

- Hike into the spectacular **Havasu Canyon** (p177) and spend the next two nights at **Havasupai Lodge**.

Day Twelve

- Spend a leisurely day exploring Havasu Canyon's waterfalls and swimming in its azure pools.

Day Thirteen

- Hike out of Havasu Canyon.

- Drive to **Hoover Dam** (p207). Take a tour of the dam, eat dinner at **Best Cellars** (p210) in Boulder City and spend the night at **Lake Mead Lodge** (p209) on Lake Mead.

Day Fourteen
- Pick up a picnic lunch and rent a boat on **Lake Mead** (p207).
- Spend the day relaxing and swimming, then drive to **Las Vegas** and catch an evening flight home.

North Rim

DRIVE-BY

- Head straight to **Grand Canyon Lodge** (p164). Enjoy the view from the back porch.
- Walk out to **Bright Angel Point** (p114) and snap some photos.

FOUR HOURS

- Follow **Cape Royal Road** (p111) to its end, where a short paved walk leads to **Angels Window** and the cape.
- Head back for lunch at **Grand Canyon Lodge** (p173).
- Stroll out to **Bright Angel Point** (p114).

ONE DAY

- Take in the view from the back porch of **Grand Canyon Lodge** (p173).
- Walk out to **Bright Angel Point** (p114).
- Pick up picnic supplies from the **North Rim General Store** and head out on **Cape Royal Road** (p111), stopping en route at viewpoints and the **Walhalla Ruins**.
- Stroll out to **Angels Window** and the cape and enjoy a rim-view lunch at the Wedding Site picnic bench.
- Attend an afternoon **ranger program**.
- Hike a section of the **Widforss Trail** (p115).
- Rest on the back porch of the lodge before leaving the park.
- Stop outside the park to dine at **Kaibab Lodge** (p165) or **Jacob Lake Inn** (p173).

TWO DAYS

Day One
- Drive along **Cape Royal Road** (p111), stopping en route at viewpoints and the **Walhalla Ruins**. At road's end, walk out to **Angels Window** and the cape.
- Lunch at the snack shop and take in an afternoon **ranger program**.
- Hike a section of the **Widforss Trail** (p115).
- Grab a drink from the **Rough Rider Saloon**, head to the back porch of the **Grand Canyon Lodge** (p173) and relax in a rocking chair.

- Stroll out to **Bright Angel Point** (p114), followed by dinner at the lodge.
- Spend the night in a **Western Cabin** (p164).

Day Two
- Have an early breakfast at the lodge, then pick up picnic supplies at the general store.
- Descend into the canyon along the **North Kaibab Trail** (p118) and hike 4.7 miles to the picnic area at **Roaring Springs**.

FOUR DAYS

Four days on the North Rim allow you to relax at quiet vistas, enjoy leisurely hikes and take a mule trip into the canyon.

Day One
- Before entering the park, stop at the **Kaibab Plateau Visitor Center** (p211) to check road conditions out to **remote viewpoints** in Kaibab National Forest (p211) and to ask which trails might work best for a day trip or short hike.
- Pick up a picnic lunch next door at **Jacob Lake Inn** (p173) and head out to **Fire Point**, **Crazy Jug** or one of the other viewpoints (see North Kaibab National Forest map, p164). Enjoy a short hike and a quiet, rim-view picnic lunch.
- Drive to the **Grand Canyon Lodge**, check in to a **Western Cabin**, then relax on the back porch of the lodge with a drink from **Rough Rider Saloon**. Dine at the lodge.

Day Two
- Have breakfast at the lodge, then browse the visitor center bookstore.
- Pick up picnic supplies at the general store and hike the **Widforss Trail** (p115).
- Dine at the lodge, stroll out to **Bright Angel Point** (p114).
- Return to the back porch for the fireside Night Moves **ranger program** (9pm).

Day Three
- Take a full-day **mule trip** (p120) into the canyon.
- For dinner, grab something from the snack shop and dine on the front porch of your cabin.
- Head to the lodge auditorium for the evening **ranger program** (8pm).

Day Four
- Breakfast at the lodge.
- Pick up picnic supplies from the general store and head out on **Cape Royal Road** (p111), stopping en route at viewpoints and the **Walhalla Ruins**.
- At **Roosevelt Point** stroll the 0.2-mile loop through secluded woodlands to a great viewpoint.
- Lunch at the Wedding Site picnic bench, then walk out to **Angels Window** and **Cape Royal**.
- Attend an afternoon **ranger program**.

One of the difficulties of seeing the North Rim is that there aren't any nearby commercial airports. This itinerary begins in Kanab, Utah, a three-and-a-half-hour drive from Las Vegas. You could fly into Las Vegas and drive to the North Rim (five-and-a-half hours) on the same day, but you'd have to adapt Day One according to your flight schedule. Alternatively, allow an extra travel day.

Day One

- Grab a picnic from the **Vermilion Espresso Bar & Café** (p216) in Kanab.
- Drive the dirt road out to **Toroweap Overlook** (p113) for lunch and a short hike.
- Visit **Pipe Springs National Monument** (p214), if time allows, then head into the park.
- Enjoy a drink on the back porch of the **Grand Canyon Lodge** (p164), then walk out to **Bright Angel Point** (p114).
- Have dinner at the lodge.
- Spend the night in a **Western Cabin**.

Day Two

- Pick up picnic supplies at the general store and drive along **Cape Royal Road** (p111), stopping en route at viewpoints and the **Walhalla Ruins**.
- At road's end, stroll out to **Angels Window** and the cape.
- Stop for lunch at the Wedding Site picnic bench.
- Attend an afternoon **ranger program**.
- Hike the **Cape Final Trail** (p118).
- Grab something from the snack shop and dine on the porch at your cabin.
- Gather around the fireplace on the back porch of the **Grand Canyon Lodge** (p164) for the Night Moves **ranger program**.

Day Three

- Hike into the canyon on the **North Kaibab Trail** (p127) and spend the night at **Phantom Ranch** (p128).

Day Four

- Climb back out of the canyon, dine at the Grand Canyon Lodge and head to the its auditorium for the evening **ranger program** (9pm).

Day Five

- After breakfast at the Grand Canyon Lodge, pick up picnic supplies at the general store.
- Hike the forested, 10-mile round-trip **Widforss Trail** (p115).
- Relax with a book at your cabin, beneath a tree along the rim or on the back porch of the lodge.
- Dine at the **Grand Canyon Lodge** (p173).

Day Six

- Breakfast at the **Grand Canyon Lodge** (p164), pick up picnic supplies at the general store and head out of the park.
- Drive out to **Fire Point**, **Crazy Jug** or another remote viewpoint (p211). (If you're seeking a longer hike, ask at the park visitor center about hikes in Kaibab National Forest.)
- Check in to the **Kaibab Lodge** (p165). Before dinner at its restaurant, grab a cold drink from the general store across the street, sit on your cabin steps, chat with fellow guests and watch the deer come out at dusk to graze.

Day Seven

- Contact **Allen's Guided Tours** (p120) to arrange a morning horseback ride in **Kaibab National Forest** (p210).
- Head back to Las Vegas for an evening flight.

TWO WEEKS

Week One

- Follow the preceding One Week itinerary.

Week Two

- Raft the **Colorado River** (p133) or take a class with the **Grand Canyon Field Institute** (p52).

Both Rims

Though the rims are about 200 miles and four hours apart, it's an easy and beautiful drive with several well-spaced sites to stop and stretch your legs.

ONE WEEK

Even if you only have one week, consider flying in and out of Las Vegas and driving around the canyon to explore both rims. This itinerary allows you to enjoy two very different Grand Canyon experiences as well as some surrounding sites.

Day One

- Fly into Las Vegas, rent a car and drive four and a half hours to Flagstaff.
- As time allows, visit **Museum of Northern Arizona** (p189), tour **Riordan Mansion** (p188) and stroll through downtown Flagstaff.
- Dine at your choice of restaurants, then relax with a drink on the third-floor verandah at the **Zane Grey Room** (p197) in the **Weatherford**.
- Spend the night at the **Monte Vista** (p193) or the **Inn at 410** (p194).

Day Two

- Start with a meal at one of Flagstaff's excellent breakfast spots.
- Drive to Tusayan and stop at the **IMAX Theater** (p94).

- Enter the park through the South Entrance and drive straight to **Mather Point** (p88).
- Enjoy the view and walk east along the **Rim Trail** (p95) as time and energy allow.
- Stop by the **Canyon View Information Plaza** (p81) to peruse the bookstore and decide which **ranger programs** you'd like to attend.
- Grab lunch at one of the cafeterias.
- Spend the afternoon hiking and riding the shuttle to viewpoints along **Hermit Road** (p86). Don't miss Hermits Rest at road's end.
- Dine at the **Arizona Room** (p169) in Bright Angel Lodge and attend the evening **ranger program**.

Day Three

- Spend part of the morning visiting sights in **Grand Canyon Village**.
- Browse through the **Hopi House** (p92) and stop by the history museum at **Bright Angel Lodge** (p91).
- Pick up picnic supplies and head into the canyon along the **Grandview Trail** (p99) to Horseshoe Mesa (6 miles round-trip).
- Relax with a drink on the back porch of **El Tovar** (p169) and stay for dinner.

Day Four

- After an early breakfast at El Tovar, leave the park via **Desert View Drive** (p88).
- On the way, hike the mile-long dirt road out to **Shoshone Point** (p95), visit the **Tusayan Ruins & Museum** (p89), stop at a few viewpoints and climb **The Watchtower** (p90).
- Drive to Cameron and stop at the **Little Colorado River Gorge Navajo Tribal Park** (p163). Here you'll find a scenic overlook and Navajo families selling crafts.
- Savor the Native American fare at **Cameron Trading Post** (p163) and shop for more crafts.
- Head to the **North Rim**, stopping for a stroll on **Navajo Bridge** (p218) and a hike through historic buildings at **Lees Ferry** (p217) as time allows.
- Pop into **Jacob Lake Inn** (p173) for a snack and a drink. Also visit the museum at the **Kaibab Plateau Visitor Center** (p211).
- Enjoy a drink on the back porch of **Grand Canyon Lodge** (p173), stroll out to **Bright Angel Point** (p114) for the sunset, then head inside for dinner.
- Spend the night in a **Western Cabin** (p164).

Day Five

- After breakfast at the lodge, pick up picnic supplies at the general store and hike part of the **Widforss Trail** (p115).
- Take **Cape Royal Road** (p111). Stop en route at viewpoints and the **Walhalla Ruins** and hike out to **Angels Window** and the cape.
- Attend an afternoon **ranger program**.
- Dine at the lodge and gather around the fireplace on the back porch for the Night Moves **ranger program**.

Day Six

- After breakfast at the lodge or a pastry from the **Rough Rider Saloon**, check road conditions at the visitors center.
- Pick up picnic supplies from the general store, then drive through **Kaibab National Forest** (p211) to remote canyon overlooks.
- Spend the night at **Kaibab Lodge** (p165). Before dinner at the lodge, grab a cold drink from the general store across the street, sit on your cabin steps, chat with fellow guests and watch the deer come out to graze.

Day Seven

- Enjoy a **horseback ride** through **Kaibab National Forest** (p210).
- Drive back to **Las Vegas** (about five hours from Jacob Lake) and catch an evening flight home.

TWO WEEKS

These extended trips to the Grand Canyon include some time visiting surrounding sites. You'll either need to drive your own car to the region or arrange to fly in and out of different airports (and return your rental car to the second one). For that reason, these trips are best for those enjoying a leisurely road trip through the USA. The two itineraries below offer one option that includes a week-long raft trip and one option that does not.

TWO WEEKS WITH A RAFT TRIP OR A CLASS

Week One

- Raft the Colorado River (p133) or take a one-week class with the **Grand Canyon Field Institute** (p52).

Week Two
Days Seven to Ten

- Drive to the North Rim, and follow the itinerary for Four Days on the North Rim.
- Adapt Day Seven to your schedule.
- During the afternoon of Day Ten, drive to the South Rim East Entrance, stopping at **Navajo Bridge** (p218), **Lees Ferry** (p217) and **Cameron Trading Post** (p163) as time allows. Save stops on Desert View Drive for when you have more time.

Day Eleven

- Wake early, grab coffee and a pastry from **Bright Angel Restaurant** (p168) and drive out to **Lipan Point** (p89) for sunrise.
- Return to the village, pick up picnic supplies from **Canyon Village Marketplace** (p167) and hike along the **Rim Trail** (p95) to Hermits Rest. If you run out of energy, hop aboard the shuttle.
- Picnic at **Hermits Rest** (p87) or somewhere en route, then hop the shuttle back to the village.
- Attend a **ranger program**.

Day Twelve
- Hike into the canyon on the **Bright Angel Trail** (p125) and spend the night at **Phantom Ranch** (p128).

Day Thirteen
- Hike out of the canyon on the **South Kaibab Trail** (p127).
- In the evening, relax with a prickly pear margarita on the back porch of **El Tovar** (p169).
- Dine at El Tovar and spend the night in Grand Canyon Village.

Day Fourteen
- In the morning stop by **Kolb Studio** (p93), the history museum at **Bright Angel Lodge** (p91) and **Lookout Studio** (p93) before picking up picnic supplies at **Canyon Village Marketplace** (p167).
- Take **Desert View Drive** (p88) out of the park, stopping to hike the mile-long dirt road to **Shoshone Point** (p95), visit the **Tusayan Ruins & Museum** (p89), and climb **The Watchtower** (p90).
- Drive to Flagstaff, stopping to visit the ancient Pueblo ruins at **Wuptaki National Monument** (p190) and hike along a lava flow at **Sunset Crater Volcano National Monument** (p190).

TWO WEEKS WITHOUT A RAFT TRIP

This trip begins in Flagstaff and ends a couple hours north of the North Rim. If you need to catch a return flight home from Las Vegas, Flagstaff or Phoenix, adjust Day Fourteen to accommodate your flight schedule or spend the fourteenth night in Kanab, Utah and allow an extra day for travel home.

Week One
- Follow the itinerary for One Week on the South Rim.
- After exiting the park on Day Seven, drive to Page and spend the night at **Uncle Bill's** (p224).

Week Two
Day Eight
- Rent a boat on **Lake Powell** (p222) – explore the coves, swim and relax.
- Hike to **Horseshoe Bend View** (p223).
- Drive to LeesFerry and spend the night at **LeesFerry Lodge/Vermilion Cliffs Bar & Grill** (p219).

Day Nine
- Walk along **Navajo Bridge** (p218) and hike through the **LeesFerry historic district** (p218).
- Continue on to the North Rim, stopping at **Jacob Lake Inn** (p173) and the Kaibab Plateau Visitors Center for a drink and a snack.
- Take an afternoon **horseback ride** through **Kaibab National Forest** (p210).

- Enjoy a drink on the back porch of **Grand Canyon Lodge** (p164), stroll out to **Bright Angel Point** (p114) for the sunset, then head inside for dinner.
- Spend the night at Western Cabin at the North Rim Lodge.

Day Ten

- After breakfast at the lodge, pick up picnic supplies at the general store.
- Hike the **Widforss Trail** (p115).
- Grab something from the snack shop and dine on the porch at your cabin.

Day Eleven

- Take a full-day **mule trip** (p120) into the canyon.
- Relax with a book at your cabin, beneath a tree along the rim or on the back porch of the lodge.
- Head to the lodge for dinner and the evening **ranger program** (8pm).

Day Twelve

- Pick up picnic supplies at the general store and drive along **Cape Royal Road** (p111), stopping en route at viewpoints and the **Walhalla Ruins**. At road's end, stroll out to **Angels Window** and the cape, then stop for lunch at the Wedding Site picnic bench.
- Attend an afternoon **ranger program**.
- Hike the **Cape Final Trail** (p118).
- Eat dinner at the lodge or the snack shop, and gather around the fireplace on the back porch of the lodge for the Night Moves **ranger program**.

Day Thirteen

- Breakfast at the lodge, pick up picnic supplies at the general store and head out of the park.
- Drive out to **Fire Point**, **Crazy Jug** or another remote viewpoint (see North Kaibab National Forest Map 6). If you're seeking a longer hike, ask at the park visitors center about hikes in Kaibab National Forest.
- Spend the night at **Kaibab Lodge** (p165). Before dinner at the lodge, grab a cold drink from the general store across the street, sit on your cabin steps, chat with fellow guests and watch the deer come out to graze.

Day Fourteen

- Head out early, pick up a picnic lunch at Jacob Lake Lodge, and drive out to **Toroweap Overlook** (p113) for lunch and a short hike.
- Visit **Pipe Springs National Monument** (p214).

GRAND CANYON NATIONAL PARK

Encompassing more than 1.2 million acres, the Grand Canyon certainly lends itself to hands-on exploration.

ACTIVITIES

The Grand Canyon's soaring cliffs and almost incomprehensible scope can be overwhelming, and each year thousands of visitors drive to the rim, peer over the edge in awe, then retreat to their cars. To truly come to terms with the canyon, it helps to throw yourself into it (please, not literally), and there's no better remedy than active exploration. You'll find an abundance of outdoor activities catered to individual interests and skill levels. Whether you explore the canyon by foot, raft, horse, mule, helicopter or bike, your visit will be greatly enhanced.

The majority of activities center on the two rims. Open year-round, the bustling **South Rim** serves as park central, drawing the bulk of visitors and offering the most recreational options. A thousand feet higher, the forested **North Rim** (open from mid-May through mid-October) is more remote and serene. Stretching between the two is the mighty 10-mile-wide canyon, laced with trails and bisected by the roaring Colorado River.

Hiking is perhaps the finest way to take in the scenery, as you escape the rim along an ancient trail, gaze up at rocky spires, search for wildlife and smell the wild sage. Choose from a superb array of hikes, from gentle half-hour rim walks to challenging day hikes and multi-day backcountry treks. **Rafting** the Colorado is a life-affirming thrill and the most exhilarating way to experience the inner canyon, while **mule trekking** offers a more leisurely means of visiting the floor. Others opt for **horseback riding** along the rim. Long stretches of roads with stunning views make for enjoyable **biking**, and gentle rim-side trails are good for **walking** and **running**. In winter the North Rim offers the adventurous plenty of terrain for **cross-country skiing** and **snowshoeing**.

Surrounding the Grand Canyon are several immense plateaus – the **Kaibab**, **Paria**, **Kanab** and **Walhalla** lying to the north, and the **Coconino** spanning the entire South Rim – and the easy-to-reach **Kaibab National Forest**, as well as numerous national wilderness and recreation areas and national monuments. Within this outdoor playground you'll find a broad network of trails and wilderness access points, campgrounds, spunky Western towns and a bevy of activities to complement your Grand Canyon experience.

This chapter offers general planning information for activities within the park and beyond. Time of year is the biggest factor when planning your trip. Use the lists and charts to decide what activities you want to do and where. More specific details are covered within the Experiencing the Grand Canyon chapter (p76), under South Rim and North Rim, respectively. Refer to Around the Grand Canyon (p174) for additional information on areas outside the park.

Hiking

Hiking is the most popular and accessible activity within the park, with plenty of options for beginners and backcountry experts alike. Many day hikes are segments of longer trails that extend into backcountry excursions. Switchbacks are common, and shade is often limited, but the dazzling views are worth the effort.

BEST SHORT HIKES ON LONGER TRAILS

For a short, scenic jaunt along a rim-to-river trail, try one of these (distances are round-trip):

✔ **South Kaibab to Cedar Ridge** (3 miles)

✔ **Bright Angel to Mile-and-a-Half Resthouse** (3 miles)

✔ **North Kaibab to Supai Tunnel** (4 miles)

✔ **Grandview to Coconino Saddle** (1.5 miles)

You can hike the canyon year-round. Though the best seasons are spring and fall, most hikers hit the trail in summer, when hot temperatures exact a toll and require special caution. Promising snow-dusted buttes and crisp blue days, winter hiking is spectacular, though only the South Rim remains open. You can still hike into the canyon from the North Rim after the first major snowfall, but you'll have to purchase a backcountry camping permit and then ski or snowshoe 44 miles to the rim. Trails are often icy in the early morning – to safeguard against glissading into the canyon, outfit yourself with a pair of crampons, which cost about $10 and are available at the Grand Canyon Village general store.

Most hikes start on either the South Rim or North Rim, with the highest concentration on the former. Ideal for kids and hikers of all levels, **rim trails** keep to the canyon's lip and afford stellar (albeit distant) vistas with little elevation change. These easily accessible, partially paved trails can get quite crowded. From the South Rim, the **river-bound trails**, most of which are drainage routes, stretch to the floor over 7 to 10 miles. The North Rim lies farther back and above the river, requiring a longer haul of 14 miles and at least one overnight en route.

Perennial favorites include the **corridor trails** – **Bright Angel**, **South Kaibab** and **North Kaibab** – which spiral from rim to river, crisscross the canyon and provide the most direct backcountry access. The legendary Kaibab is the park's only rim-to-rim hike, a 21-mile jaunt (see The Kaibab: A Rim-to-Rim Favorite, p42). Each of the corridor trails is clearly signed, carefully maintained and heavily trafficked by feet and hooves alike. Though they may feel like superhighways in summer, plan on hiking at least one of these magnificent trails, if only for a short distance. While some inevitably complain about the crowds, an equal number are content to share the vast canyon with company. You'll find plenty of less-crowded South Rim forays, like **Dipping Spring** and **Shoshone Point**, and peace is easy to find along the remote North Rim trails.

Hiking here is markedly different than hiking most anywhere else. The sheer terrain is uniquely challenging, made even more so by the environment and climate. Many trails begin with sharp descents, which translate to equally steep ascents at the end of the hike, when you're most exhausted. Add in the effects of altitude, hefty elevation changes and the desert environment, and you've got a set of circumstances that require heightened awareness and preparation. The key to enjoying the Grand Canyon on foot is to take proper precautions, respect your limitations and select hikes that best match your ability. Please refer to our comprehensive hiking charts (pp38-9, 40) and detailed trail descriptions for suggestions.

For good hiking beyond the park, head north to the **Kaibab National Forest**, where you'll find cooler summer temperatures, fewer people and a robust network of trails. Try **Snake Gulch** (which connects to **Kanab Creek**), regarded as one of the best places along the **Colorado Plateau** to see **petroglyphs**. The trailhead is off of Hwy 22, just south of Fredonia. Stop by the **Kaibab Plateau Visitor Center** (☎ 928-643-7298; open 8am-5pm) in Jacob Lake for trail information. Michael Kelsey's *Canyon Hiking Guide to the Colorado Plateau* offers detailed descriptions for dozens of hikes, many of which dip in and out of the park.

COOL TRAILS FOR A HOT DAY

Looking for a reprieve from the scorching sun? Hit one of the following trails (see the Experiencing the Grand Canyon chapter for full hike descriptions). Tip: The less-exposed, higher-altitude North Rim is the better choice when trees and shade are priorities.

✔ **Cliff Springs** (p117) – Short and sweet, this trail starts out as a sunny downhill, then cools with each step as it dips beneath overhangs, hugs a sandstone wall and ends at a misty, fern-fringed oasis.

✔ **Transept** (p115) – Wending along the rim of its namesake canyon, this trail offers a nice mix of sun and shade, open and hidden overlooks and refreshing breezes from below.

✔ **Widforss** (p115) – If you're after a longer cool hike, this is the star. The trail ribbons through aspen groves, swings by several views and offers a soothing mix of sun and shade, with a nice picnic spot at the turnaround.

✔ **Shoshone Point** (p95) – An almost entirely shaded ramble through a patch of South Rim pine forest, this trail ends at a gorgeous overlook.

DIFFICULTY LEVEL

From first-timers to veteran hikers, everyone will find suitable trails within the park. Most hikes involve some elevation change, from as little as 100ft to 7000ft. But most trails are also out-and-backs that cover the same stretch in both directions, making it easy to cater a hike to your abilities. On trails headed down to the Colorado River,

NAME	TYPE	LOCATION (STARTING)	DISTANCE (R/T)	DURATION (R/T)	CHALLENGE	ELEVATION CHANGE	FEATURES	FACILITIES	DESCRIPTION	PAGE
Rim	Day Hike	Hermits Rest/ Pipe Creek Vista	13mi (one way)	varies	easy-moderate	200ft			Popular paved and dirt point-to-point trail that winds along the South Rim, connecting the stunning overlooks.	95
SOUTH KAIBAB										
Cedar Ridge	Day Hike/ Mules	Yaki Point	3mi	1-2 hrs	moderate	1140ft			Short, steep and very scenic hike on the only corridor trail that descends along a ridgecrest. Gorgeous at sunrise.	98
Skeleton Point	Day Hike/ Mules	Yaki Point	6mi	3-5 hrs	moderate-difficult	2040ft			Panoramic views and a challenging day hike destination best not attempted in summer.	98
Bright Angel Campground	Overnight/ Mules	Yaki Point	13.6mi	2 days	difficult	4780ft			A classic backcountry excursion.	127
Phantom Ranch	Overnight/ Mules	Yaki Point	14.4mi	2 days	difficult	4714ft			Tough but rewarding hike to a cool oasis on the Colorado River.	127
South Kaibab to North Kaibab	Overnight/ Mules	Yaki Point	20.9mi (one way)	3 days	difficult	5770ft			The park's only rim-to-rim hike is a revered classic.	127
BRIGHT ANGEL										
Mile-and-a-Half Resthouse	Day Hike/ Mule	GC Village	3mi	1-2 hrs	moderate	1131ft			A short and rewarding hike along the Grand Canyon's most popular trail.	96
Three-Mile Resthouse	Day Hike/ Mule	GC Village	6mi	2-3 hrs	moderate-difficult	2112ft			Following the Bright Angel Fault, this trail zigzags down to a shaded resthouse with inner canyon views.	96
Indian Garden	Day Hike/ Mule	GC Village	9.2mi	4-6 hrs	difficult	3060ft			The grueling switchbacks of Jacob's Ladder are rewarded with the leafy bliss of Indian Garden.	96
Plateau Point	Day Hike (not in summer)/ Mule	GC Village	12.2mi	8-10 hrs	difficult	3120ft			Not recommended for summer day hikes, this sun-baked trail winds out to the edge of the Tonto Plateau for a beautiful glimpse of the inner gorge.	96

NAME	TYPE	LOCATION (STARTING)	DISTANCE (R/T)	DURATION (R/T)	CHALLENGE	ELEVATION CHANGE	FEATURES	FACILITIES	DESCRIPTION	PAGE
HERMIT										
Santa Maria Spring	Day Hike	Hermit Rd	5mi	2-4 hrs	moderate-difficult	1680ft	🏞	🚻 🚰 🛆	Beautiful and serene day hike along a steep wilderness trail to a small but lovely cliff-side spring.	101
Hermit Creek	Overnight	Hermit Rd	15.6mi	2 days	difficult	3660ft	🏞	🚻 🚰 🛆	Hard but beautiful hike to a sublime camping spot fringed with cliffs and near a creek.	130
Hermit to Bright Angel	Overnight	Hermit Rd	26.9mi one-way	3-4 days	difficult	3800ft+	🏞	🚻 🚰 🛆	A stunning inner-canyon cross-country hike along three very different trails; good Colorado River access.	131
Dripping Springs	Day Hike	Hermit Rd	7mi	3-5 hrs	moderate-difficult	1700ft	🏞	🚻 🧺 🛆	Peaceful but challenging hike to Louis 'The Hermit' Boucher's favorite hangout.	102
GRANDVIEW										
Coconino Saddle	Day Hike	Desert View Dr	1.5mi	1-2 hrs	moderate-difficult	1600ft	🏞	🚻 🛆	A steep challenge with phenomenal views.	99
Horseshoe Mesa	Day Hike	Desert View Dr	6mi	4-6 hrs	difficult	2699ft	🏞	🚻 🛆	One of the park's most popular (and steepest) day hikes.	99
Horseshoe Mesa/ Tonto Loop	Overnight	Desert View Dr	16.6mi	2 days	difficult	3699ft	🏞	🚻 🛆	A loop on the Tonto around the foot of Horseshoe Mesa promises staggering views and desert solitude.	100
OTHER HIKES										
Shoshone Point	Day Hike	Desert View Dr	2mi	30 min	easy	50ft	🏞 👪	🚻	Cool, shady walk to one of the South Rim's most sublime views.	95
Tonto	Day Hike	Yaki Point/ GC Village	13.1mi one-way	5-7 hrs	difficult	3260ft	🏞	🚻 🧺 🛆	A long, tough day hike offering a splendid look at the inner canyon along the South Kaibab, Bright Angel and Tonto Trails.	102

🏞 Views 👪 Great for Families 🚻 Restroom 🚰 Drinking Water 🧺 Picnic Sites 🛆 Backcountry Campsite

NAME	TYPE	LOCATION (STARTING)	DISTANCE (R/T)	DURATION (R/T)	CHALLENGE	ELEVATION CHANGE	FEATURES	FACILITIES	DESCRIPTION	PAGE
Bright Angel Point	Day Hike	Grand Canyon Lodge	0.6mi	20 min	easy	150ft			Short, easy paved hike to a narrow peninsula with canyon views on three sides.	114
Cape Final	Day Hike	Cape Royal Rd	4mi	1.5 hrs	easy	150ft			Flat, easy tramp along the Kaibab Plateau to a nice overlook.	118
Cliff Spring	Day Hike	Cape Royal Rd	1mi	40 min	easy-moderate	600ft			Perfect for kids, this short scenic trail passes ancient ruins, tunnels along a carved rock wall and ends at a verdant spring with views.	117
Ken Patrick	Day Hike/Mule	Near North Kaibab Trlhd	10mi (one way)	4-6 hrs (one way)	easy-moderate	800ft			Point-to-point wooded trail opening up to spectacular views at Point Imperial.	116
Nankoweap Campground	Overnight	Saddle Mountain sign on Forest Service Road 610	21.2mi to Nanko-weap Creek, 27.8 to Colorado River	2-3 days	very difficult	4800ft			A spectacular, difficult hike on an unmaintained trail with dizzying heights and stunning views.	132
Point Imperial	Day Hike	Point Imperial Parking Lot	4mi	1.5 hrs	easy	100ft			Short rim trail with views of the eastern canyon.	118
Transept	Day Hike	Grand Canyon Lodge/Cmpgrnd	3mi	45 min	easy-moderate	200ft			Enjoyable amble along a narrow dirt path rimming canyon and connecting Grand Canyon Lodge with the campground.	115
Uncle Jim	Day Hike/Mule	Near North Kaibab Trlhd	5mi	2-3 hrs	easy-moderate	600ft			A loop atop the Kaibab Plateau, with views of Roaring Springs Canyon.	117
Widforss	Day Hike	Cape Royal Rd	10mi	4-6 hrs	moderate	350ft			Lovely forested walk with some of the finest canyon views on the North Rim.	115
NORTH KAIBAB										
Supai Tunnel	Day Hike/Mule	North Rim	4mi	3-4 hrs	moderate-difficult	1410ft			Steep, spectacular hike to a red sandstone tunnel with sweeping views of the inner canyon chutes.	118
Roaring Springs	Day Hike/Mule	North Rim	9.4mi	6-7 hrs	difficult	3210ft			A North Kaibab favorite for strong hikers, this features a cascade of pools in a leafy oasis on the otherwise hot corridor trail.	118
Clear Creek	Inner Canyon	Phantom Ranch	17.4mi	7-9 hrs	moderate-difficult	1500ft			The most popular side hike on the north side of Colorado River is loaded with views and pretty falls.	132

Views · Great for Families · Restroom · Drinking Water · Picnic Sites · Backcountry Campsite

switchbacks are standard, though width and terrain vary. Trails like Grandview and Hermit, for example, are narrow and bumpy, while Bright Angel and South Kaibab are wide and rock-free.

Generally speaking, the only truly easy hikes in the Grand Canyon are those that stay above or close to the rims, along with a handful of fairly flat trails like **Uncle Jim** or short jaunts such as **Cliff Spring**. Another accessible option is to hike short segments of more challenging trails. Rangers cite the average hiking speed as 2 mph going down and 1 mph climbing up, an important consideration when selecting a trail and distance. On your first hike or two, gauge your speed to learn how long each mile might take.

The hikes in this book are organized into four difficulty levels. Remember that a single trail can have several difficulty ratings, depending on which segment you plan to hike.

Easy – Relatively gentle hikes with little elevation gain. Accessible to everyone, including kids and first-time hikers.

Moderate – These hikes involve some elevation change (usually 500ft to 1000ft) and are longer or more exposed than those rated 'easy.' Generally fine for all ability levels.

Difficult – Hikes with significant elevation change and longer mileage. Require a bit more hiking experience.

Very Difficult – Tough hikes, involving the greatest exposure and mileage, as well as substantial elevation change (2500ft to 4000ft). Better left to the most fit, experienced hikers.

When selecting a hike, don't forget about the altitude, which can quickly sap your strength, particularly when combined with the straw-dry desert environment. Don't

DOWN AND BACK IN ONE DAY? DON'T TRY IT.

Experienced hikers and fit newcomers alike are often tempted to hike from the rim to the river and back in a single day, an outing that involves close to 9000ft of elevation change. But no matter how early you start, how many previous miles you've logged or how many energy bars you eat, it's simply a bad idea – and rangers, numerous signs and this book will discourage you from trying it. In fact, rangers post themselves at key spots along the corridor trails, gently inquiring how far hikers plan to go, eyeing water supplies and climbing legs. Posted at the visitor centers and key trailheads, one particular warning poster cuts to the chase – it depicts a young, fit hiker on his hands and knees, vomiting on the trail.

While it's certainly possible for strong hikers to accomplish this haul from the South Rim in the cool air of spring and fall, attempting to do so in the summer heat is downright risky and foolish. It makes no difference if you're a fit 25-year-old or a 64-year-old trail veteran. Still not convinced? Read the gripping *Over the Edge: Death in Grand Canyon*, by Michael Ghiglieri and Thomas Myers, or ask a ranger how many costly rescues (at the hiker's expense) occur per day during the summer, many involving heat-exhausted males in their 20s.

be surprised if you're huffing after a half mile, even if headed downhill. Dehydration is also a concern along the many exposed trails beneath intense direct sun.

DAY HIKES

The Grand Canyon's trove of day hiking options ranges from quick strolls to challenging treks that cover up to 12 miles over eight or more hours on the trail. If you're venturing into the inner canyon (technically, anything below the rim), know that it is a place of extremes. Even on short hikes, preparation is key, especially in this desert climate. Regardless of whether you're hiking only a short section of the **Rim Trail** or 6 miles on the **Bright Angel**, always carry plenty of water with you. Also bring a wide-brimmed hat, sunglasses and sunscreen.

Many day hikes can be extended into the backcountry or combined into overnight excursions. See the Exploring the Backcountry (p123) for full descriptions of such hikes.

BACKCOUNTRY HIKES

If you like challenging terrain, staggeringly beautiful scenery and absolute serenity, plan an overnight hike while visiting the park. There's simply no substitute for experiencing the Grand Canyon in the heart of its vast backcountry. While the elevation change can be daunting and the distances long, backcountry hiking is far more accessible than people tend to think. Join the hundreds who trek down the **Bright Angel Trail** each year, or head to the **Tonto Trail** for a sublime backcountry escape. Provided you prepare, plan an appropriate route and itinerary, and take your time, virtually anyone with basic camping and hiking skills and a thirst for adventure can experience the wonders of being on the canyon floor.

You'll need a wilderness permit to stay overnight anywhere within the backcountry (for full details see p124). Any foray into the canyon also requires decent equipment. If you're at all nervous about tackling the backcountry alone, or feel you might need some guidance, there are plenty of group outings available, offering camaraderie and helpful instruction. For a list of outfitters, see the sections on Hiking Outfitters & Groups and Classes & Learning Vacations in this chapter.

THE KAIBAB: A RIM-TO-RIM FAVORITE

The classic South Kaibab to North Kaibab trek is a Grand Canyon favorite. Most hikers start in the south and spend two nights in the backcountry. It's 6.4 miles down from Yaki Point to the Colorado River and Bright Angel Campground, then another 7 miles to Cottonwood Campground. From there, the final 7-mile stretch snakes up to the North Rim. You'll need a backcountry permit (p124) and a lift home. Thank goodness for the nifty Transcanyon Shuttle (928-638-2820; $65 one-way), which departs daily from Grand Canyon Lodge on the North Rim at 7am, arrives at Bright Angel Lodge on the South Rim around noon, then makes the return trip at 1:30pm. Tip: Don't spend all your money buying food and water from canyon hikers – the shuttle only accepts cash!

✔ DAY HIKE CHECKLIST

Thorough preparation is the key to safe and happy day hiking in the Grand Canyon, particularly on any of the longer day hikes – you don't want to get caught without enough water or food to make it back to the rim. Here's a list of must-have items:

- ✔ **Hydration system** – Camelbak is one manufacturer; a good-sized one can double as your backpack
- ✔ **High-sodium snacks** – Nuts, pretzels, cheese, crackers, jerky, etc
- ✔ **Energy bars** – Clif Bars and the like offer your system a quick protein burst
- ✔ **Maps** – Even if you're on a short hike, it's a good idea to have a map to identify way stations, water sources and elevations, not to mention the sights you're seeing
- ✔ **Layered clothing** – Even summer temperatures can shift quickly from quite chilly (40s Fahrenheit) in the early morning to sweltering (90s and above) once the sun hits the canyon; layers of quick-drying synthetics help regulate your body temperature
- ✔ **Flashlight or headlamp** – For early morning or after-dusk hiking
- ✔ **Hat** – Broad-rimmed and not too tight will keep you cool
- ✔ **Polarizing sunglasses** – To reduce the desert glare
- ✔ **Suntan lotion** – Slather on before hitting the trail, and reapply often
- ✔ **SPF lip balm** – The sun and dry climate are especially hard on lips
- ✔ **Handkerchief or bandanna** – Douse with water to cool your skin

For longer day hikes:

- ✔ **First-aid kit** – Including moleskin for blisters
- ✔ **Walking stick** – Not for everyone, but it can come in handy on knee-jarring downs and ups
- ✔ **Signal mirror and/or whistle** – In an emergency, don't count on cell phone coverage in the canyon depths

HIKE CLASSIFICATIONS

The park service classifies canyon terrain into four specific zones, based on maintenance levels and the availability of water and facilities. These, in turn, loosely correlate to different hiking skill levels.

The heavily trafficked **corridor zone** includes well-maintained trails, often with a water source. The South Kaibab, North Kaibab and Bright Angel trails lie within this zone. Wide and well marked, these trails are regularly patrolled by NPS personnel and provide both hiking and mule access to the inner canyon. The **threshold zone** embraces less-traveled trails, such as the Hermit, that are rugged, with little or no water. The **primitive zone** encompasses little-used paths that are not maintained – best suited to experienced canyon hikers who are comfortable with route finding. The **wild zone** is just that – don't expect to find marked trails, or any trails for that matter.

All hikes listed in this book, both day excursions and backcountry forays, follow established and well-marked trails. The majority lie within the corridor and threshold zones, generally regarded as the safest areas to hike within the canyon; a section or two of the overnight treks may pass through a primitive zone.

First-time canyon hikers will be happiest and safest on the gentle rim trails, the well-tended and trafficked corridor trails or in the company of a guide. It's a great comfort to know that should an emergency arise, a ranger or other hikers are relatively close by, and there's little chance of losing the trail. Wherever you choose to roam, however, it's your responsibility to be prepared and safe.

HIKING SAFETY

It's easy to become complacent when hiking in the Grand Canyon, given the thin air, clearly marked trails and relative ease of descending into the canyon. But hiking here can be serious business. On average, there are 400 medical emergencies each year on canyon trails, and more than 250 hikers need to be rescued at their own hefty expense. It's not that hiking itself is an inherently unsafe activity, but the canyon's extreme terrain and climate lend it the potential to quickly turn dangerous.

The best safeguard for an enjoyable hike is proper planning. Learn about the trails, respect your limitations and bring ample supplies. The extra prep time should keep you out of trouble.

You'll need to pack far more food and water than you might think. In summer, as rim temperatures soar into the 90s Fahrenheit and the canyon floor exceeds 100°F, you'll need at least a gallon per day to keep yourself hydrated. Before you set out on any trail over a mile, know whether and where water is available. While pump water is available along Bright Angel and North Kaibab, pipe breakage is common. Elsewhere, such as Hermit Springs, you'll need to treat water before drinking it, either by boiling it for at least five minutes, treating it with iodine tablets or using a filter. Always err on the side of caution and bring too much water and food rather than too little.

The sun can quickly leave you dehydrated and at risk of heat exhaustion. When embarking on any of the longer day hikes, plan on beginning your hike by 6am and avoiding the sun altogether between 10am and 2pm. Take note if you haven't had to pee as often as usual or your urine is discolored. These are indicators of dehydration, which can rapidly spiral into more dire health concerns. A baseball cap or, better yet, a wide-brimmed hat will keep your head, face and neck cool. Also wear plenty of sunscreen to protect exposed skin.

Loss of appetite and thirst may be early symptoms of **heat exhaustion**, so even if you don't feel thirsty, drink plenty of water. If you *do* become dehydrated, you'll likely feel dizzy, extremely nauseous and have a headache, and your skin will be clammy but cool to the touch. If you do drink enough water, but lose salt through sweat and don't eat enough food to counterbalance that loss, there's the added risk of **hyponatremia** (low sodium blood level), which sets in with similar symptoms. Salty snacks like nuts and crackers, as well as electrolyte replacement drinks (like Gatorade), will help restore a proper balance. Bottom line: hydrate, eat smart and often and don't push yourself too hard, particularly in summer.

SAFETY TIPS FOR HIKING SMART

Heed this nuts-and-bolts advice for safe hiking in the Grand Canyon:

✔ **Down: 2x up**

Make this formula your hiking mantra. Generally speaking, it takes twice as long to hike out of the canyon as it does to descend into it. So if you'd like to hike for six hours, turn around after two. Most first-time canyon hikers slog uphill at about 1mph.

✔ **Never leave the trail**

It's always best to stay on marked trails, both for safety and erosion control. Nowhere is this more important than in the Grand Canyon, where hazards include stupefying drop-offs. It's also extremely difficult to find a hiker who has wandered off-trail. Stick to the road more traveled.

✔ **Don't hike alone**

Most of those who get in trouble in the canyon are solo hikers, for whom the risks are multiplied.

✔ **Take your time**

Given the altitude and extreme aridity, go slow to avoid overexertion. Ideally, you should be able to speak easily while hiking, regardless of the grade. Be sure to take a 10-minute break every hour to conserve energy.

✔ **Eat and drink often**

Pay close attention to your intake of food and fluids to guard against dehydration. One good strategy is to literally check your watch and have a snack and long drink of water every 20 to 30 minutes. In summer months each hiker should drink about a gallon (4 liters) of water per day; always have at least two pints of water on you. As a general rule, you should eat before you're hungry and drink before you're thirsty. Before a big hike, eat a high-energy, protein-rich breakfast and drink lots of water; afterward, drink plenty more water and treat yourself to a big dinner.

✔ **Salty snacks are your friends**

To safeguard against hyponatremia (low sodium blood level), eat plenty of carbohy-drates and salty snacks before and during your hike. Options include beef jerky, nuts, pretzels, trail mix, cheese, salami and crackers.

✔ **Take care of your feet**

In addition to sturdy, comfortable boots and medium-weight socks, your feet need special care. On long hikes, soak your feet in streams to reduce inflammation and safeguard against blisters (just be sure to dry them thoroughly before replacing your socks). After hiking, elevate your feet.

✔ **Don't be overly ambitious**

Particularly for novice hikers, it's a good idea to spend the first day or two gauging your ability and response to the climate and terrain. If you're planning long hikes, try out your desert legs on a more level hike or a short round-trip of 2 to 4 miles, then work your way up to more difficult trails.

✔ **Stay cool**

To safeguard against heat exhaustion, hike during the early morning and late afternoon and keep as cool as possible. Splash water on your face and head at streams. If you get overheated while ascending, pour water on your pulse points and place a damp ban-danna loosely around your neck.

As for critters, be on the lookout for **scorpions**, which can deliver a nasty sting and like to snooze in the shoes and clothes of backcountry campers. Day hikers are bound to encounter plenty of **mules**, who always have the right of way. If you're hiking when a train of mules approaches, stand on the inner side of the trail, turn your pack away from the animals (lest one bumps your pack and knocks you off balance) and listen for directions from the guide. Be especially careful if you're hiking with children.

HIKING RULES & PERMITS

Day hiking within the park does not require a permit, but overnight backpacking does. The only exceptions are hikers or mule riders with reservations at **Phantom Ranch**. Permits are also required for camping in undeveloped areas along the rim, such as along the Ken Patrick Trail.

Permits are in high demand, and backcountry campers must follow a specific set of regulations. Due to overcrowding and environmental concerns, rangers limit the number of people per night at each of the park's backcountry campgrounds. Plan ahead, as sites can be reserved up to four months in advance. For details on how to apply, see Exploring the Backcountry (p123).

HIKING OUTFITTERS & GROUPS

Group outings are a terrific way for first-time hikers to enjoy safe and social hiking. Even if you're an experienced hiker, group hikes offer opportunities to learn about the canyon in the company of likeminded adventurers. If you've got a hankering to explore the canyon's depths and rarely visited reaches, hiring a guide or booking an outfitted trip is certainly the safest bet.

Lots of local outfitters offer guided hiking excursions in the park. There's a wide range of trips, prices and dates, not to mention styles, so definitely peruse a few before making your choice. You can pick up a full list of accredited backcountry guide services at the visitors centers or online at **W** www.nps.gov.

Discovery Treks (☎ 888-256-8731; **W** www.discoverytreks.com) offers a wide selection of guided trips, from one-day hikes on the Grandview Trail or Marble Canyon Trail ($145 per person) to five-day backpacking excursions on the North Rim ($975). Trips include all equipment and meals. Tucson-based **Sky Island Treks** (☎ 520-622-6966; **W** www.skyislandtreks.com) caters to first-time hikers, families and expert backpackers alike. Its 'extreme itineraries' feature expedition-level treks to little-visited corners of the Grand Canyon, such as the challenging 12-night Nankoweap to Bright Angel excursion, which begins by snowshoeing into the park over Saddle Mountain. Prices vary depending on the number in your group and when you sign up. A solo client pays about $275 a day ($3575 for the trip) while two or more pay $245 a day ($3185 for the trip). For the best deal, sign up five months in advance; for a group of up to six people, the cost is $2548 per person. Kanab-based **Canyon Rim Adventures** (☎ 800-897-9633; **W** www.canyonrim adventures.com) offers camping adventures that combine hiking and biking (see Road & Mountain Biking, p48).

For short guided hikes, you can't beat the free and justly popular **ranger-led hikes**, offered year-round on the South Rim and from June to October

ACTIVITIES

TOP POST-HIKE SNACKS

Protein-rich, tasty and loaded with carbs, these snacks will recharge you after a long hot day on the trail:

✔ **Canyon Crunch Ice Cream** – Peanut-butter ice cream with a milk fudge ribbon, granola pieces, crispy rice and peanuts ($2.60 for two scoops at The Fountain, Bright Angel Lodge)

✔ **North Rim Stout** – Hearty with a touch of molasses, this special park brew hails from Flagstaff's Mogollon Brewery; for something lighter, try Kaibab Pale Ale or Bright Angel Amber ($4.80 a pint, Rough Rider Saloon, Grand Canyon Lodge)

✔ **Hiker's Salad** – Tossed greens, grilled chicken breast, tomatoes and Romano cheese ($8 at The Café, Bright Angel Lodge)

on the North Rim. Check *The Guide* for listings. If you're at all nervous about the terrain or climate, the guided **Cedar Ridge** hike, which departs daily at 7am from the South Kaibab Trailhead, is a fantastic way to assuage nerves and experience this phenomenal walk in the company of a local expert. When going with the rangers, don't forget to pack exactly what you'd bring if hiking *without* a group – while happy to share their knowledge and expertise, don't expect them to have extra water, snacks or clothing for you.

The highly respected **Grand Canyon Field Institute** (see Classes & Learning Vacations, p52) offers many naturalist-led hikes and backpacking trips for all skill levels. These fairly priced, expertly guided expeditions generally last three to nine days.

River Rafting

Ask any outdoor enthusiast, and chances are good that rafting the Colorado River is on his or her Top 10 adventure wish list. Without a doubt, it's also the most exhilarating way to experience the inner canyon. A stunning combination of raucous rapids and serene waters, the Colorado transports rafters through sinuous canyons to soft beaches for naps and picnics, hidden pools and waterfalls for cool swims, and innumerable sandy spots to sleep under the stars.

All told, the river boasts more than 160 sets of rapids over 280 river miles. Rafting season begins in mid-April and runs into September for motorized boats, November for oared vessels. While summer draws the most traffic, it also brings more afternoon thunderstorms and searing temperatures. Spring and fall are perfect times to paddle the Colorado, with sunny days in the 70s Fahrenheit and nights a cool but comfortable 50°F. No matter what time of year you go, however, the weather can be extreme, and the Colorado remains a chilly 48°F, regardless of season.

Though the park carefully regulates the number of rafts on the Colorado, visitors have several options. Most rafters join a commercial outing with one of many accredited outfitters, which offer trips lasting from three to 21 days. For a detailed description of the trip and a full list of outfitters, see Rafting the Colorado (p133).

Each year a few hundred private rafting excursions are allowed on the river. If you've got loads of whitewater experience under your paddle, you can opt to put together a noncommercial party of up to 16 members, pay a $100 fee and add your name to the waiting list for one of these berths. The only hitch – there are no less than 7500 names in front of yours, so you'd best have a dory of patience and be prepared to sit tight for about a decade. Detailed instructions and the application form are available online at **W** www.nps.gov/grca; for more tips see Permits & Costs (p135).

For those short on time, there are half- and full-day rafting trips, though not necessarily on sections within the Grand Canyon. Operating out of Diamond Creek, about four hours from the South Rim, **Hualapai River Runners** (☎ 928-769-2210, 800-622-4409) offers daylong trips in the canyon's west end. Don't want to turn your knuckles white? **Wilderness River Adventures** (☎ 800-528-6154) runs half-day rafting trips out east on the silky smooth 16-mile stretch of the Colorado that flows between Glen Canyon Dam and Lees Ferry. Xanterra offers full-day trips from the South Rim that bus rafters to Page, where they connect with the float trip.

Road & Mountain Biking

Not exactly known as a biker's park, the Grand Canyon nonetheless has some very nice stretches for two-wheeling. Hiking trails within the park are closed to bicycles, but they are welcome on all roads open to automobile traffic. Particularly enjoyable is the North Rim, where you'll find both long hauls and short spins. The best riding on the South Rim is along **East Rim Drive**, with successive scenic overlooks from Yaki Point to Desert View.

Rental bicycles are not available in the park, but you can rent in Flagstaff. For more information on self-guided biking in the Grand Canyon, pick up copies of Sarah Alley's detailed books *Bicycling America's National Parks – Arizona & New Mexico: The Best Road & Trail Rides from the Grand Canyon to Carlsbad Caverns* and *The Mountain Biker's Guide to Arizona*.

Outside the park, there's plenty of gnarly single track for mountain bikers in Kaibab National Forest, which teems with old-growth ponderosa pines, steep-sided canyons, aspen groves and velvety meadows. Stop at the Tusayan Ranger Station (☎ 928-638-2443, open 8am-5pm) for trail maps and directions.

Several outfitters offer guided biking trips that include forays into the park. Berkeley, California-based **Backroads** (☎ 800-462-2843, **W** www.backroads.com) offers a nine-day biking/camping adventure to Bryce, Zion and Grand Canyon National Parks for $1398 per person, or an inn version for $2298 per person. **High Sonoran Adventures** (☎ 480-614-3331; **W** www.hikethecanyon.com), out of Scottsdale, runs a Grand Canyon mountain biking and hiking tour that begins with lots of single tracking around the San Francisco Peaks and along the Arizona Trail before hiking on the South Rim (about $200 per person per day, all-inclusive). **Canyon Rim**

BEST BIKE RIDES IN THE PARK

Not always heralded for its two-wheeling, the Grand Canyon nonetheless offers up some great rides for those traveling with bikes, or you can pick up a rental in St George (North Rim) or Flagstaff (South Rim). Either way, stretch out your trail-tested or mule-sore legs on one of these scenic routes. Distances listed are for one-way travel.

✔ **Grand Canyon Lodge to Point Imperial** (8 miles)
A winding, shady ride through pine forests and thickets of aspen and bright orange Indian paintbrush. Ends at a picnic spot on the rim with a spectacular view.

✔ **Desert Rim Drive** (22 miles)
You'll have to concentrate to keep your eyes from wandering off the road to the stunning canyon views. This hot ride is best tackled at sunrise or in late afternoon.

✔ **Hermit Road/West Rim Drive** (10 miles)
Better for mountain bikes, but doable on a sturdy roadie or one with slicks, this relatively traffic-free ride offers a series of breathtaking overlooks. Cold drinks and ice cream await at Hermits Rest.

✔ **Point Imperial to Cape Royal** (15 miles)
Long and winding with lots of small rolling hills, this delightful pedal along a forest-fringed road eventually opens up to sage-dusted terrain and big views. Don't veer off the road when you first glimpse magical Angels Window.

Adventures, Inc (☎ 800-897-9633) offers four-day mountain biking/camping trips on the Kaibab Plateau for $795 per person, including all equipment and meals.

Fishing

Provided it's not your main source of food, fishing in the Grand Canyon can be a fun and peaceful activity. The Colorado is fairly well laden with trout and catfish, as are the permanent tributaries. Fishing is best during the winter months, when spawning trout make their way from the Colorado up Bright Angel Creek. To fish, you'll need an Arizona state fishing license, which you can pick up at Canyon Village Marketplace on the South Rim or north of the park in Lees Ferry. For nonresidents a license costs $12.50 for one day, $26 for five days or $101 for the year; the Colorado River-only license (good for a year) is a bargain at $38.50. Arizona residents pay $12.50 for one day or $28.50 for the year.

To fish along the Colorado in the park, you'll also need an overnight backcountry permit. North of the park, there's excellent angling near Lees Ferry, especially along the 16-mile stretch from the outflow of Lake Powell at Glen Canyon Dam. These waters house a trove of fat and feisty rainbow trout, and you're allowed to catch two per person per day. Several outfitters and local lodges offer guided fishing expeditions (see Lees Ferry & Marble Canyon, p217).

Mule Trips

Riding a mule down into the canyon is a time-honored park tradition. Mule trains – up to 30 animals per group – are only permitted on the corridor trails, the Uncle Jim Trail and the first mile of the Ken Patrick Trail. Not recommended for anyone scared of heights or big animals, riding 'muleback' takes some getting used to, but it's a memorable (if bumpy) means of transportation.

Rides are offered year-round from the South Rim along the Bright Angel and South Kaibab Trails, though summer treks on the latter are limited to descents only, given the heat. Reservations (up to 23 months in advance) are recommended, particularly for summer trips. To book a mule trip, call **Xanterra** (☎ 303-287-2757, 888-297-2757; W *www.xanterra.com*). A day trip costs $129 and an overnight to Phantom Ranch costs $350; for more details, see p135).

TOP THREE MULE-FREE TRAILS

Not to dis the surefooted mules, who stoically ferry their loads down impossibly steep grades in scorching temperatures, but if you'd like to take a longish hike without the added handicap of manure piles and hoof-churned dust, these trails are blessedly free of mule trains:

✔ **Widforss Trail**
✔ **Grandview Trail**
✔ **Hermit Trail**

Mule trips from the North Rim ($20-95) are offered from mid-May to mid-October only; no overnight trips are available, given the lengthy distance to Phantom Ranch. Even during the busy summer season, you stand a good chance of booking a North Rim trip as little as a week in advance. Contact **Canyon Trail Rides** (☎ 435-679-8665; W *www .canyonrides.com*) for reservations more than 10 days in advance or call or stop by the mule desk (☎ 928-638-9875) in the Grand Canyon Lodge lobby (see p164) when you arrive.

Horseback Riding

Horseback riding is offered outside the park, mostly in the lovely and cool Kaibab National Forest. Near Jacob Lake, **Apache Stables** (☎ 928-638-2891; W *www.apachestables.com*) offers trail rides along the piney trails of the Kaibab. Rides cost $30 for an hour, $55 for two hours and $40 for an evening campfire saunter (the same trip is offered via wagon for $12.50). Looking for canyon views? Choose the four-hour East Rim Ride ($95). On the **Havasupai Indian Reservation** (p176), you can travel by horseback from Hualapai Hilltop to Supai, the campground and the falls ($75 to $150). Call ☎ 928-448-2121 for reservations and information.

Cross-Country Skiing

In winter the North Rim and environs offer miles of snow-covered forest roads and a patchwork of wide meadows – that is, for those willing to make the trek. The park road officially closes from mid-October to mid-May, and visitors must ski or snowshoe the 44 miles to the rim. There are no designated trails, so you can ski or snowshoe virtually anywhere, opening up limitless options for backcountry exploration.

The South Rim boasts a few cross-country loops within the Kaibab National Forest, just south of Grandview Point. You can rent skis in Williams and Flagstaff, where you'll find several more cross-country circuits, as well as downhill facilities.

Helicopter Rides & Airplane Tours

While less of a hands-on activity than hiking, seeing the Grand Canyon from the air does offer an incredible perspective, and the tours are understandably popular. Close to 100,000 flights take almost a million passengers above the canyon each year. Tours operate out of Grand Canyon National Park Airport, just south of Tusayan, as well as the airports in Las Vegas and Phoenix. You can pick up a partial list of outfitters at the visitors centers.

The advantages of opting for an airplane tour over a helicopter excursion are lower prices and the ability to cover a lot more distance – in addition to the Grand Canyon, you'll fly over Marble Canyon and Lake Powell. Unlike airplanes, however, helicopters are permitted to dip beneath 1000ft above the rim, offering closer views of the canyon.

The flights are controversial, as flying anything over the canyon can be tricky, involving high-altitude takeoffs (the airport is at 7000ft), sudden wind shifts, unpredictable air currents and few level landing areas should an emergency arise. There have been some 60 crashes over the past half century. Stiff regulations now govern all flights crossing the canyon, to both limit noise and promote safety. More than 75% of the park airspace is off-limits to planes, and flying beneath the rim is prohibited in all but the western canyon.

See p104 for more information on trips and outfitters.

Ranger Programs

The National Park Service hosts a wealth of free ranger programs in the park, ranging from a half-hour talk on the endangered California condor to a daily three-hour guided hike down the South Kaibab Trail to Cedar Ridge. Particularly enjoyable are the evening programs, which vary in subject but often showcase the stunning night sky.

Ranger programs are offered year-round on the South Rim and between May and October on the North Rim (when the park is open). For a detailed listing of programs, refer to the park newspaper, *The Guide*, available at any entrance station (there are different versions for the South and North Rims); you can also check schedules online at **W** www.nps.gov/grca. There's also a daily ranger program at Phantom Ranch, accessed by foot or mule train only (check the bulletin board at

Bright Angel Campground or the Phantom Ranch Canteen for that day's topic). Occasionally, the rangers host special events, so be sure to check the park bulletin boards or inquire at the visitors centers.

Beyond the park, the **Kaibab Plateau Visitor Center** *(open 8am-5pm)* north of the North Rim in Jacob Lake, presents several ranger programs. Topics include the plateau's geology, the night sky and life on the Kaibab at the turn of the 20th century. Even if you can't attend one of the programs, stop by to peruse the excellent selection of books. Unlike the park visitors centers, this one is rarely crowded, and rangers will happily field your questions about the Grand Canyon and Kaibab Plateau.

Classes & Learning Vacations

The Grand Canyon's rich natural and cultural history provides endless material for discussion and discovery. Several venues offer year-round classes in a variety of subjects.

GRAND CANYON FIELD INSTITUTE

A nonprofit organization cosponsored by the Grand Canyon Association and Grand Canyon National Park, the **Grand Canyon Field Institute** *(☎ 928-638-2485; W www.grandcanyon.org/fieldinstitute)* offers more than 50 two- to nine-day classes annually in and around the park. Most instructors have advanced degrees in their field of study, have written on their subjects of expertise and have led canyon trips for several years. Courses typically include hikes that range from gentle walks on level terrain to hardcore backpacking excursions.

Subjects include cultural history, natural history and wilderness studies, women's studies, and photography expeditions on both rims (a fantastic way to explore the backcountry while honing one's photographic skills). The institute also offers **service trips**, such as Hands-on Archaeology, during which participants unearth and catalog artifacts under the guidance of park scientists, or the Hance Creek & Red Canyon Restoration, during which participants work to restore that delicate ecosystem.

Prices range from $85 for a family (children 8 and older) introduction to the canyon to $3995 for a rafting trip down the Colorado, though most cost between $300 and $600. Grand Canyon Association Members ($35 annual membership) are eligible for discounts on most institute classes. You can pick up the annual *Schedule of Courses* from the Canyon View Visitor Center; more detailed course descriptions, as well as information on registration procedures, are available in the *Catalog of Courses* on its website. You can also request information by mail from the Grand Canyon Field Institute, PO Box 399, Grand Canyon, AZ 86023.

MUSEUM OF NORTHERN ARIZONA

The **Museum of Northern Arizona** *(☎ 928-774-5211; W www.musnaz .org)* offers customized educational tours led by scientists, writers and artists. Options include hiking, backpacking, river rafting, horseback riding, van tours and hotel-based trips.

NORTHERN ARIZONA UNIVERSITY'S
GRAND CANYON SEMESTER

Northern Arizona University offers a three-month interdisciplinary **Grand Canyon Semester** (W *www.grandcanyonsemester.nau.edu; Northern Arizona University, Grand Canyon Semester, NAU Box 15018, Flagstaff, AZ 86011-5018)* that examines the region's geology, history, ecology, geography and politics, among other topics. The 18-credit-hour course, comparable to a semester abroad, spans classroom sessions in

PHOTOGRAPHY TIPS

The Grand Canyon is one of the most photographed places in the world. Views change rapidly – wait five minutes, and a butte will turn from orange to russet, or walk around a bend and gain an entirely different perspective on the same spire. Given such spectacular scenery, photography here is somewhat foolproof, but with just a bit more effort and know-how, you may just capture a prizewinner or screensaver.

Whether you're toting a disposable point-and-shoot or the snazziest new digital camera, following are a few tips to get you started. The general store in Grand Canyon Village offers the park's widest selection of camera gear, while on the North Rim you'll find film and batteries at both the Grand Canyon Lodge gift shop and the campground store.

✔ **Film** – All film has an ASA or ISO rating that designates its sensitivity to light. The most common speeds are between 100 and 400. Higher numbers are better suited to low-light settings, though the canyon is generally well lit. If you're using a standard 35mm camera, 100-speed film will work well for outdoor daylight shots; if you're shooting early or late in the day, 400 may be a better choice.

✔ **Exposure** – An exposure is a combination of shutter speed and aperture (measured in f-stops). For sharp photos, avoid shutter speeds slower than 1/125th of a second, while the higher the f-stop, the greater the depth of field (i.e., more of the scene will be in focus).

✔ **Composition** – Though landscape shots of the canyon may be a cinch, trying to capture people or a specific monument may prove tricky. Subjects often appear tiny, given the vast scale. If you're photographing someone on the rim, move closer to your subject to shift the perspective a bit. In general, position your focal point (the mule, switchbacks on the South Kaibab, the distant Colorado River, etc.) slightly off-center in the viewfinder.

✔ **Positioning** – Many of the rocky ledges that jut out from the rim make perfect perches for unobstructed shots of the canyon. Wander out onto one of these ledges (use caution!) to catch a different angle of the canyon or a view back at the rim.

✔ **Landscapes & Light** – Strong, direct sunlight can wash out the landscape in your photos. The best remedy is to photograph the canyon at sunrise or sunset, when the light is soft and golden and the contours turn peachy mauve.

Flagstaff, backcountry field trips and rafting excursions down the Colorado. While most participants are college-age students, the course is open to anyone. The semester costs about $3500 for Arizona residents and $8000 for everyone else, including dormitory accommodations and meals.

VOLUNTEER OPPORTUNITIES

The park website lists available **volunteer positions**, including year-round openings for **revegetation volunteers**. You can volunteer for a day or a month, and duties include seed collection, plant propagation and nonnative plant removal. Limited free camping may be available. Apply in advance by contacting the revegetation crew volunteer office (☎ 928-638-7964, 928-638-7857; ⓔ grca_reveg_crew@nps.gov).

ENVIRONMENTAL EDUCATION

The **environmental education** office (☎ 928-638-7662; ⓦ www.nps.gov/grca/education) offers curriculum-based, ranger-led field trips for children in grades four through six that focus on the canyon's ecology, geology and history. Workshops and educational materials are also available for teachers who would like to incorporate the lessons into their curriculum. Classes are free, but advance reservations are required.

Fun for the Kids

The park offers plenty of cool kids' activities, including mule riding, hiking and fossil hunting. Scenic hikes such as the **Rim Trail** and **Plateau Point** involve little elevation change and are perfect for small legs. On the North Rim, the **Cliff Springs Trail** is also ideal, offering such highlights as ruins, huge boulders and the springs over a 1-mile round-trip.

Many of the ranger-led programs are designed with kids in mind, such as the hugely popular fossil walks. During the summer, South Rim rangers also host a daily hour of educational activities geared toward 7- to 11-year-olds (4:30pm, Mather Campground). Evening programs feature astronomy, campfires and short walks and are good end-of-the-day options for youngsters.

The **Discovery Pack Program** begins with a 90-minute ranger talk, during which children (ages 9 to 14) and their families are given a pack with binoculars, a magnifying lens, field guides and other naturalist tools. Families then take the day to leisurely explore the park and complete the activities in their field journal.

The **Junior Ranger Dynamic Earth Program** takes kids (ages 9 to 14) on a 1-mile

SIX KID-FRIENDLY HIKES

✔ Shoshone Point
✔ Rim Trail
✔ Transept Trail
✔ Cliff Springs
✔ Bright Angel Point
✔ Cape Final Trail

hike along an unpaved portion of the rim trail and explains the geology of the canyon through hands-on activities.

For younger kids (ages 7 to 11), the **Way Cool Stuff for Kids** program uses hands-on activities to teach children about the park's plants and wildlife. Each ranger may choose a different activity. For example, one ranger builds a forest with the children, who pretend to be trees, grasses, bees and other plants and creatures.

✔ TIP

Of the park's classic corridor trails, **Bright Angel** is the easiest on little feet. Adventurous kids will enjoy the walk to Mile-and-a-Half Resthouse, which makes a perfect turnaround.

In the park's most popular program, children ages 4 to 14 can earn a **Junior Ranger** badge. Achieving the honor involves attending a ranger program (see *The Guide* for schedule) and completing a self-guided activity book, which includes wildlife detective work, drawing petroglyphs and jotting down different sensory experiences. To participate, pick up a free Junior Ranger booklet at the Canyon View Visitor Center or the Tusayan Museum.

Keep in mind that rangers are not babysitters – adults must accompany all children. Check *The Guide* for program times and locations.

The **Grand Canyon Field Institute** (**W** *www.grandcanyon.org/field institute)* offers several family-oriented classes featuring naturalist-led hikes; some excursions include meals and lodging. For kid-friendly reading on the canyon and surrounding desert, including several activity books, see Suggested Reading (p61).

Families can head just outside the park to enjoy the **IMAX** show *Grand Canyon: The Hidden Secret* (p94) or horseback rides through the Kaibab National Forest. You can also refer to Kids' Stuff at the Grand Canyon (p92) and Fun Stuff for Kids In & Around Flagstaff (p198).

You could spend days, indeed weeks, planning a trip to the Grand Canyon. Or you could hop in your car tomorrow. Either way, chances are you'd have a great time.

PLANNING THE TRIP

Last-minute travel works fine if you remain flexible, staying farther out if rooms are booked and shrugging off disappointment if you can't ride a mule or camp in the canyon. It also allows you the freedom to follow your whims, staying longer in a town you find interesting or moving on as you please.

Advance planning, however, does bring peace of mind. First, you can book accommodations to suit your needs, especially if you're traveling with children. Two-room suites and cabins are not always available at the last minute. In summer, some accommodations are booked upwards of 12 months in advance, especially those tied to specific activities. Hiking into Havasu Canyon, for example, requires a reservation at a campground or the lodge in Supai (p177), and last-minute accommodations are difficult to come by.

Second, you'll be able to book your activities. Whether you're looking for a wilderness pass, a mule to ride or a spot on a rafting trip, the earlier you make your reservations the better your chances. Advance planning also allows you to secure a spot on special excursions. The Grand Canyon Association offers wonderful trips that explore the culture, ecology and history of the Grand Canyon, but participation requires (you guessed it) advance reservations.

Third, if you have a general sense of the region before you go, you're less likely to miss points of interest on your way to or from the park. You can, for example, plan a side trip to Native American sites.

Finally, if you read up on the Grand Canyon before you go, you'll enrich your experience tremendously. As you hike down a trail, you'll be albe to identify plants and birds. As you gaze from the rim, you'll understand how the canyon was fomed. As you wander through historic buildings, you can imagine how they were once used.

If you plan an extended visit, just handle the main details (flight and room reservations, etc), then leave the rest until you arrive. But if you only have a week, particularly in summer, it's best to book all your accommodations and activities in advance.

North or South?

Once you decide to visit the Grand Canyon, the next question is, 'Which rim … or both?' Each offers a different set of experiences. Your choice will depend on the time you have, the activities you'd like to pursue and the type of experience you hope to find.

Just 80 miles north of Flagstaff and 220 miles north of Phoenix, the **South Rim** is open year-round and boasts visitors centers, several museums, historic sights, eateries, gift shops and lodges. Activity centers on Grand Canyon Village, which is literally a village, complete with a bank, grocery store, school, mechanic and post office. It's a busy place, with dozens of shuttles, a train arriving daily and hordes of tourists, particularly in summer. The elevation here is about 7000 feet, and piñon-juniper forest surrounds the village. Several hotels sit just behind the Rim Trail on the canyon's edge, including the historic El Tovar. From its dining room and porches, you can watch people stroll along the Rim Trail with the canyon beyond. Offering panoramic views, the Rim Trail stretches more than 10 miles, about 5 miles of which are paved. Drivers can choose from among 13 overlooks along two roads – Hermit Road (aka West Rim Drive) extends 8 miles west of the village, while Desert View Drive heads 25 miles east. Several spectacular trails descend into the canyon from this rim.

Though only 10 miles from the South Rim as the crow flies, the **North Rim** is a 215-mile, five-hour drive on winding desert roads from Grand Canyon Village. Because it's so remote, only about 10% of park visitors get to the North Rim, thus it offers a very different experience. At 8000 to 8800ft, this rim supports wildflower meadows and tall, thick stands of aspen and spruce, and the air is often crisp. Services are limited, and a lone historic lodge overlooks the canyon. Lodge visitors rest in rough-hewn rocking chairs on a small stone patio, and on cool evenings a fireplace crackles in the corner. While you can hike, attend ranger programs and join a mule trip, you won't find any museums or bus tours.

Opportunities to enjoy the view are more limited here than on the South Rim – you won't be able to see the canyon from as many perspectives, as overlooks are scarce on this heavily forested rim. The Kaibab National Forest stretches more than 50 miles north, and except for a few scattered lodges and campgrounds, the nearest facilities are in Kanab, Utah (80 miles north), and Page, Arizona (124 miles northeast). This is a quieter, gentler side of the Grand Canyon, and its remote beauty is well worth an extended trip.

GATEWAY TOWNS

Which rim you choose may also depend on what attractions you'd like to visit outside the park. Nearby towns such as Flagstaff or Sedona are vacation destinations in their own right.

If you visit the North Rim, you could stay a few days in Kanab, 78 miles north of the park, and visit some of the Southwest's most picturesque terrain. Grand Staircase-Escalante National Monument, Zion and Bryce Canyon National Parks, and Glen Canyon National Recreation Area all lie within two hours of Kanab.

From the South Rim, Flagstaff (78 miles from Grand Canyon Village) offers an excellent base from which to explore several Native American sites, Sedona's red rock country, and the Prescott, Kaibab and Coconino National Forests. You'll find great museums and restaurants in Flagstaff, and the surrounding area offers plenty of outdoor recreation, including downhill skiing, hiking and mountain biking.

These towns make great stops on your way to or from the park, and can also provide overflow accommodations if the park is booked. See Around the Grand Canyon (p174) for information on places to stay, sights and activities in Williams, Sedona, Flagstaff and Kanab.

PETS IN THE PARK

Pets are allowed in the park, with certain restrictions. They're allowed at rim campgrounds but cannot ride the shuttles or enter any lodges, stores or restaurants, and they must be leashed at all times. On the South Rim they can tag along on paved rim trails, but on the North Rim they're allowed only at developed stops along the road. You cannot take pets on any dirt trails or below the rim. Failure to follow these rules may lead to a $500 citation.

Kennel facilities on the South Rim (☎ 928-638-0534; open 7:30am-5pm) take pets with advance reservations and proof of vaccinations. Reserve a spot at least a week in advance in summer and at least two months in advance during major holidays. It costs $7/9 to board a cat/dog during the day. Overnight care costs $8/13.50 for a cat or a dog weighing 50 pounds or more, or $11 for dogs under 50 pounds. There are no kennels on the North Rim.

Outside the park, Kaibab National Forest is a nice shady place for dogs to play. Several motels in the surrounding area accept dogs, though you may be restricted to a smoking room or have to pay a small fee or deposit. Always ask when making a reservation, and never leave your pet in the car – the midday heat in an enclosed vehicle can kill an animal within an hour, and a night alone in the car is a dark and lonely experience.

When to Go

Facilities on the North Rim are closed from mid-October through mid-May, though you can still drive into the park and stay at the campground until the first snowfall closes the road from Jacob Lake. Snow falls as early as late October and as late as January, and annual snowfall can be more than 200 inches. Rangers stay at the North Rim year-round, and you can cross-country ski or snowshoe into the park after the road closes.

The South Rim is open year-round, though ice and snow may temporarily close roads. Some facilities have limited hours during the winter, and Yavapai Lodge closes for several months. From March through November, private cars are not allowed on Hermit Road.

SEASONAL HIGHS & LOWS

Weather is a primary consideration in deciding when to visit the park. June is the driest month, while summer thunderstorms roar through in July and August. These heavy rains can make hiking in the canyon not just unpleasant, but deadly, as flash floods can rip through side canyons with no warning. Temperatures average 85°F on the South Rim in July, the hottest month, and are generally 10 degrees cooler on the North Rim. Expect sweater weather in the evenings on the North Rim.

Temperatures on the rim average 20 degrees cooler than at the bottom of the canyon. You could wake up to frost on the rim in April and be basking in 85°F by the time you get down to the river. Summers in the gorge are mercilessly hot, averaging 101°F in June, 106°F in July, and 103°F in August. Despite the extreme heat, the summer also draws the biggest crowds; if you'd rather avoid them, visit in the spring or fall instead.

Weather is cooler and changeable in the fall. By October, highs on the South Rim average 65°F. Snow and freezing overnight temps are likely by mid- to late-September on the North Rim and by late-October on the South Rim. While fall foliage is not particularly striking on the South Rim, colors on the North Rim peak from the last week of September through mid-October. Both rims see a drop in tourists, and it is the best time to hike the inner canyon. Temperatures in the canyon average 84°F in October and 68°F in November.

The quietest season is the winter. Temperatures in January and February average 42°F on the rim and 56°F on the canyon floor. While snow adds to the dramatic beauty of the canyon, snowstorms do occasionally wreak havoc. Trails remain open, though they can be icy and dangerous near the rim.

Rates at the lodges in the park remain the same year-round, but rooms in gateway towns like Flagstaff, Kanab and Williams drop significantly during the winter.

COPING WITH THE CROWDS

Everyone has heard horror stories about the crowds at the Grand Canyon, from bumper-to-bumper traffic and long lines to fully booked hotels, campgrounds and activities. But don't worry – there are several strategies to escape the throngs.

The first trick is to avoid the South Rim in the summer. Peak season at the Grand Canyon ranges from April to September, and the park is busiest from Memorial Day to Labor Day. Visiting at other times of the year means you'll have to share the park with far fewer people.

Summer visitors may want to consider visiting the North Rim instead, as its limited services and remote location keep day-trippers to a minimum. You'll encounter few fellow hikers on its many trails. To *really* escape the crowds, plan to camp at the North Rim after the lodge closes but before the first snowfall shuts down the road to the park. You won't find any water or facilities, but you'll have the whole place pretty much to yourself.

If you do brave the South Rim, don't be discouraged by the half-hour line at the entrance station and your first encounter with the teeming village. Take a few minutes to get your bearings, then take a short stroll or hike – you'll be surprised at how easily you can leave the chaos of the village behind.

Accessing the South Rim via the East Entrance rather than the more popular South Entrance is another simple way to avoid the masses. There is usually no line here (even though it's only ten miles further from Flagstaff) and your first experiences in the park will not be marred by the craziness of the village. Stop by the Watchtower at Desert View, which offers a spectacular canyon overlook, then drive the 25 miles to the village along Desert View Drive. If you plan on camping along the South Rim, and are willing to take the chance that no campsites will be available, consider the Desert View Campground beside the East Entrance. It's typically less crowded and more peaceful than popular Mather Campground.

Because so many people stay in Flagstaff, Williams and Sedona and drive or ride the rail to the park just for the day, the South Rim quiets down considerably every

✔ WHAT TO PACK

Though it's tempting to simply toss everything into the car at the last minute, taking time to think things through as you pack can save you a lot of headaches down the road. Here are some things to remember:

✔ Sunscreen (although if you forget, it's readily available in the park)

✔ Hat (one that ties under the chin is required for all mule trips)

✔ Day pack

✔ Water bottle (ideally a strong brand, so it won't break)

✔ Hiking boots (if you plan any below-the-rim hikes, be sure your boots are well broken in)

✔ Bandanna

✔ Sunglasses

✔ Flashlight (with fresh batteries)

✔ Small binoculars

✔ Camera and extra camera batteries

✔ CDs and books on tape for children (essential during long car trips)

✔ Band-aids and antiseptic ointment (particularly for children, as rocky trails can lead to cuts and scrapes; Johnson & Johnson offers a great non-stinging, one-step cleansing and infection protection foam)

✔ Sweater (even in summer, for chilly evenings)

✔ Sunshade (for the car window)

✔ Backpack-style child carrier with sunshade for toddlers or front carrier for infants

✔ Light cotton long-sleeved pants and shirts for kids (to protect them from summer sun)

✔ Jeans and long-sleeved shirts (required for all mule trips)

✔ Children's Tylenol, infant gas relief drops, calamine lotion and aloe (for cooling sunburns)

✔ Prescription medication (and a handwritten prescription from your doctor in case you need more medicine)

✔ Ziplock bags (for storing toilet paper and snacks when you hike)

✔ Rain gear (particularly during seasonal rains in July and August)

evening. This is the time to relax on the porch of El Tovar or take a leisurely stroll along the rim. If you want to eat at El Tovar, you'll need to make advance reservations, though you can usually find a table on the small porch off the bar for drinks and hors d'oeuvres.

Lastly, don't let the threat of crowds scare you off. If you are a little flexible, you may still be able to find rooms, raft the river or book a mule trip, even if you left planning until the last minute. In fact, same-day mule trips on the North Rim are routinely available. Cancellation rates at some of the rafting companies is as high as 15%, so if you call a few weeks before your trip, there's a decent chance you can float the Colorado. If you can't book an overnight trip, consider a day rafting trip on the Hualapai Indian Reservation (p180).

Lodge vacancies are less predictable. You could call the park in mid-May and find vacancies on both rims for June, call a week later and find everything booked, then call two weeks later and find a room at El Tovar. For tips on how to find a place to lay your head, see Last-Minute Accommodations (p66).

SPECIAL EVENTS

The first three weeks of September, the park hosts the **Grand Canyon Music Festival**, featuring chamber music at Shrine of the Ages auditorium on the South Rim. Tickets cost about $18 and can be purchased in advance by contacting the festival office (☎ *928-638-9215, 800-997-8285;* **W** *www.grandcanyonmusicfest.org; PO Box 1332, Grand Canyon, AZ 86023*). Tickets are sometimes available at the door, but don't count on it.

Held annually in August on the North Rim, **Heritage Days** celebrates the region's Native American culture. Members of nearby tribes, including the Havasupai, Paiute, Hopi and Navajo (tribal participation varies from year to year), conduct this three-day program. Activities include kachina doll carving classes, musical performances and talks about the history and culture of their tribes. Call the North Rim Visitor Center (☎ *928-638-7864)* for more information.

In December the park observes the holidays with a 20ft Christmas tree in the lobby of El Tovar and Christmas Eve and Christmas night celebrations at Phantom Ranch.

Gathering Information

Gathering information on the Grand Canyon can be overwhelming, particularly in the Internet age. There's always one more website to visit, or one more book to read. Some people relish the planning process, but if you're not one of those people, don't worry, the park distributes a useful **free trip planner** – call ☎ 928-638-7888 or visit the park's website at **W** www.nps.gov/grca.

SUGGESTED READING

The Grand Canyon Association publishes an excellent trilogy on the prehistory, geology and ecology of the canyon. No more than 60 pages each, these thorough, well-written illustrated books are geared toward general audiences and ideal for anyone seeking an introduction to the region. You can buy *An Introduction to Grand Canyon Ecology*, by Rose Houk, *An Introduction to Grand Canyon Geology*, by Greer Price, and *An Introduction to Grand Canyon Prehistory*, by Christopher M Coder, individually ($7-9) or together at a discount.

History

For an extended history that reviews early Spanish and American explorers and the canyon's transformation into a tourist site, the best choice is *In the House of Stone & Light: Introduction to the Human History of the Grand Canyon*, by Donald Hughs. This very readable overview of the region is filled with historic photographs.

Living at the Edge: Explorers, Exploiters & Settlers, by Michael Anderson, offers a history of those who came to the canyon during and after the 19th century, examining the canyon's transformation from a daunting obstacle to a destination for entrepreneurs and tourists. The same author's *Along the Rim* delves into park history by describing viewpoints along the South Rim from Hermits Rest to Desert View. Take this book with you to transform a scenic drive or hike into a fascinating historical journey. Both Anderson books include lots of historic photographs.

Wallace Stegner's *Beyond the Hundredth Meridian: John Wesley Powell & the Second Opening of the West*, recalls Powell's historic first river trip down the Colorado within the context of the development of the American West. Stegner's writing will engage even those not particularly interested in the subject.

Stephen Pyne's *How the Canyon Became Grand* examines how writers, geologists, artists and explorers have transformed the canyon from a natural wonder into an American icon.

Michael Reisner's *Cadillac Desert* discusses the history of water management in the region. Though the subject may sound dry (pun intended), this book tells the dramatic story of the damming of the West, a very different account than that told in the visitors centers at Glen Canyon and Hoover Dams. The controversy surrounding the construction of Glen Canyon Dam is also addressed in *A Story That Stands Like a Dam: Glen Canyon & the Struggle for the Soul of the West*, by Russell Martin. A collection of photographs of Glen Canyon before the dam, Eliot Porter's *The Place No One Knew: Glen Canyon on the Colorado* has since become a photographic anthem of the environmental movement.

Jack Otter's *American Indians: Answers to Today's Questions* discusses Native American history and culture in a user-friendly question-and-answer format. *People of the Blue Water*, by Flora Greg Lliff, is a lovely account of this Oklahoma schoolteacher's experiences teaching Walapai and Havasupai Indians in the west end of the Grand Canyon in 1900. For a general history of the Havasupai Indians, read Stephen Hirst's *Life in a Narrow Place: The Havasupai of Grand Canyon*. If you're browsing for a Navajo rug, be sure to read *Navajo Rugs: How to Find, Evaluate, Buy & Care for Them*, by Don Dedera.

Several people's personal histories are closely entwined with that of the park. *Mary Colter: Architect of the Southwest*, by Arnold Berke, looks at the architect who built several buildings at the park and helped create the Park Service's 'rustic style.' In her book *The Harvey Girls: Women Who Opened the West*, author Lesley Poling-Kempes recalls Fred Harvey, the man largely responsible for developing the park as a tourist site and how he recruited women to work in his restaurants and hotels. William Suran's *The Kolb Brothers of Grand Canyon: Being a Collection of Tales of High Adventure, Memorable Incidents & Humorous Anecdotes* is filled with photographs and stories from the turn of the 19th century. Brad Dimock's *Sunk Without a Sound* tells the tragic story of Glen and Bessie Hyde, honeymooners who mysteriously disappeared in the canyon in 1928 while attempting to be the first man-woman team to raft in the Colorado.

Other recommended histories of the park include *Building the National Parks*, by Linda Flint McClelland; *Cowboys, Miners, Presidents & Kings: Story of the Grand Canyon Railway*, by Al Richmond; *Grand Canyon to Flagstaff Stagecoach Line: A History & Exploration Guide*, by Richard and Sherry Mangum; and *Polishing the Jewel: An Administrative History of the Grand Canyon National Park*, by Michael Anderson. The histories of the railroad and the stagecoach line include lots of wonderful historic photographs.

Activities

If you plan on any outdoor activities in the park, *Over the Edge: Death in Grand Canyon*, by Michael Ghiglieri and Thomas Myers, is an absolute must-read. Each chapter discusses deaths in the canyon from a particular cause (falling, drowning, etc.) and how these deaths could have been prevented. For the most part, these were not people engaged in radically dangerous activities – what's astounding is how many regular, middle-of-the-road tourists met their deaths by simply making poor decisions. Despite the morbid subject, it's a surprisingly funny read, and effectively impresses upon the reader the very real dangers in the park.

River runners will enjoy *Canyon*, Michael Ghiglieri's discussion of the geology and wildlife along 226 miles of wild river. Also check out *There's This River: Grand Canyon Boatman Stories*, edited by Christa Sadler. If you plan on rafting the river, peruse Buzz Belknap's *Grand Canyon River Guide*. Kim Crumbo's *A River Runner's Guide to the History of the Grand Canyon* is a good historical companion to Belknap's topographic guide.

An excellent resource on backcountry hiking is Michael Kelsey's *Canyon Hiking Guide to the Colorado Plateau* (particularly helpful are his 'Author's Experience' sections). Tom Martin's *Day Hikes from the River: A Guide to 100 Hikes from Camps on the Colorado River in Grand Canyon National Park* is another good resource.

Ecosystem & Geology

Amateur naturalists should track down *A Field Guide to Grand Canyon*, by Stephen Whitney, or *A Naturalist's Guide to Canyon Country*, by David Williams, both of which cover the region's common plants and animals. Plant lovers will also appreciate *A Field Guide to the Plants of Arizona*, by Anne Epple, while those interested in how plants can be used will enjoy *Wild Plants & Native People of the Four Corners*, by William Dunmire and Gail Tierney. Interested in geology? Consider the informative but rather technical *Grand Canyon Geology*, edited by Stanley Beus and Michael Morales.

Children's Books

Several books on the Grand Canyon will prepare children for their trip. The picture book *I See Something Grand*, by Mitzi Chandler, touches on the ecology, history and wildlife of the canyon through a discussion between a child and her grandfather. The pop-up book *Creatures of the Desert* introduces desert animals, while *101 Questions About Desert Life*, by Alice Jablonsky, is suitable for children of all ages. More of a pamphlet than a book, the Grand Canyon Association's illustrated *Fun Guide to Exploring the Grand Canyon* guides children through the park in a question-and-answer format. For children ages 9 to 16, the highly recommended *Exploring the Grand Canyon: Adventures of Yesterday & Today*, by Lynne Foster, is an engaging introduction to the region's geology, history, plants and animals. There's a hiking chapter, with detailed descriptions of trails suited to children, and about 20 pages of canyon-related activities that children can do in the car and at the park. Finally, children 8 to 12 will enjoy Marguerite Henry's *Brighty of the Grand Canyon*, a novel written through the eyes of Brighty the mule and based on true stories about a burro in the late 19th century.

Most books are available through the Grand Canyon Association (☎ 800-858-2808; W www.grandcanyon.org) or at the Canyon View Bookstore (☎ 928-638-7868).

INTERNET RESOURCES

Arizona at Your Service (W www.az.gov) The state of Arizona's tourism website, with links to hundreds of resources, from road conditions and airport information to festivals and events statewide.

Grand Canyon Association (W www.grandcanyon.org) Best online bookstore for the park, with links to the Grand Canyon Field Institute, the Grand Canyon Music Festival, helicopter tours and other useful sites.

Grand Canyon Chamber of Commerce (W www.thecanyon.com) Excellent site, with links to accommodations, restaurants and activities in Flagstaff, Sedona and Prescott.

Great Outdoor Recreation Pages (W www.gorp.com/gorp/location/az/az.htm) Dude ranches, hiking sites, rafting outfitters and other outdoor activities in Arizona.

Lonely Planet (W www.lonelyplanet.com) Home to the Thorn Tree bulletin board, where you can ask fellow travelers for their tips and share your own when you return home.

National Park Service *(W www.nps.gov/grca)* Updated information on the park, including current trail talks and a calendar of events, with link to Grand Canyon Association bookstore.

Public Lands Information Center *(W www.publiclands.org)* Consolidated information on all public lands in the United States, with links to educational programs and online shopping for recreation passes and permits, etc.

Xanterra Parks & Resorts *(W www.xanterra.com; W www.grandcanyonnorthrim.com for North Rim; W www.grandcanyonlodges.com for South Rim)* Primary in-park concessionaire, with information on special promotions, mule trips and accommodations, etc.

MAPS

Trails Illustrated/National Geographic publishes a waterproof/tearproof topographic map of *Grand Canyon National Park* that encompasses both rims, the backcountry and all trails. The best roadmap of the region is AAA's *Indian Country Guide Map*, which shows many dirt roads not included on other maps. Campgrounds and other recreational details are clearly marked on GTR Mapping's *Recreational Map of Arizona*. Maps are also available for specific hikes. For example, Earthwalk Press publishes a 1:24,000 *Bright Angel Trail Hiking Map & Guide*.

Check camping stores in Flagstaff and Kanab to find detailed topographic United States Geological Survey maps, essential for anyone planning backcountry hiking; order them in advance by calling ☎ 888-275-8747 or accessing the USGS website at W www.usgs.gov.

Two United States Forest Service maps show sights, viewpoints, primitive campsites, forest service roads and other useful locations in the surrounding Kaibab National Forest. The *North Kaibab Ranger District* map covers the forest north of the canyon, while the *Tusayan, Williams & Chalender Ranger Districts* map covers forest south of the park. They are available at the visitors centers in Flagstaff and Williams, the Tusayan and Williams Ranger Stations, and the Kaibab Plateau Visitor Center in Jacob Lake.

All but the USGS maps are available at Canyon View Bookstore on the South Rim and can be ordered in advance by calling the Grand Canyon Association at ☎ 800-858-2808. For outdoor activity maps of the entire West, peruse the map center at the **Public Land Information Center** website *(W www.publiclands.org/mapcenter)*.

USEFUL ORGANIZATIONS

Responsible for overall management of the Grand Canyon, the **National Park Service** *(☎ 928-638-7888; W www.nps.gov/grca; PO Box 129, Grand Canyon, AZ 86023)* cooperates with Xanterra, the Grand Canyon Association and other park agencies. While phoning can prove a frustrating search for a live person, you will find general information on the park. The website provides updated information, including details on automobile restrictions as the Greenway Plan (p84) is implemented. You can also call, write or visit the website to receive an advance trip planner and a backcountry planner.

National Park Service Environmental Programs instruct teachers, individuals, school and community groups about the park and the need to protect its natural resources. The environmental education office *(☎ 928-638-7662; W www.nps.gov/grca/education)* provides materials for teachers and international visitors and offers teacher-training workshops and field trips at the canyon.

Founded in 1932, the nonprofit **Grand Canyon Association** *(☎ 928-638-2481, 800-858-2828; W www.grandcanyon.org; PO Box 399, Grand Canyon, AZ 86023)* assists educational, historical and scientific programs in the park. The association operates all park bookstores, and the proceeds support park programs. In 1993 the association started the **Grand Canyon Field Institute** (p52), which offers educational courses for all ages. Visit the association website to buy books and videos on the park and peruse the various classes it sponsors.

Incorporated in 1995, the nonprofit **Grand Canyon National Park Foundation** (☎ 928-774-1760; W www.grandcanyonfoundation.org; 625 N Beaver St, Flagstaff, AZ 86001) works to preserve, protect and enhance the park. Through private, corporate and philanthropic donations, it funds wildlife restoration projects, exhibits and interpretive programs.

The **Grand Canyon Trust** (☎ 928-774-7488; W www.grandcanyontrust.org; 2601 N Fort Valley Rd, Flagstaff, AZ 86001) supports environmental projects geared toward preserving and protecting the natural resources of the Colorado Plateau. The trust has worked to control noise pollution by minimizing air tours over the canyon and helped engineer the 1996 flood flow plan to restore beaches in the canyon, among other projects.

What's It Going to Cost?

Your biggest expenses will be food and accommodations. If you camp, take day hikes and cook your own meals, you can enjoy the park for about $30 a day. If you stay at a rim-view suite at El Tovar and eat all your meals at this historic lodge, you'll spend upward of $400 a day. Add a rafting excursion, and you're talking an expensive trip. Most visitors spend somewhere between these two extremes.

A $20-per-vehicle park entrance fee covers shuttles, museums, ranger programs and some classes (for example, the photography and astronomy classes offered in the summer; see p52). If you plan to visit more than one national park in the following year, consider purchasing a **National Parks Pass** for $50 (see When You Arrive on p76 for more specifics).

Hiking is free, unless you spend the night down in the canyon (see Exploring the Backcountry, p123). Bus tours and mule trips cost extra.

Room rates in the park (unchanging year-round) range from $49 for a simple double with shared bath at Bright Angel Lodge to more than $285 for a rim-view suite at El Tovar. Most rooms average $90 to $130 per night for two people. On the North Rim, the price range between cabins and motel rooms is minimal ($91 to $116), but there's a huge difference in quality. It's well worth spending a little extra for a Western cabin. On the South Rim, some of the least-expensive rooms are at Yavapai West, and though it's not on the rim and the rooms are basic, it's one of the more peaceful spots in the park. Rim-view cabins at Bright Angel Lodge cost a bit more than doubles at the other lodges; though they don't have full rim views, they are bright, sunny and have more character than rooms at other lodges.

Most gateway towns offer accommodations to suit every budget, but your expenses will skyrocket if you stay in Sedona, one of Arizona's costliest destinations. Except for the hostel or campgrounds, it's difficult to find any lodgings for less than $80 a night.

The park cafeterias appeal to budget-conscience travelers, but consider splurging at the elegant El Tovar or the Grand Canyon Lodge, with its high ceilings, exposed beams and huge panoramic windows that overlook the canyon. All sit-down restaurants in the park (three on the South Rim, one on the North Rim) offer lower-priced children's menus. Packing picnic lunches, particularly if you buy supplies before entering the park, will save you lots of money, and you'll probably end up with a better meal than what you'll find at the cafeterias. Both rims offer plenty of great picnic spots, many with rim views.

Accommodations

Six lodges and two campgrounds are spread throughout Grand Canyon Village, and there's one campground beside the East Entrance. There is only one lodge and campground (no hookups) on the North Rim. Don't be misled, however, by the word *lodges*. Except for El Tovar and Bright Angel Lodge on the South Rim, and Grand Canyon Lodge on the North Rim, the accommodations within the park are more like roadside motels than lodges. They have clean, pleasant rooms, but don't expect rustic charm with blazing fireplaces and rough-hewn beams. Tusayan, with standard chain motels, and the towns of Williams, Flagstaff, Kanab and Sedona offer overflow accommodations, as do a few scattered lodges and motels closer to the park.

LAST-MINUTE ACCOMMODATIONS

It is possible to get last-minute accommodations at the Grand Canyon, even along the South Rim during summer peak season. Your first step should be to call **Xanterra** (☎ 888-297-2757), the official park concessionaire. Reservations may be cancelled up to 48 hours in advance, so you never know when a room may become available. If you're looking for same-day accommodations, call the lodges directly through the **North Rim switchboard** (☎ 928-638-2612) or **South Rim switchboard** (☎ 928-638-2631). There is no waiting list, so keep trying.

If you don't find a room on the South Rim, check motels in **Tusayan** (p161), only 7 miles from the South Entrance, or the motel in **Valle** (p162), about 15 miles farther south. In the middle of nowhere 32 miles east of the East Entrance is the pleasant **Cameron Trading Post & Motel** (p163), which often has vacancies. Another option is **Williams** (p182), 59 miles south of the park. Perhaps the safest bet for accommodations is **Flagstaff** (p187), 80 miles south, where you'll find a couple of wonderful historic hotels, two very nice hostels, B&Bs and lots of independent and chain motels.

The closest places to stay outside the North Rim are **Kaibab Lodge** (p165; 5 miles from the park entrance) or **Jacob Lake Inn** (p166), 30 miles north. **DeMotte Campground** (p165), across from Kaibab Lodge, is arguably the nicest campground in the region and there is also a campground in Jacob Lake. If everything is booked, you'll have to head to **Kanab** (p213), a pleasant town about 90 minutes north, where you'll find a hostel and several motels with rates from $55 to $90.

If all else fails, you can camp for free just about anywhere in Kaibab National Forest, which hugs the park on both rims. Don't camp within a quarter mile of the highway or any surface water, within a half mile of any developed campground or in meadows.

Bringing the Kids

While traveling with kids brings its own challenges, parents will find that the Grand Canyon is a very family-friendly place. The park offers plenty to do for all ages, and even the fanciest restaurants provide children's menus and crayons. Both rims also offer convenient cafeterias and plenty of picnic spots.

Of course, getting to the park, particularly the North Rim, requires lots of time in the car. Books on the desert, on wildlife and on the Grand Canyon, including several with car-friendly activities, can prepare children for the park and fuel their excitement. For kids 7 to 13, the *Puzzler's Guide to the Grand Canyon*, by Kristy McGowan and Karen Richards, is filled with crossword puzzles, mazes, hidden picture games, etc. Books on tape from your local library can help pass the hours as well. Plan plenty of stops, bring sunshades for the windows and carry water. You can take a break from the car by riding the historic **Grand Canyon Railway** (p184) into the park from Williams, featuring a predeparture old West show, strolling musicians and a staged robbery on the return trip. There are no seatbelts on shuttles in Grand Canyon Village, so you can't secure a car seat. If you take the rim-to-rim shuttle, you must provide your own car seat.

If you travel with lots of gear (stroller, backpacks, book bag, toy bag, diaper bag, etc), you might prefer to stay at **Yavapai West** on the South Rim, as it's the only place where you can park right outside your door. **Bright Angel Lodge** offers two-room cabins, and **El Tovar** has several suites, as do the chain motels in Tusayan. On the North Rim, **Pioneer Cabins** all sport two rooms (albeit tiny rooms) connected to a bathroom. Cribs and cots are available at all the lodges (there's a minimal charge for extra guests). A few suites at El Tovar accommodate up to seven guests (rather snugly) at no extra charge. See Best Family Accommodations Outside the Park (p165) for more kid-friendly lodgings.

Mule and horseback rides, several family-friendly hikes (p54) and other activities (see Fun for the Kids, p54) will wear children out, so it may not matter much where you spend the night. For more structured fun, both rims offer a **Junior Ranger Program** and several ranger-led activities that teach kids about the park history and environment. Your child must be at least 4 to participate, and most are geared toward 7- to 12-year-olds.

The 5-mile stretch of paved Rim Trail on the South Rim is suitable for strollers, but if you plan on more extensive hiking, consider a front carrier for infants or a backpack carrier for toddlers 5 and under (available at outdoor supply stores in Kanab, p213, and Flagstaff, p187).

Outside the park, parents will find plenty to keep kids happily entertained. In Kanab, kids enjoy the slapstick outdoor show at **Frontier Movie Town** (p214) and the nearby living museum at **Pipe Spring National Monument** (p214). Or consider a few days boating and swimming among the fantastic red rock scenery at Lake Powell. Also see Fun Stuff for Kids in & Around Flagstaff (p198).

Try not to pack too much in – distances are long, it's hot and dry and you'll want to spend most of your time playing. Too much time in the car and too much rushing from sight to sight can result in grumpy, tired kids and frustrated parents. Sometimes a longer stay in one place, familiarizing yourself with the area and developing a routine, can be more satisfying than trying to cover it all. Rather than simply seeing the canyon, slow down, immerse yourself and savor the smells, the tastes, the sensations and the moods of the park and the surrounding mountains and desert. This is how memories are made.

Health & Safety

EMERGENCY SERVICES

A clinic (☎ 928-638-2551; open 9am-10pm Mon-Fri) on the South Rim offers walk-in medical services, but the nearest hospital is 80 miles south in Flagstaff. There's no clinic on the North Rim – the nearest hospital is in Kanab, 80 miles north. Dial ☎ 911 (or ☎ 9-911 from your room) for emergency services on either rim.

The pharmacy on the South Rim cannot refill prescriptions (it will only accept a doctor's original prescription), so bring plenty of spare medicine. Also be sure to check the side effects of any medication, as the strong desert sun may interact with certain drugs.

PRESCRIPTIONS IN THE PARK

The small pharmacy at the South Rim clinic can fill prescriptions within 24 hours, but you must have a handwritten prescription from your doctor – be sure to carry this with you in case you lose important medication. Otherwise, you'll need to drive to the Safeway in Williams, 60 miles south. The closest pharmacies to the North Rim are 80 miles north in Kanab: Zion Pharmacy (☎ 435-644-2693 or after hours ☎ 435-644-2335; 14 E Center St; open Mon-Fri 10:30am-6:30pm, Sat 9am-2pm) and Kanab United Drugs (☎ 435-644-2418, 435-644-2418; 7 W Center St; open Mon-Fri 9am-6pm Sat 9am-12pm). Canyon Village Marketplace on the South Rim sells a wide variety of over-the-counter medications, and general stores on both rims offer a limited selection of basics.

FALLS

Just about every year people fall to their death at the Grand Canyon. Stay on the trails, and refrain from stepping over guardrails or leaning over for photographs. Absolutely do not horse around or allow children to run along the rim. There aren't as many guardrails as you may think, and several stretches have no railing at all. Parents should consider carrying toddlers in a child-carrier backpack along and below the rim.

When hiking below the rim, wear shoes or boots with good traction rather than loafers or sandals. Always turn your backpack away from mules, as they may inadvertently bump your pack and topple you into the canyon (sadly, this has happened).

DEHYDRATION, HEAT EXHAUSTION & HEAT STROKE

The canyon is a dry, hot place, and even if you're just strolling along the rim, lack of water can cause dehydration, which in turn can lead to heat exhaustion. Take time to acclimatize to high temperatures, wear a wide-brimmed hat and make sure to drink enough fluids. Hikers should drink a gallon of water per person per day. It's also a good idea to carry jugs of water in your car, should it break down. Characterized by fatigue, nausea, headaches and cramps, heat exhaustion should be treated by drinking water, eating high-energy foods, resting in the shade and cooling the skin with a wet cloth.

Long, continuous exposure to high temperatures can lead to heatstroke, a serious, sometimes fatal condition that occurs when the body's heat-regulating mechanism breaks down and one's body temperature rises to dangerous levels. Other symptoms include flushed, dry skin, a weak and rapid pulse and poor judgement or an inability to focus. Move the victim to shade, remove clothing, cover them with a wet sheet or towel and fan them continually. Hospitalization is essential for extreme cases.

Some 250 hikers a year on the most popular below-the-rim trails require ranger assistance to get out safely. Several have died. The main problems are too much sun and too little water. Time and again, hikers who have been rescued from the canyon say that their number one mistake was underestimating just how hot the canyon can be. Even if it turns out you don't need it, carrying extra water into the canyon may save someone else's life.

HYPOTHERMIA

If you hike the canyon in winter, hypothermia is a very real danger. This life-threatening condition occurs when prolonged exposure to cold thwarts the body's ability to maintain its core temperature. Symptoms include uncontrolled shivering, poor muscle control and a careless attitude. Remember to dress in layers and wear a windproof outer jacket. If possible, bring a thermos with warm fluids (even on a day trip). Treat symptoms by putting on dry clothing, drinking warm fluids and warming the victim through direct body contact with another person.

ALTITUDE SICKNESS

As the South Rim is more than 7000ft above sea level and the North Rim 8801ft at its highest point, altitude sickness is fairly common. Characterized by shortness of breath, fatigue and headaches, it can be avoided by drinking plenty of water and taking a day or two to acclimatize before attempting any long hikes.

SUNBURN

In the desert and at high altitude you can sunburn in less than an hour, even through cloud cover. Use lots of sunscreen (minimum SPF 15), especially on skin not typically exposed to sun. Be sure to apply sunscreen to young children, particularly babies. Everyone in your group should wear wide-brimmed hats. Stores on both rims carry both sunscreen and hats.

Dangers & Annoyances

Always lock your car and put valuables in the trunk, particularly if you park at a trail-head. Physical assault is rare in the park, but use caution when hiking alone.

WEATHER

Even if the sky overhead is clear, distant rainstorms can send walls of water, debris and mud roaring through side canyons without warning. Such flash floods have killed people caught in creeks and dry riverbeds. Never camp in dry washes, and be sure to check weather reports for the entire region before venturing into the canyon. Flash floods are most common during summer storms in July, August and September.

Don't underestimate the summer heat. Temperatures routinely soar past 100°F in the canyon.

In winter months, snow and ice can make trails slick and dangerous. Ask a ranger about conditions before heading out.

WILDLIFE

Do not approach or feed any wildlife, from seemingly innocuous chipmunks and squirrels to reclusive bobcats and mountain lions. In the canyon, scorpions are common and can inflict a nasty sting. If you camp out, check your boots for scorpions before putting them on. Also watch for rattlesnakes, readily identified by the segmented tips of their tails, which emit a rapid rattling sound when the snake is

ACCESS FOR ALL

Grand Canyon National Park offers many attractions and services for travelers with disabilities. Ask for an updated *Disability Guide* when you enter the park, which clearly maps out all the handicapped-accessible bathrooms, showers, campsites, guestrooms and parking lots, describes accessibility at overlooks and identifies 'windshield view' spots along the South Rim. Information is posted on the park web site (**w** www.nps.gov/grca) as well.

Many sites along the South Rim are readily accessible. Free loaner wheelchairs are usually available at the Canyon View Information Plaza. The 2-mile stretch from Mather Point to Bright Angel Lodge is easiest for those who have difficulty walking or use a wheelchair, and a golf cart runs regularly between the information plaza and Mather Point (about 200 yards). The Powell, Hopi and Pima overlooks on Hermit Road and the Yaki, Grandview, Moran and Desert View overlooks on Desert View Drive all offer wheelchair access.

All lodges except Bright Angel offer accessible guestrooms, and Mather, Desert View and Trailer Village campgrounds include a few accessible campsites. Hopi House is accessible only through a 29-inch-wide door, while steps and small doors at Kolb and Lookout Studios are more problematic. At the Tusayan Ruins & Museum, a level, paved trail leads into the museum and around the pueblo dwelling.

Descending into the canyon is a different story. The Bright Angel (South Rim) and North Kaibab (North Rim) trails are the least rocky, but even these will pose a challenge. Use extreme caution. Anyone wishing to take a certified service dog below the rim must first check in at the Backcountry Information Center on either rim.

On the North Rim, the best overlook is Cape Royal, where a fairly level, 0.6-mile paved trail leads to several canyon viewpoints. There's a wheelchair-accessible viewing platform at Point Imperial. Public spaces at Grand Canyon Lodge are easily negotiable by people with limited mobility, and four guestrooms have been specially modified. The North Rim Campground provides two accessible sites with picnic tables and one bathroom.

Limited funding has delayed purchase of wheelchair-accessible, alternative-fuel shuttles to replace the current shuttles. At press time, most of the shuttles on the green Village Route and about half those on the red Hermits Rest Route could accommodate wheelchairs. If you want to be assured a wheelchair-accessible shuttle, call ☎ 928-638-0591 a day in advance. Ask at the Canyon View Information Plaza or any of the transportation desks for a permit to drive a private car into shuttle-only areas. To obtain a permit for designated parking, inquire at an entrance station, Canyon View or the Yavapai Observation Station.

Mule rides are provisionally accessible with advance notice. Contact the **Bright Angel Transportation Desk** (*☎ 928-638-2631*), and they'll connect you with the barn to discuss your needs with the head wrangler. To secure a bus tour, call at least one week in advance to reserve a seat. The wheelchair-accessible bus has only 30 seats and the standard buses about 56; if a handicapped person books a tour, the concessionaire can limit the number of reservations.

River concessionaires can in many cases accommodate people with disabilities, even for multi-day whitewater trips. Call **Grand Canyon River Trip Information** (*☎ 800-959-9164*) for details. If you're not comfortable with rapids, **Xanterra** (*☎ 888-297-2757*) offers a bus trip to Page, where rafters meet up with **ARA Wilderness Adventures** (*☎ 928-645-3279 or ☎ 800-528-6154*) for a half-day float trip from Glen Canyon to Lees Ferry (see Activities, p222). Accessible accommodations can be arranged in advance.

disturbed. Most rattlesnakes have roughly diamond-shaped patterns along their backs. If you encounter one, inch away slowly. Those bitten will experience rapid swelling, severe pain and possible temporary paralysis. Have the victim lie down, keep the affected limb below head level and seek help immediately. Death is rare, though children are at particular risk.

FIRE
This is extremely dry country, and the slightest spark may cause a devastating wild-fire. Do not throw cigarette butts or used matches out of a car or toss them aside while hiking. Throw water on all fires, including those in fire grills, and make sure they're completely out before you leave.

GETTING LOST
The park comprises 1904 sq miles of desert terrain, and it's easy to lose one's way in its labyrinth of side canyons and sheer cliffs. Hike with a partner and don't stray from the trail under any circumstances. Whether you're hiking the backcountry or driving one of the region's many dirt roads, always carry an adequate map and bring a gallon of water per person per day.

Getting There

AIRPLANE
Both **Air Vegas Airlines** (☎ 800-255-7474; W www.airvegas.com) and **Scenic Airlines** (☎ 800-634-6801; W www.scenicairlines.com) offer daily flights from Las Vegas to Grand Canyon National Park Airport in Tusayan (about $200), 7 miles from the South Rim. If you're connecting through McCarran International Airport, you'll have to take a half-hour cab ride to North Las Vegas Airport to catch your onward flight.

Las Vegas is 290 miles from the South Rim and 277 miles from the North Rim. A 10-minute drive from the Vegas Strip, McCarran is a hub for **America West** (☎ 800-235-9292; W www.americawest.com). There are several advantages to flying into Vegas. For one, it's closer to the North Rim, and in order to attract the gambling set, airlines offer cheap flights and packages to the city year-round. Driving to the park from Vegas is also easy – aside from delays around Hoover Dam, traffic is minimal to either rim.

Phoenix is 220 miles from the South Rim and 335 miles from the North Rim. Three miles southeast of downtown, Phoenix Sky Harbor International Airport is the hub for America West and **Southwest Airlines** (☎ 800-435-9792; W www.south westairlines.com). Phoenix offers more connecting airlines and routes, but you risk getting caught in traffic. Once you do escape the city, the drive north on Highways 89 and 89A to Flagstaff is beautiful, passing through several mountain towns and Sedona's celebrated red rock country. You could easily spend a few leisurely days driving to the park. For a faster option, **America West Express** offers several flights a day from Phoenix to Flagstaff (about $250), 80 miles south of the South Rim.

TRAIN
Operated by **Amtrak** (☎ 928-774-8679, 800-872-7245; W www.amtrak.com), the Southwest Chief makes a daily run between Chicago and Los Angeles, with stops at

Flagstaff and Williams. In Williams you can connect with the historic **Grand Canyon Railway** (☎ 800-843-8724; W *www.thetrain.com*), with original 1923 Pullman cars chugging the scenic 65 miles to the South Rim (p183).

BUS

Greyhound (☎ 928-774-4573, 800-229-9424; *399 S Malpais Ln*) stops at Flagstaff to/ from Albuquerque, Las Vegas, Los Angeles and Phoenix. From the Flagstaff train depot, a shuttle heads to the park daily.

SHUTTLE

Open Road Tours (☎ 928-226-8060, 800-766-7117; W *www.openroadtours.com*) offers shuttles from Phoenix Sky Harbor to Flagstaff ($31/56 one-way/round-trip) that continue on to Williams and the Grand Canyon ($20/40 round-trip). The fare from Williams to the park is $15/30.

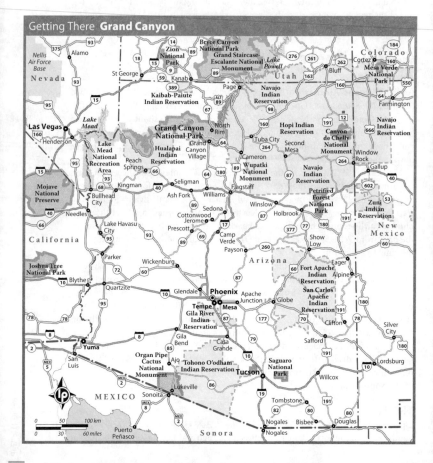

Getting There **Grand Canyon**

ORGANIZED TOURS

Among the best organized tours are those offered through the Grand Canyon Field Institute and the **Museum of Northern Arizona** (see Classes & Learning Vacations, p52). Led by experts and experienced canyon guides, GCFI trips include family-oriented tours, extended rafting and backpacking excursions, cultural and natural history tours, and photography and wilderness studies.

From the park, **Xanterra** and the **GCFI** offer a two-day/two-night all-inclusive tour of the South Rim for ages 10 and above ($572/371 for two high/low season). Participants in groups of four to 10 explore the park by foot and bus as a GCFI instructor introduces you to the region's history, geology and ecology. Call ☎ 928-638-2525 for details.

The following tours of the South Rim stop at viewpoints and selected sights; most include time for a walk along the rim. Airlines in Tusayan offer scenic canyon tours from Las Vegas (see Flyovers, p104). For details on guided rafting trips, see Rafting the Colorado (p133) and the Hualapai Indian Reservation (p180).

From Flagstaff & Williams

Open Road Tours (☎ 928-226-8060, 877-226-8060; W www.openroadtours.com) offers a one-day tour of the park for $69 per person, including a stop at the Cameron Trading Post. Departing from Flagstaff, Williams and Tusayan, **American Dream Tours** (☎ 928-527-3369, 888-203-1212; W www.americandreamtours.com) takes no more than 14 people per van on one-day trips of the South Rim ($67.50/42 adult/child); rates include a picnic lunch at Tusayan Ruins & Museum. **Grand Canyon Tours of Splendor** (☎ 866-525-2675; W www.grandcanyonsplendor.com) provides particularly comfortable vans with large aisles, reclining bucket seats and big windows; rates are $69/50 for adult/child, including a stop at the IMAX theater and a complimentary postcard of you at the Grand Canyon.

Marvelous Marv's (☎ 928-635-1935, 800-655-4948; W www.marvelousmarv.com) is run by a quirky local character who will pick you up at your hotel or campground in or around Williams for a full-day tour of the South Rim in his 15-passenger van ($70/50 adult/child; cash or traveler's checks only). Also see Grand Canyon Railway (p184) for train and combination train/bus tours out of Williams.

From Las Vegas

Grand Canyon Tour Company (☎ 800-222-6966; W www.grandcanyontourcompany.com) offers a one-day trip to the South Rim ($149 or $179 for two if you book online), as well as several plane, helicopter, bus, hiking and rafting tours of the both rims and the inner canyon. For helicopter or plane tours of the canyon from $280 per person, contact **Maverick Helicopter** (☎ 888-261-4414; W www.maverickhelicopter.com) or **Air Vegas** (☎ 800-255-7474; W www.airvegas.com). **Sundance Helicopters** (☎ 800-653-1881; W www.helicoptour.com) offers trips farther west to the Hualapai Indian Reservation, which isn't subject to the same above-the-rim air regulations enforced elsewhere in the canyon; choose from a quick flight down to the river and back (about $79 per person) or a full-day excursion that includes your flight into the canyon and a three-hour rafting trip on the Colorado ($389).

From Kanab

For customized, four-wheel-drive photography tours of remote spots along the North Rim, contact **Terry's Camera Trading Co** (☎ 435-644-5981; W www.utahcameras.com;

19 W Center St; 8am-6pm Mon-Sat). Terry has been exploring and photographing the canyon and the surrounding desert and plateau country for more than 25 years.

CAR

From **Las Vegas**, it's an easy drive to either rim. To get to the North Rim, head north on I-15 into Utah. Just past St George, take Hwy 9 east to Hurricane. You can either continue on Hwy 9 through Zion National Park, then connect with Hwy 89 down through Kanab to Fredonia, or take Hwy 59/389 southeast to Fredonia and connect with Alt 89. Alt 89 heads southeast to Jacob Lake, where Hwy 67 leads 30 miles to the park entrance station. The most direct route to the South Rim is Hwy 93 south to I-40, then east to Williams, where you'll turn north on Hwy 64 to Valle, then follow Hwy 180 into the park.

From **Phoenix**, take I-17 north to Flagstaff and continue on Hwy 180 north to the park. Another option is to take Hwy 60 northwest to Hwy 89 through Prescott, then connect with 89A, which winds northeast through forested mountains to Sedona. From there it's a short jaunt north through Oak Creek Canyon to Flagstaff. It is a beautiful drive, but traffic can be brutal in summer, particularly around Sedona. If you're continuing to the North Rim from Flagstaff, take Hwy 89 north. (At Cameron, Hwy 64 leads 32 miles west to the South Rim's East Entrance.) About 60 miles north of Cameron, Alt 89 turns east through Lees Ferry and Marble Canyon to Jacob Lake.

Car Rental

The following major car rental agencies operate out of the airports in Las Vegas and Phoenix. Options include convertibles, mini-vans and four-wheel-drive vehicles.

Avis *(☎ 800-230-4898; W www.avis.com)*
Budget *(☎ 800-527-0700; W www.budgetrentacar.com)*
Hertz *(☎ 800-654-3131; W www.hertz.com)*
National *(☎ 800-227-7366; W www.nationalcar.com)*
Thrifty *(☎ 800-367-2277; W www.thrifty.com)*

In Flagstaff, rentals are available through Avis *(☎ 928-230-4898)*, National *(☎ 928-779-1975)*, Enterprise *(☎ 928-526-1377, 800-325-8007; W www.pickenterprise.com)* and Hertz *(☎ 928-774-4452)*, though rates are higher here than in Phoenix or Las Vegas. Enterprise *(☎ 928-638-2871)* also operates out of Grand Canyon National Park Airport in Tusayan, though rates are higher still and cars may only be available from April through October.

RV & Camper Rental

Cruise America *(☎ 800-783-3768; W www.cruiseamerica.com)* rents recreational vehicles nationwide and has offices in Phoenix, Flagstaff and Las Vegas. For one-way rental, call ☎ 800-327-7799. Rates are about $1300 a week. On its website, you'll find the *Renters Assistance Guide*, which offers RV operating tips.

Motorcycle Rental

Cruise America *(☎ 480-464-7300)* rents motorcycles from its Phoenix office.

Road Conditions

To check road conditions within the park, call the automated information line at ☎ 928-638-7888. To check conditions in the Kaibab National Forest-South Rim, call the Tusayan Ranger Station (☎ 928-638-2443); for conditions in the Kaibab National Forest-North Rim, call the Kaibab Plateau Visitor Center (☎ 928-643-7298).

Ranging between 6500ft and 7500ft in elevation, roads in Flagstaff and environs may experience snow and ice from October through April. At elevations approaching 9000ft, roads along the North Rim are even more susceptible to weather. The drive up from deserts north and east of the park climbs about 4000ft, and conditions change rapidly – you may start out in sunny, dry weather in Kanab or Lees Ferry and wind up battling rain, hail or snow in Jacob Lake. The forest service's dirt roads, particularly those in Kaibab National Forest, may be impassable after even a light rain. Always check with a ranger before heading out. You'll need a high-clearance, four-wheel-drive vehicle to tackle both the 17-mile road to Point Sublime, a minimum two-hour round-trip, and the 60-mile dirt road to Toroweap. Absolutely do not attempt these drives without first telling someone where you're going, and be sure to bring plenty of water.

GRAND CANYON NATIONAL PARK

You've seen the photos, read the books and reserved your rooms. Perhaps you've watched a video or had friends regale you with their experiences.

EXPERIENCING
GRAND CANYON

Still, nothing can prepare you for that first glimpse of the Grand Canyon, with its shifting colors, dramatic stone temples and unsurpassed grandeur. The canyon remains one of the world's most spectacular sights, as much a cultural destination as a geologic phenomenon. It offers something for everyone, whether you only have time for a quick drive along the South Rim or you've set aside several weeks to explore the chasm's nooks and crannies, study its flora and fauna and raft the Colorado River. People of all ages and abilities can enjoy the park, from babies snug in carriers to fit young backpackers, strolling seniors and visitors in wheelchairs.

Sure, you'll take loads of photos and painstakingly arrange them in albums. But they can't entirely capture the sights, scents, sounds and feelings of a visit to the canyon. Those you'll have to record in your heart and spirit; no matter how short your trip may be, take the time to do just that.

When You Arrive

There's a $20-per-vehicle fee to enter the park, permitting visits to both rims within seven days of purchase. Those entering by bicycle, motorcycle or on foot pay just $10. (Be prepared to show your receipt if you leave and reenter the park.) As you enter, you'll receive a map and a copy of *The Guide*, an NPS newspaper with additional maps, current park news and information on ranger programs, hikes, accommodations and park services. There's a separate version for each rim, and each is available in English, Spanish, French and German.

If you plan a longer stay or to revisit the park, consider purchasing a $40 **Grand Canyon Pass**, which is valid for 12 months and allows unlimited visits. Better yet, a $50 annual **National Parks Pass** grants the holder and any accompanying passengers in a private vehicle free admission to any NPS site in the US. For $15 more you can purchase a **Golden Eagle** hologram for your pass, which extends access to sites administered by the US Fish & Wildlife Service, the US Forest Service and the Bureau of Land Management.

If you're 62 or older, purchase the $10 **Golden Age Passport**, which grants access to all NPS, USFW, USFS and BLM sites and is good for the holder's lifetime. A **Golden Access Passport** is free and offers the same benefits to US residents who are permanently disabled; you must offer medical proof of your disability to be eligible.

All passes are available at the park entrance stations. The Golden Age and Golden Access Passports must be purchased in person, but you can purchase a National Parks Pass in advance with a credit card (☎ 888-467-2757; Ⓦ *www.nps.gov*) or by check made payable to the National Park Foundation, Attn: Park Pass, PO Box 34108, Washington DC 20043-4108. It takes up to two weeks to receive and there is an additional cost for shipping; priority shipping (five business days) is also available.

Hours at the entrance stations vary considerably throughout the year. If the booth is unmanned, the gate is left open and you can just drive right in. Once you're in the park, no one will check to see that you have paid. Remember, however, that these fees help foot the bill for the many services the NPS provides. Please pay on your way out.

From mid-October to mid-May all services on the North Rim are closed and the 30-mile road from Jacob Lake to the North Rim entrance and all roads within the park are left unplowed. However, cross-country skiers may still enter the North Rim, free of charge. Snowmobiles are not permitted.

ORIENTATION
Entrances
There are two entrances to the South Rim. From the South Entrance (Hwy 180) it's 3 miles to Grand Canyon Village and the hub of services. The East Entrance is on Hwy 64, 32 miles west of Cameron and 25 rim-hugging miles east of Grand Canyon Village.

The only entrance to the North Rim is 30 miles south of Jacob Lake, which offers a lodge, restaurant and campground. From the entrance station it's 12.5 forested miles to the campground and another 1.5 miles to the lodge and visitors center.

Visitor Service Hubs
Almost all services on the South Rim are in Grand Canyon Village. On the North Rim, services are inside or next to Grand Canyon Lodge. Forty-four miles north of the lodge in Jacob Lake, the Kaibab Plateau Visitor Center also provides information on the park and surrounding Kaibab National Forest.

Getting Around

Free shuttle buses operate every 10 to 15 minutes along three routes on the South Rim. **Hermits Rest Route** accesses the 8-mile stretch of rim road west of Grand Canyon Village. This road is closed to private vehicles from March through November; the only way to see the overlooks then is via shuttle or on foot. You can drive to most facilities in the village, but it's easier to park your car and take one of the **Village Route** shuttles (for details see South Rim, Getting Around, p83). The

BEST RIM VIEWS OF THE COLORADO RIVER

✔ Mohave Point
✔ Hopi Point
✔ Moran Point
✔ Lipan Point
✔ Desert View

Kaibab Trail Route stops at Pipe Creek Vista, South Kaibab Trailhead and Yaki Point, the last of which is closed to private vehicles year-round. Except for an early-morning shuttle to the North Kaibab Trailhead, the only way to explore the North Rim is by car, bicycle or on foot.

The **Transcanyon Shuttle** (☎ 928-638-2820; *adult one-way/round-trip $65/110, child 12 and under one-way/round-trip $50/90; cash only*) offers rim-to-rim shuttle service from mid-May to mid-October (when the North Rim is open). Reservations are required, and infant car seats are not provided. Reserve a seat at least a week in advance to be guaranteed a spot. The shuttle departs Grand Canyon Lodge at 7am, arrives at South Rim's Bright Angel Lodge around noon, then makes the return trip at 1:30pm, arriving at the North Rim at 6:30pm. The shuttle is a godsend for rim-to-rim hikers, but it's also a good option for those who want to see both rims but don't want to bother with a car.

Call ☎ 928-638-7888 for recorded information on road and weather conditions.

Policies & Regulations

PETS

Dogs are permitted on certain developed South Rim trails but are not allowed in park lodges, below the rim or on any trails along the North Rim, unless they are certified service dogs. All pets must be on a leash. Pets are allowed in the campgrounds on both rims. (See Pets in the Park, p58)

CAMPFIRES

Open fires are only permitted in fire pits at North Rim, Desert View and Mather campgrounds. You can use camp stoves at campgrounds and in the backcountry.

WEAPONS

Weapons of any kind, including guns and bows, are prohibited on park grounds.

WILDERNESS PERMITS & REGULATIONS

A backcountry permit is required for all overnight camping below the rim and on parkland outside of designated campgrounds. See Exploring the Backcountry (p123) for details on fees and procedures for obtaining a permit.

BICYCLES

Bicycles are allowed only on roads open to other vehicles. You cannot take them on any trails in the park, including the paved sections along the South Rim.

WILDLIFE

It's illegal to feed any wildlife in the park, including squirrels and birds. This is not only for your safety, but also for the safety and well-being of the animals.

The Grand Canyon's South Rim encompasses some of the park's best and worst aspects. Here, scenic drives along the rim offer ample opportunities to enjoy gorgeous canyon vistas. Accessible to visitors of all ages and abilities, the 13-mile Rim Trail skirts the edge of the gorge and connects with Grand Canyon Village. Those wanting to descend into the canyon can choose from more than a dozen trailheads spread out along the rim or join regular mule trains on day and overnight trips. Several museums and distinctive stone buildings designed by Mary Colter illuminate the park's human history, and rangers lead a host of daily programs on subjects like geology and condors.

On the flip side, the South Rim sees the most crowds, especially in the peak summer season, when lines are long, shuttles are packed and trails are covered in boot prints. Even this, however, doesn't have to detract from your trip. Patience and a sense of humor go a long way, as does the right attitude. While people-watching from the back porch of the elegant El Tovar or chatting it up with international visitors on the train from Williams may not be quintessential wilderness experiences, they do add richness to a park visit. Despite the crowds, you'll still see deer and other wildlife, find a quiet spot to enjoy the canyon's sublime beauty and be able to hike in solitude.

SOUTH RIM HIGHLIGHTS

Shoshone Point – An easy 1-mile ramble along a dirt road to a spectacular and uncrowded overlook

El Tovar – The grande dame of national park hotels

The Watchtower – A scramble up Mary Colter's five-story stone tower offers unparalleled views of the canyon and surrounding desert

Hermit Road – An 8-mile driving tour to overlooks and the historic Hermits Rest; accessible by car (Dec-Feb only), shuttle or foot

Lipan Point – Arguably the most sublime of the South Rim's many vistas

Grandview Trail – Dropping a stunning 1200ft in the first three-quarters of a mile, this trail leads to a sagebrush-tufted mesa and offers welcome solitude

Grand Canyon Railway – Historic steam-powered Pullman cars whisk you into the park

Orientation

ENTRANCES

Most visitors enter the park via the **South Entrance**, 80 miles northwest of Flagstaff on Hwy 180. In summer be prepared to wait up to 30 minutes or more at the entrance station. A few miles north lies Grand Canyon Village, which sprawls over 3 sq miles and is the primary hub of activity. Here you'll find lodges, restaurants, two of the three developed campgrounds, the backcountry office, the visitors center, the shuttles, the clinic, bank, grocery store and other services.

The **East Entrance** lies on Hwy 64, 32 miles west of Cameron and 25 miles east of the village. At this entrance you'll find a campground, a gas station and the Desert View service hub, which offers a snack bar, a small information center, a general store, a gift shop and the Watchtower (see Desert View Drive, p88). If possible, choose this entrance if you're visiting the South Rim. It's only 10 miles farther from Flagstaff than the South Entrance, and your first views of the canyon will be much more dramatic and peaceful.

MAJOR REGIONS

The park's South Rim comprises four distinct sections: Grand Canyon Village, Hermit Road, Desert View Drive and the below-the-rim backcountry. You'll find most services in and around Grand Canyon Village, a full-fledged town that services park employees and their families. **Hermit Road** (p86) hugs the rim from the village 8 miles west to Hermits Rest, offering seven viewpoints along the way. **Desert View Drive** (p88) spans 25 miles from Grand Canyon Village through Desert View to the East Entrance, passing several excellent viewpoints, picnic areas and the Tusayan Ruins & Museum. The **Rim Trail** (p95) starts at Hermits Rest, passes Kolb Studio, the lodges, Yavapai Observation Station and Mather Point in the village, and stretches east to Yaki Point. About 5 miles of it is paved, from Maricopa Point through the village east to Pipe Creek Vista, just past Mather Point. Access to the **backcountry** is by foot or mule along established trails (see Walks & Day Hikes, p94, and Exploring the Backcountry, p123).

ESCAPING SUMMER CROWDS ON THE SOUTH RIM

Escape is easy if you know where to go:

✔ Arrive through the **East Entrance**

✔ Take the 1-mile trail to **Shoshone Point**

✔ Walk along the rim just east of **Pima Point** or east of **Mather Point**

✔ Avoid the Rim Trail through Grand Canyon Village between 9am and 5pm

✔ Hike into the canyon on the steep and narrow Hermit Trail to **Santa Maria Spring**

✔ Camp at **Desert View Campground** rather than Mather Campground

MAJOR ROADS

Hwy 180 runs north to the South Entrance from Tusayan (1 mile), Valle (22 miles) and Flagstaff (80 miles). From Williams (30 miles west of Flagstaff on I-40), Hwy 64 heads north to Valle, where it connects with Hwy 180 to the park.

Hwy 89 runs from Flagstaff 44 miles north to Cameron, where Hwy 64 heads west to the park's East Entrance. It is 25 miles from the East Entrance to Grand Canyon Village.

THE CANYON'S TEMPLES

In 1880 **Clarence Edward Dutton**, accompanied by artists Thomas Moran and William Henry Holmes, led an expedition to the canyon under the auspices of the newly formed United States Geological Survey. Dutton likened many of the canyon's elaborate mesas, buttes and pinnacles to temples in India, Egypt and China, and named them accordingly. The park's maps and interpretive signs still refer to Dutton's Brahma, Isis and Confucius Temples, to name but a few.

VISITOR SERVICE HUBS

You'll find 95% of visitor services in Grand Canyon Village, easily accessible via the blue Village Route shuttles. On the east side, **Market Plaza** includes a **grocery store** (☎ 928-631-2262), a **bank** (☎ 928-638-2437) and a **post office** (☎ 928-638-2512). The main visitors center is **Canyon View Information Plaza** (☎ 928-638-7644), just behind Mather Point.

Information

Though the park can seem overwhelming when you first arrive, it is actually quite easy to find your way. If you have questions, NPS rangers and people who staff the hotels, restaurants and services are typically helpful and friendly. The blue Village Route shuttles stop at all of the following information centers except Hermits Rest, Desert View and Tusayan Ruins & Museum. Limited hours go into effect between October and March.

CANYON VIEW INFORMATION PLAZA

Three hundred yards behind Mather Point, **Canyon View Information Plaza** encompasses the **Canyon View Visitor Center** (☎ 928-638-7644; open 8am-6pm) and **Books & More Store** (☎ 928-638-0099; open 8am-7pm), the park's most extensive bookstore. Outside, bulletin boards and kiosks display information on ranger programs, the weather, tours, etc. One display presents photos from each viewpoint – an excellent orientation to the rim. The center's bright, spacious interior includes a ranger-staffed information desk and a lecture hall, where rangers offer daily talks on a variety of subjects. The store offers a vast selection of books and videos on the park and the region.

You can take the blue Village Route shuttle directly to the plaza. Alternatively, simply stroll along the rim to Mather Point, or drive to the small lot by Mather Point and walk to the plaza. If the lot is full, you can park on the side of the road.

YAVAPAI OBSERVATION STATION

Perched on the rim, this visitors center and **bookstore** (☎ 928-638-2631; open 8am-8pm) features huge windows with expansive views of the canyon and panels that identify the major geologic features. The station lies 1.75 miles east of El Tovar and 0.6 mile west of Mather Point. As parking can be difficult, you're better off walking along the Rim Trail or hopping the blue Village Route shuttle.

DESERT VIEW INFORMATION CENTER

Housed in small stone building near the East Entrance, this staffed **information center** (☎ 928-638-7893; *open 9am-6pm*) also offers books and maps.

KOLB STUDIO

Once the home and studio of the Kolb brothers, pioneering photographers of the Grand Canyon, this **historic building** (☎ 928-638-2771; *open 8am-7pm*) houses a small but excellent bookstore and an art gallery with changing exhibits (see Sights, p93).

TUSAYAN RUINS & MUSEUM

Three miles west of Desert View, this **museum** (☎ 928-638-2305; *open 9am-5pm*) features exhibits on the park's indigenous people (see Desert View Drive, p89) and an information desk staffed by rangers.

EL TOVAR

This hotel's helpful **concierge** (☎ 928-638-2631; *open 8am-5pm*) can answer questions, arrange same- or next-day bus tours and sell stamps.

GETTING HITCHED AT THE GRAND CANYON

To be married in the park, you must first obtain a state marriage license from any Arizona courthouse. The nearest location is the **Clerk of the Superior Court** (☎ 928-779-6353) in Flagstaff. If you want an outdoor wedding, you must get a free permit from the park by writing Wedding Permit Information, Grand Canyon National Park, PO Box 129, Grand Canyon, AZ 86023. Include the exact date and time of the event, how many people will be attending, your requested location and who will be performing the ceremony. Several pastors and priests at Grand Canyon Village may be able to officiate. Otherwise, four local justices of the peace or the Flagstaff Municipal Judge can do the honors. For details on locations and other information, call 928-638-7775.

You can get married at any viewpoint along the South Rim – imagine the spectacular backdrop in your wedding photos! Outdoor weddings of more than 50 people (maximum 85) must be held at Shoshone Point, a beautiful overlook at the end of a 1-mile dirt road. Ceremonies are available by reservation from May 15 to October 15 only; call ☎ 928-638-7777 for details. Remember that summer showers are prevalent from late June to September; consider a morning wedding to minimize the possibility of rain. To make advance reservations for indoor weddings and/or receptions at park lodges, call ☎ 928-638-2525.

It's also possible to get married on the North Rim, though logistics are more complicated, given its remote location. Contact the North Rim District Ranger at the wedding permit address listed above. For catering information, call or write the **special events coordinator** (☎ 928-638-2525; *c/o Sales, Grand Canyon NP Lodges, PO Box 699, Grand Canyon AZ 86023*).

BRIGHT ANGEL, YAVAPAI & MASWIK TRANSPORTATION DESKS

In the lobbies of Bright Angel, Yavapai and Maswik Lodges, these **service desks** (☎ 928-638-2631; open 8am-5pm) can book bus tours and same- or next-day mule trips. They can also answer questions about horseback rides, scenic flights and smooth-water float trips. Bright Angel can arrange last-minute lodgings at Phantom Ranch (if available).

HERMITS REST

At the west end of Hermit Road, this beautiful stone **building** (☎ 928-638-2631; open 9am-sunset) houses a small bookstore, gift shop and snack window. For more details, see the Hermit Road driving tour (p86).

BACKCOUNTRY INFORMATION CENTER

Near Maswik Lodge, the Backcountry Information Center is open from 8am to 5pm (closed noon-1pm), including holidays. You can also phone the center weekdays between 1pm and 5pm (☎ 928-638-7875).

Getting Around

CAR

Once parked outside your hotel, your car can remain there as long as you're in the village. All services are accessible via the blue Village Route shuttle, a hassle-free alternative to traffic and parking.

If you do drive, consult the Grand Canyon Village map (Map 4) or *The Guide* for parking lot locations. You'll find lots at all the hotels and at Mather Point, though this may change as the Greenway Plan is implemented (see The Greenway Plan, p84). Small lots at viewpoints along Hermit Road and Desert View Drive usually have plenty of open spaces, even during summer peak season. Though Desert View is only 25 miles east, allow at least 45 minutes by car, even if you plan to drive nonstop. While traffic usually moves rather smoothly, the speed limit is 45mph, and cars often turn unexpectedly into the many pullouts. From March through November cars are not allowed on Hermit Road, which heads west from the village to Hermits Rest.

The park's only gas station is the **Desert View Chevron**, near the East Entrance. It's open daily from late April through September, though hours change seasonally. Gas stations in Tusayan are closer to the village. The village **auto repair** (☎ 928-638-2631) offers 24-hour emergency service and is open daily from 8am to noon and from 1pm to 5pm.

Enterprise (☎ 928-638-2871; open 9am-5pm) provides rental cars at Grand Canyon National Park Airport, in Tusayan. Pickup service is available.

SHUTTLES

Free shuttle buses ply three routes along the South Rim.

The red **Hermits Rest Route** runs west along Hermit Road from March through November. You can hop off at any of the viewpoints (it stops seven times on the way from the village to Hermits Rest), enjoy the view and a hike, then catch another shuttle farther west or back to the village. Or walk part of the way along the Rim Trail (p95) and catch the shuttle. The shuttle does not stop at all viewpoints on its return to the village.

The blue **Village Route** provides year-round transportation between most village facilities, including Canyon View Information Plaza, Yavapai Point, Market Plaza, the backcountry office, hotels, restaurants, campgrounds and parking lots. It does not stop at the clinic.

The green **Kaibab Trail Route** provides service to and from the Canyon View Information Plaza, Pipe Creek Vista, South Kaibab Trailhead and Yaki Point. The trailhead and Yaki Point are on a short road off of Desert View Drive that is closed to cars year-round.

Buses run every 10 to 15 minutes. You'll find a map of the shuttle stops and seasonal operating hours in *The Guide*. Maps are also posted at all shuttle stops and inside the shuttles themselves.

THE GREENWAY PLAN

More than 5 million people visit the Grand Canyon each year, leading at times to heavy traffic and crowded parking lots. In an effort to restrict car use, the National Parks Foundation is working with the Grand Canyon Association to develop 73 miles of dirt and paved bicycle and pedestrian paths on both rims. As the paths are developed, roads and parking lots may face restrictions.

On the South Rim three trails totaling 11 miles will connect Tusayan, Canyon View Information Plaza, the lodges and the future Heritage Education Campus. A proposed 34-mile trail will link Canyon View Information Plaza with Desert View to the east and Hermits Rest to the west. Greenway projects on the North Rim include a 6-mile trail that will connect Grand Canyon Lodge, the campground and the North Kaibab Trailhead, as well as a 14-mile trail out to Cape Royal (currently accessible only via paved road).

Four miles of Greenway trails are already in use on the South Rim. The first is part of the Rim Trail, stretching east from Yavapai Observation Station past Mather Point to Pipe Creek Vista. The second trail connects Canyon View Information Plaza with Grand Canyon Village.

The plan is dependent in part on private and corporate donations. For updated information and details on how to contribute, contact the **Grand Canyon Foundation** (☎ *928-774-1760;* ₩ *www.grandcanyonfoundation.org).*

HIKERS' SHUTTLES

The green **Kaibab Trail Route shuttle** ferries hikers from Canyon View Information Plaza to the South Kaibab Trailhead. In June and July it runs every 10 to 15 minutes from 4am to 9pm, in August it runs every 10 to 15 minutes from 4:30am to 8:30pm, and in September it runs every 30 minutes from 5am to 7:45pm.

An early-morning **express hikers' shuttle** leaves from Bright Angel Lodge and the Backcountry Information Center for the South Kaibab Trailhead daily at 4am, 5am and 6am from June to August; 5am, 6am and 7am in May and September; 6am, 7am and 8am in April and October; and 8am, 9am and 10am between November and March.

TAXI

Grand Canyon Coaches (☎ 928-638-0821) and **Fred Harvey's 24-Hour Taxi** (☎ 928-638-2822) offer taxi service to and from Tusayan and within the park.

ORGANIZED TOURS

Narrated **bus tours** west to Hermits Rest or east to the Watchtower depart twice daily from Maswik, Yavapai and Bright Angel Lodges. These offer a good introduction to the canyon, as drivers stop at the best viewpoints, point out the various buttes, mesas and pleateaus, and offer historical anecdotes. Tickets are available at the lodge transportation desks or from the El Tovar concierge. Children under 16 ride for free when accompanied by an adult.

Two-hour tours to Hermits Rest ($15.75) depart daily at 9am and 4pm. A 90-minute **sunrise tour** or two-hour **sunset tour** to Hermits Rest ($12.25) depart at various times throughout the year (the sunrise tour can leave as early as 4am in summer).

Four-hour Desert View Drive tours ($28) depart daily at 9am and 12:30pm and include an hour at the Watchtower. In summer a **sunset tour** of Desert View Drive departs at 4pm.

A **combination tour** ($34) allows you to choose any two of the above options.

Driving Tours

Two scenic drives follow the rim on either side of the village – **Hermit Road** to the west and **Desert View Drive** to the east. The rim dips in and out of view as the road passes through the piñon-juniper and ponderosa stands of Kaibab National Forest. Pullouts along the way offer spectacular views and interpretive signs that explain the canyon's features and geology.

✔ TIP

Bring water with you on the Hermit Road shuttle – no water is available until Hermits Rest.

Resist the temptation to simply jump out of your car and snap a photo. It takes a while to absorb each view. If you're short on time, select a few choice overlooks to enjoy at length. Breathe in the desert air, watch for birds, peer down at the river and wonder at the forces that carved this canyon.

Though you might expect bumper-to-bumper traffic, this is generally not the case. Yes, there's a constant stream of cars, but you'll rarely come to a standstill and can usually find plenty of parking at the viewpoints. The road to Yaki Point and the South Kaibab Trailhead is closed year-round to all traffic except bicycles and the green Kaibab Trail Route shuttle. From March 1 to November 30, Hermit Road is closed to all traffic except bicycles and the red Hermits Rest Route shuttle. Both scenic drives may close due to snow or ice buildup from November through March, call ☎ 928-638-7888 for current road and weather conditions.

If you don't have a car or don't want to drive, **bus tours** of both scenic drives leave several times daily year-round (see Organized Tours, p85). Alternatively, you can hike the Rim Trail (p95) to any of the viewpoints along Hermit Road. In summer it's nice to combine shuttle rides with hiking.

Canyon View Bookstore sells an **audio guide** on tape or CD with more information on what you'll see along the rim. Some viewpoints offer good river views, while others are best for sunrises or sunsets. Everyone has a favorite – find your own among the following.

HERMIT ROAD
Route: Grand Canyon Village to Hermits Rest
Distance: 8 miles
Speed Limit: 35mph

This popular drive offers several exceptional views. It begins at the west end of Grand Canyon Village and ends at Mary Colter's distinctive Hermits Rest, built as a rest stop for early park tourists.

Trailview Overlook

This overlook offers a great view of **Bright Angel Trail** (p96), the lush vegetation at **Indian Garden** and **Grand Canyon Village** on the rim to the east. The Havasupai Indians first blazed Bright Angel Trail to access Indian Garden and grow crops. In 1890-91 prospectors Pete Berry and Ralph Cameron improved the trail, and in 1898-99 Cameron extended it to the river. Realizing there was more money to be made in tourism than in mining, he imposed a $1 toll in 1903 and charged tourists hiking or riding mules down the trail. The National Park Service constructed alternative trails from Hermits Rest and Yaki Point until 1928, when it gained control of Bright Angel. If you arrive early in the morning, you may see tiny specks of a faraway mule train descending into the canyon.

Maricopa Point

In 1890 prospector Daniel Lorain Hogan discovered what he believed to be copper 1100ft below this viewpoint. He filed a mining claim for the area, including 4 acres on the rim, and set about to make his fortune. After more than 40 years of minimal success, Hogan realized that the real money at the canyon was in tourism, so in 1936 he built tourist cabins, a trading post and a saloon on the rim. In 1947 he sold the property to Madelaine Jacobs for $25,000.

Ironically, it was Jacobs who would make her fortune off mining interests here. Learning that the gray rock Hogan had ignored in his quest for copper was rich in uranium, she sold out to Western Gold & Uranium. From 1956 through 1969 the Orphan Mine just southwest of this point produced more than a half million tons of uranium ore. Tourists still visited the point during the mining, though the experience must have been somewhat marred by the noise and radioactive dust.

Today you can see the metal remains of the tramway and elevator that moved the ore to the rim. Some areas above the rim are fenced off, in part due to a slight risk from radioactivity.

Powell Memorial

Erected in 1915, the **Powell Memorial** honors John Wesley Powell, the one-armed Civil War veteran, ethnologist and geologist who led the first white-water trek through the canyon on the Colorado in 1869. Though it doesn't offer the best river view, this is a good spot to think about that first bold run along the unexplored, wild Colorado. The park was officially dedicated at this spot in 1920.

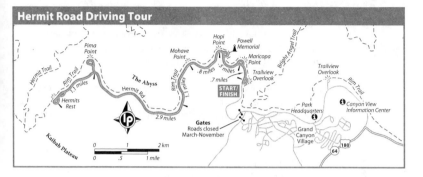

Hopi Point

Arguably one of the park's best viewpoints, Hopi Point juts out farther than any other overlook along Hermit Road and offers spectacular views of the canyon and Colorado River a mile below. This is a popular place to watch the sunset and is often crowded on summer evenings. Until completion of Hermit Road in 1912, Hopi Point was the westernmost spot on guided tours.

Mohave Point

If you only have time for a couple stops, Mohave and Hopi are good choices. This is a particularly good place to see the Colorado, as three rapids – **Salt Creek**, **Granite** and **Hermit** – are visible below and downstream. Hermit Rapids are named after one of the park's most famous residents, Louis Boucher (aka 'The Hermit'), a Canadian immigrant who worked as a prospector and tourist guide and lived alone at Dripping Springs in Boucher Canyon (below Hermits Rest) from 1889 to 1912. Thirteen canyon features are named after him.

The Abyss

From here the canyon does indeed look like an abyss. If you're at all acrophobic, consider stopping at a different viewpoint – sheer cliffs drop 2600ft to the Redwall limestone below.

Pima Point

In 1912 the Atchison, Topeka & Santa Fe Railway completed Hermit Camp, a tourist hub with tent cabins, restrooms, showers and a blacksmith forge 3000ft below Pima Point, accessible from a trailhead at Hermits Rest. The camp was a popular mule train destination, and a tramway was built in 1926 to transport supplies. By 1930 tourists favored Phantom Ranch, the stone lodge and cabins built along the river in 1922 by Mary Colter, and Hermit Camp was abandoned. In 1936 the railway intentionally torched the camp, the remains of which are still visible from the rim.

Hermits Rest

Prospector Ralph Cameron held the rights to Bright Angel Trail, prompting the Atchison, Topeka & Santa Fe Railway to develop other trails and services for canyon tourists. In 1909 the railway began work on Hermit Road. It commissioned Mary Colter to design a resthouse at the end of the road, constructed an 8.5-mile trail from the rim into the canyon and built a camp at the end of the trail (remnants are still visible from Pima Point). Colter's Hermits Rest, a beautiful stone and wood shelter, offered tourists a place to freshen up before descending into the canyon or after the arduous journey back to the rim.

Today, Hermits Rest features a small gift shop and snack bar. You can still take Hermit Trail into the canyon (see Hermit Trail Hike, p100). If you just want to stretch your legs, hike down about 10 minutes and search the walls for exposed fossil beds.

DESERT VIEW DRIVE
Route: Mather Point to East Entrance
Distance: 25 miles
Speed Limit: 45mph

The Desert View Drive begins at Mather Point and heads west for 25 miles to the park's East Entrance. Seven well-marked viewpoints, a small museum and ancient puebloan site and Mary Colter's Watchtower line the road. A leisurely drive, with plenty of time for every stop, takes about four hours. See Walks & Day Hikes for details on **Shoshone Point** (p95), a wonderful 1-mile walk along a dirt road to a picnic spot and viewpoint off Desert View Drive.

Mather Point
As it sits right beside the parking lot used for Canyon View Information Plaza (300 yards away), Mather is the most crowded of all the viewpoints. However, you can walk east along the rim about a mile to Pipe Creek Vista to escape the crowds (see Rim Trail Hike, p95). From Pipe Creek you can take the shuttle back to the information plaza.

Yaki Point
From this spot in 1924 the NPS began the two-year process of blasting rock to create **South Kaibab Trail** (p98), an effort to bypass Ralph Cameron's Bright Angel Trail. Closed year-round to private vehicles, the viewpoint lies just north of Desert View Drive and is accessed by the green **Kaibab Trail Route** shuttles.

Grandview Point
Peter Berry (another prospector-turned-entrepreneur) and his partners built the **Grandview Toll Trail** in 1893 to access copper claims more than 2000ft below on Horseshoe Mesa. In 1897 he built the Grand View Hotel here on the rim, and when he wasn't hauling copper, he led tourists into the canyon on foot and by mule. When the railroad arrived 13 miles west of here in 1901, tourists gravitated toward those facilities, and Berry closed his business in 1908. His mining venture petered out about the same time. Today, thousands make a steep descent into the canyon via Berry's Grandview Trail (p99), while others enjoy canyon views from the spot where his hotel once thrived.

Moran Point

This point is named after Thomas Moran, the landscape painter who spent just about every winter at the canyon from 1899 to 1920 and whose work was instrumental in securing the canyon's national park status. From here you can see down the river in both directions, and, particularly in the early morning or evening light, it's easy to see what drew Moran and hundreds of other artists to the canyon.

✔ TIP

Check *The Guide* or the kiosk at Desert View Information Plaza for sunrise and sunset times.

Tusayan Ruins & Museum

While 'museum' may be a slight exaggeration, as there are only a few displays of pottery and jewelry, the beautiful stone building is worth a stop. Don't miss the 4000-year-old twig figures of animals (see Grand Canyon History, p227). From here you can take a short self-guided walk through the remains of an **ancient Pueblo village** that was excavated in 1930. Tree-ring analyses date the structure to 1185, and archaeologists estimate that about 30 people lived here. Look in *The Guide* for details on ranger-led tours. This is a shaded area with bathrooms, but there are no canyon views.

Lipan Point

Perhaps the most spectacular viewpoint on the South Rim, Lipan Point offers an unobstructed view of **Hance Rapids** on the Colorado and is a

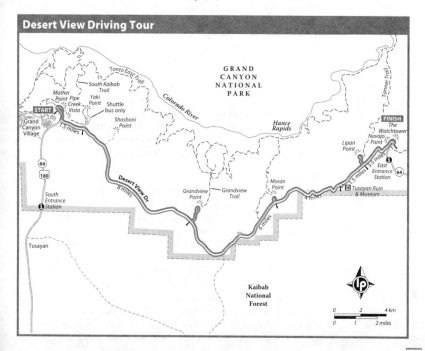

Desert View Driving Tour

splendid spot to watch the sunset. The panoramic view includes the distant **Echo and Vermilion Cliffs**.

Navajo Point
This spot overlooks the river below and vast Navajo Indian Reservation to the east.

The Watchtower
Designed by Mary Colter and built in 1932, this 70ft circular stone tower was inspired by ancient Pueblo watchtowers. You'll enter through the gift shop, above which a small terrace offers beautiful views. Continue up a small flight of stairs to the **Hopi Room**, where you can rest on a bench and admire the wall murals that depict the snake legend and a Hopi wedding, among other scenes. Second- and third-floor balconies also overlook this room. A final flight of steps leads to the fourth floor, where binoculars and big windows offer expansive views in every direction. This is the South Rim's highest overlook (7522ft). From here you can see the canyon and the Colorado River, the **San Francisco Mountains**, the **Navajo Indian Reservation**, **Echo Cliffs** and the **Painted Desert**.

Sights
MAP 4
While the canyon itself is the primary attraction, several buildings and museums offer a fascinating historical perspective that will enrich your park experience. You'll learn how Pueblo Indians carved out a living, why early explorers saw the canyon primarily as an obstacle, whether prospectors struck it rich, how artists interpreted the canyon, and how entrepreneurs and railways ultimately transformed it into one of the world's most famous tourist destinations. Of particular interest are the many buildings designed by visionary architect Mary Colter (p242).

Interpretive displays at each of the viewpoints described in Driving Tours (p85) provide pertinent geologic and historical tidbits. Read the Desert View driving tour for details about **The Watchtower** and **Tusayan Ruins & Museum**, and consider purchasing the self-guided **Walking Tour of Grand Canyon Village Historical District** ($1), at park bookstores.

EL TOVAR
Built in 1905 for the Atchison, Topeka & Santa Fe Railway, El Tovar remains a grande dame of national park lodges. Architect Charles Whittlesey designed the four-story lodge as a blend between a Swiss chalet and the more rustic style that would come to define national park lodges in the 1920s. Spacious rooms (many with sleigh beds and rim overlooks), a dining room with panoramic views, and wide, inviting porches with rocking chairs offered visitors a comfortable and elegant place to relax after a long journey to the park.

Today, the public spaces look much as they did when the lodge opened (though many of the rooms are smaller; see Places to Stay, p158), and it remains the most luxurious lodge on the South Rim. Moose and elk trophies, reproduction Remington bronzes and craftsman-style furniture lend the interior a classic Western feel. A gift shop and restaurant adjoin the lobby, and the helpful concierge can book bus tours and answer questions. The lodge sits about 100 yards from the rim, and though it bustles with throngs of tourists by day, the scene mellows in the evening. The back porch, a nice spot to relax with a drink, looks out over a small lawn, one of the park's few grassy areas and a great place for small children to play.

BRIGHT ANGEL LODGE

By the 1930s tourism to the park had boomed, and Fred Harvey decided to build a more affordable alternative to the El Tovar. Designed by Mary Colter, the log-and-stone Bright Angel Lodge was completed in 1935. Just off the lobby is the **History Room**, a small museum devoted to Fred Harvey, the English immigrant who, in conjunction with the Atchison, Topeka & Santa Fe Railway, transformed the Grand Canyon into a popular tourist destination. Don't miss the fireplace, built of Kaibab limestone and layered with stones that represent the canyon strata from river to rim.

On the lodge grounds is the **Buckey O'Neill Cabin**, now a guesthouse. Built in the 1890s by William Owen O'Neill, the cabin is the longest continually standing building on the rim. Nicknamed 'Buckey' because he 'bucked the odds' in a card game, O'Neill moved to Arizona in 1879 and worked as an author, journalist, miner, politician and judge. Drawn to a copper deposit near Anita, about 14 miles south of today's Grand Canyon Village, he lived in this cabin and worked on the side as a tour guide. As was the case with so many other prospectors, Buckey found mining to be an unprofitable venture, so he eventually sold his land to the railways and went on to become mayor of Prescott, Arizona. He was one of Teddy Roosevelt's Rough Riders in the Spanish American War and died the day before the assault on San Juan Hill. Today, the lucky few who make reservations well in advance can stay in his cabin (see Bright Angel Lodge, p159).

HISTORY OF THE BRIGHT ANGEL

In one form or another, the Bright Angel Trail has been in continuous use for thousands of years. It was originally forged by the Havasupai Indians to access present-day Indian Garden, where they grew crops and farmed until the early 20th century. In the early 1890s prospectors Ralph Cameron and Pete Berry – who built the Grand View Hotel – improved the trail, eventually extending it to the river. Seeing a golden opportunity, in 1903 Cameron imposed a $1 toll on anyone using the trail, a widely criticized decision. In response, the Atchison, Topeka & Santa Fe Railway and others constructed toll-free alternative trails, such as the Hermit, to draw the burgeoning mule tourism trade. In 1928 the park service took the reigns of the Bright Angel and lifted the toll, thus ending mule traffic on the Hermit.

YAVAPAI OBSERVATION STATION

Panoramic views of the canyon unfold behind plate glass windows with accompanying plaques that identify the various landmarks and explain how they were formed. If this sparks your curiosity, consider attending a ranger talk about canyon geology (check *The Guide* for locations and times).

KIDS' STUFF AT THE GRAND CANYON

The park offers a slew of diverse and cool things to do with the younger set. A few of our favorite picks:

✔ Visit the **mule corral** (p103) to watch wranglers ready mules for treks into the canyon
✔ Earn a **Junior Ranger Badge** (p55)
✔ Pick up a disposable camera at Canyon Village Marketplace and attend Eastman Kodak's *Photography Just for Kids* (check *The Guide* for current programs)
✔ Walk the **Rim Trail** (p95) to Hermits Rest and reward yourself with an ice cream
✔ Hike into the canyon on the **South Kaibab** (p98); on the North Rim try **Cape Final** (p118), **Cliff Spring** (p117) or part of **Widforss Trail** (p115)
✔ Take a family class through the **Grand Canyon Field Institute** (p52)
✔ Bump along the North Rim on a mule or take a half-day ride to Supai Tunnel on the **North Kaibab Trail** (p118)
✔ Join a ranger for a **Fossil Walk** (p106)
✔ Stargaze from the back porch of **Grand Canyon Lodge** (p164)

GRAND CANYON DEPOT

Designed by Francis Wilson for the Atchison, Topeka & Santa Fe Railway, this depot was completed in 1909 (eight years after the first train arrived in the village from Williams). It's one of three remaining log depots in the country and one of only 14 log depots ever constructed in the US. The logs are squared on three sides to create a flat-walled interior. The first floor was used for passenger services, and the second floor was a two-bedroom apartment for the ticket agent. Today, a Grand Canyon Railway train pulls into the station daily from Williams (see Riding the Rails, p183).

HOPI HOUSE

Another beautiful stone building designed by Mary Colter for Fred Harvey, **Hopi House** (☎ 928-638-2631; 8am-8pm May-Aug, 9am-5pm Sep-Apr) was built largely by Hopi Indians and was finished a few weeks before completion of El Tovar in 1905. It was modeled after the pueblos at Old Oraibi, a Hopi settlement on the Third Mesa in eastern Arizona that vies with Acoma, New Mexico, for the title of longest continually inhabited village in the US. The interior does resemble an ancient pueblo, featuring adobe walls and concrete walls made to look like dirt, corner fireplaces and a timbered ceiling. Exterior ladders and interior staircases connect each story. In the park's early days, Hopi Indians lived here, sold crafts and entertained travelers with nightly dances. Today, it's a wonderful place to shop for high-quality Native American jewelry, basketwork, pottery and other crafts.

VERKAMP'S CURIOS

In 1898 John G Verkamp sold souvenirs from a tent outside Bright Angel Lodge to persevering travelers who arrived at the canyon after long, arduous stagecoach rides. He was a little before his time, however, as there weren't enough customers to make a living, and he closed down his operation after only a few weeks. Arrival of the railroad in 1901 opened up the canyon to more and more tourists, and in 1905 Verkamp returned to build the craftsman-style **Verkamp's Curios** (☎ *928-638-2242; 9am-6pm May-Aug, 9am-8pm Sep-Apr*) at its present location, beside Hopi House and across the parking lot from El Tovar. He lived on the second floor and sold his wares from the first. Today, Verkamp's ancestors run the curio shop.

LOOKOUT STUDIO

Like Mary Colter's other canyon buildings, **Lookout Studio** (circa 1914) was modeled after stone dwellings of the Southwest Pueblo Indians. Made of rough-cut Kaibab limestone (the stone that comprises the upper canyon walls), with a roof that mirrors the lines of the rim, the studio blends into its natural surroundings. The interior features an arched stone fireplace, stone walls and a timber-framed ceiling. You'll find a small **souvenir shop** (☎ *928-638-2631; 8am-8pm May-Aug, 9am-5pm Sep-Apr*) and a tiny back porch offers spectacular canyon views.

KOLB STUDIO

Born in Pennsylvania, photographers Ellsworth and Emery Kolb first came to the Grand Canyon in 1902. The brothers built the studio in 1904, expanded it in 1915 and again in 1925, and made their living photographing parties traveling the Bright Angel Trail. In 1911 they filmed their own trip down the Green and Colorado Rivers, and canyon visitors clamored to their small auditorium to see the film, in which both brothers repeatedly tumble into the water. Emery continued to show the film to audiences twice daily until his death at 95 in 1976. Today, their **studio** (☎ *928-638-2771; open 8am-7pm*), perched on the edge of the canyon, holds a small but well-stocked bookstore and an art-gallery with changing exhibits. You can still see clips of the original Kolb river picture, though it's no longer projected on a full screen.

SURE SHOTS

Visitors can choose from among dozens of scenic vistas on both rims for that quintessential Grand Canyon photo. When sunrise breaks over the South Rim, grab your camera and head to **Yaki**, **Yavapai** or **Lipan Points**. With a telephoto lens you can get great shots of the Colorado River from Lipan, **Pima** or **Hopi Points**. **Hermits Rest** and Pima Point are good bets for sunset shots, as is Hopi Point, though the latter is a highlight of the sunset bus tour and accompanying crowds.

Sunrise is spectacular at **Cape Royal** on the North Rim, while at sunset, visitors can simply perch on the back patio of the Grand Canyon Lodge. For the most dramatic river shots, however, you'll have to drive more than 60 miles to **Toroweap Point**, much along dirt roads several hours from North Rim facilities.

GRAND CANYON CEMETERY

More than 300 people are buried here, many whose lives are intricately woven into the history of the canyon, including the Kolb brothers, John Verkamp, Ralph Cameron and John Hance, who ran a hotel a few miles from Grandview Point.

RED HORSE STATION

The first stagecoach to the South Rim left Flagstaff on May 19, 1892. Eventually, stages made the 11-hour ride to the park thrice weekly, and three stations along the way allowed visitors to stretch their legs, dust off and prepare for the next leg of the journey. **Red Horse** (originally called Moqui Station) was built 16 miles south of the village in the 1890s; in 1902 Ralph Cameron, who controlled Bright Angel Trail, moved the building to its present site (on the Bright Angel Lodge grounds) and converted it into the Cameron Hotel. It served as a post office from 1907 to 1935. When Mary Colter designed Bright Angel Lodge in the early '30s, she insisted the station be preserved and incorporated into the lodge.

IMAX THEATER

Shown on a screen up to eight times the size of conventional cinema screens, with 14-speaker surround sound, the 34-minute *Grand Canyon – The Hidden Secrets* plunges you into the history and geology of the canyon through the eyes of ancient Indians, John Wesley Powell and a soaring eagle. The film is splendid and offers a cheaper, safer aerial perspective of the canyon than would a flight. The **theater** *(Map 2; ☎ 928-638-2468; open 8:30am-8:30pm Mar-Oct and 10:30am-6:30pm Nov-Feb)* is in Tusayan, just outside the South Entrance.

> ✔ TIP
>
> If you plan on hiking and don't want to leave computers, passports or other valuables in the car, Bright Angel Lodge offers a storage service for a small fee.

Walks & Day Hikes

Hiking along the South Rim is among park visitors' favorite pastimes, with options for every skill level. The popular river-bound corridor trails (**Bright Angel** and **South Kaibab**) span the 7 to 10 miles to the canyon floor, following paths etched thousands of years ago by drainage routes. Several turnaround spots make these trails ideal for day hikes of varying lengths. Both can get packed during summer with foot and mule traffic. For more solitude, opt for a less-trodden trail like **Hermit** or **Grandview**.

Most of the trails start with a super steep series of switchbacks that descend quickly to the dramatic ledge of **Coconino sandstone** about 2 miles beneath the rim. Hike another 3 miles and you'll hit the sun-baked **Tonto Platform**, which after another couple miles opens up to inner gorge vistas. From the platform it's a fast and furious pitch to the canyon floor and Colorado River. Most day hikers will want to stay above the Tonto Platform, particularly in summer.

Day hiking requires no permit, just preparation and safety. In the following descriptions, distances listed are one-way, while duration is round-trip, unless otherwise noted. (Hiking time depends largely on each hiker's ability.) Elevation change marks the difference between the trailhead and the destination point. Since most of the trails offer multiple turnaround spots, the respective distances and elevations are summarized under the trail heading and detailed in the description. Day hikes that can extend into overnight excursions are noted in the text; for full descriptions of overnight hikes, see Exploring the Backcountry (p123).

RIM TRAIL
Distance: Varies (up to 13 miles one-way)
Duration: Varies
Challenge: Easy-Moderate
Elevation Change: 200ft

Stretching from Hermits Rest on the rim's western edge through Grand Canyon Village to Pipe Creek Vista, the Rim Trail connects a series of scenic points and is hands-down the easiest long walk in the park. By no means a nature trail, it's paved from Maricopa Point (1.5 miles west of Kolb Studio) to Pipe Creek Vista (1.3 miles).

Still, flexibility is a big draw, it being easy to literally jump on for a segment (or three) and hike for as long or little as you like. Every viewpoint is accessed by one of the three shuttle routes, which means you can walk to a vista and shuttle back, or shuttle to a point, walk to the next and shuttle from there. A helpful map inside *The Guide* shows the shuttle stops and hiking distances along each segment of the trail.

The trail passes many of the park's historical sights, including **El Tovar**, **Hopi House**, **Kolb Studio**, **Lookout Studio** and **Verkamp's**. The 3 miles or so that wind through the village are usually packed with people, but the farther west you venture, the more you'll break free from the crowds. Out there the trail runs between Hermit Road and the rim, and though some segments bump up against the road, elsewhere you can't hear a sound from the shuttle buses.

One very pretty stretch is the mile east of Pima Point, where the trail is set far back from the road, offering stunning views and relative solitude. Winding through piñon-juniper woodlands, it passes several viewpoints; see the Hermit Road driving tour (p86) for details. Mohave and Hopi Points offer great views of the Colorado River, with three visible rapids (**Salt Creek**, **Granite** and **Hermit**) below and downstream.

Its accessibility makes the Rim Trail a terrific option for families. It's also a lovely stroll at sunrise, sunset or under a starry sky, times when the crowds really thin out. Runners also favor this trail before the heat hits. When you first arrive in the park, stretch your legs along the trail to take in the canyon air and get the lay of the land.

SHOSHONE POINT
Distance: 1 mile one-way
Duration: 30 minutes round-trip
Challenge: Easy
Elevation Change: 50ft

The gentle and cool amble out to Shoshone Point, accessible only by foot or bike, can be a welcome pocket of peace during the summer heat and crowds. This little-known hike is also ideal for children. Chances are you won't see another person, which means you can hoard the spectacular views all to yourself.

The trail starts from a dirt pullout along Desert View Drive, 1.2 miles east of Yaki Point or 6.3 miles west of Grandview Point. There's no official trailhead or signpost, so look for the dirt road barred by a closed and locked gate. The park service deliberately downplays this trail, which they kindly make available from May to October for weddings and other private events. Be respectful of any events you may stumble upon. When it hasn't been reserved for a special gathering, and during winter months, hikers are welcome on the trail.

It's a fast and mostly flat walk along the forested trail, which weaves through junipers before opening up in a clearing. This is a great spot for a family gathering, as you'll find picnic tables, barbecue grills and portable toilets. Nearby, Shoshone Point juts out into the canyon, offering magnificent views of the North Rim's full sweep. Unlike the other scenic points, there are no safety railings here. You can walk to the tip of the slender plateau, where it feels almost possible to reach out and touch **Zoroaster Temple**.

BRIGHT ANGEL TRAIL – SHORT DAY HIKE
Distance: 1.5 miles to Mile-and-a-Half Resthouse;
3 miles to Three-Mile Resthouse
Duration: 1-2 hours; 2-3 hours round-trip
Challenge: Moderate; Moderate-Difficult
Elevation Change: 1131ft; 2112ft

BRIGHT ANGEL TRAIL – LONG DAY HIKE
Distance: 4.6 miles to Indian Garden; 6.l miles to Plateau Point
Duration: 4-6 hours; 8-10 hours round-trip
Challenge: Difficult
Elevation Change: 3060ft; 3120ft

The most popular of the corridor trails, the **Bright Angel** is wide, well graded and easy to follow. It's equally attractive to first-time canyon hikers and seasoned pros, as well as mule trains, making it a heavily trafficked route. But the din doesn't lessen the sheer beauty. The steep and scenic 7.8-mile descent to the Colorado is punctuated with four logical turnaround spots, including two well-appointed resthouses for opportunities to seek shade and hydrate. Even if you're wary of crowds, you won't regret taking a jaunt of some length on the Bright Angel.

The trail follows a natural route along the Bright Angel Fault and was first used by the Havasupai to reach the glistening water source at Indian Garden and the inner canyon recesses. In the late 19th century, miners improved the trail, enlisted the help of mules and began charging a toll for usage. While numerous individuals and groups, including the Atchison, Topeka & Santa Fe Railway, wrangled for control, the reigns eventually went to the National Park Service in 1928.

Unlike the South Kaibab, there's both shade and seasonal water on the Bright Angel. Still, the summer heat can be crippling – day hikers should either turn around at one of the two resthouses (a 3- to 6-mile round-trip) or hit the trail at dawn to safely make the longer hikes to Indian Garden and Plateau Point (9.2 and 12.2 miles round-trip). Hiking to the Colorado for the day is not an option.

Apropos for the oft-crowded Bright Angel, the trailhead is smack in Grand Canyon Village, just west of Kolb Studio and Bright Angel Lodge. There's ample nearby parking, or you can take the shuttle bus to the Hermits Rest transfer stop and walk from there. The piñon-fringed trail quickly drops into some serious switchbacks as it follows a natural break in the cliffs and soon passes through two tunnels – look for the Indian pictographs on the walls of the first. After passing through the second, **Mile-and-a-Half Resthouse** comes into view, just under an hour's hike from the top, with restrooms, an emergency phone and drinking water from May to September. Turning around here makes for a 2.5-hour round-trip.

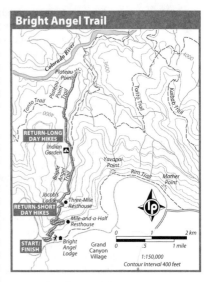

Continuing downward through different colored rock layers, more switchbacks eventually deposit you at **Three-Mile Resthouse**, with seasonal water and an emergency phone but no restrooms. Down below, you'll see the iridescent green tufts of Indian Garden tucked into a canyon fold, as well as the broad expanse of Tonto Platform, a nice visual reward if this is your turnaround point.

After leaving the cool reprieve of the resthouse, you'll hit a grueling set of switchbacks known as **Jacob's Ladder**, which twist through Redwall cliffs. A bridge ferries you across the Transcanyon, and soon after you descend into the cool leafiness of **Indian Garden**, where Havasupai still farmed up until a century ago. Now, it's a popular campground, with a ranger station, toilets, year-round drinking water, shaded picnic tables and a mule corral. If this is your day-hike destination, linger in the soothing, albeit crowded, spot – eat lunch under a cottonwood, nap on the grass and splash your feet in the creek. It's a hard and hot 4.6-mile climb back up to the rim – particularly the thigh-burning Jacob's Ladder. The round-trip takes about seven hours.

From the campground, if you turn left and head west across Garden Creek, you'll soon reach the **Plateau Point Trail** junction, a spur off the **Tonto Trail**. This ribbon of a trail unfurls north for just under a mile over the flat, barren and yucca-studded **Tonto Platform**, dead-ending at **Plateau Point** for a stunning view of the inner gorge. Though

✔ **TIP**

If you're headed into the canyon, decide just how long you'd like to hike, then turn around once a third of the time has elapsed.

it's a popular year-round destination for strong day hikers, rangers nonetheless discourage anyone from making the round-trip trek in summer. The long exposed stretch can be brutally hot, with the 12-mile round-trip taking up to 10 hours.

From Indian Garden, Bright Angel continues north to the river and is soon intersected by the east-west Tonto Trail. For a description of overnight hikes along the Bright Angel, refer to Exploring the Backcountry (p125).

SOUTH KAIBAB
Distance: 1.5 miles to Cedar Ridge; 3 miles to Skeleton Point
Duration: 1-2 hours round-trip; 3-5 hours round-trip
Challenge: Moderate; Moderate-Difficult
Elevation Change: 1140ft; 2040ft

The **South Kaibab** is arguably one of the park's prettiest trails, combining stunning scenery and adventurous hiking with every step. The only corridor trail to follow a ridgeline instead of a drainage route, the red-dirt path traverses the spine of a crest, allowing for unobstructed 360-degree views. Blasted out of the rock by rangers in the mid-1920s, the South Kaibab is steep, rough and wholly exposed. The dearth of shade and water, combined with the sheer grade, make ascending the South Kaibab particularly dangerous in summer, and rangers discourage all but the shortest of day hikes. The main passersby during summer are mule trains taking the shortest route to Phantom Ranch, backpackers planning to ascend Bright Angel and day hikers out for a quick peek. The trail sees a fair number of rescues, with up to a half dozen on a hot June day. Even if you're just hiking a few miles, plan on bringing a gallon of water.

Look down, not just up

When hiking out of the canyon, it helps to gauge your progress by stopping occasionally to look *back* at how far you've climbed – instead of only up toward the rim, which can sometimes feel daunting and overwhelming, especially when you're tired.

Summer day hikers should turn around at **Cedar Ridge**, perhaps the park's finest short day hike, about a three-hour round-trip. It's a dazzling spot, particularly at sunrise, when the deep ruddy umbers and reds of each canyon fold seem to glow from within. During the rest of the year, the continued trek to **Skeleton Point**, 1.5 miles beyond Cedar Ridge, makes for a fine day hike – though the climb back up is a beast in any season.

The trailhead is 4.5 miles east of Grand Canyon Village along Yaki Point Road, just shy of the point itself. To keep crowds in check during high season, you're only permitted to park at the trailhead between December and February; all other times require a ride aboard either the **Kaibab Trail Route shuttle** (p84) or the far more direct **express hikers' shuttle** (p84). Water and toilets are available at the trailhead.

From the mule corral the trail starts out deceptively gentle, with a long, well-graded switchback that leads to the end of a promontory about 20 minutes from the top. Here the cliff-hugging trail opens up to a shaggy promontory, which juts off the elbow of a switchback and offers a sweeping panorama of the purplish Tonto Platform far below. The ledge, unfortunately dubbed 'Ooh Aah Point,' is a nice spot for rest and refreshment. It's also a good juncture to gauge how you're feeling and consider turning back, ascending the 780ft to the top for a round-trip hike of a little over 1.5 miles.

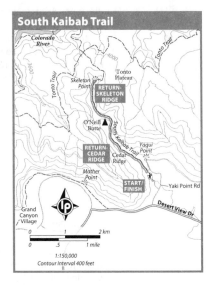

Soon after, things turn serious, as the trail takes a sharp nosedive and begins to zigzag down a series of steep, tight switchbacks, making its way down the red sandstone. After about 30 minutes, the trail straightens out some when it hits the gorgeous **Cedar Mesa** and its namesake ridge, a striking red-tinged mesa. Stop long enough for a snack and perhaps a visit to the pit toilet. But what you'll linger for are the lovely vast views of Bright Angel Canyon, Devil's Corkscrew and the North Rim. This is considered the last 'safe' turnaround in summer, and the ascent from here takes one to two hours.

The trail then meanders off the mesa toward **O'Neill Butte**, wraps around to the east, then levels out onto another plateau known as **Skeleton Point**, from which you can see the Colorado River. From here settle in for a hefty, scree-covered descent on switchbacks that grind through the Redwall limestone before fanning out onto the flat skirt of the Tonto Platform. After traversing the platform, you'll reach its edge and the junction of the **Tonto Trail**, some two to three hours from the top. About 19 miles to the west, the Tonto connects with the **Grandview Trail** (p99), while a mere 4.1 miles to the east are **Indian Garden** and **Bright Angel Trail**, making for a terrific long day hike (p96). For a description of backcountry hikes on the South Kaibab, refer to Exploring the Backcountry (p127).

GRANDVIEW TRAIL
**Distance: 0.75 mile to Coconino Saddle; 3 miles to Horseshoe Mesa
Duration: 1-2 hours round-trip; 4-6 hours round-trip
Challenge: Moderate-Difficult; Difficult
Elevation Change: 1600ft; 2699ft**

One of the steepest trails in the park – dropping 1200ft in the first three-quarters of a mile – Grandview is also one of the finest and most popular day hikes. The payoff following the stunning (and grueling) descent is an up close look at one of the inner canyon's sagebrush-tufted mesas and a spectacular sense of solitude. The trail spirals down to a sprawling horseshoe-shaped mesa, where Hopi Indians once collected minerals. In 1892 miner Pete Berry improved the former Indian route and constructed the current trail to access his Last Chance Mine at **Horseshoe Mesa**.

For the next 15 years mules carted high-grade copper from there to the rim (see History, p227)

The trailhead, right beside where the hotel once stood, is at Grandview Point, 12 miles east of the village on Desert View Drive, with year-round parking. While rangers don't recommend the trek to Horseshoe Mesa in summer (there's no water on the very exposed trail, and the climb out is a doozy), it's not overly long and certainly doable for strong hikers strapped with a hydration system and hiking early or late. For a shorter but still rewarding option, you can hike to **Coconino Saddle** and turn around there. Though it's only 1.5 miles round-trip, it packs a quick and precipitous punch as you plunge 1600ft over less than a mile. With the exception of a few short level sections, the Grandview is a rugged, narrow and rocky trail and probably not the best choice for those skittish of heights or occasional loose footing. The steep drop-offs can be a bit scary, but although the trail is no longer maintained, Berry's metal-reinforced switchbacks have held up quite nicely.

Steep from the start, the trail first wends down the north end of **Grandview Point** and Kaibab limestone along cobbled and cliff-edged rock stairs fringed with occasional flowers like fiery orange Indian paintbrush, straw-yellow arnica and blue delphinium. The views from the trailhead and just below are extraordinary, so even if you don't plan to hike, do walk down the trail a short way to take in the vistas. After about 30 or so minutes, you'll reach the **Coconino Saddle**, where the trail crosses the slender spur between Hance and Grapevine Canyons. It's a stunning overlook and nice leafy spot for a snack and a rest in the shade. From here the trail is more exposed and eventually narrows to a ribbon as it traverses the ruddy Supai sandstone. A little over 2 miles past Coconino you'll hit a second saddle, connecting to **Horseshoe Mesa**, then a short dip later reach pit toilets and remnants of old miners' cabins. There are traces of mining all over the mesa, from the speckled soil to old machinery and mineshafts. Although the many hollowed-out caves may look enticing, it's forbidden, not to mention very dangerous, to enter them.

For **backpackers**, three different trails descend 1000ft from Horseshoe Mesa to the **Tonto Trail** – the easiest to follow is the one that heads west near the pit toilets. Take it to hike a 7-mile loop around the foot of the mesa, following the Tonto and East Horseshoe Mesa Trails and rejoining Grandview a little ways up from the mesa, making for a 16.6-mile round-trip from the rim. Camping overnight on Horseshoe Mesa or the Tonto requires a backcountry permit (p124). From the Tonto you can also hike 7 miles east to join New Hance Trail at the Colorado River, or 20 miles west to the South Kaibab Trail (p127).

HERMIT TRAIL
Distance: 2.5 miles to Santa Maria Spring
Duration: 2-4 hours round-trip
Challenge: Moderate-Difficult
Elevation Change: 1680ft

This wilderness trail descends into pretty Hermit Canyon by way of a cool spring. It's a rocky trip down, with some knee-wrenching switchbacks and long traverses that wend through the Supai cliffs. But if you set out early in the morning and take it slow, the Hermit offers a wonderfully serene day hike and a peek into secluded nooks. Offering several good turnaround spots and a clear shot to the Colorado River, the trail is equally appealing to both day hikers and backcountry adventurers.

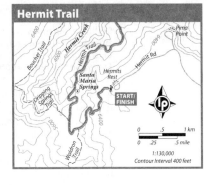

In 1912 the Atchison, Topeka & Santa Fe Railway developed the trail (originally called El Tovar) for tourists to avoid tolls on the then privately controlled Bright Angel Trail. Mule trains ferried travelers to cushy Hermit Camp, which boasted a fancy stone cabin outfitted with a stove, glass windows, beds, and Navajo rug-adorned wood floors, and supplies arrived via tram from Pima Point. The trail was eventually renamed in honor of Louis 'The Hermit' Boucher (see The Hermit, p241). When the NPS gained control of Bright Angel in 1928, luring away the mule tourism business, the Hermit was abandoned. Though officially untended since then, the trail is in remarkably good condition.

The best destinations for day hikers are to **Santa Maria Spring** (5 miles round-trip) or to **Dripping Springs** via a spur trail (6.5 miles round-trip). For a shorter but still worthwhile hike, turn around at the **Waldron Trail** junction in Waldron Basin, a round-trip of just under 3 miles with 1600ft of elevation change. The upper section of the Hermit is well shaded in the morning, making it a cool option in summer.

The **Hermit Trailhead** is at the end of its namesake road, 8 miles west of Grand Canyon Village and about 500ft from Hermits Rest. Although the road is only accessible via shuttle bus during the summer peak season, overnight backpackers are permitted to park at the lot near the trailhead throughout the year, and day hikers may do so in winter.

✔ **TIP**

Arming yourself with a hydration system like a Camelbak, which can double as your daypack, is a great idea, particularly for longer day hikes or backpacking trips. You'll be able to carry more water – hands-free – and the easy-to-use bite valves will encourage you to drink more.

The rocky trail weaves down Hermit Basin toward Hermit Creek along a cobblestone route indented with steps and fraught with washouts. You'll reach the rarely used **Waldron Trail** (jutting off to the south) after about 1.5 miles and 1200ft of descent, followed some 30 minutes later by the spur trail headed for **Dripping Springs**. The trail then traces over some flat rocks (a great picnic spot) before descending steeply to **Santa Maria Spring**, a cool, shady haven, marked by a pretty stone shelter adorned with green foliage and a welcome wooden bench. The lush scene belies the spring, however, which is actually more of a trickle. You can drink the water provided you treat it.

DRIPPING SPRINGS TRAIL
Distance: 3.5 miles one-way
Duration: 3-5 hours round-trip
Challenge: Moderate-Difficult
Elevation Change: 1700ft

An excellent day hike of moderate length and difficulty, Dripping Springs is a must-do for South Rim hikers curious to see why Louis Boucher made this secluded spot his home. The trailhead is at Hermits Rest, and for the first 2 miles you'll be on the Hermit Trail. At the junction with the Dripping Springs Trail, turn left and head west along the narrow path as it climbs and meanders along the slope's contours. In a mile you'll hit the Boucher Trail and turn left, following the Dripping Springs Trail as it wends up toward the water source, which sprouts from an overhang not far beneath the rim. Droplets shower down from the sandstone ceiling, misting a myriad of leafy ferns.

TONTO TRAIL (SOUTH KAIBAB TO BRIGHT ANGEL)
Distance: 13.1 miles one-way
Duration: 5-7 hours one-way
Challenge: Very Difficult
Elevation Change: 3260ft

A stellar choice for strong hikers seeking solitude, this full-day excursion links the two corridor trails along a 4.1-mile section of the peaceful, winding Tonto Trail. It's long, difficult and best suited for any season but summer. That said, it is doable in the hot months, provided you're on the trail by 5am and are a very experienced hiker. The Tonto is an unpatrolled wilderness trail with no facilities along its undulating, sun-baked desert terrain – under no circumstances is this route an option for moderate hikers during the summer.

The full Tonto is a 95-mile east-west passage along the entire length of the Tonto Platform, from Red Canyon to Garnet Canyon. Unlike the corridor trails, the Tonto does not extend to the rim, nor does it involve significant elevation change, remaining around 4000ft. But it is by no means easy or level – the trail jumps up and down as it follows the contours and drainage routes while paralleling the river and rim. The Tonto crosses numerous trails, including the Grandview, then 20 miles west the South Kaibab, and another 13 miles west the Hermit. Most hikers hop on the Tonto to connect to other trails. The segment described here – from The Tipoff on South Kaibab to Indian Garden on Bright Angel – is considered the central portion and officially referred to as the Tonto Trail.

From the South Kaibab Trailhead it's a hefty and hot 4.4-mile descent to the Tonto Trail junction, dropping 3260ft in elevation to the edge of the Tonto Platform. Just past the junction there's an emergency telephone and a toilet, a final reminder you're about to step foot onto more wild and unpatrolled terrain.

Heading west on the Tonto, you'll hug the contours as the trail crosses the agave-dotted plateau and darts in and out of gulches. Deep in a canyon fold, the trail skirts through a canopy of cottonwoods near a drainage; just past here on the left is a terrific spot for camping (for back-country permit information see p124). The trail remains in shade through midmorning. As the day progresses, however, the Tonto bakes and the surrounding landscape is completely parched – you don't want to be caught here midday in summer. After about two hours you'll stumble into lush **Indian Garden**, the perfect shady oasis for cooling off before the haul up to the rim. From here it's a steep, hot and mule-churned 4.6 miles up the Bright Angel – the first 1.5 miles are the toughest.

Other Activities

The South Rim offers a multitude of outdoor activities in all seasons.

MULE RIDES

One- and two-day mule trips into the canyon depart every day of the year from the corral west of Bright Angel Lodge. The seven-hour day trip ($129) takes riders down the **Bright Angel Trail** to **Indian Garden**, then follows the **Plateau Point Trail** to **Plateau Point**, an overlook of the Colorado River. Here you can hop down and stretch your legs, enjoy the view and pre-pare for the 6-mile return trip. Riders stop for lunch at Indian Garden. **Overnight trips** ($350) follow the Bright Angel Trail to the river, travel east on the **River Trail** and cross the river on the **Kaibab Suspension Bridge** to spend the night at **Phantom Ranch**. It's a 5.5-hour, 10-mile trip to Phantom Ranch. The return trip is an hour shorter, as riders return via the 8-mile South Kaibab Trail. Two-night trips to Phantom Ranch ($452 per person, or $764 for two) are offered between mid-November and March 31. Overnight trips include accommodations and all meals.

Don't plan a mule trip assuming it's the easiest way to travel below the rim. It's a bumpy ride on a hard saddle, and unless you are used to riding a horse regularly, you will be sore. Riders must be at least 4ft 7in tall, speak fluent English and weigh less than 200lbs. Personal backpacks, fanny packs, purses or bags of any kind are not allowed on the mules. Anything that could possibly fall off and injure someone in the canyon below will be confiscated till your return.

When you arrive at the corral, the wranglers will give you a small bag (a 15lb ice bag) that is just big enough for a bathing suit, a change of clothes and a few personal items

These will be put in saddlebags for the trip – your bag will not necessar-ily be on your mule, so don't put anything in it you may need during the ride. Carry sunscreen and any medications in your pocket. You must wear a hat that secures to your head, a long-sleeved shirt and long pants (preferably jeans) or you will not be allowed on the mule. You should also wear sun-glasses, but they must also secure to your head. The wranglers will give each rider a water pouch and will provide additional water with meals. Be sure to eat something before you leave – it's a long, tiring ride to lunch.

To book a mule trip more than 24 hours and up to 23 months in advance, call **Xanterra** (☎ 303-287-2757, 888-297-2757; W www.xanterra.com).

If you arrive at the park and want to join a mule trip the following day (pending availability), stop by the **transportation desk at Bright Angel Lodge**. If the trips are booked, join a waiting list, then show up at the lodge at 6:15am on the day of the trip and hope there has been a cancellation. If riding a mule is important to you, reserve this trip well in advance. Mule rides on the North Rim (p120) are usually available the day before the trip.

If you're not planning a mule trip, just watching the wranglers prepare the mules can be fun, particularly for young children. In summer stop by the mule corral at 8am; in winter they get going about an hour later.

For information on horseback riding, see Kaibab National Forest (South Rim), on p175.

FLYOVERS

Based at Grand Canyon National Park Airport in Tusayan, three helicopter companies and two airlines offer scenic rides over the canyon. It's a popular activity, logging 90,000 scenic flights per year and more than a million passengers. Be aware, however, that as of 2001, 355 people have been killed in 58 accidents in and around the park, a particularly high number. Also, noise pollution has led to regulations on the number and height of scenic flyovers. Consider enjoying an aerial view from the safety and comfort of the IMAX Theater (p94).

Standard routes include a 30-minute flight over the western canyon, a 40-minute eastern tour along the rim to the confluence of the Colorado and Little Colorado rivers, and a 50-minute loop that bridges the two by crossing the North Rim forest. On most flights you'll see Coconino Plateau, Dragon Head and the Painted Desert.

Contact the following companies for specific rates, as each offers several options. Ask about trips to Havasu Canyon on the Havasupai Indian Reservation (p180). Flights from Tusayan operate year-round, departing daily on demand between 8am and 5pm; each chopper carries up to six passengers, while a minimum of four is required on each flight.

AirStar Helicopters (☎ 928-638-2623, 800-962-3869;
W www.airstar.com)

Grand Canyon Helicopters (☎ 928-638-2764, 800-541-4537;
W www.grandcanyonhelicoptersaz.com)

Papillon Grand Canyon Helicopters (☎ 928-638-2419, 800-528-2418;
W www.papillon.com)

Air Grand Canyon (☎ 928-638-2686, 800-247-4726;
W www.airgrandcanyon.com)

Grand Canyon Airlines (☎ 928-638-2407, 800-638-2407;
W www.grandcanyonairlines.com)

RIVER RAFTING

Xanterra and **Grand Canyon Airlines** (☎ 928-638-2407) offer a full-day excursion (adult/child 12 & under $111/61) from mid-March to mid-November that starts at 7am daily with a bus ride from Maswik Lodge in the village to Glen Canyon Dam, where passengers connect with an ARA Wilderness Adventures rafting trip (no rapids) to Lees Ferry. The bus returns you to the South Rim by 6:30pm.

See Rafting the Colorado (p133) and the Hualapai Indian Reservation (p181) for other rafting trips. River trips on the Hualapai Reservation depart from Peach Springs, a four-hour drive from the village.

MOUNTAIN BIKING

Mountain bikers have limited options inside the park, as bicycles are only allowed on roads (this will change as the Greenway Plan develops; see p84). Hermit Road offers a scenic ride west to Hermits Rest, about 16 miles round-trip from the village. Keep in mind that shuttles ply this road every 10 to 15 minutes between March and November. They are not permitted to pass bicyclists, so you'll have to pull over each time one drives by. The rest of the year, traffic is minimal, making this a very pleasant ride.

Alternatively, you could ride out to the East Entrance along Desert View Drive (p88), a 50-mile round-trip from the village. The route is largely shuttle-free but sees a lot of car traffic in summer. Just off Desert View Drive, the 1-mile dirt road to **Shoshone Point** is an easy, nearly level ride that ends at this secluded panoramic vista, one of the few places to escape South Rim crowds. For details see Day Hikes (p94).

The only section of the Rim Trail open to cyclists is the stretch from Mather Point to Pipe Creek Vista – part of the park's new Greenway trail system. A cycling and walking path now leads from Canyon View Information Plaza to Grand Canyon Village, and construction is underway on paths south to Tusayan and east to Desert View.

Options outside the park include **Kaibab National Forest** (p174), just south, which offers several mountain biking trails. The closest bike rental is in Flagstaff (p187).

FISHING

You can fish anywhere along the Colorado as long as you have an Arizona fishing license with a trout stamp. There are several good fishing spots near Phantom Ranch, though the most popular area is the 15-mile stretch of water east of **Lees Ferry** (p217). Several lodges there offer gear and guided trips. Nonresident fishing permits (one-day/five-day $12.50/26) are available at Canyon Village Marketplace.

CROSS-COUNTRY SKIING

From November through March, depending on snowfall, the surrounding national forest offers several trails for cross-country skiing and snowshoeing. Trails around **Grandview Point** may be groomed. Contact the **Tusayan Ranger Station** (☎ 928-638-2443) for current information. You can rent skis from several outdoor shops in Flagstaff (p187), where you'll also find plenty of cross-country and downhill trails.

ROCK CLIMBING

Though rock climbing is allowed anywhere in the canyon, it is not recommended. Remember that most of the rock at the canyon is crumbly shale and not conducive to rock climbing. Contact **Vertical Relief Rock Climbing** in Flagstaff (p191) for information on climbing throughout the region.

continued on p108

CAR REPAIR

The garage in Grand Canyon Village is open for servicing and repairs weekdays from 8am to 5pm. Call ☎ 928-638-2631 for 24-hour emergency towing.

GROCERIES & CAMPING SUPPLIES

In Market Plaza, **Canyon Village Marketplace** (☎ *928-631-2262; open 7am-9pm*) is the park's only full-size grocery. The store also sells and rents sleeping bags, tents, backpacks, camping stoves and lanterns, as well as cross-country skis in the winter. It offers the park's largest selection of gear and can even tackle simple repairs.

At the East Entrance near Desert View Campground, **Desert View Marketplace** (☎ *928-638-2393; open 8:30am-6pm summer, 9:30am-5pm Oct-May*) sells basic grocery items, including canned goods, milk, cereal, beer and cheese. It also offers a few camping necessities like flashlights, water purification tablets and thermal blankets.

Several stores in Flagstaff sell and rent outdoor gear (see Around the Grand Canyon, p198).

FILM PROCESSING

A one-hour processing desk in Canyon Village Marketplace is open daily from 9am to 5pm.

INTERNET ACCESS

Just behind the garage, the **library** (☎ *928-638-2718; open noon-5pm Mon-Fri, 9am-1pm Sat*) is in a small brown building that looks like an old schoolhouse. It provides Internet access at $3 for 50 minutes. You can call them up to a month in advance and reserve a time, as they can get very busy, but reservations are not required.

In Tusayan, access the web at **Jennifer's Coffeehouse & Bakery** (p171), across from the IMAX Theater.

KENNELS

Pets must spend the night either in your tent or trailer at the campgrounds, or in the **kennel** (☎ *928-638-2631*). See Pets in the Park (p58).

LOST & FOUND

If you lose something in or near the lodges or restaurants, call the main switchboard (☎ *928-638-2631*) and ask to be connected to the place where you last had the item. People will often turn in lost items to the front office. Otherwise, ask to be connected to lost and found, where all items are eventually returned. If you lose something elsewhere in the park, call Grand Canyon National Park **Lost and Found Office** (☎ *928-638-7798*).

The park asks that you turn in found items to Canyon View Information Plaza.

MEDICAL SERVICES & EMERGENCIES

Dial 911 for emergency medical care (from lodge rooms dial 9-911). The **clinic** (☎ *928-638-2552)* offers walk-in medical care Monday through Friday 9am to 7pm and Sunday 10am to 4pm. A **dentist** (☎ *928-638-2395)* is also available.

MONEY

In Market Plaza, **Bank One** (☎ *928-638-2437; open 9am-4pm Mon-Thu, 10am-5pm Fri)* offers the only ATM on the South Rim.

POSTAL SERVICE

You'll find a full-service **post-office** (☎ *928-638-2512; open 9am-4:30pm Mon-Fri, 11am-3pm Sat)* in Market Plaza. You can buy stamps from machines in the lobby, which is open daily from 5am to 10pm. The concierge at El Tovar also sells stamps.

RELIGIOUS SERVICES

Just west of Market Plaza and accessed by the blue Village Loop shuttle, **Shrine of the Ages** hosts several church services, including Baptist, Catholic and Mormon services on Saturday and Sunday. Service times are posted at the shrine, Mather Campground and the information kiosk near the post office. Every evening at 7pm (weather permitting) a inter-denominational service is held outdoors along the Rim Trail, about 10 minutes west of the Hermits Rest shuttle stop.

SHOWERS & LAUNDRY

The **Camper Services Building** near Mather Campground *(open 6am-11pm)* provides a coin laundry and pay showers. The last laundry load must go in by 9:45pm.

TELEPHONES

All park lodgings offer in-room telephones and pay phones in the lobbies. You'll also find pay phones at Market Plaza and Canyon View Information Plaza.

TRASH & RECYCLING

The park recycles paper, newspaper, magazines, cardboard, aluminum and steel cans, plastic and glass. Tan recycling dumpsters stand beside regular trash dumpsters throughout the park.

continued from p105

RANGER PROGRAMS

Free ranger programs are one of the park's greatest treasures. Lasting 30 minutes to four hours, the talks cover subjects ranging from fossils to condors to Native American history. Programs are held throughout the park and often involve a short walk. *The Guide* provides a complete listing of current ranger programs, including a short description and the location, time and duration of each program. A kiosk at Canyon View Information Plaza also clearly explains current programs.

The **Cedar Ridge Hike** is one regular offering. It involves a strenuous 3-mile hike (three to four hours round-trip) 1140ft below the rim on the South Kaibab Trail. While you can take this trail by yourself, the ranger will explain canyon geology and history as you hike. It departs from the South Kaibab Trailhead at 7am. Take the green Kaibab Trail Route shuttle from Canyon View Information Plaza to access the trailhead.

On the one-hour **Geology and Fossil Walks**, both offered daily, you can brush up on your knowledge of brachiopods and learn about the canyon's rich history. The Fossil Walk is an easy half-mile one-way walk to exposed fossil beds along the rim, a particularly nice activity if you plan on hiking into the canyon from Hermits Rest. If you attend the ranger talk, you'll be able to recognize fossils that lie about 10 minutes down the trail.

During the week following summer solstice, the Tucson Amateur Astronomy Association (see Classes & Learning Vacations below) offers a **'Star Party'** nightly at Yavapai Point, featuring a slide presentation followed by telescope viewing of the June sky.

Each **evening program** at Mather Amphitheater examines a significant aspect of the canyon's natural or cultural history. Subjects change nightly; check the kiosk at the Canyon View Information Plaza or call ☎ 928-638-7610.

See Fun for the Kids (p54) for information on ranger programs geared toward kids.

CLASSES & LEARNING VACATIONS

Several organizations offer one-day classes and extended learning vacations. While most require advance reservations, a couple of programs operate like ranger talks and are open on a drop-in basis.

If you plan on photographing the canyon (who doesn't?), consider taking part in the park's **photography program**. In summer months Eastman Kodak, in conjunction with the National Park Foundation, sends a representative to the park to teach photographic interpretation and techniques for capturing the canyon on film. Programs include a *Morning Light Photography Walk*, *Photography Just for Kids*, *Pixels Schmixels – A Digital Photography Talk* and an evening slide show, *Grand Canyon – Picturing Its Treasures*. Check *The Guide* for details on current classes.

Periodically, volunteers from the **Tucson Amateur Astronomy Association** offer a free slide presentation on the night sky. Participants can then check out the stars and planets through telescopes while volunteers answer questions long into the night. Check *The Guide* for current schedules or contact the **Canyon View Visitor Center** *(☎ 928-638-7644)* before you arrive in the park.

The North Rim offers park visitors a more peaceful perspective on the canyon. Hwy 67 winds 44 miles south from Jacob Lake through meadows and tall aspens to **Grand Canyon Lodge**, a large wood-and-stone hotel on the canyon rim. Guest cabins line either side of the road, and a horseshoe-shaped covered boardwalk offers a postal window, gift shop, small snack shop and saloon. A mile north is a one-story motel, a campground and general store.

That's just about all you'll find. There are no shuttles, no museums, no paved rim trails, no shopping centers, schools or garage, no bus tours or float trips. And thanks to its remote location and limited accommodations, you won't find the crowds that you do on the South Rim.

At 8200ft, this rim is about 10 degrees cooler – even on summer evenings you'll need a sweater. From the lodge, huge windows offer panoramic views of the canyon, while a small back porch with a stone fireplace and rough-hewn rocking chairs perches directly on the rim. Several excellent trails, including the wonderful Widforss Trail, wind through the aspens and pines, offering subtle glimpses of the canyon.

NORTH RIM HIGHLIGHTS

✔ **Western Cabins** – Relax in a wicker rocking chair on the front porch of one of these spacious log cabins

✔ **Grand Canyon Lodge** – Enjoy incredible canyon views from the lodge's intimate back porch or classic dining room

✔ **Widforss Trail** – Hike through stands of white fir, spruce, ponderosa pine and aspen to a spectacular canyon overlook

✔ **Fireside Ranger Talk** – Gather on the back porch of Grand Canyon Lodge for a ranger talk beneath the stars

✔ **Cape Royal** – Stroll to canyon views and picnic among the piñon pines

✔ **Bright Angel Point** – Perch on this canyon overlook for quiet stargazing or a dramatic daytime panorama

Orientation

The only entrance to the North Rim lies 30 miles south of Jacob Lake and 14 miles north of the rim. Visitors can access several remote overlooks (see Toroweap Overlook, p113, and Kaibab National Forest, p210) along dirt roads just outside the gate; though you don't need to pay the park entrance fee to visit these, you still need backcountry permits to camp.

MAIN REGIONS

The North Rim is divided into five main regions: Grand Canyon Lodge, the campground, Cape Royal Road, Point Sublime and remote overlooks outside the park's main entrance. The 1.5-mile **Transept Trail** links the lodge and campground.

VISITOR SERVICE HUBS

Most visitor facilities cluster around Grand Canyon Lodge, and there's a general store and gas station beside the campground. Forty-four miles north at Jacob Lake you'll find a few campgrounds, a restaurant, a lodge, a gas station and a visitor center. Between the rim and Jacob Lake are a lodge, a campground and a general store that sells fuel.

Information

To reach the Grand Canyon Lodge front desk, the saloon, the gift shop or the general store, call the North Rim switchboard at ☎ 928-638-2612. To book a mule trip, duck inside the lodge to the **Mule Desk** (☎ 928-638-9875). Adjacent to the lodge, the **North Rim Visitor Center** (☎ 928-638-9875; open 8am-7pm) offers a small bookstore. The **North Rim Backcountry Office** (☎ 928-638-7868; open 8am-noon, 1-5pm) lies just north of the campground. In Jacob Lake you'll find the very helpful **Kaibab Plateau Visitor Center** (☎ 928-643-7298; open 8am-5pm, closed Dec–mid-May), where you can also purchase backcountry permits.

All services on the North Rim are closed from mid-October through mid-May, but rangers are on hand. Day-trippers are welcome year-round (no charge). You can stay at the campground until the first heavy snowfall closes the road from Jacob Lake; after that you'll need a backcountry permit (available directly from rangers after the backcountry office closes).

 ✓ TIP

If you intend to spend most of your time at the North Rim, consider starting in Flagstaff, taking a short detour to the South Rim, then heading up to the North Rim. Get an early start from Flagstaff, enter the park via the South Entrance and head east along Desert View Drive. If time allows, stop by **Shoshone Point** (p95), and don't miss the historic **Watchtower** (p90). Exit the park via the East Entrance, lunch in Cameron and continue about four hours north to the North Rim.

Getting Around

The only way to tour the North Rim is by car, bicycle or motorcycle. You'll find a **Chevron gas station** beside the campground (open 7am-7pm in summer, 8am-5pm in spring/fall), and there's another gas station at Jacob Lake, but the nearest **service garage** is Judd Auto (☎ 928-643-7107; open 7am-7pm), 75 miles north in Fredonia.

The **Transcanyon Shuttle** (☎ 928-638-2820; adult one-way/round-trip $65/110, child 12 and under one-way/round-trip $50/90; cash only) takes passengers to the South Rim, departing from the Grand Canyon Lodge at 7am daily. Reserve at least a week in advance (see p78 for more details). A **hikers' shuttle** ($5 first passenger, $2 each additional passenger) to the North Kaibab Trail departs daily at 5:20am and 7:20am, also from Grand Canyon Lodge. You must sign up for it at the front desk; if no one signs up the night before, it will not run.

Driving Tours

There are no bus tours on the North Rim, so the only way to take in the following driving tours is by car or bicycle. You can hike to Point Imperial (see Ken Patrick Trail, p116), but no trails connect the viewpoints.

CAPE ROYAL ROAD
Route: Grand Canyon Lodge to Cape Royal
Distance: 23 miles
Speed Limit: 45mph

From Grand Canyon Lodge head 3 miles north to the turnoff for **Point Imperial** and **Cape Royal**. The road splits about 5 miles east of Hwy 67; you can head 3 miles north to Point Imperial or 15 miles south to Cape Royal. The road to Cape Royal winds through the woods past several picnic areas and an ancient Pueblo site, but you can only see the canyon from the viewpoints. Even in summer you won't find crowds – you can enjoy a leisurely picnic and probably not see another soul. The road descends gradually (from 8200ft at Grand Canyon Lodge and 8803ft at Point Imperial to 7865ft at Cape Royal), and the vegetation changes to that of the upper Sonoran. Shrub-like piñon pines and sagebrush replace the tall aspens and ponderosa pines characteristic of the North Rim. This road may be closed in the late fall and early spring. There are bathrooms at Point Imperial and Cape Royal.

Point Imperial
At 8803ft, Point Imperial is the highest overlook on either rim. Expansive views of the canyon's eastern half and the desert beyond include **Nankoweap Creek** (directly below the viewpoint), the **Vermilion Cliffs**, the **Painted Desert** and the **Little Colorado River**. An interpretive sign identifies the sights and geologic formations, and there are several picnic tables. Just past the parking lot lies the trailhead for the **Nankoweap Trail** (p132), a difficult below-the-rim trail with lots of thornbushes.

Vista Encantada
Less crowded than Point Imperial or Cape Royal, this viewpoint offers several picnic tables right along the rim.

Roosevelt Point
From here you can see the confluence of the Little Colorado and Colorado Rivers, the **Navajo Reservation**, the **Painted Desert** and the **Hopi Reservation**. The pleasant

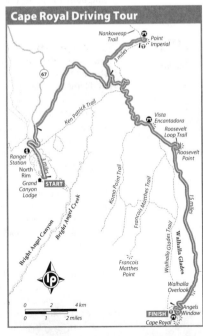

Cape Royal Driving Tour

0.2-mile round-trip **Roosevelt Point Trail** loops through secluded wood land and offers spectacular views.

Walhalla Overlook & Walhalla Glades

On the east side of the road is the **Walhalla Overlook**; on the west side a short path leads to an **ancient Pueblo site**. From 1050 to 1150 AD, **Walhalla Glades** was the summer home of a small farming village of about 20 people. Because it sits below most of the North Rim, snow melted earlier and enabled villagers to grow beans, corn and squash. In winter they returned to the warm canyon depths. A short self-guided walk leads past six small ruins – pick up a walking tour brochure from a small box at the trailhead just off the road.

Cape Royal

The North Rim's busiest overlook, Cape Royal offers a 0.3-mile paved, level walk to **Angels Window**, a natural arch, and **Cape Royal**, arguably the best view from this side of the canyon. The narrow overlook by Angels Window juts into the canyon and drops dramatically on three sides. Though there are railings, it's rather harrowing – don't walk to the tip if you have vertigo, and keep toddlers secured in carriers or holding an adult's hand at all times. Trailside signs explain vegetation along the walk, and it's plenty wide for wheelchairs, though they can't access the overlook. Scattered amid the piñon pines and sagebrush at the far end of the parking lot are several shaded picnic tables. To the left, the **Wedding Site picnic bench** features great canyon views – an ideal spot for a sunrise picnic breakfast.

POINT SUBLIME
Route: Grand Canyon Lodge to Point Sublime
Distance: 17 miles
Speed Limit: 45 mph

A 17-mile dirt road (four-wheel-drive vehicles only) leads to a **Point Sublime**, an overview that juts into the canyon and offers amazing views. From here you can see the Colorado River and a panorama of both rims. You probably won't see anyone else here, and it's a rough road even in the best of weather. Check in with a ranger at the visitors center before attempting the drive, and allow two hours one way. There's a picnic area at the point, and you can camp with a backcountry permit. The quickest route is to head 2.7 miles north of Grand Canyon Lodge on Hwy 67 and turn left on the unpaved road to the point. Alternatively, you can reach Point Sublime from DeMotte Campground in Kaibab National Forest; contact the Kaibab Plateau Visitor Center or the North Rim Visitor Center for directions.

Just over 4 miles west of Hwy 67 on the road to Point Sublime, you'll reach an old dirt road that heads south about 4.5 miles to **Tiyo Point**, a quiet overlook and good backcountry campsite (no facilities). You can't drive or bike the road, but it's a moderate hike, and you'll have the point to yourself.

One of the park's most impressive overlooks, this remote spot is far from any facilities. To access it, you must drive about 90 miles northeast of the park entrance, then 61 miles south on a dirt road. But if you're looking for a quiet spot to enjoy the canyon, it's worth the drive. Sheer cliffs drop to **Vulcans Throne**, a lava neck that rises 50ft from the middle of the Colorado River directly below, while **Lava Falls**, perhaps the roughest water in the canyon, is visible 1.5 miles downstream. Twenty-five miles east is the mouth of **Havasu Canyon**. There are no guardrails, so use extreme caution, and do not venture too close to the edge.

A few moderate hikes offer chances to stretch your legs in this desert landscape. The 2.9-mile **Esplanade Loop Trail** begins at the campground. For a shorter hike, try the easy **Saddle Horse Canyon Trail**, a 1.6 mile round-trip to the canyon rim. The trailhead is 5.7 miles south of the ranger station.

You don't need to pay a park entry fee, and you must bring your own water. To get here, drive 9 miles west of Fredonia on Hwy 389 and look for a dirt road and the sign 'Toroweap 61.' Take this road (usually passable to cars) 55 miles south to the Tuweep Ranger Station, staffed year-round. A free primitive campground lies about 5 miles beyond the ranger station and a mile from the rim. At 4552ft, Toroweap is lower than either rim. Piñon pines, junipers, cacti and small flowering desert plants cover the plateau, and it can get very hot.

> **✔ TIP**
>
> Accessible along forest service roads in Kaibab National Forest outside the park, several remote overlooks on the North Rim offer backcountry camping (p212). Camping at remote spots within the park requires a backcountry permit.

Walks & Day Hikes

Decidedly quieter than the South Rim, the North Rim can seem like a whole different park. Even with the additional 1000ft of altitude and the sensation you've taken a giant step back from the canyon, it's somehow more intimate. And so it is with the hiking.

A piney fringe hugs much of the canyon's rim, buffering hikers from the steeps, while willowy groves of aspens and ponderosa pines pop up here and there to shade the trails. Wildflowers provide bursts of colors, like lipstick-red penstemon, purple lupine and magenta paintbrush, while birds soar and sing overhead. Some claim this rim is less scenic – the Colorado is far less visible, trans-canyon views are scarce and there aren't as many rock ledges jutting out for sunset views. But wilderness lovers and avid hikers in the know disagree, gleefully making the longer journey to

FOR COFFEE LOVERS

Before hitting the trail, early-rising hikers on the North Rim can grab a latte ($3.73 with tax) from 5:30am to 10:30am at the Espresso Bar, in the Rough Rider Saloon at Grand Canyon Lodge. While you're there, load up on pastries and bananas.

swap crowds and craggy views for the serene cool calm that awaits on the softer side of the canyon.

There's a wider selection of hikes on the North Rim, most accessible to all skill levels and several good for kids. The majority of trails weave through the peaceful upper realm atop the Kaibab Plateau, with only the North Kaibab descending into the canyon's rugged depths. The Colorado River is a 14-mile haul from the rim, requiring an overnight en route (p127). Even if the river isn't your destination, hiking the North Kaibab for a half day is a wondrous trip, quickly passing through multiple temperate zones.

While in general the North Rim is cooler and breezier than the South, it's all relative – hiking here still necessitates the same level of preparation and caution. Hit the longer trails by sunrise, carry plenty of water and don't push yourself in the desert heat.

You don't need a permit to hike on the North Rim unless you plan to camp along rimside trails or beneath the rim). In the following descriptions, distances listed are one-way, while duration is round-trip, unless otherwise noted. (Hiking time depends largely on each hiker's ability.) Elevation change marks the difference between the trailhead and the destination point. The North Kaibab offers day hikers multiple turnaround spots; respective distances and elevations are summarized under the trail heading and detailed in the description.

BRIGHT ANGEL POINT
Distance: 0.3 miles one-way
Duration: 20 minutes round-trip
Challenge: Easy
Elevation Change: 150ft

Though it tends to be busy, this short and easy paved trail is a must for all ages. Beginning from the back porch of Grand Canyon Lodge, the trail wraps up, down and out along a narrow finger of an overlook that dangles between The Transept and Roaring Springs Canyon. Breezes sometimes carry the echo of rushing water up from Roaring Springs several thousand feet below. The sensation of being suspended in air above the canyon is uplifting. Along the way, there are some nooks for private overlooks and even picnics – look for the spot right near the trail's end, off to the right.

From the oft-packed overlook take in the spectacular views out toward Bright Angel Canyon. You'll have unfettered views of mesas, buttes, spires and temples, as well as a straight shot of the South Rim, 11 miles away. On a clear day you'll even see the distant **San Francisco Peaks**. This pretty trail is a good choice for a quick post-arrival walk to stretch your legs. It's a very popular spot at both sunrise and sunset; but if you have a good flashlight or headlamp, visit the point after dusk for unequaled stargazing.

TRANSEPT TRAIL
Distance: 1.5 miles one-way
Duration: 45 minutes round-trip
Challenge: Easy-Moderate
Elevation Change: 200ft

Conveniently connecting Grand Canyon Lodge to the campground, the Transept makes for an enjoyable and level walk. Skirting the rim of its namesake canyon, the narrow dirt path darts in and out of the aspens and oaks often enough that it's easy to forget there's a drop-off on one side. While it doesn't offer unobstructed panoramic canyon views like the Rim Trail (p95), it's a lovely and cool stroll, passing prehistoric ruins, benches and several side trails to overlooks. Watch for the occasional lizard, as well as deer tramping through the lupine. The mostly rock-free trail is a good choice for kids of all ages, a post-dinner amble or a trail run.

You can access the trail from the steps off the back patio at Grand Canyon Lodge (the Bright Angel Point Trail veers off from the Transept) or from behind the general store at the campground.

WIDFORSS TRAIL
Distance: 5 miles one-way
Duration: 4-6 hours round-trip
Challenge: Moderate
Elevation Change: 350ft

Arguably the finest rim trail in the park, this lovely hike through stands of spruce, white fir, ponderosa pine and aspen leads to **Widforss Point**, one of the best canyon views on the North Rim. As is the case with most North Rim trails, the pine needle-cushioned route winds mainly through the woods and offers only periodic glimpses of the canyon through the trees. It's a much more subtle view of the canyon than that presented by dramatic panoramas along the South Rim, and the focus is equally shared with flower-laced wooded glades zipping with hummingbirds. Tall trees offer shade, fallen limbs provide pleasant spots to relax, and you likely won't see more than a few people on this wilderness trail.

After an initial climb, the canyon will come into view. Soon after, the trail jags away from the rim and dips into gullies of lupines and ferns. From Widforss Point (elevation 7900ft), a small rocky ledge shrouded with pines, you can see five temples: **Zoroaster**, **Brahma**, **Deva**, **Buddha** and **Manu**. A picnic table and campsite just off the rim is a nice spot for lunch before tackling the 5-mile return to the trailhead. Though the total elevation change is only 350ft, rolling terrain makes the first couple of miles a moderate challenge. It's a

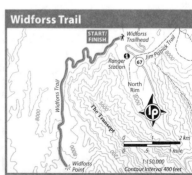

Widforss Trail

10-mile full-day trip if you hike to the overlook and back, but even if you just walk an hour or so up the trail, the peaceful cool forest and occasional rim views make this a great choice.

To get to the trailhead, turn left on the dirt road about 0.3 mile south of Cape Royal Road and follow it for a mile to the Widforss Trail parking area. Self-guided trail brochures are available at the trailhead and at the visitors center. This is a particularly pretty hike in late September or early October when the leaves are golden. In summer it can be a bit buggy on the trail, so be sure to bring along insect repellant.

KEN PATRICK TRAIL
Distance: 10 miles one-way
Duration: 4-6 hours one-way
Challenge: Easy-Moderate
Elevation Change: 800ft

Offering rim and forest views, this peaceful trail ascends and descends numerous ravines as it wends through an old, deep forest, crosses **Cape Royal Road** after 7 miles and continues for another 3 miles to **Point Imperial** (elevation 8803ft), the highest point on the North Rim. To hike the entire point-to-point route in either direction, it's necessary to arrange a car shuttle. An easier and equally enjoyable option is to fashion it into an out-and-back hike of your desired length. The trail was named in memory of a popular Grand Canyon park ranger who was murdered in 1973 by an escaped convict while on assignment at California's Point Reyes National Seashore.

From the North Kaibab Trail parking lot the trail veers northeast into the forest. Mules frequently travel the first wooded and sandy mile, and it can be rather smelly and soggy. After a mile the mules head off on the Uncle Jim (see below), while the Ken Patrick veers to the left. Beyond this junction the trail grows increasingly serene and at times faint but discernible. You'll pass the old Bright Angel Trail on the right after 4 miles, as well as areas of blackened brush, evidence of a prescribed burn that spread out of control in the spring of 2000. If you'd like to camp anywhere along the trail, you'll need a backcountry permit (p124); there's no water source between the trailhead and Point Imperial, so factor that into your planning.

For excellent views and a shorter, mule-free walk, park along Cape Royal Road and pick up the Ken Patrick on its final 3-mile jaunt to Point Imperial. This stretch is the steepest but also the prettiest. The trail alternates between shady conifer forests and panoramic views of Nankoweap Canyon, the Little Colorado River gorge, Marble Platform and the Painted Desert, and the San Francisco Peaks far to the south. Allow three to four hours for the round-trip journey. Another option is to start at Point

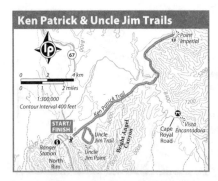

Ken Patrick & Uncle Jim Trails

Imperial and walk the 3 miles to Cape Royal Road. Hikers can shuttle a car or arrange a pickup at the turnout, one-tenth of a mile west of where the trail crosses the road.

UNCLE JIM TRAIL

Distance: 2.5 miles one-way
Duration: 2-3 hours round-trip
Challenge: Easy-Moderate
Elevation Change: 600ft

This spur trail is named for a hunting advocate and forest service warden who shot hundreds of mountain lions on the North Rim to protect resident deer. The trail branches off the Ken Patrick, makes a wide loop atop the Kaibab Plateau, then doubles back to the start. Uncle Jim shares the Ken Patrick Trailhead (see p116), which is near the mule corral on the east edge of the North Kaibab Trail parking lot, 1.5 miles north of Grand Canyon Lodge.

The trail starts with a gentle climb into the woods and winds through gambel oak, ponderosa pine, white fir and aspen woodland. Views are intermittent, offering quick glimpses of Roaring Springs Canyon. The trail sees a lot of mule traffic, and it shows – particularly on the first mile, where the soft dirt path, worn into sandy grooves by hooves, can be hard on the feet.

After about 20 minutes of walking, the more heavily used Uncle Jim Trail spurs off to the right, while the Ken Patrick veers to the left. After a bit of down and up, the trail soon splits into the 2-mile loop out to the point – it makes little difference if you go left or right. Near the tie-up area for mules at **Uncle Jim Point**, you'll have a terrific view of the North Kaibab switchbacks, Roaring Springs, the Walhalla Plateau and the South Rim. Stop for a picnic amid the big rocks near the point before your return.

CLIFF SPRING TRAIL

Distance: 0.5 mile one-way
Duration: 40 minutes round-trip
Challenge: Easy-Moderate
Elevation Change: 600ft

Though some stretches require a bit of scrambling over rock, this sweet little wooded trail is relatively easy. The trailhead lies on a curve of the Cape Royal Road, across the street from **Angels Window Overlook**, 13.7 miles south of the Point Imperial turnoff and a half mile before the road's end at Cape Royal.

After about 120 yards the trail meanders past a small **Pueblo Indian granary**, used by the canyon's early inhabitants to store corn, beans and squash. The oak-lined route continues down a short, rocky descent into a ravine, then cuts alongside a huge hollowed-out boulder. Eventually, it reaches a small spring that drips into mossy green pools. Look for it beneath a large overhang on the cliff side of a chest-high boulder. It's a pretty and peaceful spot, fringed with ferns and verdant thistle and cooled by steady breezes. There's a second, stronger spring just past the sign.

CAPE FINAL TRAIL
Distance: 2 miles one-way
Duration: 1.5 hours round-trip
Challenge: Easy
Elevation Change: 150ft

If you don't have much time or are unaccustomed to hiking, this flat, easy hike to an overlook on the Kaibab Plateau is a good choice. It's easy to miss the trailhead on Cape Royal Road, 11.8 miles south of the Point Imperial turnoff and 2.5 miles north of the road's end at Cape Royal. Look for a small, unmarked dirt parking lot.

After a pleasant stroll through cool ponderosa pines, the trail ends at Cape Final. Here the thick forest gives way to piñon, sagebrush and cliff rose, all of which thrive in the hot, dry canyon updrafts. The overlook offers expansive views of **Unkar Creek Canyon**, **Vishnu Temple** and, by the river, **Unkar Delta**, a 300-acre span of alluvial terraces. This delta served as the Pueblo people's winter farming grounds until the late 12th century; archaeologists have uncovered at least 94 structures, including large storage rooms, living quarters and kivas.

POINT IMPERIAL
Distance: 2 miles one-way
Duration: 1.5 hours round-trip
Challenge: Easy
Elevation Change: 100ft

From the Point Imperial parking lot this trail heads northeast along the rim through areas burned by the 2000 fire. The trail ends at the park's northern border, where it connects with the Nankoweap Trail (p132) and US Forest Service roads. Though this trail rolls gently along the rim, offering views of the eastern canyon, the high elevation (8800ft) can make it seem more difficult.

NORTH KAIBAB TRAIL
Distance: 2 miles to Supai Tunnel; 4.7 miles to Roaring Springs
Duration: 3-4 hours round-trip; 6-7 hours round-trip
Challenge: Moderate-Difficult; Difficult
Elevation Change: 1410ft; 3210ft

The North Kaibab is one of the park's prettiest, most diverse trails, offering an awesome array of scenery on its 14.2-mile descent to the Colorado River. Following the **Bright Angel Creek** drainage, the route has gone through numerous permutations over its thousands years of use as an inner canyon trail. The current route, which steeply descends Roaring

Springs Canyon, was established by the park service in the late 1920s.

The trailhead lies 2 miles north of Grand Canyon Lodge. The modest parking lot is often full soon after daylight; you can also park along the roadside, walk from the lodge or campground, or hop the **daily hikers' shuttle** (p110).

Most day hikers on the North Kaibab opt for the 4-mile round-trip to **Supai Tunnel**; only strong hikers should continue to **Roaring Springs**, a hard hike just shy of 10 miles round-trip. At first the sandy trail remains shaded, hugging the forest of aspens and pines. After about 15 minutes you'll reach **Coconino Overlook**, a flat ledge that offers clear views of Roaring Springs and Bright Angel Canyons. For those wanting just a taste of the North Kaibab, this is a good turnaround spot, making for a 1.5-mile round-trip.

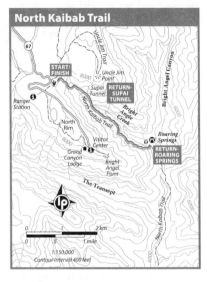

Twenty or so minutes later you'll reach a tree-shaded glen with a seasonal water tap and pit toilets – an ideal rest area for hikers and mule riders on half-day trips. Just around a bend is **Supai Tunnel**, a short red corridor that leads to clear views of the canyon's narrow chutes followed by a very steep set of switchbacks beside an impressive drop-off. You'll follow the folds of the canyon on the descent to **Redwall Bridge**, which crosses Roaring Springs Creek. Soon after, you'll reach Roaring Springs itself, a cascade of cool puddles that will soothe tired feet. Potable water is available from May to September, so you can refill before the arduous return to the rim, a 9.4-mile round-trip in all. On the way back, as you emerge from Supai Tunnel, look up at the magnificent striped rocks in layers of slate gray, brown and white.

For a description of overnight hikes on the North Kaibab, see Exploring the Backcountry (p127).

✔ TIP

Vandalism or theft of the park's cultural or archaeological resources is a violation of federal law; if you witness such a violation, please contact the park service's confidential **Silent Witness Program** (☎ 928-638-7767).

Other Activities

With a similar array of activities as the South Rim but less people doing them, the North Rim offers the chance to get outdoors *and* get away from it all.

MOUNTAIN BIKING

You can fashion a terrific extended ride out to Point Imperial and on to Cape Royal, about 45 miles each way from Grand Canyon Lodge. The park's 35mph speed limit ensures slow traffic, and the pine-fringed road offers a good riding surface. For a short, sweet ride that's well suited to families, take the **Bridle Path**, which leads from the North Kaibab Trailhead to the campground (0.5 mile) and lodge (1.5 miles).

Mountain bikes are allowed on blacktop roads only. The one exception is the 17-mile dirt road to Point Sublime (p112). In the surrounding Kaibab National Forest, you'll find several excellent mountain bike trails and dirt roads to canyon overlooks; see Kaibab National Forest (North Rim), on p211.

MULE RIDES

Canyon Trail Rides offers one-hour mule trips along the rim and half- or full-day trips into the canyon. The full-day, seven-hour trip ($95) departs at 7:25am daily and descends about 4000ft to **Roaring Springs**. Lunch and water are provided. Half-day trips 2000ft below the rim to **Supai Tunnel** ($45) leave at 7:25am and 12:25pm. Riders spend about 75 minutes on the mule each way, and there is water at Supai Tunnel. If you're not used to riding, this trip is far gentler on your muscles than full-day trips, and it still lets you experience the inner gorge. Riders must weigh less than 200lbs and be at least 8 years old for the half-day trip and 12 years old for the full-day trip. A one-hour rim ride ($20) along the Ken Patrick Trail is available for children 7 or older and adults weighing less than 220lbs.

To make advance reservations, call ☎ 435-679-8665 or access the company's website at W www.canyonrides.com. Credit cards are not accepted, so be prepared to send a check or money order. To make reservations within 10 days of your visit, call or stop by the mule desk (☎ 928-638-9875) in the Grand Canyon Lodge lobby. Unlike mule trips on the South Rim, you can usually book a trip when arrive at the park.

FISHING

The nearest place to purchase the required Arizona fishing license is Jacob Lake Lodge, 44 miles north of the rim. See Activities, Fishing (p49), and Lees Ferry & Marble Canyon (p218) for information on fishing the Colorado.

HORSEBACK RIDING

At Jacob Lake, **Allen's Guided Tours** (☎ 435-644-8150) offers one-hour ($25), two-hour ($35) and half-day ($45) rides through Kaibab National Forest. Full-day rides ($65) visit an overlook of the eastern canyon and include lunch. Though there is no age limit, think carefully before taking a child under 5 on a ride. Reservations are not required for short rides – just stop by the corrals (on Hwy 67 about a mile north of Jacob Lake Lodge). It's difficult to reach the business by phone – if you want to arrange a half- or full-day trip, stop by the corrals on your way in to the park.

CROSS-COUNTRY SKIING

Once the first heavy snowfall closes Hwy 67 into the park (as early as late October or as late as January), you can cross-country ski the 44 miles to the rim and camp at the campground (no water, pit toilets). Camping is permitted elsewhere with a backcountry permit, available from rangers year-round.

You can ski any of the rim trails, though none are groomed, while experienced skiers may head into the canyon along the North Kaibab. If you plan on descending into the canyon, be sure your skis are properly equipped, as it can be a treacherous trek.

RANGER PROGRAMS

Ranger programs include a talk on ancient Pueblo Indians at Walhalla Overlook and a 1.5-mile nature walk and discussion of fire ecology at the recently burned area near Point Imperial. Several evening programs (including the geology talk and historical tales of the North Rim) are held around the fireplace on the back porch of Grand Canyon Lodge – a highlight of any visit. When skies are clear, guests gather on the back porch to gaze through telescopes while a ranger describes the night sky; these aren't always scheduled, so be sure to ask at the visitors center. Check *The Guide* for a schedule of other programs.

Children enjoy the **Discovery Pack Program** and the **Junior Ranger Program**, during which they attend ranger talks, fill out a Junior Ranger book, then are sworn in as Junior Rangers (see p55).

CLASSES

There are no regularly scheduled classes on the North Rim, though many classes offered through the Grand Canyon Field Institute and other organizations encompass both rims and the canyon interior (see p52).

FUEL

You'll find a gas station (open 7am-7pm) on the access road to North Rim Campground.

GROCERIES & CAMPING SUPPLIES

Just beside the campground, the **North Rim General Store** (☎ 928-638-2611; open 8am-8pm) offers a small but thorough selection of groceries. You'll find steak, frozen meat, eggs, cheese, diapers, beer, wine and firewood, among other essentials. The closest full grocery store is in Kanab, a 90-minute drive north.

The general store also sells a limited selection of camping gear, including fuel, insect repellant and lanterns, as well as mats and sleeping bags. Hours vary according to demand. Willow Canyon Outdoor Co (p217) in Kanab sells outdoor gear, books and maps.

LOST & FOUND

If you lose an item anywhere on the North Rim, contact the visitors center (☎ 928-638-7864) or Grand Canyon Lodge (☎ 928-638-2612).

MEDICAL SERVICES & EMERGENCIES

The nearest clinic and pharmacy is in Kanab, 80 miles north. In an emergency call ☎ 911; from your cabin or room dial ☎ 9-911.

MONEY

There's neither a bank nor an ATM on the North Rim. The nearest ATM is in Jacob Lake, 44 miles north of the lodge.

POSTAL SERVICE

You'll find a postal window (open 11am-4pm, Mon-Fri 8am-1pm Sat) on the covered boardwalk beside the lodge.

RELIGIOUS SERVICES

A bulletin board in the lodge provides information on North Rim religious services.

SHOWERS & LAUNDRY

Pay showers and laundry facilities (open 7am-7pm) are on the access road leading to the campground. Water must be pumped up more than 3000ft from Roaring Springs to the rim, so use these services sparingly.

TELEPHONES

All rooms have telephones. You'll also find pay phones at the general store and outside the main entrance to the lodge. Cell phones usually work if you're close to the rim.

TRASH & RECYCLING

The park recycles paper, newspaper, magazines, cardboard, aluminum and steel cans, plastic and glass. Tan recycling dumpsters stand beside regular trash dumpsters throughout the park.

EXPLORING THE BACKCOUNTRY

The Grand Canyon's backcountry is an exhilarating place guaranteed to provide a unique backpacking experience. Adventure enthusiasts should plan to spend at least a night or two deep in the inner gorge – walking the sandy banks of the Colorado, exploring the side canyon tributaries, sleeping beneath the vast swath of stars and listening to the nightly serenade of chirping frogs.

From the rim, where the majority of park visitors stay put, it's impossible to truly appreciate the rich wilderness that lies below, nor is it possible to tell how that wilderness may affect you. Dip down to the canyon floor along the main corridor trails and immerse yourself in scenes of otherworldly beauty. Some people love it and return every year, while others decide the canyon's inner reaches aren't for them. Either way, the experience will add a whole new perspective to your visit.

Overnight backpacking trips and rafting excursions on the Colorado River are the most popular means of experiencing the backcountry. This chapter offers descriptions of some of the more accessible overnight hikes, as well as options for making a trip-of-a-lifetime passage down the Colorado.

Backcountry Hiking

Most hikes described in this chapter involve travel along the well-maintained **corridor trails**, which lead from the rim down to the Colorado and back again. The most common rim-to-river-to-rim route is a descent on the South Kaibab (p127) followed by an ascent up the Bright Angel (p125), but backpackers have an endless variety of options. The corridor trails offer access to several **threshold** and **primitive** trails, which are not patrolled by rangers, are short on water and are hard to follow in places. A few of the longer hikes involve segments along these more remote paths.

The backcountry is a vast land of extremes – over-the-top views, bone-dry conditions and scorching temperatures. For most, it's an entirely unfamiliar and inhospitable area, in terms of both terrain and climate, where rote situations can quickly turn dangerous. Hiking in the backcountry requires keen preparation and caution, even if you're a veteran with thousands of hiking miles under your feet. Each year's numerous canyon rescues involve both inexperienced hikers and strong backpackers. For more information on key safety issues, see Hiking Safety (p44). On long out-and-back hikes along unmaintained trails, you might consider stashing water along the route to ensure you won't run dry.

Generally speaking, you shouldn't put together a hiking itinerary that is beyond the capabilities of any one member of your group. If you'd like to hike the backcountry but don't want to go solo (a bad idea anyway), there are lots of group hike offerings (p46). Before setting out on any backcountry excursion, check trail conditions at one of the backcountry offices or call park headquarters at ☎ 928-638-7888.

PERMIT INFORMATION

Overnight hikes into the canyon require a backcountry permit. Control of camper numbers is very tight, and demand often far exceeds available slots. If you're caught camping in the backcountry without a permit, expect a hefty fine and possible court appearance.

Permits cost $10, plus an additional $5 per person per night for sites below the rim, or $5 per person per night for undeveloped rim sites; the fee is nonrefundable and payable by check or credit card. If you plan on backcountry camping in the canyon at least three separate times in a given year, the $25 Frequent Hiker Membership Card will save you at least $5.

Reservations are accepted in person or by mail or fax beginning the first day of the month, four months prior to the planned trip – for instance, if you'd like to hike the Bright Angel in June, you'll want to apply on or after February 1. Detailed instructions and the permit request form is available online at W www.nps.gov/grca, as well as in the *Backcountry Trip Planner*, available throughout the park. Submit your request by fax to 928-638-2125, or send it to Grand Canyon National Park, Backcountry Reservations Office, PO Box 129, Grand Canyon, AZ 86023. Permits must be picked up in person at the Backcountry Reservations Office on the South Rim or at the North Rim ranger station by 9am on the day your hike begins.

When applying, be prepared to give very detailed information, including your specific itinerary, the number in your party (no more than 11), where you'll be spending each night, and even license plate information for cars left at trailheads. Once a permit is granted, itinerary changes are not permitted, except for emergencies. You're permitted to list three alternative dates and routes, which can markedly increase your chances of securing a permit.

If you're willing to be flexible about where and when you hike, you can show up in person at the **Backcountry Reservations Office** (☎ 928-638-7868 on the North Rim; ☎ 928-638-7875 on the South Rim; open 8am-noon and 1-5pm). Add your name to a waiting list by submitting a request in writing for a permit for the following day. The waiting list can take anywhere from a day to a week to clear, and the wait tends to be longer on the South Rim. Requests are accepted in person only, but you can get an idea of how long the waiting list is by calling the Backcountry Reservations Office in advance.

BACKCOUNTRY CAMPING

The park offers three types of backcountry camping. Three backcountry campgrounds, **Indian Garden**, **Bright Angel** and **Cottonwood**, lie along the main corridor trails between the South and North Rims. Hikers on these trails can also stay at **Phantom Ranch** (p128). Campgrounds have a two-night limit, except between November 15 and February 28, when a four-night limit is in effect. All provide picnic tables, pit toilets and seasonal or year-round potable water sources. Most are adjacent to a ranger station.

The threshold and primitive zones contain 18 designated campsites: Cape Final (one campsite), Horseshoe Mesa (one campsite), Monument Trail area (five campsites), Hermit Trail (two campsites), Point Sublime (one campsite), Pasture Wash (three campsites), Swamp Ridge (two campsites), Tapeats

Creek (two campsites) and Deer Creek (one campsite). All sites feature a two-night limit, level tent sites and pit toilets.

The park also recognizes at-large camping, or dispersed camping, which simply means an area without facilities or any designated campsites, where camping is limited to seven nights.

BRIGHT ANGEL TRAIL
Distance: 18.6 miles round-trip
Duration: 3 days
Challenge: Difficult
Elevation Change: 4380ft descent

The most popular path from the rim to the bottom of one of the world's deepest chasms, the Bright Angel is a wide, well-maintained and easy-to-follow corridor trail – fun for first-time canyon hikers and veterans alike. Sweeping canyon views take your mind off the knee-pounding 7.8-mile descent to the Colorado River.

The path follows a natural break in the cliffs along Bright Angel Fault as it winds down to the productive freshwater spring at Indian Garden and on to the inner canyon. Native Americans were the first to use the route. Arriving in the late 19th century, prospectors improved the trail, introduced mules and began charging a toll. Tourism quickly outpaced mining, and by 1928 the NPS gained control.

Between mid-May and mid-September, extreme heat and sun mandate shorter hiking days. The NPS often restricts summer hiking to mornings and evenings, keeping hikers off the trail between 10am and 4pm. Plan to start hiking at first light – 4:30am in summer and 6:30am in spring and fall. Take advantage of the trail's four day-use resthouses to get out of the sun and hydrate. These open-walled, roofed enclosures offer shade, picnic tables, nearby toilets and an emergency telephone. The two upper resthouses provide drinking water from May to September.

Mules have the right-of-way, so hikers must step aside for mule trains to pass. In winter and early spring the upper reaches can be icy, and you may want to wear crampons.

If you didn't secure a backcountry permit in advance, visit the **Backcountry Information Center** where walk-ins get preference to fill vacancies or cancellations. Permits are not required for day hikes, so this is always an option.

The Bright Angel Trailhead lies just west of Kolb Studio and Bright Angel Lodge in Grand

Canyon Village on the South Rim. Ride the shuttle bus to the Hermits Rest transfer stop. The trailhead sign is visible just steps away.

Day 1: Bright Angel Trailhead to Indian Garden Campground
(2-3 hours, 4.6 miles, 3060ft descent)

The Bright Angel Trailhead (6860ft) is both exhilarating and intimidating. The canyon unfolds before you in all its glory, hikers bustle around making last-minute adjustments to their backpacks, and wranglers acquaint first-time mule riders (is there any other kind?) with the curious beasts. You may even reread the interpretive sign at the trailhead to delay your first steps down a trail that looks like it drops off the edge of the planet.

Take a deep breath and start slowly. If you suffer vertigo, look to the left for a while or just stop and close your eyes – the first five minutes are the hardest. Before you know it, you'll grow accustomed and the trail gets interesting.

Quickly pass through **First Tunnel**. Indian pictographs adorn the wall above the piñon- and juniper-lined trail. After passing through **Second Tunnel**, you'll reach **Mile-and-a-Half Resthouse** (5720ft), 45 minutes from the trailhead. Anyone starting late or hiking for the first time should turn around here, allowing 2.5 hours round-trip.

About 200 yards before **Two-Mile Corner** look for more pictographs on a boulder. As you approach **Three-Mile Resthouse** (4920ft), 90 minutes from the trailhead, your views expand over the Redwall limestone cliffs to Indian Garden and Tonto Platform below. Day hikers turning back here should allow five hours round-trip.

The sinuous switchbacks of **Jacob's Ladder** descend through sheer Redwall cliffs. Beyond, mesquite clumps grow from seasonal streambeds as you cross the trans-canyon water pipeline and reach Indian Garden, 45 minutes from Three-Mile Resthouse. Havasupai Indians farmed here until the early 20th century.

The year-round **Indian Garden Campground** (3800ft; 50-camper limit) is an inviting stop, with cottonwoods, a ranger station, a toilet and a resthouse with picnic tables. Year-round drinking water is available just before the Plateau Point Trail junction. Each of the campground's 15 sites offers a picnic table shaded by an open-walled, roofed enclosure. Indian Garden is a day-hike destination only for very strong hikers, who should allow seven hours round-trip.

Day 2: Day Hike to Colorado River
(6-8 hours, 9.4 miles, 1388ft descent, 1388ft ascent)

Passing the Tonto Trail junction at a half mile, the Bright Angel Trail follows year-round Garden Creek as it cuts through the dramatic sandstone cliffs of **Tapeats Narrows**. Below, you'll cross the creek twice before arriving at a barren saddle.

In front of you is **Devils Corkscrew**, a massive set of switchbacks through the arid Vishnu schist and the trail's last big descent. At the base of the switchbacks, the trail meets Pipe Creek, whose lush streamside habitat contrasts sharply with the surrounding desert. To the west, Garden Creek tumbles over a dramatic waterfall to join Pipe

Creek. Ninety minutes from Indian Garden you'll reach the **River Resthouse**.

The welcome sight of the Colorado and Pipe Creek Beach below heralds the unsigned junction (2446ft) with the **River Trail**. Follow this undulating trail upstream for 30 minutes, enjoying views of Zoroaster Temple (7123ft), then cross the **Silver Suspension Bridge**. Linking the Bright Angel and South Kaibab Trails, the trail continues a short distance to the black Kaibab Suspension Bridge.

You'll find a ranger station, toilet, drinking water and telephone just prior to the footbridge over Bright Angel Creek. Cross the footbridge and turn left at the junction, following the creek upstream to **Bright Angel Campground**, 1.5 miles from the start of the River Trail. **Phantom Ranch** (2546ft) is 0.3 mile farther. A right turn at the junction leads to the boat beach, Anasazi ruins and the Kaibab Suspension Bridge. After a picnic, return to Indian Garden to camp. If you'd like to take in different campgrounds, hike to Bright Angel Campground the first night, then up to Indian Garden Campground the second night, breaking the ascent into two days.

Day 3: Indian Garden Campground to Bright Angel Trailhead
(4-5 hours, 4.6 miles, 3060ft ascent)
Retrace your steps up to the South Rim.

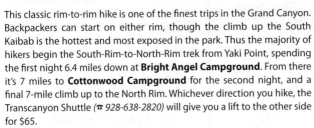

SOUTH KAIBAB TO NORTH KAIBAB
Distance: 20.9 miles one-way
Duration: 3 days round-trip
Challenge: Difficult
Elevation Change: 5770ft

This classic rim-to-rim hike is one of the finest trips in the Grand Canyon. Backpackers can start on either rim, though the climb up the South Kaibab is the hottest and most exposed in the park. Thus the majority of hikers begin the South-Rim-to-North-Rim trek from Yaki Point, spending the first night 6.4 miles down at **Bright Angel Campground**. From there it's 7 miles to **Cottonwood Campground** for the second night, and a final 7-mile climb up to the North Rim. Whichever direction you hike, the Transcanyon Shuttle (*☎ 928-638-2820*) will give you a lift to the other side for $65.

This hike can easily be adapted to start and finish on the South Rim by descending the South Kaibab, then picking up the Bright Angel, via the River Trail, for the return (see above). For a full description of the North Kaibab Trail, see p118.

Day 1: South Kaibab Trailhead to Bright Angel Campground
(6.8 miles, 4-6 hours, 4780ft descent)
From the South Kaibab Trailhead the trail starts out gentle before spiraling steeply down to **Cedar Mesa**, where you'll have a slight reprieve. Past

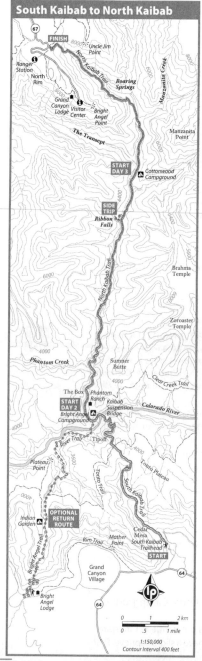

FINISH
Uncle Jim Point
Ranger Station
North Rim
Grand Canyon Lodge
Visitor Center
Bright Angel Point
North Kaibab Trail
Roaring Springs
Manzanita Creek
The Transept
Manzanita Point
START DAY 3
Cottonwood Campground
SIDE TRIP
Ribbon Falls
North Kaibab Trail
Brahma Temple
Zoroaster Temple
Phantom Creek
Sumner Butte
Clear Creek Trail
The Box
Phantom Ranch
START DAY 2
Bright Angel Campground
Kaibab Suspension Bridge
Colorado River
River Trail
Tipoff
Plateau Point
Tonto Trail
Tonto Plateau
Indian Garden
OPTIONAL RETURN ROUTE
Rim Trail
Bright Angel Trail
Mather Point
Cedar Mesa
South Kaibab Trailhead
South Kaibab Trail
START
Grand Canyon Village
64
Bright Angel Lodge
64

0   1   2 km
0   .5   1 mile
1:150,000
Contour Interval 400 feet

Skeleton Point it continues its precipitous drop over scree through the Redwall cliffs, eventually opening up onto the Tonto Platform. Traverse the agave-studded plateau past the Tonto Trail junction, then take a long pause and deep breath at **The Tipoff**, which provides an emergency phone and toilet and marks the start of the steep descent into the inner gorge. After another challenging 1.5 miles and pretty views of Phantom Ranch, you'll reach the **River Trail** junction, which skirts the south side of the Colorado and connects to the Bright Angel Trail. Soon you'll cross the river via the skinny black **Kaibab Suspension Bridge**; turn left after crossing the bridge to see an ancient **Anasazi dwelling**. Just shy of a mile from here is the **Bright Angel Campground**.

As an alternative to camping at Bright Angel Campground, you can stay at **Phantom Ranch.** This picturesque riverside ranch is the only accommodation within the canyon. Dating from 1922, the cluster of buildings – which include a main lodge and cabins – is fringed with towering cottonwoods and fruit orchards planted more than a century ago. Used predominantly by people who descend the corridor trails on mules, the ranch is very popular and often fully booked. Spots not taken by mule excursions go to hikers who don't feel like toting camping gear. **Reservations** (☎ 888-297-2757) must be made far in advance, and you must check in at the Transportation Desk at Bright Angel Lodge by 4pm on the day prior to your hike. You can also try your luck with a same-day opening by calling ☎ 928-638-2631, as cancellations for dorm beds do occur and are doled out on a first-come, first-served basis each morning at Bright Angel Lodge.

Cozy private cabins sleep four to 10 on bunks and cost $77.46 per person for the first two people and $11.30 for each additional guest; dormitor-style bunks in single-sex cabins outfitted for 10 are $27.97 per person. Bunk prices include bedding, soap, shampoo and towels; meals are extra. The ranch – or rather a mule – also provides a duffel delivery service for $53.80 each way. Reservations for the family-style meals – a predawn breakfast ($18) and dinner

($20-30) served at 5pm and 6:30pm sittings – must be made at the same time as room reservations; preordered sack lunches ($9) are also available. If you'd rather skip the expensive meals, you may bring your own food and stove. Campers from nearby Bright Angel Campground can also eat here with advance reservations. After dinner each night, from 8pm to 10pm, the dining room converts into a canteen and serves guests beer, wine and hot drinks ($2-6). There are also board games, books, magazines and plenty of lively conversation.

Day 2 Option: Bright Angel Campground to South Rim

(9.3 miles, 6-9 hours, 4460ft ascent)

If you'd rather opt for a shorter excursion or return to the South Rim, take the River Trail from the campground, pick up the Bright Angel and begin the 9.3-mile ascent, which takes between six and nine hours (see the preceding route description). Provided you've planned ahead, you could also spend a second night on the trail at **Indian Garden Campground**.

Day 2: Bright Angel Campground to Cottonwood Campground

(7.3 miles, 2-4 hours, 1600ft ascent)

Just past Phantom Ranch, the North Kaibab Trail starts its gentle, steady climb along Bright Angel Creek through **The Box**, a mile-long section of narrow canyon walls laced with vertical seams of red gneiss. Where you emerge from The Box, **Phantom Creek** cuts through the canyon's west wall and **Sumner Butte** towers overhead to the east. Several bridges aid the trail's snake-like path along the next half mile of the creek to a wide amphitheater dripping with white silicate.

From here the corridor widens, and the points and buttes of the North Rim come into view. The next couple of miles roll gently through this low-desert terrain, with occasional seeps where tadpoles reside and fresh mint grows in abundance; the water here is high in mineral content and hard on water filters.

A sign for Ribbon Falls (see the Side Trip below) should signal hikers to stay on the east side of Bright Angel Creek during periods of maximum runoff, though foot trails on the west side of the creek may lead you to believe otherwise. Just past the sign you'll crest a knoll and see a bridge below; continue straight to reach **Cottonwood Campground**, another 30 minutes up Bright Angel Creek. Surrounded by a hearty stand of cottonwoods, the campground provides drinking water (May 15 to October 15), pit toilets, a phone, a ranger station and an emergency medical facility.

Side Trip: Ribbon Falls

(1 mile, 2 hours)

The lush oasis at Ribbon Falls is certainly worth a visit for anyone hiking the North Kaibab Trail, and it makes a good day-hike destination from Bright Angel Campground or Phantom Ranch.

Cross the bridge north of the Ribbon Falls sign and turn left to reach Ribbon Creek. Here the trail turns west up a narrow sandstone canyon and climbs quickly up the creek bed. Follow the signed route up the canyon's south side to the grotto behind **Ribbon Falls** – a fairyland of green heather moss and rust-stained rock.

Return the way you came, using caution on the potentially slippery descent along the creek bed. Turn left when you reach Bright Angel Creek, then right to cross the bridge and rejoin the North Kaibab Trail. From here it's north to Cottonwood Campground and south to Bright Angel Campground.

Day 3: Cottonwood Campground to North Kaibab Trailhead
(6.8 miles, 5-7 hours, 4170ft ascent)

The trek up the North Kaibab to the rim is a straightforward haul, beginning along Bright Angel Creek, then snaking along the south side of the spectacularly steep Roaring Springs Canyon. From the campground head north and follow the creek for the first 1.5 miles. The trail then skirts the foot of west-facing Manzanita Point, and **Manzanita Creek** makes an impressive entrance from the east. You're treated to just under a mile more of relatively gentle climbing before reaching a Y-junction, where a unmaintained path – the old Bright Angel Trail – heads north to the Ken Patrick Trail (p116). The North Kaibab continues west, crosses the creek, enters Roaring Springs Canyon and starts its arduous upward climb.

HERMIT TRAIL TO HERMIT CREEK
Distance: 15.6 miles round-trip
Duration: 2 days round-trip
Challenge: Difficult
Elevation Change: 3640ft

Day 1: Hermit Trail to Hermit Creek
(7.8 miles, 4-6 hours, 3640ft descent)

From the Hermit Trailhead a steep rocky path descends 2.5 miles to Santa Maria Spring (for a full description of the day hike, see p100). Backpackers continue past the spring as the trail levels for a mile or so before zigzagging over loose rocks.

Soon after descending the Redwall via a series of extremely steep, compressed switchbacks known as the **Cathedral Stairs**, the Hermit hits the **Tonto** (6.6 miles from the trailhead). One mile west of the junction are stone remnants of the old **Hermit Camp** and near that the cliff-rimmed **Hermit Creek Campground**, a glorious place to sleep.

From the campground it is another 1.5 miles to the Colorado River, which you can reach by turning down Hermit Creek just before Hermit Camp or following the creek right from the campground. **Hermit Rapids** mark the confluence of the creek and the Colorado.

Day 2: Hermit Creek to Hermit Trailhead
(7.8 miles, 6-8 hours, 3640ft ascent)

For an out-and-back hike, retrace your steps for the arduous but gorgeous climb back to the trailhead. For a longer wilderness excursion, you can pick up the eastbound Tonto and intercept the Bright Angel (see p131 for a full description).

HERMIT TRAIL TO BRIGHT ANGEL TRAILHEAD
Distance: 26.9 miles
Duration: 3-4 days
Challenge: Difficult
Elevation Change: See individual days

Not for first-time hikers, this stunning trek may require some route finding, particularly along the undulating and unmaintained Tonto. But you'll find ample water sources and plenty of camping spots.

Day 1: Hermit Trailhead to Monument Creek
(11.6 miles, 5-7 hours, 3640ft descent)
Descend 4 miles past Santa Maria Spring, then turn right at the Tonto Trail junction for the 14.5-mile eastbound passage to the Bright Angel Trail. From the junction it's 3.8 miles to **Monument Creek**, providing water and designated trailside camping sites. Alternatively, you can spend the first night at Hermit Campground, then backtrack a mile to embark on the Tonto your second morning.

For a quick side trip, head 2 miles down the drainage to Granite Rapids on the Colorado; look for the trail sign just south of the monument spire.

Day 2: Monument Creek to Indian Garden Campground
(10.7 miles, 4-6 hours, 600ft)
The Tonto snakes along the contour, reaching Cedar Spring after 1.3 miles and Salt Creek in another 30 minutes; there's seasonal water and camping, as well as a pit toilet just above the campsite at Salt Creek. From there it's just under 5 miles to Horn Creek – don't drink (or even treat to drink) the water here, as it's been found to have a high radioactive level. In under an hour you'll be at verdant Indian Garden, with treated water available year-round.

Day 3: Indian Garden Campground to Bright Angel Trailhead
(4.6 miles, 3-5 hours, 3800ft ascent)
Load up on water at the campground before beginning the hot grind back to the South Rim, the first 2 miles of which are the toughest. It's best to get a very early start so that you're still in the shade for the grueling Jacob's Ladder switchbacks. You'll stay cool and have a spectacular view as the sun inches its way down the red Supai sandstone. (For a full description of the Bright Angel Trail, see p125)

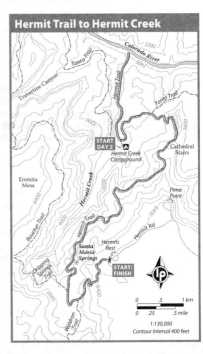

Hermit Trail to Hermit Creek

CLEAR CREEK TRAIL
Distance: 8.7 miles one-way
Duration: 7-9 hours round-trip
Challenge: Moderate-Difficult
Elevation Change: 1500ft

In excellent condition and easy to follow, the enjoyable Clear Creek Trail is one of few inner-canyon trails on the north side of the Colorado and easily the most popular side hike. The views into the gorge and across the canyon are magnificent. There's no water at the creek, so bring plenty with you.

Pick up the trail 0.3 mile north of Phantom Ranch. Heading east off the North Kaibab, the trail switchbacks up to the base of Sumner Butte, levels for a bit, then ascends to the Tonto Platform. It then meanders along the contours and canyon folds, passing beneath both Zoroaster and Brahma Temples on the left. Nine miles later it drops down to the streambed.

It's an excellent full-day excursion for strong day hikers from Phantom Ranch and Bright Angel Campground. Even the first few miles provide gorgeous views, making it equally worthwhile for those desiring a shorter hike. Overnighters will find nice cottonwood-fringed camping spots near the creek.

Lots of trails follow the creek's tributaries, leading to surprises like inner quartzite canyons. The northeast fork of Clear Creek leads up to **Cheyava Falls**, the canyon's tallest (best viewed in spring), but it's a long haul – 10 miles round-trip from Clear Creek. The trail was first developed in 1933 by the Civilian Conservation Corps as a way to access these falls.

NANKOWEAP TRAIL
Distance:: 21.2 miles to Nankoweap Creek round-trip;
27.8 miles to Colorado River round-trip
Duration: 2-3 days round-trip
Challenge: Very Difficult
Elevation Change: 4800ft

For very strong hikers seeking solitude and comfortable with heights, the spectacular Nankoweap is an exhilarating challenge. This unmaintained trail is by no means suited for first-time canyon visitors. It can be tricky to follow in spots and requires a fair amount of maneuvering along steep ledges. But the wilderness experience and sweeping views of Marble Platform make it a worthwhile detour.

Day 1: Nankoweap Trail to Nankoweap Creek
(10.6 miles, 6-8 hours, 5498ft descent)
To reach the trailhead (signed Saddle Mountain), drive north to exit the park. About a mile south of Kaibab Lodge, turn right onto the unpaved forest service Road 610 and drive east for 15 miles to the trailhead.

After the first mile the trail becomes more pronounced, just in time for a somewhat terrifying teeter along a sandstone ledge beside a sheer drop. Take a break at **Marion Ridge** before traversing more ledges past stunning rock pillars to **Tilted Mesa**, about 2.5 hours from the trailhead.

A grueling series of switchbacks and tiered ledges winds down from the mesa, including spots that require careful scrambling. A couple miles later you'll reach **Nankoweap Creek**, a resplendent green oasis in the barren canyon. This is a fine place to camp and the first source of water on the trail.

Day 2: Nankoweap Creek to Colorado River

(3.3 miles, 1-2 hours, 550ft descent)
From the creek, the trail is fairly faint but heads downstream a few easy miles to the **Colorado**, ending with a gorgeous view of Marble Canyon and limitless places to camp. This spur trail is also a nice day-trip option from Nankoweap Creek.

Day 3: Colorado River to Nankoweap Trail

(14.9 miles, 10-12 hours, 6048ft ascent)
This is an out-and-back hike, so once you've had your fill of the scenery, turn around and carefully retrace your steps. It's a very long, tough climb out, so be sure to leave at daybreak.

Rafting the Colorado

The Colorado is the King Kong of rivers, with two of its 160-plus rapids rated as Class 10 (equal to a standard Class V) and many others rated 5.

The biggest single drop (from the top to the base of the rapids) is 30ft, and nearly 20 rapids drop 15ft or more. Perhaps you have an adventurous spirit but have never gone white-water rafting. Well, it's safer than you might think. The Colorado is a forgiving river – just hang on tight, always wear your life vest and do everything your guide tells you.

But a trip down the Colorado offers much more than the quick thrills of roller-coaster rapids. The true grandeur and scope of the canyon is perhaps best grasped looking up from the river, not down from the rim. Glimpse the region's human history in ruins and rock art, ancient footpaths or the wreckage of an explorer's boat. Hike to mystical grottos and waterfalls or venture up amazing slot canyons. View wildlife in its native habitat, from a resting condor to grazing bighorn sheep or a ringtail cat that wanders through camp. Watch for subtle changes as light dances across canyon walls. Absorb the tranquility on stretches of flat water between all those rapids, and spend a few days living simply in a primitive setting.

Given two or three weeks, you can run the entire 279 miles of river through the canyon between Lake Powell and Lake Mead. If that's more vacation than you've got, you can raft one of three shorter sections (each 100 miles or less) in four to nine days. Or raft a combination of two shorter sections. Choosing to run the river via motorboat rather than raft shortens the descent by a few days.

Start planning your trip by contacting the Grand Canyon River Trip Information Center, also called the **River Permits Office** (☎ 928-638-7843 or ☎ 800-959-9164; W www.nps.gov/grca/river; c/o Grand Canyon National Park, PO Box 129, Grand Canyon, AZ 86023).

WHAT KIND OF BOAT?

Do you want to descend the river via oar, paddle or motor power? Your choice will determine the size of the boat, the number of passengers, the noise level, navigability and stability on the rapids, and the duration of your trip.

The most commonly used boat on the Colorado is an 18ft neoprene raft seating three to five passengers and a guide who rows a set of long wooden oars. Its high center of gravity provides greater stability while giving the guide more power down the big rapids.

Less common is a 14ft neoprene raft on which as many as six passengers and a guide all use single-blade paddles. This style is better suited to high and fast water.

Dories – 17ft rigid, flat-bottomed boats – comfortably seat up to four passengers and a guide who rows a set of long wooden oars. Trips by dory take one or two days longer than rafting trips.

Motorboats typically comprise inflatable pontoons lashed together to create a 33ft craft. They seat from eight to 16 passengers and two or three guides.

Hard-shell kayaks are most often used on private trips, while some commercial operators provide inflatable kayaks on request.

WHEN TO GO

The Grand Canyon stretch of the Colorado sees 22,000 annual visitors and is run year-round, though access to some sections is limited under certain conditions. Most commercial trips operate between April and October, and June, July and August are the peak months. But unless you enjoy triple-digit temperatures, summertime is just too hot. The only way to stay cool would be to engage in water fights with fellow rafters (controlled releases from Glen Canyon Dam keep water temperatures between 48ºF and 55ºF year-round). Monsoon rains in July and August also spawn flash floods and increased sediment that turns the water a murky reddish-brown.

Instead, veteran river guides suggest you plan a trip in April or between mid-September and mid-October, when air temperatures are mild and rafters can tackle day hikes not possible in summer. Drawbacks of a spring/fall excursion include occasional storms, headwinds and shorter daylight hours.

RAFTING COMPANIES

Most people join a commercial trip, on which operators provide the boat, all rafting and camping gear, cooking equipment and food. Guides double as chefs and prepare all meals. Oar-powered rafting trips cost $200 to $300 per day, while trips via motorboat cost $225 to $325 per day. Children must be 12 or older. The trips are very popular, so make reservations six to 12 months in advance.

Arizona River Runners (☎ *602-867-4866, 800-477-7238;* W *www.raft arizona.com; PO Box 47788, Phoenix, AZ 85068-7788)* offers motorboat trips ($225-265 per person per day) that last from three to eight days.

Grand Canyon Dories (☎ *209-736-0805, 800-877-3679;* W *www.oars .com/gcdories; PO Box 216, Altaville, CA 95221)* specializes in dory trips down the full length of the river or a combination of the upper and middle sections. Trips ($220-300 per person per day) last from 13 to 22 days.

OARS (☎ *209-736-2924, 800-346-6277;* W *www.oars.com; PO Box 67, Angels Camp, CA 95222)* offers oar-powered rafting trips and paddle trips on request. Trips ($240-315 per person per day) last from five to 17 days and take in combinations of river sections.

Outdoors Unlimited River Trips (☎ *928-526-4546, 800-637-7238;* W *www.outdoorsunlimited.com; 6900 Townsend Winona Rd, Flagstaff, AZ 86004)* specializes in paddle trips, which cost $10 per day more than other options. Trips ($210-270 per person per day) last from five to 15 days. Some spring and fall trips stretch one or two days longer to allow more hiking.

PERMITS & COSTS

When you join a commercial river trip, the operator will take care of your permit. If you plan a private trip, you must apply for your own permit. Be prepared for a very long wait. Only 25% of all permits are allocated to private trips – far less than demand. The waiting list wavers between eight and 20 years.

To add your party to the list, contact the River Permits Office (see contact information on p134). You'll need to complete a New Additions Application, which can only be submitted by mail or fax each February with a non-refundable $100 fee. Once on the waiting list, each person must submit a Continuing Interest Form each year by January 31. Once you receive a launch date, the permit costs $100 per person.

When arranging a trip, many private rafters go through an outfitter to rent the boat and gear and arrange food and shuttles. For a complete list of outfitters, see W www.nps.gov/grca/river/support_companies.htm. A good choice is the reputable **Professional River Outfitters Inc** (☎ *800-648-3236, 928-779-1512; PO Box 635, Flagstaff, AZ 86002)*.

PUT-IN & TAKEOUT POINTS

Fifteen miles below the Glen Canyon Dam near Page, Lees Ferry is the only put-in point for boats. The takeout point is more than 300 miles downstream at South Cove on Lake Mead. (The old takeout point at Pierce Ferry is no longer used due to low lake levels.) Though boats must ply the full course, rafters may join, leave or rejoin a river excursion at several points.

RIVERSIDE CAMPING

There are no developed campsites or facilities anywhere along the Colorado. Groups are self-sufficient, packing in all necessary food and gear. Rafters camp on pristine, sandy beaches, often near clear side streams. Tamarisk stands provide wisps of shade on most beaches. Usually, only one group will

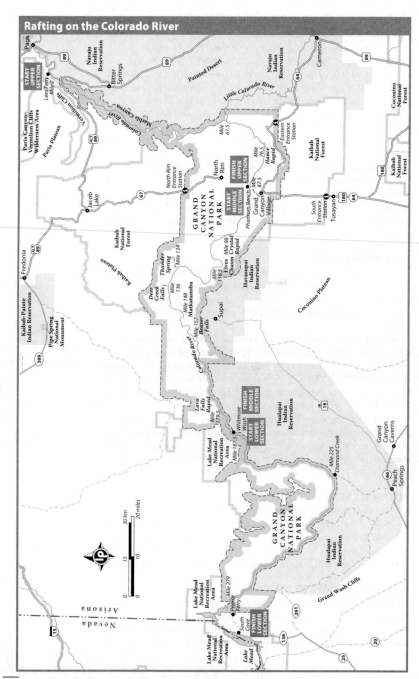

Rafting on the Colorado River

camp on any given beach, affording everyone heaps of privacy. Smaller beaches allow just enough room for tents, while other beaches are expansive, with room for volleyball or Frisbee.

SIDE HIKES

The canyon's waterfalls are difficult to reach unless you start from the Colorado, and the park's many slot canyons also lie along the river. Several excellent day hikes lead to impressive falls, inviting pools and sandstone narrows. Visits to these remote spots can be the most rewarding part of a river trek.

THE COLORADO RIVER
Distance: 279 miles
Duration: 15-19 days
Start: Lees Ferry
End: South Cove, Lake Mead

Lasting between 15 and 19 days, trips along the full stretch of river between Lees Ferry and South Cove are typically only offered in April, May, September and October. In the stifling heat of July and August, trips are curtailed – they still start at Lees Ferry, but the takeout point is at Diamond Creek (Mile 225), and they last 12 or 13 days.

Upper Section: Lees Ferry to Phantom Ranch
(Beginning to Mile 87.5)
From Lees Ferry the upper section passes through Marble Canyon and Granite Gorge. **Marble Canyon** extends to the confluence with the Little Colorado River at Mile 61.5. Near Mile 77 the appearance of granite-speckled black Vishnu schist marks the start of **Granite Gorge**. From the boat beach near Phantom Ranch, rafters may hike out to the South Rim.

This stretch features 28 rapids, 17 of which are rated 5 or higher. Nine rapids drop 15ft or more, including **Hance Rapid** (Mile 76.5), which boasts the Colorado's largest single drop, a whopping 30ft. Operators run this section between May and October. Oar-powered rafts take five to seven days, while motorboats take two to four days.

Middle Section: Phantom Ranch to Whitmore Wash
(Mile 87.5 to Mile 187.5)
Rafters hike from the South Rim to the boat beach near Phantom Ranch to raft the middle section through **Granite Gorge** and **Middle Granite Gorge**, where Tapeats sandstone meets the Vishnu schist.

This section holds the Colorado's biggest white water. It also offers the most technically challenging rapids – **Crystal Rapid** (Mile 98) and renowned **Lava Falls Rapid** (Mile 179.5). From Lava Falls Rapid the next 80 miles downstream is a geologic marvel. Columnar basalt lines the canyon walls for thousands of vertical feet, forming impressive geometric patterns.

To leave Whitmore Wash, rafters take a helicopter from the Hualapai Indian Reservation (the only place in the canyon helicopters are allowed to land) to the Bar 10 Ranch, 10 miles north of the canyon rim.

The middle section encompasses 38 rapids, 23 of which are rated 5 or higher – both Crystal and Lava Falls Rapids are rated a 10. Eight rapids drop between 15ft and 18ft. Operators run this stretch between May and July. Between July and September trips continue to **Diamond Creek** (Mile 225). Oar-powered rafts take seven to nine days, while motorboats take four to five days.

Side Hike: Elves Chasm

(10 minutes)

Ferns, orchids and scarlet monkeyflowers drape the lush rock walls of this grotto, where a waterfall tumbles over intricate, multicolored travertine formations. It takes just five minutes to scramble up trout-filled Royal Arch Creek from Mile 116.5 to **Elves Chasm**. When you reach this sublime grotto, dive into the pool and swim to the base of the waterfall. Clamber up through the cave to an opening above a moss-draped rocky chute, then jump back into the pool below.

Side Hike: Thunder Spring

(4.5 hours, 5 miles, 1400ft ascent, 1400ft descent)

Thunder Spring, the roaring 100ft waterfall that gushes out of the Muav limestone at Thunder Cave, is the source of Thunder River, one of the world's shortest rivers. Over its half-mile course it plunges more than 1200ft to the confluence with Tapeats Creek.

Just before Mile 134, follow the **Thunder River Trail** upstream along cottonwood-shaded **Tapeats Creek**, crossing it twice. You'll reach the first crossing, a thigh-deep ford of rushing water, in about 45 minutes. The second crossing, an hour later, is via a fallen log. Leaving Tapeats Creek, you'll slowly zigzag up an open slope for 30 minutes to expanding views of **Tapeats Amphitheater** and **Thunder Spring** (3400ft) – you'll hear the roar before seeing the waterfall. Enjoy a picnic in the shade at the base of the fall before retracing your steps.

You can make this a six-hour near-loop hike by continuing on the Thunder River Trail beyond the waterfall, traversing Surprise Valley and descending the Deer Creek Trail (see below) to the Colorado.

Side Hike: Deer Creek Trail

(2.5 hours, 3 miles, 800ft ascent, 800ft descent)

Downstream of Granite Narrows below Mile 136, **Deer Creek Falls** tumbles into the Colorado. From this welcoming trailhead you head 500ft up a steep, bushy slope to a stunning overlook. From here the trail leads into **Deer Creek Narrows**, an impressive slot canyon whose walls bear remarkable pictographs. The narrows end in an inviting cascade. Above, lush vegetation lines the trail as it meanders along the cottonwood-shaded creek. The trail crosses the creek and ascends open, rocky slopes to **Deer Creek Spring**, the trail's second waterfall. From here retrace your steps back to the river. Despite having to scramble up and down steep slopes over loose rocks and follow narrow, exposed trails, this hike is one of the inner canyon's best.

Side Hike: Matkatamiba
(20 minutes, 0.8-mile round-trip)
Matkatamiba, named for a Havasupai family and nicknamed Matkat, is a very narrow Redwall limestone slot canyon that meets the Colorado at Mile 148. So, wet or dry? You must quickly decide how to spend the next 10 minutes heading up to Matkat's acoustically perfect natural **amphitheater**, lined by ferns and wildflowers. On the tricky wet route, you head upstream through the creek – wading when possible, crawling on all fours and using handholds to pull yourself over slippery boulders.

But hang on, you get wet on the dry route too, since the first 25ft of both routes start by wading through a chest-deep pool, clambering over a boulder as wide as the creek, then wading through yet another pool. Here the dry route leaves the creek and ascends 100ft of steep rock to an exposed trail that overlooks the narrow chasm. At a sculpted curve where the amphitheater emerges, the two routes merge. The wet route is too dangerous to descend, so return via the dry route.

Side Hike: Beaver Falls
(4 hours, 8 miles round-trip)
The blue-green spring-fed waters of Havasu Creek plunge over a series of five breathtaking waterfalls to the Colorado. Beaver Falls, which tumbles over travertine formations with one prominent fall, is the cascade nearest to the river. (Most backpackers hike in only as far as Mooney Falls, so Beaver Falls – 2 miles farther – is almost the exclusive domain of rafters.)

The slot canyon near Mile 157 doesn't hint at what lies farther up **Havasu Creek**. A few minutes from the Colorado, the rock walls part to reveal wild grapevines, lush ground cover and tall cottonwoods along the level creekside trail. On this gentle hike, you'll spend about 20 minutes in water as you ford the creek, cross deep pools and wade upstream through knee-deep water. Once through the first and biggest water obstacle – the lovely, chest-deep **Big Kids Pool** – you'll emerge and climb a log staircase through a Muav limestone tunnel. The trail continues upstream to the base of a cliff near the confluence with Beaver Creek. Scramble up the cliff to reach an **overlook** of Beaver Falls. Retrace your steps, relaxing and swimming in the several pools.

Lower Section: Whitmore Wash to South Cove

(Mile 187.5 to beyond Mile 279)
Rafters join the river at Whitmore Wash via helicopter from Bar 10 Ranch. **Lower Granite Gorge**, the third and last of the canyon's sister granite gorges, starts at Mile 215, marked by the appearance of metamorphic and igneous rock. Though it features more flat water than other stretches, this section still boasts great white water,

including 11 rapids, 7 of which are rated 5 or higher. The two biggest drops are 16ft and 25ft. Oar-powered rafts take four to five days, motorboats three to four days.

In July and August the trip wraps up at Diamond Creek (Mile 225). Trips in May and June, however, continue downstream beyond the canyon's terminus at **Grand Wash Cliffs** to South Cove on Lake Mead. Oar-powered rafts take passengers as far as Mile 240, where they hop a motorboat for the one-hour ride to South Cove.

MAP SECTION

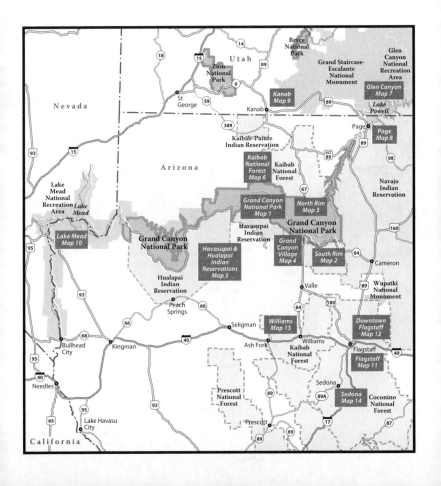

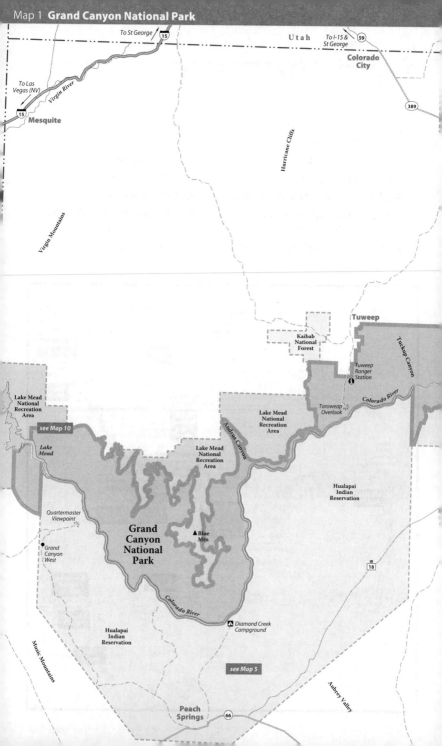

Map 1 **Grand Canyon National Park**

To St George

15

U t a h

To I-15 &
St George

59

Colorado City

To Las
Vegas (NV)

Virgin River

15

Mesquite

389

Hurricane Cliffs

Virgin Mountains

Tuweep

Kaibab
National
Forest

Tuckup Canyon

Tuweep
Ranger
Station

Lake Mead
National
Recreation
Area

Colorado River

Toroweap
Overlook

see Map 10

Lake
Mead

Lake Mead
National
Recreation
Area

Andrus Canyon

Lake Mead
National
Recreation
Area

Hualapai
Indian
Reservation

Quartermaster
Viewpoint

**Grand
Canyon
National
Park**

▲Blue
Mtn

Grand
Canyon
West

IR
18

Colorado River

Music Mountains

Hualapai
Indian
Reservation

▲Diamond Creek
Campground

see Map 5

Aubrey Valley

**Peach
Springs**

66

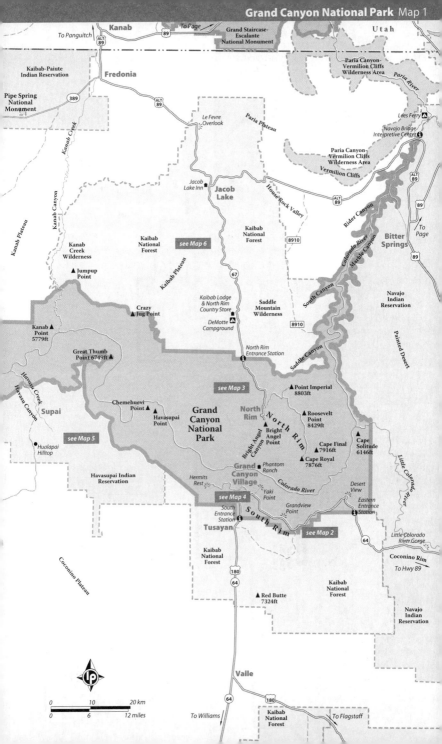

Map 2 **South Rim**

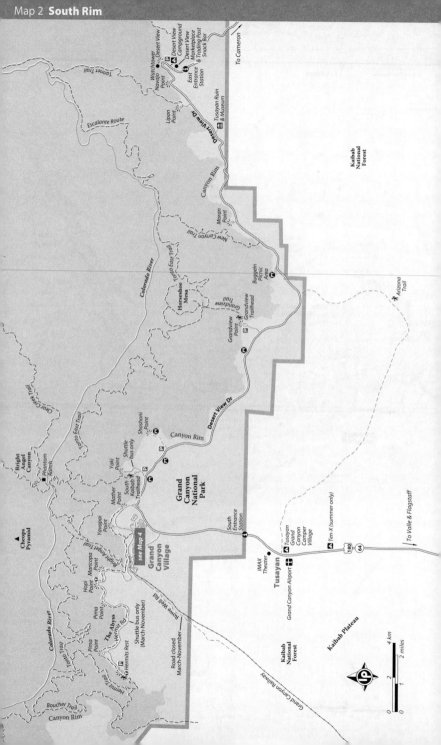

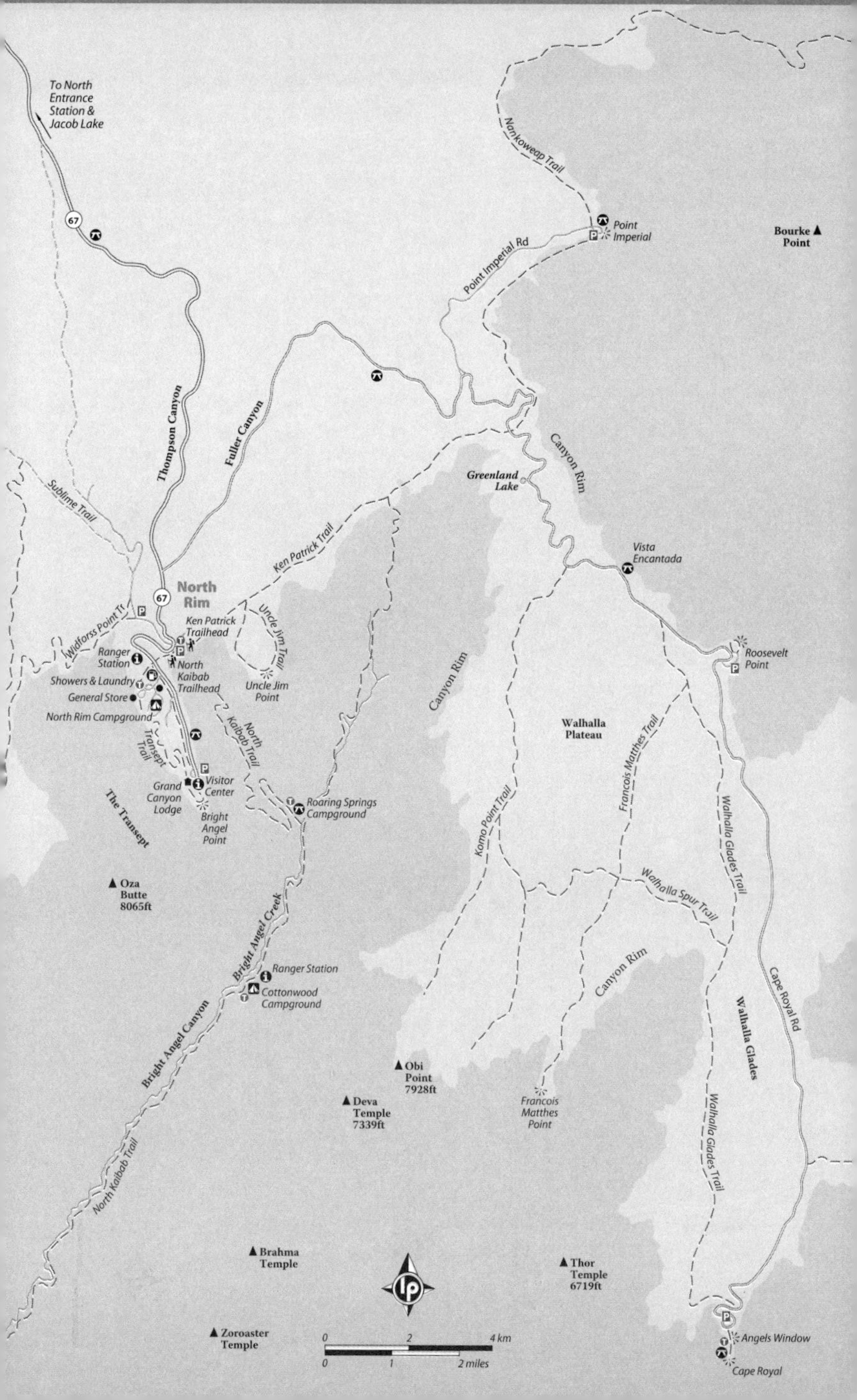

Map 3 **North Rim**

To North
Entrance
Station &
Jacob Lake

67

Nankoweap Trail

Point Imperial Rd

P Point
Imperial

Bourke ▲
Point

Thompson Canyon

Fuller Canyon

Sublime Trail

Ken Patrick Trail

Greenland
Lake

Canyon Rim

Vista
Encantada

Widforss Point Tr

67

North Rim

Ken Patrick
Trailhead

Uncle Jim Trail

P Roosevelt
Point

Ranger
Station

North Kaibab
Trailhead

Uncle Jim
Point

Showers & Laundry
General Store
North Rim Campground

North Kaibab Trail

Canyon Rim

Walhalla
Plateau

Francois Matthes Trail

Walhalla Glades Trail

Transept Trail

Grand
Canyon
Lodge

Visitor
Center

P

Roaring Springs
Campground

Komo Point Trail

The Transept

Bright
Angel
Point

Walhalla Spur Trail

▲ Oza
Butte
8065ft

Bright Angel Creek

Ranger Station

Cottonwood
Campground

Canyon Rim

Walhalla Glades

Cape Royal Rd

Bright Angel Canyon

▲ Obi
Point
7928ft

North Kaibab Trail

▲ Deva
Temple
7339ft

Francois
Matthes
Point

Walhalla Glades Trail

▲ Brahma
Temple

▲ Thor
Temple
6719ft

▲ Zoroaster
Temple

0   2   4 km

0   1   2 miles

P
Angels Window

Cape Royal

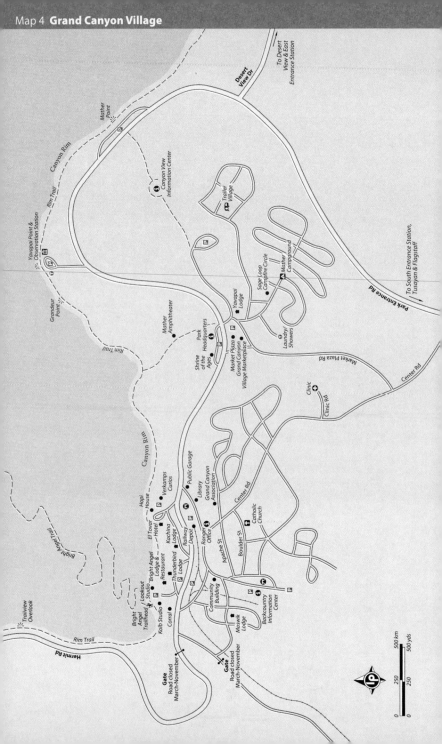
Map 4 Grand Canyon Village

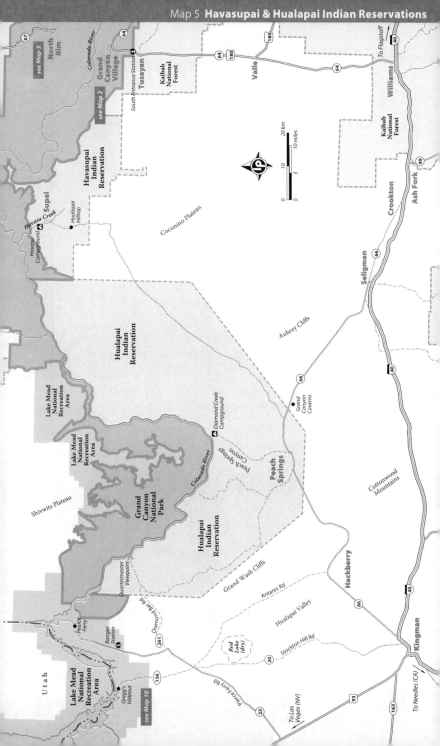

Map 5 **Havasupai & Hualapai Indian Reservations**

Map 6 **Kaibab National Forest North Rim**

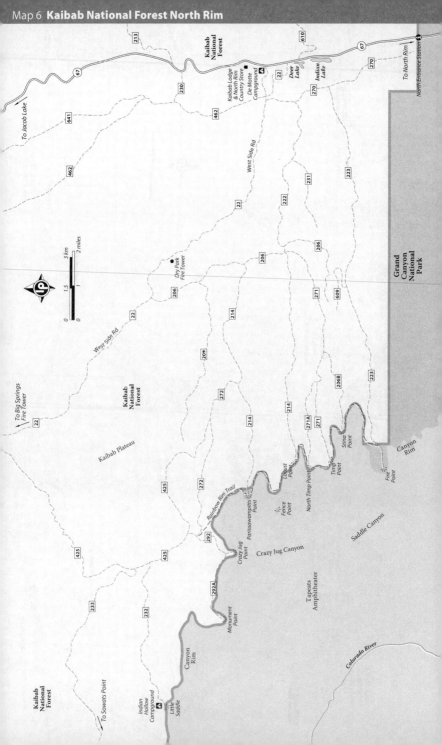

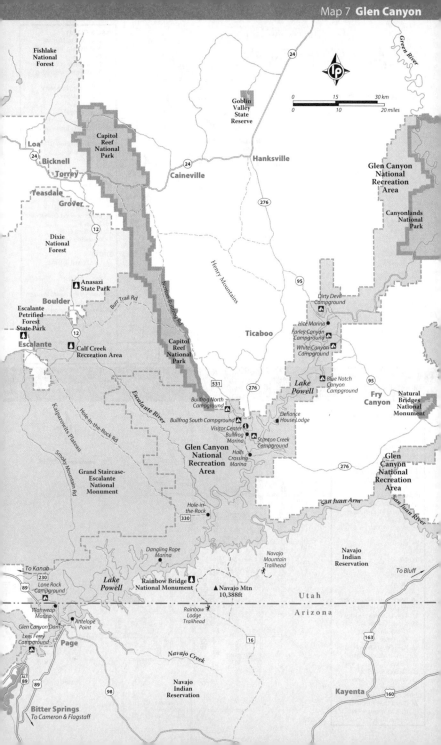

Map 7 **Glen Canyon**

Fishlake
National
Forest

Green River

24

0   15   30 km
0   10   20 miles

Capitol
Reef
National
Park

Loa

24

Bicknell

Torrey

Caineville

24

Hanksville

Goblin
Valley
State
Reserve

Glen Canyon
National
Recreation
Area

Teasdale

Grover

276

Canyonlands
National
Park

12

Dixie
National
Forest

Anasazi
State Park

Burr Trail Rd

Herry Mountains

95

Dirty Devil
Campground

Boulder

North Bullfrog Rd

Ticaboo

Hite Marina
Farley Canyon
Campground

Escalante
Petrified
Forest
State Park

12

Capitol
Reef
National
Park

White Canyon
Campground

Escalante

Calf Creek
Recreation Area

531

276

Lake
Powell

Blue Notch
Canyon
Campground

95

Fry
Canyon

Natural
Bridges
National
Monument

Escalante River

Hole-in-the-Rock Rd

Kaiparowits Plateau

Smoky Mountain Rd

Bullfrog North
Campground

Bullfrog South Campground

Visitor Center
Bullfrog
Marina

Defiance
House Lodge

Stanton Creek
Campground

Glen
Canyon
National
Recreation
Area

Glen Canyon
National
Recreation
Area

Halls
Crossing
Marina

276

Grand Staircase-
Escalante National
Monument

Hole-in-
the-Rock

330

San Juan Arm

San Juan River

Dangling Rope
Marina

Navajo
Mountain
Trailhead

Navajo
Indian
Reservation

To Bluff

To Kanab

230

Lone Rock
Campground

89

Lake
Powell

Rainbow Bridge
National Monument

Navajo Mtn
10,388ft

Utah

Wahweap
Marina

Glen Canyon Dam

Antelope
Point

Rainbow
Lodge
Trailhead

Arizona

Lees Ferry
Campground

Page

89

ALT
89

98

Navajo Creek

16

163

Navajo
Indian
Reservation

Kayenta

160

Bitter Springs
To Cameron & Flagstaff

Map 8 **Page**

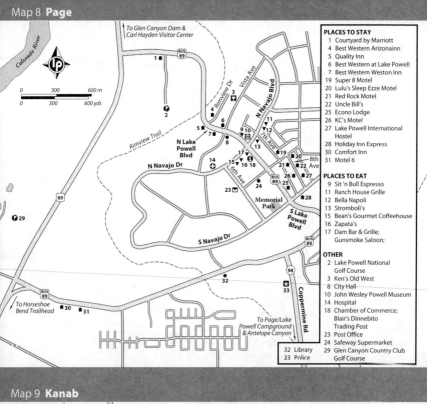

PLACES TO STAY
1 Courtyard by Marriott
4 Best Western Arizonainn
5 Quality Inn
6 Best Western at Lake Powell
7 Best Western Weston Inn
19 Super 8 Motel
20 Lulu's Sleep Ezze Motel
21 Red Rock Motel
22 Uncle Bill's
25 Econo Lodge
26 KC's Motel
27 Lake Powell International Hostel
28 Holiday Inn Express
30 Comfort Inn
31 Motel 6

PLACES TO EAT
9 Sit 'n Bull Espresso
11 Ranch House Grille
12 Bella Napoli
13 Stromboli's
15 Bean's Gourmet Coffeehouse
16 Zapata's
17 Dam Bar & Grille; Gunsmoke Saloon;

OTHER
2 Lake Powell National Golf Course
3 Ken's Old West
8 City Hall
10 John Wesley Powell Museum
14 Hospital
18 Chamber of Commerce; Blair's Dinnebito Trading Post
23 Post Office
24 Safeway Supermarket
29 Glen Canyon Country Club Golf Course
32 Library
33 Police

Map 9 **Kanab**

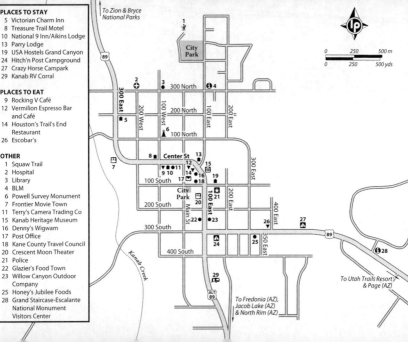

PLACES TO STAY
5 Victorian Charm Inn
8 Treasure Trail Motel
10 National 9 Inn/Aikins Lodge
13 Parry Lodge
19 USA Hostels Grand Canyon
24 Hitch'n Post Campground
27 Crazy Horse Campark
29 Kanab RV Corral

PLACES TO EAT
9 Rocking V Café
12 Vermilion Espresso Bar and Café
14 Houston's Trail's End Restaurant
26 Escobar's

OTHER
1 Squaw Trail
2 Hospital
3 Library
4 BLM
6 Powell Survey Monument
7 Frontier Movie Town
11 Terry's Camera Trading Co
15 Kanab Heritage Museum
16 Denny's Wigwam
17 Post Office
18 Kane County Travel Council
20 Crescent Moon Theater
21 Police
22 Glazier's Food Town
23 Willow Canyon Outdoor Company
25 Honey's Jubilee Foods
28 Grand Staircase-Escalante National Monument Visitors Center

Map 10 **Lake Mead**

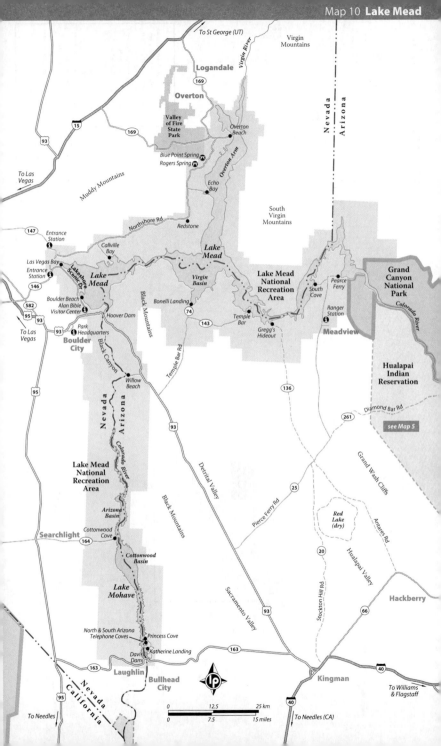

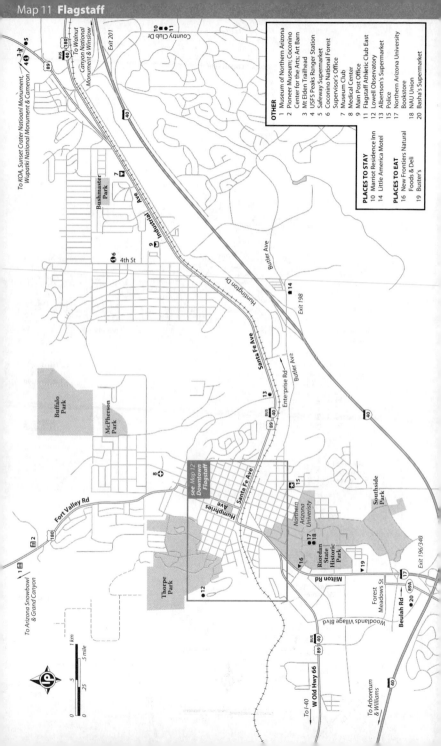

Map 11 **Flagstaff**

OTHER
1   Museum of Northern Arizona
2   Pioneer Museum; Coconino
    Center for the Arts; Art Barn
3   Mt Elden Trailhead
4   USFS Peaks Ranger Station
5   Safeway Supermarket
6   Coconino National Forest
    Supervisor's Office
7   Museum Club
8   Medical Center
9   Main Post Office
11 Flagstaff Athletic Club East
12 Lowell Observatory
13 Albertson's Supermarket
15 Police
17 Northern Arizona University
    Bookstore
18 NAU Union
20 Basha's Supermarket

PLACES TO STAY
10 Marriot Residence Inn
14 Little America Motel

PLACES TO EAT
16 New Frontiers Natural
    Foods & Deli
19 Buster's

To KOA, Sunset Crater Natioanl Monument,
Wupatki National Monument & Cameron

To Walnut
Canyon National
Monument & Winslow

To Arizona Snowbowl
& Grand Canyon

To Arboretum
& Williams

To I-40

Country Club Dr

Exit 201

Bushmaster Park

4th St

Butler Ave

Huntington Dr

Exit 198

Santa Fe Ave

Industrial Ave

Buffalo Park

McPherson Park

Enterprise Rd

Butler Ave

Fort Valley Rd

see Map 12
Downtown
Flagstaff

Humphries Ave

Santa Fe Ave

Northern Arizona University

Riordan State Historic Park

Thorpe Park

Milton Rd

Forest Meadows St

Southside Park

Woodlands Village Blvd

Beulah Rd

W Old Hwy 66

Exit 196/340

1 km

.5 mile

.5

.25

0

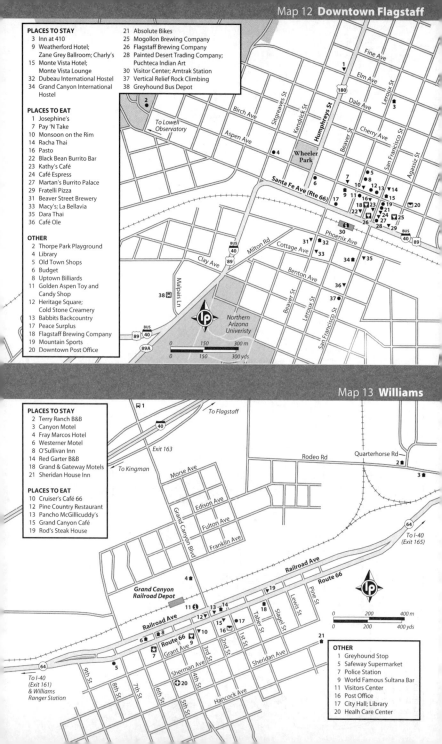

Map 12 Downtown Flagstaff

PLACES TO STAY
3 Inn at 410
9 Weatherford Hotel;
 Zane Grey Ballroom; Charly's
15 Monte Vista Hotel;
 Monte Vista Lounge
32 Dubeau International Hostel
34 Grand Canyon International
 Hostel

PLACES TO EAT
1 Josephine's
7 Pay 'N Take
10 Monsoon on the Rim
14 Racha Thai
16 Pasto
22 Black Bean Burrito Bar
23 Kathy's Café
24 Café Espress
27 Martan's Burrito Palace
29 Fratelli Pizza
31 Beaver Street Brewery
33 Macy's; La Bellavia
35 Dara Thai
36 Café Ole

OTHER
2 Thorpe Park Playground
4 Library
5 Old Town Shops
6 Budget
8 Uptown Billiards
11 Golden Aspen Toy and
 Candy Shop
12 Heritage Square;
 Cold Stone Creamery
13 Babbits Backcountry
17 Peace Surplus
18 Flagstaff Brewing Company
19 Mountain Sports
20 Downtown Post Office

21 Absolute Bikes
25 Mogollon Brewing Company
26 Flagstaff Brewing Company
28 Painted Desert Trading Company;
 Puchteca Indian Art
30 Visitor Center; Amtrak Station
37 Vertical Relief Rock Climbing
38 Greyhound Bus Depot

Northern
Arizona
Univeristy

Map 13 Williams

PLACES TO STAY
2 Terry Ranch B&B
3 Canyon Motel
4 Fray Marcos Hotel
6 Westerner Motel
8 O'Sullivan Inn
14 Red Garter B&B
18 Grand & Gateway Motels
21 Sheridan House Inn

PLACES TO EAT
10 Cruiser's Café 66
12 Pine Country Restaurant
13 Pancho McGillicuddy's
15 Grand Canyon Café
19 Rod's Steak House

OTHER
1 Greyhound Stop
5 Safeway Supermarket
7 Police Station
9 World Famous Sultana Bar
11 Visitors Center
16 Post Office
17 City Hall; Library
20 Healh Care Center

Grand Canyon
Railroad Depot

To I-40
(Exit 161)
& Williams
Ranger Station

Map 14 **Sedona**

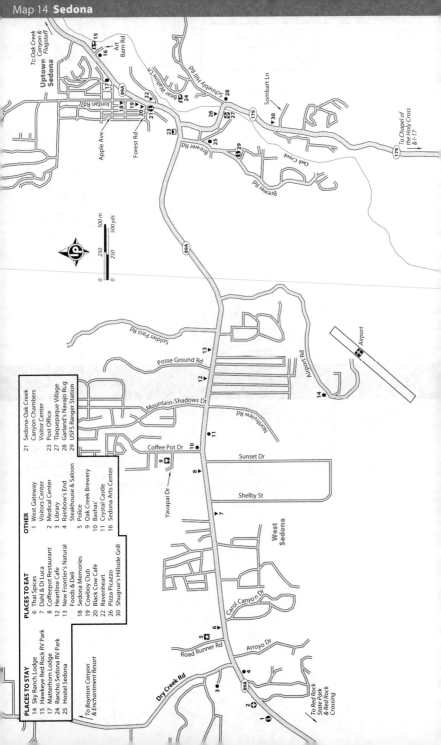

To Oak Creek Canyon & Flagstaff

Uptown Sedona

Art Barn Rd

Jordan Rd

Apple Ave

Forest Rd

Bear Wallow Ln

Schnebly Hill Rd

Sombart Ln

To Chapel of the Holy Cross & I-17

Brewer Rd

Oak Creek

Brewer Rd

Soldier Pass Rd

Posse Ground Rd

Mountain-Shadows Dr

Northview Rd

Airport Rd

Airport

Coffee Pot Dr

Sunset Dr

Yavapai Dr

Shelby St

West Sedona

Carol Canyon Dr

Arroyo Dr

Road Runner Rd

Dry Creek Rd

To Red Rock State Park & Red Rock Crossing

To Boynton Canyon & Enchantment Resort

500 m
500 yds
0   250
0   250

PLACES TO STAY
14 Sky Ranch Lodge
15 Hawkeye Red Rock RV Park
17 Matterhorn Lodge
24 Rancho Sedona RV Park
25 Hostel Sedona

PLACES TO EAT
6 Thai Spices
7 Dahl & Di Luca
8 Coffeepot Restaurant
12 Heartline Cafe
13 New Frontier's Natural
   Foods & Deli
18 Sedona Memories
19 Cowboy Club
20 Black Cow Café
22 Ravenheart
26 Pizza Picazzo
30 Shugrue's Hillside Grill

OTHER
1 West Gateway
   Visitors Center
2 Medical Center
3 Library
4 Rainbow's End
   Steakhouse & Saloon
5 Police
9 Oak Creek Brewery
10 Bashas'
11 Crystal Castle
16 Sedona Arts Center
21 Sedona-Oak Creek
   Canyon Chambers
   Visitor Center
23 Post Office
27 Tlaquepaque Village
28 Garland's Navajo Rug
29 USFS Ranger Station

Legend

ROUTES

———————— .... Freeway
———————— .... Primary Road
———————— .... Secondary Road
———————— .... Tertiary Road
– – – – – – – .... Dirt Road
–)– – – –(– .... Tunnel
– – – – – – – .... Trail

ROUTE SHIELDS

[80] Interstate Freeway
[101] US Highway
[95] State Highway
[G4] County Road

HYDROGRAPHY

.... River; Creek
.... Canal
.... Lake
.... Spring; Rapids
.... Waterfalls
.... Dry; Salt Lake
.... Swamp; Mangrove

AREAS

.... National Park
.... Wilderness Area
.... National Forest

BOUNDARIES

— ·· — ·· — ...... State Boundary

POPULATION SYMBOLS

◉ **STATE CAPITAL** .... State Capital
❶ **Large City** .... Large City
❶ **Medium City** .... Medium City
● **Small City** .... Small City
• Town; Village .... Town; Village

MAP SYMBOLS

⬛ .... Place to Stay   ▼ .... Place to Eat   ● .... Point of Interest

Airfield	Cave	Mountain	RV Park
Airport	Church	Museum	Shopping Mall
Archeological Site; Ruin	Cinema	Park	Skiing - Cross Country
Bank	Footbridge	Parking Area	Skiing - Downhill
Baseball Diamond	Gas Station	Pass	Telephone
Battlefield	Hospital	Picnic Area	Toilet - Public
Bike Trail	Information	Police Station	Trailhead
Bus Station; Terminal	Lookout	Pool	Tram Stop
Cable Car; Chairlift	Mine	Post Office	Transportation
Campground	Monument	Pub; Bar	Volcano

Note: Not all symbols displayed above appear in this book.

Notes

GRAND CANYON NATIONAL PARK

Accommodations in the park range from historic lodges, with dark beams and overstuffed chairs, to rustic cabins and standard motel rooms.

PLACES TO STAY

The South Rim boasts the majority of accommodations, while the North Rim offers just one lodge and one campground. Those descending into the canyon will find a lodge and several backcountry campgrounds. Be sure to book early, particularly if you have a specific lodging in mind (perhaps a rimside cabin on the North Rim or the wonderful Buckey O'Neill Cabin on the South Rim). If you haven't booked ahead, you still have a chance of finding a great room – a 48-hour advance cancellation policy means that rooms open up all the time (see Last-Minute Accommodations, p66).

SOUTH RIM

Visitors to the park's South Rim have six lodges and three campgrounds to choose from. **Mather** and **Trailer Village** take reservations and are open year-round, while **Desert View** is open May through September and does not accept reservations. There is a seven-day limit at all three campgrounds. If you don't find a spot in the park, you can always pitch your tent free of charge in the surrounding Kaibab National Forest (p174).

Xanterra (☎ 888-297-2757; W *www.xanterra.com*) operates all park lodges, as well as Trailer Village. You can make reservations up to 23 months in advance. Visit Xanterra's South Rim website (W *www.grandcanyonlodges.com*) for more information. For same-day reservations call the South Rim switchboard (☎ 928-638-2631).

If you can't find a room within the park, consider a chain motel in Tusayan or a roadside joint in Valle. If you want more than just a place to lay your head, however, head to Flagstaff, Williams or Sedona (see Around the Grand Canyon, p174). Several historic hotels and bed-and-breakfasts in Flagstaff and Williams and gorgeous but expensive inns in Sedona offer far more character than you'll find at most lodgings in or near the park.

Inside the Park

CAMPING

The **National Park Service** (☎ *800-365-2267;* W *http://reservations.nps .gov)* operates Mather and Desert View campgrounds. Reservations for Mather are accepted up to five months in advance till the day before your arrival.

Mather Campground

(Map 4; 317 sites; family site $15, group site $40, backpacker site $4; open year-round; Grand Canyon Village) Though you might imagine Mather to be uncomfortably crowded and noisy, it's actually a pleasant and relatively quiet place to camp. Piñon and juniper trees offer plenty of shade, sites are well dispersed and the flat ground offers a comfy platform for your tent. If you're longing for pristine wilderness, look elsewhere, but if you just want a guaranteed site with ample facilities, this is your best bet. You'll find pay showers, laundry facilities, drinking water, toilets and grills. Next door a small general store stocks camping supplies, drinks and basic food items like cereal and canned goods. Pay phones stand just outside, and a full grocery store is a short walk away.

Mather accepts reservations between April 1 and November 30 – the rest of the year it's first come, first served. Family sites (the official name for standard sites) hold up to six people. Group sites hold up to 40 people, but there

CAMPING RULES

The most important rule to remember when camping in the park or surrounding Kaibab National Forest is to **leave no trace.** With so many annual visitors, the park environment is particularly vulnerable to overuse or carelessness.

✔ Pack out all trash (including food scraps)

✔ Keep fires in grills (no open campfires); backpackers should use small portable stoves

✔ Refrain from gathering wood; instead, purchase wood at Canyon Village Marketplace or the North Rim General Store

✔ Never leave fires unattended; extinguish them thoroughly with water

✔ Keep all food and fragrant items (soap, deodorant, toothpaste, etc.) in your car or hang your backpack from a tree overnight to keep coyotes and other critters at bay

✔ If pit toilets are unavailable, bury human waste 6 inches deep and at least 200ft from trails, campsites or water sources

✔ Wash dishes at least 200ft from water sources and scatter strained dishwater (waste breaks down slowly in the dry desert climate)

is no minimum – if you don't mind spending the extra money, you can reserve one all to yourself. Disabled sites are closer to the facilities and on more level ground. If you don't have a car or would just like some distance between you and your fellow campers, ask for a backpacker site.

If you think you'll arrive late or need to cancel a reservation, call the campground at ☎ 800-388-2733. If you're hoping for same-day reservations, just show up in person and hope for the best. As crowds diminish in September, some loops are closed. By December only one loop remains open.

Desert View Campground

(Map 2; 50 sites; $10; open mid-May–mid-Sep; 25 miles east of Grand Canyon Village) Set back from the road in a quiet piñon-juniper forest near the East Entrance, this first-come, first-served campground is a peaceful alternative to the more crowded and busy Mather Campground. Sites are spread out enough to ensure a bit of privacy. You'll find toilets and drinking water but no showers or hookups. A small cafeteria/snack shop serves breakfast, lunch and dinner, while nearby is a general store that offers basic camping supplies and staples like pasta, canned food, milk, beer and wine.

The best time to secure a spot is midmorning, when people are packing up camp. Don't drive in after dark assuming you'll get a site, as it's at least 25 miles to another campground. Before you arrive, call the East Entrance Station *(☎ 928-638-0105)* to confirm whether any sites are available. Call the Desert View Information Center *(☎ 928-638-7893)* to confirm the campground's operating dates.

Trailer Village

(Map 4; ☎ 928-638-2631; 84 sites; $24; open year-round; Grand Canyon Village) As its name implies, this is basically a trailer park, offering little in the way of natural surroundings. Expect RVs lined up tightly at paved pull-through sites amid a rather barren, dry patch of ground. Check for spots with trees on the far north side. You'll find picnic tables and barbecue grills, while a coin laundry and showers are a quarter mile away at Mather Campground. Rates are for two people; there is a $2 charge for each additional person over 16 years old.

LODGING

To reach any lodge, call the central **switchboard** *(☎ 928-638-2631)*. Photographs, including pictures of the rooms, are posted on Xanterra's South Rim website *(W www.grandcanyonlodges.com)*.

El Tovar

(Map 4; double/suite $123-285; open year-round; Grand Canyon Village) Featuring replica Remington bronzes, Arts & Crafts–style chairs, stained glass and exposed beams, this quintessential 1905 national park lodge (see Sights, p90) lures visitors seeking more than a roadside motel. Wide inviting porches wreathe the rambling wood structure, offering pleasant spots to people-watch and admire canyon views. Even if you're not a guest, stop by to relax with a book on the porch swing or a drink on the patio. The public spaces hint at the genteel elegance of the park's heyday.

The original guestrooms were remodeled to accommodate private baths, thus many of the standard double rooms are incredibly small – ask for the slightly more expensive deluxe room. Doubles with one double bed cost $123, while deluxe doubles with two queens or one king cost $175. You can put a cot or a crib in a deluxe double at no extra charge for children ($11 for adults), but if your party is more than three people, consider getting a suite rather than multiple doubles. The capacity varies by suite – standard suites sleep three, four, or seven ($225-255), while porch suites sleep three, four or five ($225-280).

Those in a mood to splurge can stay in one of three rim-view suites ($285) – one sleeps three, another five and the third sleeps seven. All offer private porches with full canyon views. These are the only rooms in the park with a full rim view, and they're often booked more than a year in advance. Don't expect sleigh beds and antiques, but the furnishings are several steps up from a standard motel. All rooms have a full bath.

Bright Angel Lodge & Cabins

(Map 4; double/cabin $49-241; open year-round; Grand Canyon Village) Built in 1935, the log-and-stone Bright Angel (see Sights, p91) offers travelers more historic charm and nicer rooms than you'll find at most other lodgings. Unfortunately, the public spaces have neither the quiet elegance nor rustic Western character found at El Tovar. You will find two restaurants (p168), a snack bar and a small, nondescript bar with a TV. But if you want to relax with a drink, you're much better off walking a few doors down to El Tovar.

In 2001 all rooms at Bright Angel were refurbished in keeping with architect Mary Colter's original design. The least expensive rooms in the park are the $49 doubles, which offer a double bed, a desk and a sink. While the bathroom is down the hall, there are no TVs and the rooms are nothing special, this is a great price for a perch right on the rim (no views). Powell suites ($110) feature two bedrooms and a tub but no shower or TV. Each holds up to seven people.

Cabins at Bright Angel, many decorated in rustic Western style, offer more character. There are several options, starting with a standard cabin for $84. Another excellent value are **rim-view cabins** ($105), which are bright and airy, with a queen bed, a full bath, a refrigerator, a partial canyon view and doors that open right out onto the Rim Trail. Four out of the 15 rim-view cabins have a fireplace ($128).

One of the more interesting places to stay on either rim, the **Buckey O'Neill Cabin** ($240) is a spacious, Western-style cabin with a king bed, separate sitting room, refrigerator, dry bar, two TVs, a full bath and front and back doors. Built in the 1890s, the cabin was home to Buckey O'Neill, a prospector who believed he found copper in Anita, 14 miles south of the canyon. It's the second-oldest building in the park (see Sights, p91), offering a real sense of history and an escape from the tourist throngs. Canyon breezes more than compensate for the lack of an air conditioner. As with rim-view suites at El Tovar, the cabin is usually booked more than a year in advance.

Kachina & Thunderbird Lodges

(Map 4; double $115-125; open year-round; Grand Canyon Village) Beside the Rim Trail between El Tovar and Bright Angel, these lodges offer standard motel-style rooms with two queen beds, full bath and TV. Rooms with views of the parking lot cost $115; it's worth spending an extra $10 for rimside rooms ($125), some with partial canyon views. The drab concrete buildings resemble elementary schools, but they're a short stroll from El Tovar's lovely public spaces. Neither lodge has a lobby

BEST PLACES TO STAY IN THE PARK

✔ Buckey O'Neill Cabin at Bright Angel Lodge (p159)
✔ Rim-view cabins at Bright Angel Lodge (p159)
✔ Rim-view suites at El Tovar (p158)
✔ Desert View Campground (p158)
✔ Western cabins at Grand Canyon Lodge (p164)

or front desk – guests at Kachina check in at El Tovar, while those at Thunderbird check in at Bright Angel.

Maswik Lodge

(Map 4; double/cabin $67-119; open year-round; Grand Canyon Village) A quarter mile from the rim, Maswik Lodge (named for the Hopi kachina who guards the canyon) comprises 16 two-story wood-and-stone buildings set in the woods. Rooms at Maswik North cost $119 and feature private patios, high ceilings and forest views. Rooms at the less expensive Maswik South ($77) are smaller and don't offer much of a view. There's less foot traffic and general bustling about here than at the rim, but the rooms are standard motel rooms. You'll find a cafeteria (p168) and a bar with a pool table and big-screen TV. Small cabins are available in the summer only ($67).

Yavapai Lodge

(Map 4; double $91-103; open Apr-Oct; Grand Canyon Village) Sure, it's your basic motel, but there are some hidden pluses to this place. For one, it lies more than a mile from the traffic and chaos of the central village. Though it may not boast rim views, it is close to Canyon View Information Plaza and within walking distance of the grocery store, post office and bank in Market Plaza. The lodgings are stretched out amid a peaceful piñon and juniper forest, yet you can pull your car right up to your door. Rooms in Yavapai East ($103) are in six two-story buildings and are air-conditioned, while rooms in Yavapai West ($91) are spread out in 10 single-story buildings and are not air-conditioned. These are basic, clean motel rooms with tubs, showers and TVs. Yavapai closes from November through March, though it does open for the Thanksgiving and Christmas holidays.

Phantom Ranch

(Map 2; double or dorm $23-78) This Mary Colter classic, the only lodge on the canyon floor, can only be reached on foot or by mule. Stretching along the Colorado River, stone cottages offer both private and dormitory-style rooms. For more details, see Exploring the Backcountry (p123).

Outside the Park

If you can't find a vacancy in the village, try one of the chain motels in nearby Tusayan. Otherwise, consider the roadside motel in Valle or one of the many lodgings in Williams, Flagstaff or Sedona (see Around the Grand Canyon, p174). See Kaibab National Forest (South Rim) for information on dispersed camping in the woodlands that hug the park (p174).

TUSAYAN

Several motels line a half-mile strip of Hwy 64 just outside the park's South Entrance in Tusayan. Though some offer a touch more character than what you'd find at any other roadside motel, don't expect anything particularly memorable.

Ten-X Campground

(Map 2; ☎ 928-638-7851; 70 sites; $10; open mid-Apr–Sep; 2 miles south of Tusayan) This woodsy and peaceful first-come, first-served forest service campground fills up early. (It may soon accept reservations – call to check.) You'll find large sites, picnic tables, fire rings and barbecue grills (the campground host sells firewood), water and toilets, but no hookups and no general store. Pine needles make for soft sleeping grounds. An amphitheater hosts daily programs on everything from canyon geology to nature programs for children; check the bulletin board for times.

Grand Canyon Camper Village

(Map 2; ☎ 928-638-2887; 300 sites; tent/RV $18/23) A mile south of the park on Hwy 67, this private campground provides a playground. So, if you have kids, it's got that going for it. Beyond that, there's not much here to recommend. Sites are on dirt with no shade or natural surroundings. There are toilets and pay showers, though, and if you really do need a place to camp, it's a safe and relatively quiet choice.

Rodeway Inn – Red Feather Lodge

(☎ 928-638-2414, 800-538-2345; W www.redfeatherlodge.com; double $94-119) This motel offers well-kept rooms in two buildings, as well as an adjacent restaurant, a fitness center and an outdoor pool. Built in 1997, the three-story hotel features elevators and interior doors, while the older two-story motor lodge offers outside entrances and stairs.

Seven Mile Lodge

(☎ 928-638-2291; double $68) This simple motel doesn't take reservations. Rooms open up at 9am daily and are usually filled by early afternoon in the summer. Show up early and chances are you'll find a vacancy.

Grand Canyon Quality Inn & Suites

(☎ 928-638-2673, 800-228-5151; W www.grandcanyonqualityinn.com; double/suite $128/178) This is one of the better options in Tusayan, featuring spacious rooms and suites, a bright, modern restaurant, an outdoor pool and hot tub, and an 8-foot indoor hot tub set in an atrium. All suites have two rooms, while suites with king beds include pullout couches in the sitting area.

Best Western Grand Canyon Squire Inn

(☎ 928-638-2682, 800-622-6966; double $135-150) Rooms at this Best Western range from $135 for a standard double (in a two-story 1973 annex, no elevator) to $150 in the main hotel (spacious interior rooms and elevators). With plenty of stuff to keep kids and adults alike busy, this is the only resort-like accommodation in Tusayan. You'll find a restaurant, a coffee shop, a popular sports bar, a bowling alley, pool tables, a beauty salon, exercise room, coin laundry, tennis courts and an outdoor pool.

CHAIN MOTELS

While a room with character adds to any vacation, sometimes you just need a place to rest your head. If it's late, you're tired and you don't want any surprises, head to one of the region's many chain motels. When you call to book a room, try to gauge the quality of the motel. Ask when the motel was built, whether or not the rooms have interior entrances, if there's a pool and how many floors there are. Chain motels are mapped throughout this book.

Hilton (☎ 800-445-8667; W www.hilton.com) perches at the high end of the scale, with full-service hotels that cater to upscale business travelers. Among the mid-range options, **Holiday Inn Express** (☎ 800-465-4329; W www.holidayinnexpress.com) and **Hampton Inn** (☎ 800-426-7866; W www.hampton-inn.com) offer clean, spacious rooms and often adjoining pools and restaurants. Following close behind are **Fairfield Inn** (☎ 800-228-2800; W www.fairfieldinn.com), **Days Inn** (☎ 800-329-7666; W www.daysinn.com), **Quality Inn** (☎ 800-228-5151; W www.qualityinn.com), **Radisson** (☎ 800-333-3333; W www.radisson.com) and **Ramada** (☎ 800-272-6232; W www.ramada.com). **Motel 6** and **Super 8** are generally the least expensive and offer minimal services, while **Best Western** (☎ 800-937-8376; W www.bestwestern.com) is inconsistent (many are true dives).

Grand Hotel

(☎ 928-638-3333, 888-634-7263; W www.visitgrandcanyon.com; double $139) There's a distinct Western motif in this hotel's open public spaces, including a big fireplace, high ceilings, woven rugs, stone floors and faux pine beams. Though new, the decor has an old look, and it works. Tour buses come for the 7pm Indian dance show at the restaurant, and nightly live country music caps off the theme. While the rooms are nothing special, they are relatively big, and the ones out back face the woods. You'll also find an indoor pool and hot tub.

Holiday Inn Express

(☎ 928-638-3000, 888-538-5353; double/suite $140-159/$250) Holiday Inn Express offers predictable quality, featuring modern, comfortable interior rooms, an indoor pool and complimentary continental breakfast. Though attractive, two-room suites cost $250 – the same amount you'd pay for a canyon-view suite at El Tovar. Doubles are more reasonable.

VALLE

About 25 miles south of the park, Valle sits the intersection of Hwy 64 to Williams and Hwy 180 to Flagstaff. There is no town here – just a gas station and a few places to stay and eat.

Flintstones Bedrock City

(☎ 928-635-2600; tent/RV $13/17; open Mar-Oct) Strangely out of place, Bedrock City is a kitschy, though worn, roadside attraction and campground. Built in 1972, it features a life-size Fred and Barney, a Flintmobile and other memorabilia. You'll find coin showers and a laundry, a snack bar (think Bronto Burgers and Dino Dogs) and a recreation area complete with 'concreteosaurs.' Unless you're a real Flintstones fanatic, or you're drawn to the quirky Americana charm of the place, there's no reason to stay here. It's a dry, dusty, windy spot – a tough place to pitch a tent.

Grand Canyon Inn

(☎ 928-635-9203; double $60-70) This motel is parceled out on either side of Hwy 64, offering standard motel rooms, a restaurant (open 7:30am-2pm, 6pm-9pm) and an outdoor pool. All rooms have TVs and air conditioners, while the larger ones also provide telephones. Next door you'll find a gas station and mini-mart.

CAMERON

A tiny, windswept community 32 miles east of the park's East Entrance and 54 miles north of Flagstaff, Cameron sits on the western edge of the Navajo Indian Reservation. There's not much to it – in fact, the town basically comprises just the **Cameron Trading Post & Motel** (☎ 928-679-2231, 800-338-7385; **W** *www.camerontradingpost .com; double/suite $79-179, RV site $16)*. In the early 1900s Hopis and Navajos came to the trading post to barter wool, blankets and livestock for flour, sugar and other goods. Today visitors can browse a large selection of quality Native American crafts, including Navajo rugs, basketry, jewelry and pottery. Of course, you'll also find the ubiquitous T-shirts, roadrunner knickknacks and other canyon kitsch.

The spacious rooms, many with balconies, feature hand-carved furniture and a Southwestern motif. They are spread out in three two-story adobe-style buildings: the Navajo (doubles with two double beds), the Hopi (two-room suites and doubles with one or two queen beds) and the Apache (doubles with two queen beds). The nicest is the Hopi, set around a lovely, lush garden with fountains and benches – a peaceful spot to sit and relax. Ask for a room with a garden view or a view of the **Little Colorado River Gorge**, which winds around the back of the hotel. RV sites offer hookups, and there's a good on-site restaurant (p172). If you're driving to the North Rim and need a place to stay en route, or if rooms in the park are booked, this is a great option.

NORTH RIM

Accommodations within the park are limited to one lodge and one campground. Within 45 minutes of the rim you'll find two motels, three campgrounds and free dispersed camping in the surrounding Kaibab National Forest. Other than that, it's spectacularly empty country up here. The road from Jacob Lake to the North Rim closes after the first snowfall, and the lodge is closed from mid-October through mid-May. When the road and lodge close, you can still ski or snowshoe in to stay at the campground.

If the following lodgings are booked, try your luck 80 miles north in Kanab, Utah (p213), or 84 miles northeast in Lees Ferry, which offers three motel-style lodges. There are also a few motels in tiny Fredonia (p212), 7 miles south of Kanab.

Inside the Park

Reservations for North Rim Campground are accepted up to five months in advance till the day before your arrival. Xanterra (☎ 888-297-2757; **W** *www.xanterra.com)* operates Grand Canyon Lodge, and reservations are accepted up to 23 months in advance. For same-day reservations call the North Rim switchboard (☎ 928-638-2612).

North Rim Campground

(Map 3; ☎ 800-365-2267; W http://reservations.nps.gov; 83 sites; $15; 1.5 miles north of Grand Canyon Lodge) Set back from the road beneath ponderosa pines, this campground offers pleasant sites on level ground blanketed in pine needles. Sites that overlook The Transept are an additional $5, but be forewarned that these are pretty windy spots. **Hiker/biker sites** for travelers without cars are available for $4, as are group and handicapped-accessible sites. If you don't have a reservation, arrive early and hope for the best.

The 1.5-mile Transept Trail (p115) links the campground and lodge, and within walking distance you'll find coin-operated showers and a laundry, as well as a small general store that sells limited supplies. The campground remains open once snow closes the road from Jacob Lake, but there are no services (pit toilets only), no water and you must have a backcountry permit (available from onsite rangers after the backcountry office closes).

Grand Canyon Lodge

(Map 3; ☎ 928-638-2612, 888-297-2757; W www.grandcanyonnorthrim.com; double/cabin $91-116) You'll catch only glimpses of the canyon on your approach to the South Rim. But walk through the front door of Grand Canyon Lodge to the sunroom and there, framed by three huge picture windows, is the canyon in all its glory. You'll have driven 44 miles past wildflower-strewn fields and stands of aspens and pines to get here, and this first view of the canyon is magical, unspoiled by traffic, shuttles or masses of tourists. Take a moment to breathe it in.

The original lodge was built in 1928 by the Union Pacific Railroad, but the train (and masses of tourists) never did arrive. The building burned down in 1932 and was rebuilt in 1937. Made of wood, stone and glass, with a 50-foot-high lobby and a lovely dining room with panoramic canyon views, this is the kind of lodge you imagine should be perched on the rim. On a horseshoe-shaped boardwalk around the driveway are a small snack shop (about five tables), a Western saloon that also serves coffee and pastries, a post office window, a gift store and the visitor center.

Accommodations vary significantly in everything but price. There are no rooms in the lodge itself. Farthest up the driveway (less than a mile), simple **motel rooms** cost $91. Comprising the majority of accommodations here, cabins lie scattered on either side of the road just north of the lodge. **Frontier cabins** ($92) actually occupy half a cabin – a small room with two beds, a tiny bathroom (shower only) and a desk. Someone else occupies the other half, and the walls are thin, so you can hear every word, cough or alarm clock. If you book a **Pioneer cabin** ($101), you get the whole cabin – two small rooms (one with a double bed and twin bed, the other with two twins) connected by a bathroom (shower only). On the other side of the road are **Western cabins** ($106), buffered by trees and more space. These spacious cabins provide full baths, gas fireplaces and small porches with wicker rocking chairs – well worth the additional $10. Four Western cabins overlook Bright Angel Canyon, allowing lucky guests to settle back in a rocking chair and enjoy the view. They cost $116 (only $25 more than a tiny Frontier cabin) and are booked more than a year in advance.

Outside the Park

DeMotte Campground and Kaibab Lodge are 18 miles (about a 30-minute drive) from the rim, while Jacob Lake lies 44 miles north. Outside these small hubs, you won't find anything but peaceful forest and grazing deer.

DeMotte Campground

(Map 1; 23 sites; $12; open Jun-Sep) Set on a slight hill in a spruce, fir and aspen forest, this lovely campground (among the nicest in the region) overlooks a grassy meadow just off Hwy 67. Across the street is a small general store with basic supplies, while the restaurant and bar at Kaibab Lodge are just down the road. It's at 8760ft, so be prepared for cool temperatures, even in summer. The campground is first come, first served, so choose a site before heading for the canyon. Don't plan on driving in at night and finding a spot, as it fills up quickly. The weather dictates when the campground opens and closes for the year – call the Kaibab Plateau Visitor Center *(☎ 928-638-2389)* to check before you arrive.

Kaibab Lodge

(Map 1; ☎ 928-638-2389; W www.canyoneers.com; Hwy 67; cabin $80-110; open mid-May–mid-Oct) If Grand Canyon Lodge is booked, this friendly, low-key lodge is your best option. Cabins are spread out in two lines of cabins within a short walk of the main lodge. Cabins 7 and 8 are the nicest, each with two bedrooms, three beds and rough-hewn interiors. Rooms 10 through 16 share one cabin – doors open onto a big porch where you can sit

BEST FAMILY ACCOMMODATIONS OUTSIDE THE PARK

✔ Sheridan House Inn (Williams, p185)
✔ Little America Inn (Flagstaff, p193)
✔ Utah Trails Resort (Kanab, p215)
✔ Parry Lodge (Kanab, p215)
✔ Best Western Grand Squire Inn (Tusayan, p161)
✔ Canyon Motel (Williams, p185)
✔ Comfi Cottages (Flagstaff, p193)
✔ The Grand-Gateway Motels (Williams, p185)
✔ Kaibab Lodge (North Rim, above)
✔ Junipine Resort (Sedona, p202)

with a drink and watch deer graze. Though the newer cabins are more expensive, they're smaller (quite tiny, actually), have only one room and don't overlook the meadow. For groups, Sam's Cabin ($110) sleeps six, the Deerview ($130) mobile home sleeps two to four, and the Meadowview cabin ($150) sleeps up to eight. Handicapped-accessible rooms are also available. The lodge operates a restaurant and a bar with a fireplace. When the lodge is closed, call ☎ 800-525-0924 to seek information or make advance reservations.

JACOB LAKE

Set at 8000 feet amid ponderosa pines, this crossroads (Alt 89 and Hwy 67) is biggest hub of activity between the rim (44 miles south), Kanab (38 miles north) and Lees Ferry (46 miles east). That said, there's nothing here but the lodge, campgrounds and very helpful Kaibab Plateau Visitor Center (☎ 928-643-7298). The drive up from Lees Ferry and Kanab climbs several thousand feet, so be prepared for changeable weather and bring a sweater.

Jacob Lake Campground

(Map 1; Hwy 67; 43 sites; $12; open mid-May–mid-Oct) This first-come, first-served forest service campground (no hookups) spreads out beneath Ponderosa pines. Jacob Lake Inn (featuring a restaurant, ice cream and tasty baked goods) is just across the street, and ranger programs are offered every evening.

Kaibab Camper Village

(Map 1; ☎ 928-643-7804; W www.canyoneers.com; 50 tent sites, 80 RV sites; tents/RVs $12/22; open mid-May–mid-Oct) Set back a half mile from Hwy 67 on a forest service road just south of Jacob Lake Inn, this peaceful, privately run operation offers camping in the national forest. Though surrounded by dense woods, the campground itself has just enough trees for shade and opens on a big field. You'll also find showers and pit toilets.

Jacob Lake Inn

(Map 1; ☎ 928-643-7232; W www.jacoblake.com; Hwy 67; double/cabin $72-91; open 6:30am-10pm year-round) Just 44 miles north of Bright Angel Point, this spot offers motel rooms and simple cabins with tiny bathrooms (no TVs or phones). Cabins are tightly packed amid the ponderosa pines, and there's a small playground. Though things seem a bit rundown, no one seems to mind. Just about everyone heading up to the canyon stops here, piling out of dusty vehicles to breathe in the mountain air, shop for canyon souvenirs and grab a cookie or ice cream before continuing to the rim. The inn also operates a restaurant (p173).

✔ TIP

Gas is available around the clock at Jacob Lake Inn – just pay at the pump with a credit card.

Meals are often an after-thought on a trip to the Grand Canyon, but the park does provide a decent variety of dining options. On either rim you can choose between basic cafeteria eats or upscale continental cuisine.

PLACES TO EAT

El Tovar and Grand Canyon Lodge offer creative menus with surprisingly good food, although their top-end prices make them ideal for a special meal rather than everyday dining. Picnicking is a great way to not only save money, but also enjoy some quiet moments. Prices listed below are for dinner – expect lower prices for breakfast and lunch. If you're visiting the park for more than a day, buy a small cooler to stow picnic supplies and keep drinks cold – consider a backpack-style cooler so you can easily carry it with you. In-room refrigerators are a rarity in park lodges, but you can get ice at Canyon Village Marketplace, Desert View Marketplace and the North Rim General Store.

SOUTH RIM

Inside the Park

Most South Rim restaurants are located in Grand Canyon Village.

GROCERIES

While there is a full-service grocery store in the village, you may want to stock up outside the park, where the prices and selection are better.

Canyon Village Marketplace *(Map 4;* ☎ *928-631-2262; open 7am-9pm)*
The biggest source for supplies on either rim, this market offers everything you'd expect from your local grocery store. You'll find canned goods, meat, cheese, beer, wine, firewood, diapers and over-the-counter medications, though no pharmacy. A deli serves sandwiches and soup.

Desert View Marketplace *(Map 2;* ☎ *928-638-2393; open 8:30am-6pm)*
At the East Entrance, near The Watchtower, Desert View Campground and Desert View Trading Post Snack Bar, this general store sells simple groceries and souvenirs. Expect the same goods you'd find at any convenience store.

TEN GREAT PICNIC SPOTS

✔ **Cedar Ridge** (p98)
✔ **Indian Garden** (p97)
✔ **Yavapai Overlook** (p91)
✔ **Santa Maria Spring** (p101)
✔ **Widforss Point** (p115)
✔ **Uncle Jim Point** (p117)
✔ **Shoshone Point** (p95)
✔ **Point Imperial** (p111)
✔ **Hermits Rest** (p87)
✔ **Cape Royal Wedding Site** (p112)

BUDGET

Bright Angel Fountain

(Map 4; ☎ 928-638-2631; open 8am-8pm) On the rim at Bright Angel Lodge, this cafeteria-style fountain serves burgers, hot dogs, premade sandwiches, yogurt, ice cream, soda and milk. The most expensive thing on the menu is the hamburger, for $3.85.

Hermits Rest Snack Bar

(Map 2; ☎ 928-638-2351; open 9am-sunset) To call it a snack bar is a slight exaggeration. This walk-up window outside Hermits Rest on the rim's west end sells candy, cookies and drinks.

Desert View Trading Post Snack Bar

(Map 2; ☎ 928-638-2360; dishes $2-6; open 7:30am-6pm) The only place to eat on the east end of the rim (aside from the general store), this small snack bar serves a limited breakfast, lunch and dinner. Menu items include burgers, corn dogs, premade sandwiches and soda, and cold cereal, eggs and French toast in the morning.

The Deli at Marketplace

(Map 4; ☎ 928-631-2262; open 7am-8pm) This counter in the village grocery store is the best place to find a fresh-made sandwich for a picnic. If you prefer, you can sit at one of the few indoor tables and enjoy such hot dishes as pizza and fried chicken. In the morning the deli offers donuts and coffee.

MID-RANGE

Bright Angel Restaurant

(Map 4; ☎ 928-638-2631; entrées $8-13; open 6:30am-10pm) This busy family-style restaurant in the back of Bright Angel Lodge offers burgers, fajitas, lasagna, roast turkey and other simple dishes. Of the three South Rim restaurants that offer waiter service, this is the least inviting. With few windows and no canyon views, it's a bit dark and resembles a basic, nondescript coffee shop. Families with small children gravitate here, and it can get loud. The restaurant serves coffee from 6am and does not take reservations.

Maswik & Yavapai Cafeterias

(Map 4; ☎ 928-638-2631; entrées $6-10) Based in their respective lodges, these are, well…cafeterias. Expect cafeteria food, service and seating. Though fairly predictable, the food is pretty good – a nice variety and not too greasy. You'll find pizza, burgers, fried chicken, Mexican fare and other hot dishes, as well as beer, soda and milk. Maswik is open daily from 6am to 10pm, while Yavapai closes an hour earlier.

TOP END

El Tovar Dining Room

(Map 4; ☎ 928-638-2631; entrées $12-22; open 6:30-11am, 11:30am-2pm, 5-10pm) If at all possible, eat at least one meal at the historic El Tovar. The memorable surroundings feature dark wood, tables set with china and white linen, and huge picture windows with views of the rim and canyon beyond. The service is excellent, the menu creative, the portions big and the food very good – much better than you might expect at a place with captive customers

✔ **TIP**

El Tovar does not take reservations for breakfast or lunch. To avoid lunchtime crowds, eat before the Grand Canyon Railway arrives at 12:15pm, as passengers often make lunch at El Tovar their first stop.

that knows it's the only gig in town. Options at breakfast ($4-9) include fresh-squeezed orange juice, El Tovar's pancake trio (buttermilk, blue corn-meal and buckwheat pancakes with pine nut butter and prickly pear syrup) and cornmeal-encrusted trout with two eggs. Lunch ($8-15) and dinner menus are equally creative. Though you're welcome to dress up to match the elegant setting, you'll be perfectly comfortable in jeans as well. Reservations are required for dinner. Call Xanterra *(☎ 888-297-2757)* to make reservations up to six months in advance (one month in advance if you're not a hotel guest).

DRINKS WITH A VIEW

At the end of a tiring mule trek or a long, dusty hike into the canyon, sit back with a cold drink and soak up one of the following scenic views:

✔ The Rim Trail and the canyon beyond from the back porch of **El Tovar** (p169)

✔ Flagstaff's historic downtown from the second-floor wrap-around porch at Weatherford's **Zane Grey Room** (p193)

✔ Spectacular canyon views from a rocker on the back porch of **Grand Canyon Lodge** (p173)

✔ Deer grazing in the meadow from a cabin stoop at **Kaibab Lodge** – grab a cold beer from the bar inside or the general store across the street (p173)

Arizona Room

(Map 4; ☎ 928-638-2631; entrées $8-21; open 4:30-10pm) A wonderful balance between casual and upscale, this restaurant in Bright Angel Lodge is one of the best options for dinner on the South Rim. Antler chandeliers hang from the ceiling, and picture windows overlook a small lawn, the rim walk and the canyon beyond. It's a bright, busy place. Doors open at 4:30pm, and by 4:40 you may have an hour wait – reservations are not accepted. There is no indoor bar, but you can sit outside on the small deck,

watch passersby on the Rim Trail and enjoy a drink while you wait (an expensive wait at $7.60 for a margarita). Entrées include steak, chicken and fish dishes, while appetizers include such creative options as toasted cumin onion rings.

Phantom Ranch

(Map 1; ☎ 928-638-2631; entrées $20-30) On the canyon floor, Phantom Ranch offers family-style meals that feature hearty stews, steaks and vegetarian fare, as well as sack lunches ($9). There are two dinner sittings (5pm and 6:30pm), and breakfast ($18) is served predawn. You must make reservations before your trip into the canyon (up to 23 months in advance).

NIGHTLIFE IN THE GRAND CANYON

The park isn't exactly a nightlife hot spot, but for those who still have energy at the end of the day, there are a few places to go.

If you're on the North Rim, stop by the **Rough Rider Saloon** for a drink and a browse of the Teddy Roosevelt memorabilia. In nice weather take your drink to the stone patio off the back of adjacent **Grand Canyon Lodge**. Rough-hewn rocking chairs line the canyon rim, a fire blazes in the fireplace, and rangers offer talks, sometimes providing telescopes to let guests stargaze.

On the South Rim, the patio off the bar at **El Tovar** is a great spot to sit with a prickly pear margarita and watch people strolling along the rim. Inside is a dark and cozy lounge, with big, cushioned chairs and stained glass. Sports fans can catch a game on the big-screen TV at **Maswik Lodge Sports Bar**. The dark, windowless bar at **Bright Angel** doesn't offer much in the way of character, but it's fun to look at the historic photos on the bar. All bars close at 11pm, and drinks are prohibited along the rim itself.

On Thursday nights park employees head to Tusayan, just outside the park's South Entrance, for dancing at the **Grand Hotel** (10:30pm-1am; see p162). Some opt to catch the latest scores at the popular sports bar in the **Best Western Squire Inn** (p161), which also features a video arcade, pool tables and a bowling alley.

At campground amphitheaters in the summer, rangers on both rims offer evening talks on a variety of subjects. Check *The Guide* for program descriptions, times and locations.

Outside the Park

For places to eat in Flagstaff, Williams and Sedona, see Around the Grand Canyon (p174).

TUSAYAN

This restaurant and hotel hub lies just outside the South Entrance along Hwy 64. Considering the number of annual tourists that pass through, however, there really isn't much here. It's about a half-mile strip of fast-food franchises and restaurants that adjoin the chain hotels.

PLACES TO EAT

Mexican Kitchen

(☎ 928-638-1105; entrées $6-10; open 11am-9pm) Sporting bright turquoise walls and Southwestern chairs, this tiny café in the Grand Canyon Village Shops (opposite the IMAX Theater) offers decent Mexican food, including tacos and fajitas (no beer or wine). The friendly, low-key spot is a welcome alternative to the bigger, tourist-oriented restaurants in town and on the rim. The café may start serving breakfast – call to find out.

Jennifer's Coffeehouse & Bakery

(☎ 928-638-3433; entrées $2-7; open 7am-5pm) Also in the Grand Canyon Village Shops, this is where USFS rangers come to grab a sandwich and escape the tourists. It's a small place with high tables, Internet access ($3 for 15min), coffee, pastries and a limited menu. Breakfast items include Belgian waffles ($4.50) and eggs with bacon ($5). Sandwiches are made to order, including a veggie sandwich ($6.95). Ask the staff to pack a picnic for you if you'd rather enjoy your meal in the forest or at the park.

Quality Inn Restaurant

(☎ 928-638-2673; open 24hrs, buffet 7-9:30am, 11am-2:30pm and 5:30-9pm) A great option for hungry families, this hotel serves daily buffets in its indoor atrium at breakfast (adults/children $7.50/4.50), lunch ($8/4.50) and dinner ($15/7.50). It's bright and airy, you can get a drink from the bar, and children under 5 eat free.

We Cook Pizza & Pasta

(☎ 928-638-2278; entrées $10-23; open 11am-10pm) Though it beats eating at Pizza Hut (except in price), there's nothing particularly compelling about the dishes here – the most creative pizza toppings are broccoli and Asiago cheese. There's no table service; you place your order and wait for your number to be called.

Canyon Star

(☎ 928-638-3333; entrées $11-21; open 7:30am-9:30pm) In the Grand Hotel, this spacious restaurant with high ceilings and faux wooden beams strives for a Western feel. To set the mood and attract tour bus crowds, a Native American dance performance is held every evening at 7pm followed by live country music. The food is overpriced and nothing special, though some options are more interesting than others, including portobello mushroom lasagna.

GOOD SPOTS FOR GROCERIES

Though both rims have general stores that offer basic supplies, several stores outside the park offer a better selection at better prices.

- ✔ New Frontiers Natural Marketplace (Flagstaff and Sedona)
- ✔ Safeway (Flagstaff, Williams and Page)
- ✔ Glazier's Food Town (Kanab)
- ✔ Albertsons (Flagstaff and Boulder City, SW of Lake Mead)
- ✔ Bashas' (Flagstaff and Sedona)

VALLE

If you're on your way to or from the park and cannot wait till Williams or Tusayan, stop by the **Grand Canyon Inn Restaurant** *(☎ 928-635-9203; entrées $4-12; open 7am-9pm)* for standard American fare. Alternatively, kids may enjoy the snack bar at **Bedrock City** (p162), a silly, fun spot to expend their pent-up energy.

CAMERON

In Navajo country 32 miles east of the park's East Entrance, the **Cameron Trading Post Dining Room** *(☎ 928-679-2231 or ☎ 800-338-7385; entrées $7-17; open 6am-10pm)* is a nice spot for a meal. The bright, airy interior features Southwestern decor, high ceilings and big windows with views of red sandstone formations. The menu offers well-prepared Native American dishes, including a huge Navajo taco (fried dough with whole beans, ground beef, chili and cheese) – a small one is more than enough for a hungry adult. Browse the trading post for crafts following your meal.

NORTH RIM

The same solitude that attracts so many visitors to the North Rim also means you'll have limited dining options. If you don't have dinner reservations at Grand Canyon Lodge, you'll either have to eat at the snack bar, visit the general store for picnic items, or drive to Kaibab Lodge (25 minutes) or Jacob Lake Inn (50 minutes).

Inside the Park

Visitors can contact park restaurants through the North Rim switchboard *(☎ 928-638-2612)*.

North Rim General Store

(Map 3; open 8am-8pm) Though you won't find a deli here, you can pick up supplies for a picnic at one of the many spots along Cape Royal Road (p111). Hours may vary according to demand.

Café on the Rim

(Map 3; entrées $4-6; open 7am-9pm) This small cafeteria beside the lodge serves surprisingly good food. The limited menu includes made-to-order sandwiches, pizza, a chicken and rice bowl (with crisp, fresh green beans) and ice cream. There are a few indoor tables, but you're better off taking your plate outside to enjoy the high mountain air.

Rough Rider Saloon

(Map 3; open 5:30-10:30am, 11:30am-11pm) If you're up to catch the sunrise or enjoy an early morning hike, stop at this small saloon on the boardwalk beside the lodge for an espresso and a muffin or pastry. Starting at 11:30am the saloon serves coffee, beer, wine and mixed drinks. Teddy Roosevelt memorabilia lines the walls, honoring his role in the history of the park – ask the bartender for the book about Teddy to browse while you drink. This is the only bar in the lodge, so if you want to take a drink out to the back patio or up to your room, stop here first.

Grand Canyon Lodge Dining Room

(Map 3; entrées $9-20; open 6:30-10am, 11:30am-2:30pm, 4:45-9:45pm) Some people get downright belligerent if they can't get a window seat at this wonderful spot, but the windows are so huge, it really doesn't matter where you sit. The solid menu includes several vegetarian options. Dinner reservations are required. Make arrangements when you book your room, or call Xanterra (☎ *888-297-2757)* to place a reservation up to six months in advance.

Outside the Park

North Rim Country Store

(Map 1; ☎ 928-638-2383; open 7am-9pm) Just across Hwy 67 from Kaibab Lodge and DeMotte Campground, this small store and gas station sells a small selection of groceries, including canned goods, cereal, cheese, juice and beer.

Kaibab Lodge

(Map 1; ☎ 928-638-2389; W *www.canyoneers.com; Hwy 67, 18 miles north of North Rim; entrées $7-14; open 6-9:30am, 5-9:30pm; closed mid-Oct–mid-May)* There's something comforting about this lodge. Perhaps it's the setting, hugged on two sides by a lovely meadow and on a third by Kaibab National Forest. Or maybe it's because there's nothing overly 'grand' about it there – no crowds, no breathtaking views. It's a simple, low-key place, where the biggest excitement comes from counting deer that wander from the woods to graze. In a bright, casual room flanked by windows that overlook the meadow, the restaurant serves basic, tasty dishes like pasta and burgers. The lobby bar serves drinks, and continental breakfast is offered in the mornings.

Jacob Lake Inn

(Map 1; ☎ 928-643-7232; W *www.jacoblake.com; Hwy 67, 44 miles north of North Rim; entrées $7-13; open 6:30am-9pm)* This busy, almost festive place is filled with visitors either coming from or headed to the North Rim. The inn does not accept reservations, and the last sitting is at 8pm. A window overlooks the forest, and on every table is a guide describing the Navajo rugs that cover the walls. The lunch menu offers tasty sandwiches, from the standard grilled cheese to cranberry cream cheese chicken, while the dinner menu includes steak, chicken, fish and vegetarian selections. An adjacent ice cream counter offers delicious cookies and desserts and serves breakfast and lunch.

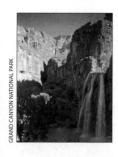

GRAND CANYON NATIONAL PARK

Grand Canyon National Park borders Kaibab National Forest to the north and south, Lake Mead National Recreation Area to the west and Glen Canyon National Recreation Area to the northeast.

AROUND THE
GRAND CANYON

Divided into two distinct ecosystems by the canyon, the Kaibab National Forest offers fantastic outdoor activities and a peaceful escape from park crowds. Formed by Hoover and Glen Canyon Dams, respectively, Lakes Mead and Powell lure parched Southwesterners with fishing, swimming, water sports and extended houseboat trips. Marble Canyon spirals southwest from Glen Canyon Dam to Lees Ferry, a dusty desert outpost where most Colorado River trips begin. Though the national park encompasses the vast majority of the canyon, visitors can enjoy breathtaking views, explore the inner canyon and raft the river from the Hualapai and Havasupai Indian Reservations, several hours west of Grand Canyon Village.

Four gateway towns – three south of the South Rim and one 90 minutes north of the North Rim – provide overflow accommodations for visitors to the Grand Canyon. Each presents its own distinct character, offering visitors more than just a place to sleep. Kanab is an ideal base for exploring national parks in northern Arizona and southern Utah, while Flagstaff and Sedona are destinations in their own right, promising a wide range of accommodations, restaurants, shops, outdoor activities and attractions.

Kaibab National Forest (South Rim)

The park's South Rim is bordered by the piñon-juniper and ponderosa pine woodland of Kaibab National Forest. Offering several great mountain-biking trails, unlimited camping, hiking and cross-country skiing, the forest extends outdoor recreation options beyond the park. You won't find spectacular canyon views, but you won't find the crowds either. Bring plenty of water, as natural water sources are scarce in this arid region. You'll likely spot elks, mule deer, turkeys and coyotes, and on rare occasions you may encounter a mountain lion, black bear or bobcat.

ORIENTATION & INFORMATION

The forest's Tusayan Ranger District (327,267 acres) borders Grand Canyon National Park to the north, the Navajo Indian Reservation to the east, private and state-owned lands to the south and the Havasupai Indian Reservation to the west. The main road through the forest is Hwy 64/180, which connects Williams and Flagstaff with the canyon. Hwy 64 accesses the district's northeast corner.

If you plan on hiking or camping in the forest, maps are available at the Williams visitor center and at the park's Canyon View Information Plaza bookstore. **Tusayan Ranger Station** (☎ *928-638-2443;* W *www.fs.fed.us/r3/kai; open 8am-4:30pm)* sits just outside the canyon's South Entrance.

SIGHTS & ACTIVITIES

Built by the Civilian Conservation Corp in 1936 as a fire tower, the 80ft **Grandview Lookout** offers great views of the region for those willing and able to climb all those stairs. From the park's Desert View Drive (p88), turn at the sign for 'Arizona Trail' between mileposts 252 and 253, about 2 miles east of Grandview Point. You can **hike** or **bike** 1.3 miles on a dirt road to the lookout. Alternatively, take unpaved Forest Road 302, just past Grand Canyon National Park Airport, in Tusayan.

You can also ride or hike here via the **Tusayan Bike Trail**, a moderate bike trail on an old logging road. The trailhead is 0.3 mile north of Tusayan on the west side of Hwy 64/180. It's 16 miles from the trailhead to the lookout. If you don't want to ride all that way, three interconnected loops offer 3-, 8- and 9-mile round-trips.

From the lookout you can hike or ride part or all of the still-evolving **Arizona Trail**, a 24-mile one-way ride to the south boundary of the Tusayan Ranger District. This is an excellent and relatively easy ride. Eventually, the Arizona Trail will span the state more than 750 miles from north to south. The northern segment of the trail unfolds beneath ponderosa pines and gambel oaks; farther south, the trail passes piñon-juniper stands, sage and grasslands. Bring plenty of water, as there are no dependable sources along the trail. Ask at the ranger station about other hikes.

Apache Stables (☎ *928-638-2891;* W *www.apachestables.com)* offers several horseback rides through the forest. The strenuous four-hour East Rim ride ($95; ages 14 and up) winds through the Kaibab to a canyon view on Desert View Drive; this is the only ride that offers rim views, though it does not go along the rim or into the canyon. The one-hour ride through the forest costs $30 (ages eight and up), while the two-hour ride costs $55 (ages 10 and up). You can take a one-hour evening saunter to a campfire and return on a wagon ($41; ages eight and up). For riders of all ages, the outfitter offers a campfire wagon ride, in which trail riders rendezvous with the wagon for a cookout beneath the stars. It costs $12.50 for ages six and up, $6.25 for children two to five and is free for kids under two. For both campfire trips you must bring your own food (think hot dogs and marshmallows) and drinks – if you bring a small cooler, the staff will put it on the wagon.

In the winter the United States Forest Service (USFS) maintains a groomed **cross-country skiing loop** 0.3 mile north of Grandview Lookout.

PLACES TO STAY

The USFS **Ten X Campground** *(Map 2; $10; open mid-Apr–Sep)* is set in the woods 2 miles south of Tusayan. You'll find picnic tables, water and toilets but no showers or hookups. This is a pleasant, quiet campground and an excellent alternative to the park's Mather Campground.

Free dispersed camping is allowed in the national forest as long as you refrain from camping in meadows, within a quarter mile of the highway or any surface water, or within a half mile of any developed campground. Dispersed camping is not allowed inside the national park.

Havasupai Indian Reservation
MAP 5

One of the canyon's true treasures is Havasu Canyon, a hidden valley with four gorgeous, spring-fed waterfalls and inviting azure swimming holes in the heart of the 185,000-acre Havasupai Reservation. Because the falls lie 10 miles below the rim, most trips are combined with a stay at either Havasu Lodge in Supai or at the nearby campground. Situated 8 miles below the rim, Supai is the only village within the Grand Canyon.

ORIENTATION & INFORMATION

The reservation lies south of the Colorado River and west of the park's South Rim. From Hualapi Hilltop, a three- to four-hour drive from the South Rim, a well-maintained trail leads to Supai, waterfalls and the Colorado River. Information is available from the Havasupai Tourist Enterprise (☎ 928-448-2141; PO Box 160, Supai, AZ 86435). Visitors pay an entry fee of $20 when they arrive in Supai. The local post office distributes its mail by pack animals – postcards mailed from here bear a special postmark to prove it. Liquor, recreational drugs and nude swimming are not allowed. Trail bikes are not allowed below Hualapai Hilltop, and fires are prohibited – campers must cook with gas stoves or canned heat. Be sure to purify your water. There is a small emergency clinic in Supai.

HIKING

Two moderate to difficult trails are on the reservation, and lead to waterfalls and a swimming hole.

HUALAPAI TRAIL TO SUPAI
Distance: 8 miles one way
Duration: 3 to 5 hours one way
Challenge: Moderate
Elevation Change: 2000ft

Before heading down to Supai, you must secure reservations to camp or stay in the lodge. Do not try to hike down and back in one day – not only is it dangerous, but it also doesn't allot enough time to see the falls, as they lie farther down, in **Havasu Canyon**.

The trail descends steep switchbacks for 1.5 miles, levels off in a dry creek bed and winds through the canyon for the remaining 6.5 miles to the village. About 1.5 miles before Supai the trail meets Havasu Creek. Follow the trail downstream to the village. Shade trees line the creek, and the sheer walls of the canyon rise dramatically on either side of the trail.

HAVASU CANYON TO WATERFALLS & THE COLORADO RIVER

Distance: 9 miles one way
Duration: 7 to 8 hours one way
Challenge: Moderate-Difficult
Elevation Change: 1200ft

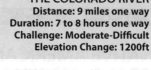

Just over a mile beyond Supai is 75ft-high **Navajo Falls**. Next comes **Havasu Falls**, which drops 100ft into a sparkling blue pool surrounded by cottonwoods, a popular swimming hole. **Havasu Campground** sits a quarter-mile beyond Havasu Falls. Just past the campground, the trail passes **Mooney Falls**, which tumbles 200ft down into another blue-green swimming hole. To get to the swimming hole, you must climb through two tunnels and descend a very steep trail (chains provide welcome handholds). Limestone walls tower over the creek and falls. After a picnic and a swim, continue about 2 miles to **Beaver Falls** and the **Colorado River**. The trail passes small pools and cascades and crosses the creek many times. The river lies 10.5 miles from Supai and 8 miles beyond the campground. Camping is prohibited beyond Mooney Falls, so it's a strenuous hike to the river and back. It's recommended that you don't attempt to hike to the river; in fact, the reservation actively discourages it. Enjoy the waterfalls instead.

PLACES TO STAY & EAT

In Supai, **Havasupai Lodge** (*Map 5;* ☎ *928-448-2111; PO Box 159, Supai, AZ 86435; 24 rooms; $80*) offers motel rooms, all with canyon views, two double beds, air conditioning and private showers. There are no TVs or telephones. Reservations are essential; the lodge is often booked months in advance for the entire summer, and unless you plan to camp, there's nowhere else to stay. A **café** serves breakfast, lunch and dinner daily, and a **general store** sells basic groceries and snacks.

Two miles past Supai Village is **Havasu Campground** (*Map 5;* ☎ *928-448-2121; Havasupai Camping Office, PO Box 160, Supai, AZ 86435; 340 sites; $10*), whose sites span three-quarters of a mile along the creek between Havasu and Mooney Falls. You'll find picnic tables, pit toilets and a spring for drinking water (purify it first). While there are no showers, you can swim in the river and pools. Fires are not permitted. This campground is often packed in summer, so be sure to hike its length before choosing a spot to pitch your tent.

Rates do not include the $20 per person entrance fee into the reservation. Remember: It's 8 miles to the lodge and more than 10 miles to the campground from Hualapai Hilltop. It is absolutely essential that you make reservations in advance; if you hike in without a reservation, you will have to hike all the way back up to your car at the trailhead.

GETTING THERE & AROUND

Seven miles east of Peach Springs on historic Route 66, a signed turnoff leads to the 62-mile paved road to Havasu Canyon. At Hualapai Hilltop you'll find the parking area, stables and the trailhead into the canyon. To get to Supai, park your car and then hike, ride or fly the 8 miles down to the village. If you plan

NATIVE AMERICANS OF THE GRAND CANYON

The Havasupai, which translates as 'people of the blue-green waters' and the Hualapai ('pine-tree people') share the Yuman language and are together referred to as Northeastern Pai. Their legends tell them that mankind originated on a mountain near the Colorado River. They left their Mojave relatives behind and headed to Meriwitica, near Spencer Canyon (a tributary of Grand Canyon). The Hualapai stayed near Meriwitica, but a frog, enticed by the stream and lush vegetation, led the Havasupai east to Havasu Canyon. Archeological records indicate that the Northeastern Pai arrived at the Grand Canyon around AD 1150, and the Havasupai have occupied Havasu Canyon since about that time.

Before the American Indian Wars of the 19th century, the Hualapai and Havasupai were left pretty much to themselves. They developed complex systems of irrigation and spent summers farming within the canyon, at places like Havasu Canyon and Indian Garden. During the winter, they hunted on the plateau. They dressed in sewn buckskin and made coiled baskets and brown or red pottery. Their biggest contact was with other Indian tribes, and through trade with the Hopi, the Northeastern Pai acquired peaches, figs, wheat, melons, cattle and horses. In the 1850s, American trappers, traders and pioneers began to intrude into their lives, and by 1880 both the Havasupai and Hualapai were contained in reservations.

William Wallace Bass set up camp on the rim near Havasu Canyon and began taking tourists down to the Havasupai village in about 1890. He became friendly with the Havasupai, bringing them medicine during an epidemic of measles and employing them in his camp. More and more visitors came to the Grand Canyon during the early 20th century, and the Havasupai community became less and less isolated. They sold peaches in Williams and Flagstaff, found jobs at Grand Canyon Village and began adopting Anglo clothes and speaking English.

Today, over 10,000 tourists visit Havasu Canyon every year, and the Havasupai's lives and economic survival are integrally related to the tourist industry that has developed in and around Grand Canyon National Park. They are well known for their basketry and beadwork. Though tourism has not been as integrated into the lives of the Hualapai, they too have come to depend upon the tourist industry. They operate a hotel in Peach Springs and a campground on the rim, lead scenic tours and operate commercial rafting trips on the Colorado River. Like the Havasupai, the Hualapai are renowned for their basketry. You will also find Hualapai dolls at trading posts and in and around the canyon.

West of the Grand Canyon lies the 2410-sq-mile **Hopi Reservation** (☎ 928-734-3283) and the 27,000-sq-mile **Navajo Reservation** (☎ 928-871-6436). Like the Havasupai and Hualapai, the Hopi and Navajo story is one of the destruction, relocation and rebirth as a subject for the tourist gaze.

Hopi and Navajo crafts, more than those of the other canyon tribes, became an important part of the park's tourist development. In the early 20th century, Fred Harvey hired Hopi to live in the Hopi House, demonstrate their crafts, wear their native costumes and perform dances for the tourists. Today, Hopi Kachina dolls and Navajo rugs are some of the most sought-after Indian crafts.

According to Hopi religion, Kachinas are several hundred sacred spirits that live in the San Francisco Mountains north of Flagstaff. At prescribed intervals during the year, they come to the Hopi Reservation and dance in a precise and ritualized fashion. These dances maintain harmony among all living things and are especially important for rainfall and fertility. Kachina dolls, traditionally carved from the dried root of the cottonwood tree and elaborate in design and color, represent these sacred spirits. While some Kachina dolls are considered too sacred for public display or trade, the Hopi carve Kachinas specifically to be sold to the general public. You can buy these, as well as pottery, basketwork and jewelry at the Hopi House in Grand Canyon Village, at the Watchtower (where Navajo weavers often demonstrate their craft) and at the Cameron Trading Post, east of the East Entrance.

When visiting an Indian reservation, please be respectful and keep in mind certain rules of etiquette. Many tribes ban all forms of recording, be it photography, videotaping, audiotaping or drawing. Others permit these activities if you pay a certain fee, and others still allow them only in certain places or at certain times. Ask permission before taking any pictures, recordings or videos. Kivas (ceremonial spaces) are always off-limits to visitors.

Ceremonials and powwows are religious events. Many do not have a fixed date and are arranged a couple of weeks ahead of time. The tribal office can inform you of upcoming public events. Do not applaud, chat or ask questions during ceremonials and powwows. Most reservations ban the sale or use of alcohol, and drugs are banned from all reservations. Activities such as camping, fishing, hunting and backpacking require tribal permits – be sure to get the appropriate permits before engaging in any activities. When in doubt, ask.

For more on the Grand Canyon's native tribes, see History (p227).

on hiking or riding down, you must spend the night either in Peach Springs (ideally), Grand Canyon Caverns or in one of the motels along Route 66.

The motels in Seligman are about 90 miles from Hualapai Hilltop. Don't plan on spending the night prior to your hike on the South Rim, as it's a three- to four-hour drive from there to Hualapai Hilltop.

Don't let place-names confuse you: Hualapai Hilltop is on the Havasupai Indian Reservation, not the Hualapai Reservation, as one might think.

Mule or Horse Rides into the Canyon
If you don't want to hike to Supai, you can arrange for a mule or horse to carry you in and out. It costs $120 round-trip for rides to the lodge, and $150 round-trip for rides to the campground. It's about half that price if you hike in and ride out, or vice versa. Mules depart Hualapai Hilltop at 10am year-round. Call the lodge or campground (wherever you'll be spending the night) in advance to arrange a ride.

Helicopter Rides into the Canyon
On Thursdays, Fridays, Sundays and Mondays from mid-March through October, a helicopter ($85 one-way) shuttles between Hualapai Hilltop and Supai from 10am to 1pm. You can't call to make advance reservations; you just arrive at the parking lot and sign up. There's no hangar or anything – just a helicopter in the dirt. Call **Havasupai Tourist Enterprise** (☎ 928-448-2141) before you arrive to be sure the helicopter is running. From November to mid-March the helicopter operates on Fridays and Sundays only.

Papillon Grand Canyon Helicopters (☎ 800-528-2418) offers a daily flight from Grand Canyon National Park Airport, in Tusayan, to Supai for $442 round-trip. Flights depart Tusayan at 9:40am – you can spend the day in the canyon and return on the 3:30pm flight, or you can return at 10am or 3:30pm on a later day.

Hualapai Indian Reservation
MAP 5
This reservation borders many miles of the Colorado River northeast of Kingman and includes the only road to the river within the Grand Canyon. In 1988 the Hualapai opened 'Grand Canyon West,' and they market their section of the canyon as being 'untouched by our 20th-century world. No buildings, no traffic, no noise.' As an alternative to the remote North Rim or the touristy South Rim, Grand Canyon West does indeed offer visitors a chance to enjoy the canyon with less chaos. You won't find the historic buildings or sublime views, and it's a bit of a drive to get here, but that's part of its charm.

ORIENTATION & INFORMATION
The Hualapai reservation covers the southwest rim of the canyon, bordering Havasupai Reservation to the east and Lake Mead National Recreation Area to the west. **Hualapai Office of Tourism** (☎ 888-255-9550; *Hualapai Reservation, PO Box 538, Peach Springs, AZ 86434*) staffs an office at Hualapai Lodge (see p181) in the blink-and-you'll-miss-it town of Peach Springs. The reservation entrance fee is $6.30 per day per person. You can buy passes at Hualapai Lodge.

SIGHTS & ACTIVITIES

Grand Canyon West Tours

A 4.5-mile bus tour along the canyon rim costs adult/child $35/22 for and includes a barbecue lunch and plenty of local lore and information from a Hualapai guide. Tours last about two hours and depart several times a day from the Grand Canyon West airport terminal.

Quartermaster Viewpoint

Available at the terminal, a $10 per person permit allows you to drive the 4 miles to **Quartermaster Viewpoint**, which offers good views of the lower Grand Canyon. A five-minute hike on a rough trail brings you to a small bluff with an even better view. Though the views aren't quite as good as those along the South Rim, they do offer a much more peaceful perspective. Beside the parking lot are picnic tables and an outhouse. Ask for directions when you purchase your permit.

Diamond Creek Road

This 22-mile unpaved scenic road heads north from Peach Springs to the Colorado River. At road's end you'll find picnic tables and a camping area (see p181). Don't forget to purchase an entrance permit ($6.30) from the Hualapai Lodge front desk before driving down the road.

Rafting

Hualapai River Runners (☎ 928-769-2219, 888-255-9550; W www.river-runners.com) offers one-day rafting trips on the Colorado from Diamond Creek to Pierce Ferry Landing. Its motorized rafts hold up to 10 people. This is your only opportunity for a one-day white-water rafting trip within the Grand Canyon. Trips leave from Hualapai Lodge and cost $265 per person (including a souvenir mug). Package deals are offered through Hualapai Lodge. Trips run weekdays from May through October. Children must be at least eight years old. Ask about overnight trips to Lake Mead.

PLACES TO STAY & EAT

The only place to stay in Peach Springs is the modern **Hualapai Lodge** (☎ 928-769-2230, 888-255-9550; 900 Rte 66; $75), with interior rooms and the **Diamond Creek Restaurant**. The restaurant serves standard American fare (entrées $4 to 9) and is open daily for breakfast, lunch and dinner.

On the Colorado, at the end of Diamond Creek Road, is the small and basic **Diamond Creek Campground**, a beach camping spot along the river. The elevation here is 1900ft, so the campground is extremely hot in summer. You'll find toilets and a picnic table but no drinking water. Camping costs $10 per day per person and includes entrance fees. The campground holds about 10 people – contact the Hualapai Office of Tourism (☎ 888-255-9550) in the Hualapai Lodge for availability.

Thirteen miles east of Peach Springs on Route 66 is **Grand Canyon Caverns & Inn** (☎ 928-422-3223; W www.gccaverns.com; MM 115, Rte 66; single/double $52/57), offering basic motel rooms, a pool and a **restaurant** (entrées $3-7; open 7am-7pm) serving burgers and fried food. The hotel also operates tours of **Grand Canyon Caverns**, 21 stories below ground via elevator. One-hour tours are on a paved, well-lit trail, while two-hour tours (ages 12 and up) go off-trail. The restaurant and caverns sit a mile behind the rooms and pool.

Thirty-five miles east of Peach Springs, in Seligman, you'll find several inexpensive, simple motels; the best is **Historic Route 66 Motel** (☎ *928-422-3204; 500 W Rte 66; $42*).

GETTING THERE & AROUND

There are no regular shuttles or buses to Peach Springs or the Hualapai Reservation. River trips include a shuttle to the reservation from Hualapai Lodge in Peach Springs.

Driving to Grand Canyon West involves travel along dirt roads. Call or stop by Hualapai Lodge to check road conditions before heading out – if there has been a lot of rain, roads may be impassable. Three miles west of Peach Springs is Buck & Doe Rd, which leads about 50 miles to Grand Canyon West. Grand Canyon West can also be reached from Hwy 93. Head north from Kingman about 26 miles, northeast along the paved Pierce Ferry Rd (toward Lake Mead) for about 30 miles, then 21 miles along the dirt Diamond Bar Road.

Williams

MAP 7 • TEL 928 • POP 2910 • ELEVATION 6780FT

A pretty dead spot by day, Williams comes to life in the evening when the Grand Canyon Railway returns with passengers from the South Rim. Though this small town can't compete with Flagstaff's restaurants, historic downtown or myriad sights, it is a friendly place and caters to canyon tourists.

ORIENTATION & INFORMATION

Inside the historic train depot, the **visitors center** (☎ *928-635-4061, 800-863-0546; 200 W Railroad Ave;* W *www.visitwilliams.com; open 8am-5pm*) offers a small bookstore with titles on the canyon, Kaibab National Forest and other areas of interest. You'll find USFS rangers at both the visitors center and **Williams Ranger Station** (☎ *928-635-2633; 742 S Clover Rd; 8am-4pm Mon-Fri*).

Other services include the **library** (☎ *928-635-2263; 113 S 1st St)*, **post office** (☎ *928-635-4572; 120 S 1st St)*, **Health Care Center** (☎ *928-635-4441; 301 S 7th St)* and **police station** (☎ *928-635-4461; 501 W Rte 66)*.

The famed Route 66 passes through the main historic district as a one-way street headed east; Railroad Ave parallels the tracks and Route 66 and heads one-way west. Most businesses lie along these two roads.

SIGHTS & ACTIVITIES

There are plenty of opportunities for **hiking** and **biking** in nearby Kaibab, Coconino and Prescott National Forests. Ask at the visitors center or at the ranger station for maps and information.

RIDING THE RAILS

On September 17, 1901, the Grand Canyon Railway departed Williams to carry its first passengers to the South Rim – and so began the modern era of the canyon as a tourist destination. Absent the hurdle of a long and arduous stagecoach ride, tourists could now visit the rim in relative comfort. By 1968 car travel had made the train obsolete – only three passengers were on that year's final trip to the rim. In 1989 Max and Thelma Biegert bought and restored the train and resumed passenger service after a 21-year absence. Today the railway runs a steam locomotive from Memorial Day through September and a diesel locomotive the rest of the year.

Passengers can choose from among five classes of service. **Coach class** (adult/child $58/25 round-trip) features a 1923 Harriman-style Pullman car with reversible seats and large wood-framed windows that open to let in the desert breeze; complimentary soda is included. **Club class** ($79/46) offers a mahogany cash bar and complimentary juice and pastries. In air-conditioned **1st class** ($116/83), the spacious seats recline, and champagne and appetizers are offered during the return trip. Not open to children under 11, the **deluxe observation dome class** ($137/104) features a cash bar and upper-level seating in a glass-enclosed dome. The **luxury parlor car** ($147/114) offers incredibly comfortable cushioned window seats and an open-air rear platform. A 1952 parlor car doubles as a café, selling coffee, candy, box lunches, sunscreen, water and film.

Even if you're not a train buff, or if you generally shirk from traveling en masse, the train can be a lot of fun if you get into the spirit. A banjo player or another kind of musician wanders the aisles, joking with passengers and strumming such folk classics as *I've Been Working on the Railroad*. Something about riding the rails, waving your arms out the window or pretending to be FDR stumping on the rear platform brings the kid out in people. A mock horseback chase and train robbery enliven the return trip.

The train departs the 1908 Williams Depot at 10am, following a 9:30am Wild West shoot-out by the tracks (a slapstick performance to put you in the mood). You'll arrive at Grand Canyon Depot at 12:15pm. The return train pulls out at 3:30pm, arriving back in Williams at 5:45pm. Most people approach it as a day trip, but you can purchase a one-way ticket or spend a few days in the park and return on a later train. Packages are available through the Fray Marcos Hotel, in Williams, and lodgings at the rim. For reservations and details about accommodations, bus tours and meal packages, contact the **Grand Canyon Railway** (☎ *800-843-8724;* Ⓦ *www.thetrain.com*).

Grand Canyon Railway

Following a 9:30am **Wild West show** by the tracks, the historic Grand Canyon Railway departs for its two-hour ride to the South Rim. If you're only visiting the rim for the day, this is a lively and relaxing option. You can leave the hassle of the car behind and enjoy the park by foot, shuttle or tour bus.

Grand Canyon Deer Farm

Children love the **deer farm** (☎ 928-635-4073, 800-926-3337; W www.deer farm.com; 6752 E Deerfarm Rd; adult/child $6.75/3.95, under 3 free; open 8am-7pm, shorter winter hours). Blanketed in wood chips, a trail leads through an open area where the deer roam free. A smaller pen is home to goats (always eager to munch on food, shirts, strollers, whatever). Just $2 buys enough deer food to keep kids busy for a while. There are a few other animals, though you're asked not to feed them. It's 8 miles east of Williams.

PLACES TO STAY
Camping & Budget

Free dispersed camping is allowed throughout Kaibab National Forest.

Providing 96 RV hookups and an area for tents, **Railside RV Ranch** (☎ 928-635-4077, 888-635-4077; W www.thegrandcanyon.com/railside; 877 Rodeo Rd; 10 tent sites; tent/RV $17/20) is the closest campground to downtown Williams. There's no shade, and the sites are right beside the tracks, so it can get loud. To get here turn east from Grand Canyon Blvd onto Edison Ave (three blocks north of the tracks), then left on Airport Rd. After one block, turn right onto Rodeo Rd – the campground is on the left, just before the tracks.

. The welcoming **Red Lake Campground & Hostel** (☎ 928-635-4753, 800-581-4753; 28 sites, 7 double rooms; tent/RV/room $10/14/10-33) sits 8 miles north of I-40 on Hwy 64 (exit 165). Options include dorm rooms, as well as private rooms with three beds and a shared bath. Offering wooded sites and a camp store, **Ponderosa Forest RV Park & Campground** (☎ 928-635-0456, 888-635-0456; 56 sites; tent/RV $14/21) is at exit 178 off I-40, 14 miles east of Williams.

Three pleasant **USFS campgrounds** ($10 to $12) offer year-round camping but no hookups. Take exit 161 off I-40 and head north 2 miles to reach **Cataract Lake Campground**.

Kaibab Lake Campground is 4 miles northeast of town; take exit 165 off I-40 and go north 2 miles on Hwy 64. Nine miles southeast of town is **Whitehorse Lake** ($10), which offers a hiking trail and fishing; from town, drive 8 miles on 4th St and turn left on FR 110. Swimming is not allowed in any of the lakes. Contact the visitors center or the Williams Ranger Station (see Orientation) for information.

Amid 27 acres of ponderosa-pine forest a half mile north of I-40 at exit 167, **Circle Pines KOA** (☎ 928-635-2626, 800-562-9379; W www.circlepineskoa .com; tent/RV/cabin $20/30/35) is open year-round and offers plenty of activities for children and adults alike. Options include live music and hayrides on the weekends, miniature golf, an indoor pool, two hot tubs, bike rentals and horse stables. A **café** with outdoor seating serves breakfast and dinner.

Mid-range

Canyon Motel (☎ 928-635-2552, 800-482-3955; 1900 E Rodeo Rd; $70-97) Stone cottages and rooms in two railroad cabooses and a former Grand Canyon Railway coach car offer a kitschy alternative to a standard motel. Resting on sections of old track, the train cars sport private decks, and even though they're a little bit on the cramped side, kids love the experience. Several cars provide bunk beds, and campfires highlight the evenings. The little cottages feature white walls and wood floors, with kitchenettes and king or double beds.

O'Sullivan Inn (☎ 928-635-2349, 877-405-3280; 422 W Rte 66; $45) Rooms at this friendly motel are a step up from typical motel rooms; they include frilly curtains, bedspreads and a teddy bear on the bed to make you feel at home. Some rooms have interior doors.

The Grand & Gateway Motels (☎ 928-635-9590, 800-635-9590; W www .thegrandmotel.com; 234 E Rte 66; 24 rooms; single/double/suite/apt $38/49/55-65/120) Built in 1936 along Route 66 and listed on the National Register of Historic Places, this classic roadside motel is capped by a metal-tiled stucco roof made to look like the original faux adobe walls. Each room is different, and all feel like you're stepping into a time warp – you can imagine yourself road-tripping to the Grand Canyon before the days of chain motels. Many of them are designed like little apartments and some of them have little balconies. There are several deluxe units that offer two or three rooms, with a sink, refrigerator and microwave ($55 to $65). Comprising two bedrooms, a full kitchen and living room, a mini-apartment ($120) sleeps six to eight guests. Ask for a room in the original Grand Motel section, as rooms in the newer Gateway Motel across the street lack the same character.

Westerner Motel (☎ 928-635-4312, 800-385-8608; 530 W Rte 66; single/double/suite $38/44/68) Of the independent motels lining Route 66, this is one of the better ones. While there is nothing historic or charming about the place, it's a clean and well-run roadside spot. Wood and plastic chairs and potted flowers sit outside the rooms. The two-bedroom, three-bed suite includes a refrigerator and microwave.

Top End

Sheridan House Inn (☎ 928-635-9345, 888-635-9345; W www.thegrand canyon.com/sheridan; 460 E Sheridan; double/suite $145-210; closed Jan-Feb) Steve and Evelyn Gardner are the gracious hosts at this pine-fringed hilltop inn on the far south end of town. Guests can relax on a bench swing that looks out on the distant mountains, a welcome respite from the busy town center. Included in the rates are a full hot breakfast and buffet-style dinner, served on the outdoor deck. You're encouraged to help yourself to a fridge full of complimentary beer, soda, juice and water. Downstairs you'll find a pool table and fully stocked bar – fix yourself a drink and relax on adjacent flagstone patio. While not historic, the rooms are nicely appointed (nothing too cutesy) and offer CD players, TVs, VCRs and full marble baths (some are huge). The family unit ($185) features two rooms, one with a bunk bed and each with a TV & VCR. The inn's video library includes a selection of children's videos.

Terry Ranch Bed & Breakfast (☎ *928-635-4171, 800-210-5908;* W *www .terryranchbnb.com; 701 Quarterhorse Rd; 4 rooms; double $115-145, $10 more on weekends)* Rooms in this bed-and-breakfast boast antique oak and cherry furniture, king- or queen-size beds, private baths (three with claw-foot tubs), TVs and fireplaces. Terrycloth bathrobes and a basket of toiletries in the bathrooms are a nice touch. Homey Old West touches include a wraparound porch, quilt bedspreads, hardwood floors, Southwestern rugs, log cabin–style walls and leather breakfast plates. To get here turn east from Grand Canyon Blvd onto Edison Ave (three blocks north of the tracks), then left on Airport Rd. Drive one block, then turn right onto Rodeo Rd. Terry Ranch is just past the tracks, on the corner of Rodeo and Quarter Horse St.

Red Garter Bed & Bakery (☎ *928-635-9371, 800-482-3955;* W *www.red garter.com; 137 W Railroad Ave; 4 rooms; double $90-130)* Up until the 1940s, gambling and girls were the draw at this 1897 bordello-turned-B&B across from the tracks. The largest room was once reserved for the house's 'best gals,' who would lean out the window to flag down customers. Set back from the road, the other three rooms are smaller and less interesting, though quieter. The breakfast of cold cereal, instant oatmeal and pastries from the downstairs bakery is nothing special, and the staff isn't particularly friendly. But innkeeper John Holst grew up in Flagstaff and knows the area well. He's happy to get out a map, offer suggestions and relate the saucy history of the bordello and the town.

Fray Marcos Hotel (☎ *928-635-4010, 800-843-8724;* W *www.thetrain .com; 235 N Grand Canyon Blvd; 196 rooms; double $120)* This sprawling hotel caters primarily to passengers heading to the rim on the Grand Canyon Railway. While the spacious lobby, with a flagstone fireplace and painting of the canyon, hints at the elegance of days past, the Southwestern-style rooms are what you'd expect at any standard hotel. A lounge serves simple meals, and an adjacent restaurant serves breakfast, lunch and dinner. You'll also find a fitness room, pool and hot tub. Ask about room/railway packages (see Riding the Rails, p183).

PLACES TO EAT

If you're looking for a good meal, head to Flagstaff. But if all you want is a decent place to grab a bite, several restaurants in Williams feed and entertain the tourist crowd.

Pine Country Restaurant (☎ *928-635-9718; 107 N Grand Canyon Blvd; entrées $5-11; open 7am-10pm)* This family restaurant offers reasonably priced American basics and delicious pies. Though the menu offers few surprises, the food is good, and the price is right.

Pancho McGillicuddy's Mexican Cantina (☎ *928-635-4150; 141 W Railroad Ave; entrées $7-14; open 11am-10pm)* Directly across from the train station, this bustling spot is popular with hungry passengers. Don't expect great Mexican food, as the kitchen cooks for the palate of Midwestern tourists, but it's a lively place to hang out. The restaurant is housed in an 1893 tavern, and musicians perform on the outdoor patio on summer evenings.

Rod's Steak House (☎ *928-635-2671; 301 E Rte 66; entrées $8-23; open 11:30am-9:30pm)* Locals say the service here depends on owner Stella's mood, so don't rely on service with a smile. The food, however, is consistently good. The cow-shaped sign and menus spell things out – if you want a steak and potato, this is the place to come. They've been staples since the restaurant opened in 1946, though there are a few non-cow items on the menu.

Cruisers Café 66 *(☎ 928-635-2445; 233 W Rte 66; entrées $6-17; open 3-10pm)* Housed in an old Route 66 gas station, with photos of gas stations on the walls and meals served on a hubcap, this café is a fun place for kids. Expect the usual diner fare, such as burgers and grilled cheese, as well as more elaborate entrées, like mesquite-grilled ribs (cooked on the outdoor patio). In summer you can sit outside and enjoy live music.

Grand Canyon Café *(☎ 928-635-1255; 125 W Rte 66; entrées $4-7; 8am-3pm & 5pm-8pm Mon-Fri, 8am-2pm Sat)* A good choice for a quick meal, this small fast-food café serves an eclectic mix. You can order a South Rim (ham and cheese) and other canyon-themed sandwiches or choose such Far Eastern offerings as chow mein or fried rice.

ENTERTAINMENT

Stop by the quirky **World Famous Sultana Bar** *(☎ 928-635-2021; 301 W Old Rte 66; open 10am-1am)* for a beer and a game of pool. Expect the once-over when you walk in – they don't see many tourists here.

GETTING THERE & AROUND

Greyhound *(☎ 928-635-0870, 800-229-9424; W www.greyhound.com)* stops at the Chevron gas station at 1050 N Grand Canyon Blvd. **Amtrak** *(☎ 800-872-7245; W www.amtrak.com)* stops on the outskirts of town. **Open Road** *(☎ 928-226-8060, 800-766-7117)* offers two shuttles a day to the canyon ($10) and to Flagstaff ($10), as well as a connecting shuttle from Flagstaff to Phoenix Sky Harbor International Airport ($30).

DETOUR: GRAND FALLS

The Grand Falls give an insight into Southwestern hydrography. The Little Colorado River is a minor tributary of the Colorado, and like many Arizonan rivers, it is nearly dry for much of the year. During spring runoff, however, the river swells, and the Grand Falls come into being. The 185ft drop is impressive, with muddy-brown spray giving the falls their local nickname of 'Chocolate Falls'. The best time for viewing is March and April, although earlier in the year can be good if there has been enough winter precipitation. Occasional summer storms will also fill the falls.

The falls are on the Navajo Reservation. Drive 14 miles east of Flagstaff along I-40 to the Winona exit, then backtrack northwest about 2 miles to Leupp Rd. Head northeast on Leupp Rd for 13 miles to the signed turn for Grand Falls. An unpaved road, passable by car, leads 10 miles to the river and a quarter-mile trail goes to a falls overlook. The Navajo tribe allows free access to the falls, where there are basic picnic facilities.

Flagstaff

MAP 11 • TEL 928 • POPULATION 60,000 • ELEVATION 7000FT

People come to Flagstaff for many reasons – to attend Northern Arizona University, to break up an interstate jaunt or perhaps to stay while visiting the South Rim. Many end up moving here – that's the kind of place it is. With a pedestrian-friendly historic downtown, lots of great restaurants, fun brewpubs, leisurely coffeehouses, interesting hotels, fantastic scenery and proximity to myriad outdoor activities, Flagstaff is a wonderful city, well worth a few days before or after a trip to the canyon.

ORIENTATION & INFORMATION

Approaching Flagstaff from the east, I-40 parallels Old Route 66. Their paths diverge at Enterprise Rd – I-40 veers southwest, while Old Route 66 curls northwest, hugging the railroad tracks, and is the main drag through the historic downtown. Northern Arizona University sits between downtown and I-40. From downtown, I-17 heads south toward Phoenix, splitting off at Hwy 89A, a scenic winding road through Oak Creek Canyon to Sedona. Hwy 180 is the most direct route northwest to Tusayan and the South Rim (80 miles), while Hwy 89 beelines north to Cameron (59 miles), where it meets Hwy 64 west to the canyon's East Entrance. Those headed to the North Rim (193 miles) stay on Hwy 89 past Cameron, linking up with Alt 89 to Jacob Lake, then Hwy 67 to the rim.

You'll find the **visitors center** *(Map 12; ☎ 928-774-9541, 800-842-7293,* Ⓦ *www.flagstaff.az.us; 1 E Rte 66; open 8am-5pm)* inside the Amtrak station. For information on hiking, biking and camping in the surrounding national forest, contact the **Coconino National Forest Supervisor's Office** *(Map 11; ☎ 928-527-3600; 2323 Greenlaw Lane; open 7:30am-4:30pm Mon-Fri).* The **USFS Peaks Ranger Station** *(Map 11; ☎ 928-526-0866; 5075 N Hwy 89; open 7:30am-4:30pm Mon-Fri)* provides information on the Mt Elden, Humphreys Peak and O'Leary Peak areas north of Flagstaff. The **Mormon Lake Ranger Station** *(☎ 928-774-1147; 4373 S Lake Mary Rd)* focuses on the area south of town.

Other services include the **library** *(Map 12; ☎ 928-774-4000; 300 W Aspen Ave),* **post office** *(Map 12; ☎ 928-779-3589; 104 N Agassiz St),* **medical center** *(Map 11; ☎ 928-779-3366; 1200 N Beaver)* and **police station** *(Map 11; ☎ 928-556-2316; SE cnr Butler & Lone Tree).*

SIGHTS

The various museums and sights in and around Flagstaff are all interesting and well worth a visit.

Riordan Mansion State Historic Park

Centered on a beautiful 13,000-sq-ft mansion, this **park** *(Map 11; ☎ 928-779-4395; 409 Riordan Rd;* Ⓦ *www.pr.state.az.us; admission $5; open 8:30am-5pm May-Oct, 10:30am-5pm Nov-Apr)* is a must for anyone interested in the Arts & Crafts movement. Having made a fortune from their Arizona Lumber Company, brothers Michael and Timothy Riordan had the house built in 1904. The craftsman-style design was the brainchild of Atchison,

Topeka & Santa Fe Railway architect Charles Whittlesey, who also designed El Tovar, on the South Rim. The exterior features hand-split wooden shingles, log-slab siding and rustic stone. Filled with Edison, Stickley, Tiffany and Steinway furniture, the interior is a shrine to Arts & Crafts and looks much as it did when the Riordans lived here. Visitors are welcome to walk the grounds and picnic, but entrance to the house is by guided tour only. Tours leave daily and on the hour; advance reservations are accepted. The visitors center offers a good selection of books on the Arts & Crafts movement, as well as exhibits on Flagstaff's history and architecture.

The Arboretum

More than just an attraction for gardeners and plant lovers, this 200-acre **arboretum** (☎ 928-774-1442; 4001 S Woody Mountain Rd; W www.thearb .org; admission $4; open 9am-5:15pm Apr-Dec, closed mid-Dec–Mar 31) is a lovely spot to take a break and rejuvenate your spirit. Two short wood-chip trails hug a meadow and wind beneath ponderosa pines, passing an herb garden, native plants, vegetables and wildflowers, among other growing things. Plan a picnic at one of the tables scattered throughout the gardens. The arboretum offers tours (11am to 1pm), as well as a summer adventure program for children ages four to 12.

Lowell Observatory

Atop the aptly named Mars Hill a mile west of downtown, this **national historic landmark** (Map 11; ☎ 928-774-3358; W www.lowell.edu; 1400 W Mars Hill Rd; admission $4; open 9am-5pm Apr-Oct, noon-5pm Nov-Mar) was built in 1894 by Percival Lowell. In 1896 Lowell bought a 24-inch Clark refractor telescope for $20,000 ($6 million in today's dollars) and spent the next 20 years looking for life on Mars. Though he never did spot a Martian, the observatory has witnessed many important discoveries, the most famous of which was the first sighting of Pluto, in 1930. In the '60s NASA used the Clark telescope to map the moon. Weather permitting, visitors can stargaze through the telescope (8pm Monday to Saturday June to August, varying times the rest of the year). The short, paved Pluto Walk climbs through a scale model of our solar system, providing descriptions of each planet. You can stroll the grounds and museum on your own, but the only way to see the telescopes is on a tour (10am, 1pm and 3pm in summer; 1pm and 3pm in winter). Even those with a passing interest in astronomy will enjoy the tours, as guides do a great job of explaining things in everyday terms.

Museum of Northern Arizona

If you have time for only one sight in Flagstaff, come here. In an attractive craftsman-style stone building amid a pine grove, this small but excellent **museum** (Map 11; ☎ 928-774-5213; W www.musnaz.org; 3001 N Fort Valley Rd; $5; open 9am-5pm) features exhibits on local Indian archaeology, history and customs, as well as geology, biology and the arts. Don't miss the wonderful collection of Hopi katsina (the museum's spelling for 'kachina') dolls and a lovely display of Native American basketry and ceramics. The bookstore specializes in regional subjects. Check the website for information on changing exhibits, weekend craft demonstrations and one- to three-day workshops for children and adults. The museum also offers customized trips to the Grand Canyon (see Classes & Learning Vacations, p52).

Pioneer Museum & Center for the Arts

Housed in the old 1908 county hospital, the **Pioneer Museum** *(Map 11; ☎ 928-774-6272; 2340 N Fort Valley Rd; 9am-5pm Mon-Sat)* preserves Flagstaff's early history in photographs and an eclectic mix of memorabilia – for example, a 1920s-era permanent-wave machine (for curling hair) that looks more like a science-fiction torture device.

Behind the museum, the **Coconino Center for the Arts** *(☎ 928-779-2300)* exhibits work by local artists and hosts various performances and programs. The adjacent **Art Barn** *(☎ 928-774-0822)* has been displaying and selling local artisans' work for three decades. Here you'll find a good selection of jewelry, photography, painting, pottery and kachina dolls, among other objects. Hours at both venues vary.

Sunset Crater Volcano National Monument & Wupatki National Monument

In AD 1064 a volcano erupted on this spot, spewing ash across 800 sq miles, spawning the Kana-A lava flow and leaving behind 8029ft **Sunset Crater**. The eruption forced farmers to vacate lands they had cultivated for 400 years. Subsequent eruptions continued for more than 200 years. The visitor center *(☎ 928-526-0502; W www.nps.gov/sucr; open 8am-6pm)* houses a seismograph and other exhibits pertaining to volcanology, while viewpoints and a 1-mile interpretive trail through the **Bonito lava flow** (formed ca 1180) grant visitors a firsthand look at volcanic features. A shorter 0.3-mile loop is wheelchair accessible. You can also climb **Lenox Crater** (7024ft), a 1-mile round-trip that climbs 300ft. More ambitious hikers and mountain bikers can ascend **O'Leary Peak** (8965ft; 8 miles round-trip), the only way to peer down into Sunset Crater (aside from scenic flights).

The first eruptions enriched the surrounding soil, and ancestors of today's Hopi, Zuni and Navajo Indians returned to farm the land in the early 1100s. By 1180 thousands were living here in advanced, multistory buildings, but by 1250 their pueblos stood abandoned. About 2700 of these structures lie within **Wupatki National Monument** *(☎ 928-679-2365; W www.nps.gov/wupa; HC33, Box 444A, Flagstaff, AZ 86004; open 8am-6pm)*, though only a few are open to the public. A short, self-guided tour of the largest dwelling, **Wupatki Pueblo**, begins behind the visitors center. **Lamaki**, **Citadel** and **Nalakihu Pueblos** sit within a half-mile of the loop road just north of the visitors center, and a 2.5-mile road veers west from the center to **Wukoki Pueblo**, the best preserved of the buildings. In April and October rangers lead visitors on a 16-mile round-trip weekend backpacking tour ($50; supply your own food and gear) of **Crack-in-Rock Pueblo** and nearby petroglyphs. Chosen by lottery, only 13 people may join each tour; apply two months in advance via the website or in writing.

Covered by a single $5 entrance fee, both monuments lay along Park Loop Rd 545, a well-marked 36-mile loop that heads east off Hwy 89 about 12 miles north of Flagstaff then rejoins the highway 26 miles north of Flagstaff.

Visitors can choose from among several picnic grounds. Rangers offer interpretive programs in summer.

Walnut Canyon National Monument

The Sinagua cliff dwellings at Walnut Canyon (☎ 928-526-3367; W www.nps.gov/waca; admission $3; open 9am-6pm) are set in the nearly vertical walls of a small limestone butte amid this forested canyon. The mile-long **Island Trail** steeply descends 185ft (more than 200 stairs), passing 25 rooms. A shorter, wheelchair-accessible **Rim Trail** affords several views from a distance.

Meteor Crater

A huge meteor crashed into our planet almost 50,000 years ago and produced this crater, which is 570ft deep and almost a mile across. It was used as a training ground for some of the Apollo astronauts; the on-site museum has exhibits about meteors and space missions. Descending into the crater is not allowed, but you can walk the 3.5-mile Rim Trail. However, apart from a big hole in the ground, there's not much to see, and some readers suggest that it is an overpriced attraction.

The **crater** (☎ 928-289-2362, 800-289-5898; W www.meteorcrater.com) is privately owned and operated, and national park passes are not accepted. Hours are 6am to 6pm mid-May to mid-September, and 8am to 5pm the rest of the year. Admission is $12 for adults and $6 for six- to 17-year-olds.

Meteor Crater RV Park (☎ 800-478-4002) has 71 RV sites with hookups for $20. Showers, coin laundry, a playground, a coffee shop and groceries are available.

ACTIVITIES
Hiking & Biking

Ask at the USFS ranger stations for maps and information about the scores of hiking and mountain biking trails in and around Flagstaff. Another useful resource is *Flagstaff Hikes & Mountain Bike Rides*, by Richard and Sherry Mangum, available at the visitors center, La Bellavia restaurant (p194) and Babbit's Backcountry Outfitter (see Shopping, p198), among other places.

Consider tackling the steep, 3-mile one-way hike up 9299ft **Mt Elden**. Arizona Snowbowl offers several trails, including the strenuous 4.5-mile one-way hike up 12,633ft **Humphreys Peak**, the highest point in Arizona; wear decent boots, as sections of the trail cross crumbly volcanic rock. In summer ride the **scenic chairlift** at Arizona Snowbowl to 11,500ft *(adult/child $9/5; open daily 10am-4pm Jun-Aug, Fri-Sun only through mid-Oct)*, where you can hike, eat lunch on the Agassiz Deck and take in the desert and mountain views. Children under 7 ride for free.

Skiing

The **Arizona Snowbowl** (☎ 928-779-1951; adult/child $40/22) is small but lofty, with four lifts that service 30 runs between 9200ft and 11,500ft. You can cross-country ski along 30 groomed trails at the **Flagstaff Nordic Center** (☎ 928-779-1951; $10; Hwy 180, 15 miles north of Flagstaff), which offers lessons, rentals and food. Past the Nordic Center off Hwy 180, you'll find plenty of USFS cross-country skiing pullouts, where you can park and ski for free.

Rock Climbing
Vertical Relief Rock Climbing (*Map 12; ☎ 928-556-9909; 205 S San Francisco St; 10am-11pm Mon-Fri, noon-8pm Sat-Sun*) provides 6000 sq ft of artificial indoor climbing walls. Routes range from beginner to the most difficult grades. The center also offers classes and information on nearby climbs.

Horseback Riding
MacDonalds Ranch (*☎ 928-774-4481; W www.macdonaldsranch.com*) offers one- or two-hour guided trail rides and hay rides through Coconino National Forest at Arizona Snowbowl. **Hitchin' Post Stables** (*☎ 928-774-1719; 4848 Lake Mary Rd*) offers trail rides to Walnut Canyon and other destinations upon request. **Horse-drawn carriage** rides depart from Heritage Square on summer weekend evenings.

Fishing
Fly-fishing opportunities abound in Oak Creek and the lakes surrounding Flagstaff and Williams. **Babbit's Fly-Fishing** (*☎ 928-779-3253; 15 E Aspen Ave; 10am-6pm Mon-Fri, 10am-4pm Sun*) and **Peace Surplus** (see Shopping, p198) provide information and equipment. Babbits offers guided trips.

Swimming
The kid-friendly pool at **Flagstaff Athletic Club East** (*Map 11; ☎ 928-526-8652; 3200 N Country Club Dr; open 5am-7pm*) includes a children's play area with a mushroom fountain, as well as swimming lanes for adults. It costs $5 per person to use the pool (lockers and changing rooms are available); for $12 per person you can use the indoor pool, tennis courts, gym, sauna and other club facilities.

PLACES TO STAY
Camping
Free dispersed camping is permitted in the national forest surrounding Flagstaff.

Woody Mountain Campground (*☎ 928-774-7727; 2727 W Rte 66; 146 sites; tent/RV $18/23; open Mar-Oct*) offers a pool, playground and coin laundry. **Fort Tuthill County Park** (*☎ 928-774-3464, 774-5130; exit 337 off I-17; tent/RV $9/13; closed Oct-Apr*) sits 5 miles south of downtown. It has 100 family sites with water and sewer only, and 150 group sites without utilities. One of the biggest campgrounds, **Flagstaff KOA** (*☎ 928-526-9926; 5803 N Hwy 89; 201 sites; tent/RV $21/27; open year-round*) lies a mile north of I-40 off exit 201, 5 miles northeast of downtown. Across from the Sunset Crater Volcano National Monument visitors center (p190), the USFS-run **Bonito Campground** (*☎ 928-526-0866; 43 sites; $10; closed Oct-May*) provides running water and restrooms but no showers or hookups.

✔ **TIP**

If you've forgotten basics like shampoo or a toothbrush, the only convenience store in the historic downtown is the Pay 'n' Take (p195), on Aspen Avenue.

See Sedona, Places to Stay (p201), for information about USFS campgrounds in Oak Creek Canyon, 15 to 30 miles south of town.

Budget

Dozens of nondescript, independent motels, with rates ranging from $30 to $50 line Old Route 66 and the railroad tracks east of downtown (exit 198 off I-40). Check the room before you pay – some are worse than others, and many are loud. You're better off at one of the hostels or historic hotels downtown.

Hostels

Sharing the same owner, the independent **Grand Canyon International Hostel** (Map 12; ☎ 928-779-9421, 888-442-2696; 19 S San Francisco St; dorm/double $16-19/$34-37) and **Dubeau International Hostel** (Map 12; ☎ 928-774-6731; 19 W Phoenix Ave; dorm/double $16-19/$34-37) offer budget travelers friendly service and clean, well-run accommodations. Guests can choose either dorms (four-person maximum at the Grand Canyon Hostel) or private doubles with shared bathrooms; rates include breakfast. Internet access ($2 for 30 minutes), kitchens and laundry facilities are available. Housed in a historic building with hardwood floors and Southwestern decor, the Grand Canyon Hostel provides a TV room with a VCR. The Dubeau offers a nonsmoking lounge with a fireplace, as well as a jukebox, foosball and a pool table; consequently, it can be a bit loud. For information on either hostel, visit Ⓦ www.grandcanyonhostel.com.

Mid-range

Chain motels line Milton Road (exit 196 off I-40) and cluster around exit 198 off I-40.

Weatherford Hotel (Map 12; ☎ 928-779-1919; Ⓦ www.weatherfordhotel .com; 23 N Leroux St; weekday/weekend $55/61) This historic three-story brick hotel offers eight small, pleasant rooms, five with private baths and all with a turn-of-the-20th-century feel. Hosting two bars and live music (p197), this can be a loud place – if you need silence in the evening, consider staying elsewhere. The third-floor **Zane Grey Room** welcomes hotel guests and visitors with an 1882 bar, a fireplace and an original Thomas Moran painting. Perch along the adjoining wraparound verandah with a drink, admire the distant San Francisco Peaks, and watch passersby on the busy streets below.

Monte Vista (Map 12; ☎ 928-779-3631, 800-545-3068; Ⓦ www.hotel-montevista.com; 100 N San Francisco St; double/suite $50/120) A huge neon sign towers over the roof of this classic 1926 hotel. Feather lampshades, antique furniture, bold colors (just try to find a plain white wall) and eclectic decor lend each room its own personality, and many are named for movie stars who slept in them. The Humphrey Bogart room features black-satin bedding, black walls and a yellow ceiling, while the Jane Russell room flaunts a red rug, red walls and a chair in the shape of a high-heeled shoe. In the late '70s a woman died in the rocking chair of the Bon Jovi room and is said to haunt the room. Creepier still is the Gary Cooper room, supposedly haunted by two prostitutes who were stabbed and thrown out its window in the 1930s. The hotel houses a basement bar (deep enough to keep noise to a minimum), a restaurant and an adjoining Aveda spa. Rates are $10 to $20 more on weekends, less when things are slow.

Top End

Little America Motel *(Map 11;* ☎ *928-779-7900, 800-865-1401;* W *www.little america.com; 2515 E Butler Ave; double/suite $100/150)* When you reach the adjacent truck stop, don't drive away thinking you have the wrong place. Behind an unassuming exterior is a wonderful hotel with an elegant lobby and spacious rooms, which are beautifully appointed with faux antique furniture, goose-down pillows and rich bedding, refrigerators and large bathrooms. Small patios in each room open on 500 acres of grass and woods, with a playground and a pool with a small bar. Other amenities include room service, a coffee shop and an upscale restaurant. This oasis in the most unexpected of places, minutes from downtown, is great for families.

Comfi Cottages *(*☎ *928-774-0731, 888-774-0731;* W *www.comficottages com; 8 bungalows; $105-260)* If you're tired of hotels and motels, consider these bungalows, which are spread out in residential areas around town and all less than a mile from the historic district. Most were built in the 1920s and '30s and have a homey old feel to them, with wood floors, Arts & Crafts kitchens and little lawns. Cabinets are filled with breakfast foods, and each cottage includes a TV, VCR, telephone, bicycles, tennis rackets, a barbecue grill, a picnic table and picnic baskets. The smallest cottage has one bedroom and one bath, while the largest has four bedrooms and four baths.

ROMANTIC ROOMS

✔ Inn at 410 (Flagstaff, p194)
✔ Briar Patch Inn (Sedona, p202)
✔ Garland's Oak Creek Lodge (Sedona, p202)

Inn at 410 *(Map 12;* ☎ *928-774-0088, 800-774-2008;* W *www.inn410 .com; 410 N Leroux St; 9 rooms; $135-190)* This elegant and fully renovated 1894 house offers spacious, beautifully decorated bedrooms, each with a refrigerator and private bath, most with a fireplace or whirlpool and many with four-poster beds and garden views. Rates include a full gourmet breakfast and afternoon snack.

Marriott Residence Inn *(Map 11;* ☎ *928-526-5555, 800-331-3131;* W *www .marriott.com; 3440 N Country Club Dr; studio suite/2-room suite $109-169/$169-219)* The peaceful location and spacious, apartment-like rooms with fully equipped kitchens, laundry facilities and complimentary continental breakfast set this apart from other chain-motel rooms. Rooms out back open on fields and a picnic area.

PLACES TO EAT

Of all the towns in the region, Flagstaff offers the best restaurants. The food is better than anything in nearby Williams and is often more reasonably priced than meals in upscale Sedona. Arizona State University influences the food scene here (as it does everything else), and you'll find several great coffee shops and brewpubs.

Budget

La Bellavia *(Map 12;* ☎ *928-774-8301; 18 S Beaver St; entrées $3-8; open 6:30am-9pm)* Be prepared to wait in line at this popular breakfast spot. The seven-grain French toast with bananas, apples or blueberries is excellent. In addition to the standard eggs Benedict, you'll find eight English muffin/ poached egg dishes, including eggs José (green chilies, tomatoes and Muenster cheese), eggs Sardo (sautéed spinach and artichoke hearts) and eggs California Benedict (smoked turkey and avocado). If you're lucky, one of the few tables outside will be free. Lunch includes a grilled portobello-mushroom sandwich and a grilled salmon salad, as well as standard options like grilled cheese, burgers and a tuna melt. Credit cards are not accepted.

Macy's *(Map 12;* ☎ *928-774-2243; 14 S Beaver St; up to $6.25; open 7am-10pm)* Two doors down from La Bellavia, this crunchy café caters to the vegan/vegetarian crowd. (A coin laundry lies between the two restaurants, so you can pop in a load and relax with your latte and book). Bob Dylan music plays from the speakers while patrons sit around wooden tables chatting, reading or typing at computers. 'Wheat free Wednesday' gives you an idea of what kind of food you'll find here. Choices include tofu hot dogs, hummus, seitan and baked tofu. There's also a bit of the usual fare, like pastries, scrambled eggs, yogurt and granola. On late afternoons and evenings, the café presents live music, including Tuesday folk funk, Saturday Celtic and Friday jazz. Monday is chess-club night. Credit cards are not accepted.

Café Espress *(Map 12;* ☎ *928-774-0541; 16 N San Francisco St; entrées $5-8; open 7am-5pm Sun-Thu, 7am-9pm Fri-Sat)* A sunny, bright café offering coffee and tea drinks, pastries, smoothies and fresh-squeezed juices, this is a great choice for breakfast, lunch or dinner. There's something here for everyone, from the spinach pesto tofu scramble and Italian vegetable frittata to corned beef hash and biscuits and gravy. One order of blueberry wholegrain pancakes is big enough to satisfy two hungry adults. The lunch and dinner menus are equally eclectic, including mahi-mahi tacos, salmon BLTs, turkey burgers and black bean–chicken salad.

Kathy's Café *(Map 12;* ☎ *928-774-1951; 7 N San Francisco St; entrées $4-6.50; open 6:30am-3pm)* This low-key coffee shop is a dependable choice for classic diner fare. Options include omelets (spice things up a bit by adding chorizo, avocado, green chili or crab) and grilled ham and cheese, as well as such twists as a Navajo taco and a tofu stir-fry.

Black Bean Burrito Bar *(Map 12;* ☎ *928-779-9905; 12 E Rte 66; entrées $4-8; open 11am-9pm)* If you're hungry, head to this tiny spot for a massive burrito wrapped in foil. Sure, you can get a beef and bean burrito, but why go for the standard when you can try a steamed vegetable or Thai peanut tofu burrito? Choose from six different salsas, take your plastic basket to the counter and chow down while you people-watch.

Martans Burrito Palace *(Map 12;* ☎ *928-773-4701; 10 N San Francisco St; entrées $4-8; open 8am-2pm Mon-Fri, 8:30am-1pm Sun)* This local-favorite hole-in-the-wall specializes in chilaquiles (scrambled eggs, red enchilada sauce, cheese and onions on a tortilla). Just about everyone in town recommends it for quick, tasty, low-key Mexican.

Cold Stone Creamery *(Map 12;* ☎ *928-214-8440; open 1-9pm Mon-Thu, noon-10pm Fri-Sat, noon-9pm Sun)* Better than your standard ice-cream store, this popular spot offers all kinds of treats, from gummy bears and brownies to fruit, which are then folded into your ice cream.

Pay 'n' Take *(Map 12; ☎ 928-226-8595; 12 W Aspen Ave; open 7am-10pm Mon-Wed, 7am-1am Thu-Sat, 9am-10pm Sun)* More a convenience store than a restaurant, this low-key local institution is a great place to kick back with a beer or a cup of coffee. Help yourself to whatever you'd like from the wall refrigerators, and eat at one of the few small round tables. If you prefer, have a pizza delivered to the store, or bring in takeout from the Thai restaurant down the street. Folks here are always happy to shoot the breeze, and the small bar serves coffee drinks as well as beer and wine.

Mid-range

Dara Thai *(Map 12; ☎ 928-774-0047; 14 S San Francisco St; entrées $7-13; open 11am-10pm Mon-Sat, noon-9pm Sun)* Plants and wooden booths give this low-key Thai spot a comfortable feel. To suit every taste, food is available in spice levels, from one to five. The service is friendly, and the food consistently good, with clean flavors and large portions. Consider ordering a selection of appetizers – deep-fried banana slices dipped in tempura batter; lime, ginger, peanut and toasted coconut wrapped in spinach leaves with brown-sugar dip; or chicken satay (marinated in yellow curry) with peanut sauce and cucumber dip.

Racha Thai *(Map 12; ☎ 928-774-3003; 104 N San Francisco St; entrées $7-13; open 11am-3:30pm Tue-Sat, 4:30-9pm Tue-Thu & Sun, 4:30-10pm Fri-Sat)* Though it doesn't have the warm feel of Dara Thai, Racha Thai serves delicious food in a casual setting. Locals argue which Thai restaurant is better, but it's really splitting hairs. They're both very good. Perhaps the best way to decide is to let your stomach lead the way – they are on opposite sides of the track. Be prepared for hot stuff if you order spice level five.

Café Olé *(Map 12; ☎ 928-774-8272; 119 S San Francisco St; entrées $5-11; open 5-9pm Tue-Sat)* For some of the best Mexican food in the region, stop by this brightly colored joint (think chili-pepper strings and wall murals). It's a friendly, family-run place – the Aguinaga family has been perfecting their recipes for more than a decade. The food veers towards New Mexican–style, featuring green and red chili sauce, and everything is fresh and healthy (no lard in the beans; minimal frying). For spice lovers, this is some Mexican food with a real kick.

Pasto *(Map 12; ☎ 928-779-1937; 19 E Aspen Ave; entrées $8-16; open 5-10pm)* An excellent option for Italian, cozy Pasto serves dinner only. This is not your run-of-the-mill bland, heavy Italian – dishes here are hearty, fresh, creative and full of flavor. The rear outdoor patio is an intimate spot for a quiet meal.

Monsoon on the Rim *(Map 12; ☎ 928-226-8844; 6 E Aspen Ave; entrées $6-8; open 11:30am-9pm)* Offering good food, patio dining and a large, modern interior just off Heritage Square, Monsoon is busy with tourists and locals alike. The limited menu features Chinese standards (kung pao chicken, ginger beef etc), but you can also get a turkey, teriyaki or Asian burger – thinly sliced vegetables replace fries. Available à la carte, the sushi is pretty tasty. Look for interesting daily specials.

Beaver Street Brewery *(Map 12; ☎ 928-779-0079; 11 S Beaver St; entrées $5-12; open 11am-10pm)* Very popular for its microbrewery (five handmade ales are usually on tap) and delicious pizzas, burgers and salads, Beaver Street packs in the families, businessmen, outdoorsy types and students – just about everyone.

Fratelli Pizza *(Map 12; ☎ 928-774-9200; 112 E Rte 66; entrées $6-16; open 11am-10pm Sun-Thu, 11am-2am Fri-Sat)* Except for a small counter along the window, there's nowhere to sit at this tiny takeout and delivery pizza joint. Sauce choices include red, barbecue, pesto and white (olive oil with garlic, basil and oregano), and toppings range from standard pepperoni to grilled chicken, walnuts, artichoke hearts and cucumber. There are lots of pizza places in town, but this is consistently voted the best, is close to downtown and offers the option of a slice to go ($1.80).

Buster's *(Map 11; ☎ 928-774-5155; 1800 Milton Rd; entrées $8-21; open 11:30am-10pm)* Locals recommend this place as an old standby. The food is always good, and it boasts Flagstaff's best fresh-seafood selections. Hang out at the oyster bar with a cold beer.

New Frontiers Natural Foods & Deli *(Map 11; ☎ 928-774-5747; 1000 S Milton Rd; entrées $5-8; open 8am-8pm)* A good place to shop for a picnic, this deli makes great salads and sandwiches. The menu leans toward 'healthy,' including turkey breast, hot dogs on whole-wheat buns, falafel and tempeh burgers. You can also get good smoothies and organic juices.

Top End

Josephine's *(Map 12; ☎ 928-779-3400; W www.josephinesrestaurant.com; 503 N Humphreys St; entrées $15.50-18.50; open 11am-2:30pm & 5:30-9pm Mon-Sat)* Occupying a 1911 Arts & Crafts bungalow, this restaurant offers a creative and eclectic menu, fresh ingredients and pleasant patio dining (though Humphreys St is a bit loud). Inside you'll find a great old stone bar, fireplace, craftsman light fixtures and dining tables in each room (including upstairs). It feels more like someone's home than a restaurant. Dinner features such dishes as seared ahi tuna with ginger mango salsa and cilantro rice; tortilla-encrusted halibut; and lemon-tarragon roasted chicken. Though a bit pricey, it's a good option for an upscale meal. Consider stopping for lunch – crab cakes, pecan-encrusted fish tacos and a turkey and Brie sandwich are welcome changes from typical lunch fare. They also have a good salad selection and an extensive wine list.

ENTERTAINMENT

Flagstaff hosts all sorts of festivals and music programs – call the visitor center or log on to its website for details. On summer weekends, people gather on blankets for fun evenings at Heritage Square. Live music (folk, Celtic, children's etc) starts at 6:30pm, followed at 9pm by a movie projected on an adjacent building. Various activities keep kids entertained until the film starts.

Flagstaff Symphony Orchestra *(☎ 928-523-5661, 888-520-7214; W www.flagstaffsymphony.org)* holds eight annual performances in the Ardrey Auditorium, on the NAU campus.

Several downtown bars present live music. In the Weatherford Hotel (p21), **Charly's** fireplace and brick walls offer a cozy setting in which to hear blues (Mondays), jazz, folk and other genres. Head upstairs to stroll the verandah outside the popular **Zane Grey Room**, which overlooks the historic district. In the Monte Vista Hotel (p21), the hopping **Monte Vista Lounge** hosts DJs most nights, and on weekends welcomes diverse bands, from country to hip-hop to rock. Popular with students and outdoorsy types,

the **Flagstaff Brewing Co** *(Map 12; ☎ 928-773-1442;* W *www.flagbrew.com; 16 E Rte 66; open 11am-1am)* and **Mogollon Brewing Co** *(Map 12; ☎ 928-773-8950;* W *www.mogollonbrewing.com; 15 N Agassiz St; open 3pm-12:30am Mon-Fri, noon-12:30am Sat-Sun)* serve up handcrafted beer and a variety of live music. Housed in a 1931 taxidermy museum (hence its nickname, 'The Zoo'), the log cabin–style **Museum Club** *(☎ 928-526-9434;* W *www .museumclub.com; 3404 E Rte 66)* has been a nightclub since 1936. Today, its cowboy spirit, country music and spacious wooden dance floor attract a lively crowd. The Zoo also provides free taxi service home.

If you're just after a game of pool and a beer (great selection), head to the smoke-free **Uptown Billiards** *(Map 12; ☎ 928-773-0551; 114 N Leroux St; open 1pm-1am Mon-Sat, 3-11pm Sun)*.

SHOPPING

For Native American crafts and an excellent selection of books on regional topics, stop by **Painted Desert Trading Co** *(Map 12; ☎ 928-226-8313; 2 N San Francisco St; open 10am-6pm Mon-Sat, noon-5pm Sun)*. The smaller **Puchteca Indian Art** *(Map 12; ☎ 928-774-2414; 20 N San Francisco St; 9am-5:30pm Mon-Sat, 10am-4pm Sun)* specializes in Hopi pottery and jewelry. **Old Town Shops** *(Map 12; 120 N Leroux St)* is a cluster of several independent stores, including a wine shop and a soap-and-bath store.

For books on regional hiking, biking, skiing and camping, as well as gear, clothing, rentals and USGS maps, stop by **Babbits Backcountry Outfitter** *(Map 12; ☎ 928-774-4775; 12 E Aspen Ave; open 10am-6pm Mon-Sat, noon-5pm Sun)* or **Peace Surplus** *(Map 12; ☎ 928-779-4521;* W *www.peacesurplus .com; 14 W Rte 66; open 8am-9pm Mon-Fri, 8am-8pm Sat, 8am-6pm Sun)*.

AROUND THE GRAND CANYON

The smaller **Mountain Sports** *(Map 12; ☎ 928-226-2885; 24 N San Francisco St; open 10am-7pm Mon-Sat)* sells clothes and regional books. **Northern Arizona University Bookstore** *(Map 11; ☎ 800-426-7674; W www.book store@nau.edu; S San Francisco St at Mountain View Dr; open 8am-6pm Mon-Thu, 8am-5pm Fri, 10am-4pm Sat, closed Sun)* offers one of the best selections of books about Native Americans and the region, as well as field guides and children's books.

Children love browsing through classic and educational toys at **Golden Aspen Toy & Candy Shop** *(Map 12; ☎ 928-556-3043; 3 E Aspen Ave; open 10am-7pm Mon-Fri, 10am-8pm Sat, 8am-7pm Sun)*, and parents may find a few things to keep little ones busy in the car.

GETTING THERE

Flagstaff Pulliam Airport is 4 miles south of town off I-17. **America West Express** *(☎ 800-235-9292; W www.americawest.com)* offers several daily flights from Phoenix Sky Harbor International Airport. **Greyhound** *(Map 12 ☎ 928-774-4573, 800-229-9424; W www.greyhound.com; 399 S Malpais Lane)* stops in Flagstaff en route to/from Albuquerque, Las Vegas, Los Angeles and Phoenix. **Open Road Tours** *(☎ 928-226-8060, 877-226-8060; W www.openroadtours.com)* offers shuttles to the Grand Canyon ($20 one-way, with a stop at Williams) and Phoenix Sky Harbor (one-way/round-trip $31/56).

Operated by **Amtrak** *(☎ 928-774-8679, 800-872-7245; W www.amtrak .com)*, the *Southwest Chief* stops at Flagstaff on its daily run between Chicago and Los Angeles.

GETTING AROUND

Mountain Line Transit *(☎ 928-779-6624; $0.75)* services four local bus routes Monday through Saturday; pick up a user-friendly map at the visitors center. Those with disabilities can use the company's on-call VanGo service.

Several major car rental agencies operate from the airport, including Avis, Budget, Hertz and National (see Planning, Car Rental, p74). You can also rent a car downtown through **Budget** *(Map 12; ☎ 928-213-0156; 175 W Aspen Ave)* and **Enterprise** *(☎ 928-774-9407; 100 N Humphreys St)*.

If you need a taxi, call **Friendly Cab** *(☎ 928-774-4444)* or **Sun Taxi** *(☎ 928-774-7400, 800-483-4488)*. **Absolute Bikes** *(Map 12; ☎ 928-779-5969; 18 N San Francisco St; W www.absolutebikes.net; open 9am-7pm Mon-Fri, 10am-6pm Sat, 10am-4pm Sun)* rents mountain and road bikes ($25 to $45 per day).

Sedona

MAP 14 • TEL 928 • POPULATION 16,000 • ELEVATION 4700FT

Nestled amid crimson sandstone formations at the south end of lovely Oak Creek Canyon, Sedona is popular with New Age types, who believe this area is the center of vortexes that radiate the Earth's power. The combination of scenic beauty and mysticism attracts throngs of tourists year-round. You'll find all sorts of alternative medicines and practices, from psychic channeling, past-life regression, crystal healing, shamanism and drumming workshops to more traditional massages, yoga, tai chi and acupressure. The surrounding canyons offer excellent hiking and mountain biking, and the town itself bustles with art galleries and expensive gourmet restaurants. Unlike nearby Flagstaff, Sedona's economy is almost entirely tourism driven, and in summer the traffic and the crowds in town and on the trails can be oppressive. Just be patient and let Sedona's famous beauty soothe your soul.

ORIENTATION & INFORMATION

The town's main drag is Hwy 89A, which leads south to Prescott (57 miles) and north to Flagstaff (28 miles) through Oak Creek Canyon. You'll find most of the restaurants, stores and hotels along this stretch. The north end of town is the pedestrian center, with plenty of restaurants and boutiques.

The **Sedona-Oak Creek Canyon Chamber of Commerce Visitor Center** (☎ 928-282-7722, 800-288-7336; Ⓦ www.sedonachamber.com; Forest Rd at Hwy 89A; open 8:30am-5pm Mon-Sat, 9am-3pm Sun) and the **West Gateway Visitors Center** (☎ 928-204-5818; Hwy 89A, west of hospital; open 8:30am-5pm Mon-Fri) offer oodles of information. The **Oak Creek Visitors Center** (☎ 928-203-0624; open 8am-4:30pm) is in Oak Creek Canyon, 4 miles north of town and 3 miles south of Slide Creek State Park.

Other services include a **USFS Ranger Station** (☎ 928-282-4119; 250 Brewer St; open 9am-5pm Mon-Fri), the **library** (☎ 928-282-7714; 3250 White Bear Rd), **post office** (☎ 928-282-3511; Hwy 89A at Hwy 179), **medical center** (☎ 928-204-3000; 3700 W Hwy 89A) and **police station** (☎ 928-282-3100; 100 Road Runner Rd).

A Red Rock Pass is required to park anywhere in the surrounding national forest ($5 per day, $15 per week). You can buy one at the visitors centers, Circle Ks and at some trailheads. In summer, the **ranger station** (☎ 928-525-3948; Hwy 89A, 5 miles south of Flagstaff) at Oak Creek Vista sells Red Rock Passes, hiking guides and maps.

SIGHTS
Chapel of the Holy Cross

Perched between spectacular red-rock towers, 3 miles south of town, this modern, nondenominational **chapel** (☎ 928-282-4069; open 9am-5pm) was built in 1956 by Marguerite Brunwige Staude in the tradition of Frank Lloyd Wright. There are no services.

Slide Rock State Park

Popular for picnicking and swimming, this **state park** (☎ 928-282-3034; $8 per car; open 8am-7pm Memorial Day–Labor Day, 8am-5pm Sep-May) features a natural rock chute that whisks swimmers through Oak Creek. Bring a blanket and a cooler, or buy drinks and snacks at the small park store. To avoid the long lines and entrance fee, you can park your car on the shoulder just north of the entrance and hike down to the rock chute (follow the crowds).

Red Rock State Park

This **park** (☎ 928-282-6907; $6 per car; open 8am-5pm) includes an environmental education center, a visitors center, picnic areas and 5 miles of well-marked trails in a riparian habitat amid gorgeous scenery. Ranger-led activities include nature walks, bird walks and full-moon hikes during the warmer months. While popular, it's not quite as packed as Slide Rock, as there's no place to swim.

Sedona Arts Center

The **arts center** (☎ 928-282-3809, 888-954-4442; **W** *www.sedonaartscenter .com; Hwy 89A, west of hospital; open 10am-5pm)* features changing exhibits of local and regional artists, a gift shop, classes in performing and visual arts and a variety of cultural events.

ACTIVITIES

Hiking and **mountain biking** trails crisscross the surrounding red-rock country and the woods and meadows of Oak Creek Canyon. Available at the visitors centers and ranger stations, *The Recreation Guide to Red Rock Country* describes hiking and biking trails for all skill levels and includes a map of **scenic drives**. One popular hiking trail in Oak Creek Canyon is the **West Fork Trail**, which follows the creek for 7 miles – the canyon walls rise more than 200ft in places. Wander up as far as you want, splash around and turn back when you've had enough. The trailhead lies about 3 miles north of Slide Rock, in **Call of the Canyon Recreation Area**.

Oak Creek holds several good **swimming** holes. If Slide Rock is too crowded, check out **Grasshopper Point** ($7), a few miles south. Southwest of town you can splash around and enjoy splendid views of Cathedral Rock at **Red Rock Crossing**, a USFS picnic area along a pretty stretch of Oak Creek – look for the turnoff about 2 miles west of the hospital on Hwy 89A.

For **horseback riding**, call **Trailhorse Adventures** (☎ 928-282-7252; **W** *www.trailhorseadventures.com)*, which offers one- and two-hour rides ($30/50), breakfast rides ($60) and half-day trips ($75).

PLACES TO STAY

Sedona hosts several beautiful bed-and-breakfasts, creek-side cabins and full-service resorts, but be prepared to spend a lot of money. Rates at chain motels range from $70 to $120, which is reasonable by Sedona standards. Contact the **Sedona Bed & Breakfast Guild** (**W** *www.bbsedona.net)* for lodging information and suggestions.

Camping

Dispersed camping is not permitted in Red Rock Canyon. The **USFS** (☎ 928-282-4119) runs the following campgrounds along Hwy 89A in Oak Creek Canyon (none with hookups).

Manzanita 18 sites; open year-round; 6 miles north of town
Bootlegger 10 sites; no water; 8.5 miles north
Cave Springs 82 sites; showers; 11.5 miles north
Pine Flat East and **Pine Flat West** 57 sites; 12.5 miles north

All are nestled in the woods just off the road. It costs $15 to camp, but you don't need a Red Rock Pass. Reservations are accepted for Pine Flat West and Cave Springs; call ☎ 877-444-6777.

Rancho Sedona RV Park (☎ 928-282-7255, 888-641-4261; 30 sites; 135 Bear Wallow Lane; $33-52)* includes a laundry, showers and 30 RV sites, most

IN SEARCH OF THE NEW AGE

Sedona is the foremost New Age Center in the Southwest and is one of the most important anywhere. The term 'New Age' loosely refers to a trend toward seeking alternative explanations or interpretations of what constitutes health, religion, the psyche and enlightenment. Drawing upon new and old factual and mystical traditions from around the world, New Agers often seek to transform themselves psychologically and spiritually in the hope that such personal efforts will eventually transform the world at large.

You can't miss the New Age stores in town – many of them have the word 'crystal' in their names. They sell books, crystals and various New Age paraphernalia; distribute free maps showing vortex sites; provide information; and arrange various spiritual or healing events. The **Center for the New Age** (☎ 928-282-2085; W www.sedonanewagecenter.com; 341 Hwy 179) is open daily and is a good place to start.

Sedona's offerings include mainstream services such as massage, nutrition counseling, acupressure, meditation, and yoga and tai chi classes, as well as more estoeric practices such as herbology, psychic channeling, aura photography, astrology, palmistry, tarot-card and runes readings, aromatherapy, past-life regression, crystal healing, shamanism, drumming workshops, reflexology, hypnotherapy and more.

The four best-known vortexes, or high-energy sites where the earth's power is said to be strongly felt, are in Sedona's Red Rock Mountains. These include **Bell Rock**, near the village of Oak Creek (east of Hwy 179), **Cathedral Rock**, near Red Rock Crossing, **Airport Mesa**, along Airport Rd, and **Boynton Canyon**. Local maps show these four main sites, although some individuals claim that others exist.

New Agers are generally gentle folk, but some have been criticized for performing rituals, such as chantings or offerings, in scenic areas. If you want to participate in such public rituals, please keep your vocal interactions with the planet to a peacefully personal level, pick up your offerings when you're through, and leave nothing behind but your love, energy and blessings.

with full hookups. Another option is **Hawkeye Red Rock RV Park** (☎ 928-282-2222; 40 Art Barn Rd; 43 sites; tent/RV $19-31).

Budget
Hostel Sedona (☎ 928-282-2772; 5 Soldiers Wash Dr; W www.hostelsedona .com; dorm/single/double $15/30/35) This pleasant, quiet hostel sits in the woods behind Burger King just off Hwy 89A. Tea, coffee and kitchen facilities are provided.

Mid-range
Sky Ranch Lodge (☎ 928-282-6400, 888-708-6400; W www.skyranch lodge.com; $75-159) At the top of Airport Rd, with spectacular views of the town and surrounding country, this lodge offers spacious motel rooms, six landscaped acres, and a pool and hot tub. Rates vary according to type of bed and your view. Some include balconies, fireplaces, kitchenettes and/or refrigerators. Also available are cottages ($189), with vaulted ceilings, kitchenettes and private decks. Away from the strip and its tourist hordes, this is an excellent option for reasonable accommodations.

Garland's Oak Creek Lodge *(☎ 928-282-3343; W www.garlandslodge .com; Hwy 89A, 8 miles north of Sedona; single/double $130-165/190-225; closed mid-Nov–Apr)* Set back from Oak Creek, on eight secluded acres with broad lawns, an apple orchard and woods, this lodge offers nicely appointed Western log cabins, many with fireplaces. Rates include a full hot breakfast, 4pm tea and a gourmet dinner. It feels a bit like a private club – guests stroll the grounds, drinks in hand, and speak in hushed tones. The staff is even a tad snobby. Catering to adults who crave quiet and service, Garland's is not kid-friendly, charging $60 extra for any child over the age of two.

Slide Rock Lodge *(☎ 928-282-3531; 6401 N Hwy 89A; $80-95)* Just south of Slide Rock State Park, this motel is a simple strip of rooms set against the red rock and ringed by trees. Rooms are pretty basic, with a bed and couch, but they are quiet and clean.

Matterhorn Lodge *(☎ 928-282-7176, 800-372-8207; W www.matter hornlodge.com; 230 Apple Ave; 23 rooms; weekday/weekend $89/119)* All rooms at this motel include refrigerators and have balconies or patios that overlook uptown Sedona and Oak Creek. Though it abuts the highway, it's nice to be within walking distance of the shops and restaurants.

Top End

Briar Patch Inn *(☎ 928-282-2342, 888-809-3030; W www.briarpatch inn.com; 3190 N Hwy 89A; $169-325)* Nestled in nine wooded acres along Oak Creek, this lovely inn offers 17 log cottages with a Southwestern decor and Native American art. All cottages include patios, many have fireplaces, and several lie beside the burbling creek. There's a small meadow with grazing sheep and a creek-side cottage for massages. Accompanied by a classical guitarist, a delicious breakfast buffet is served on a stone patio that overlooks the creek. This friendly, relaxed, unpretentious spot is a welcome change from the attitude found at other upscale places in town.

Junipine Resort *(☎ 928-282-3375, 800-742-7436; W www.junipine.com; 8351 N Hwy 89A; 50 units; weekday/weekend $125-170/$175-225)* In woodland 8 miles north of Sedona, this resort offers spacious, nicely decorated one- and two-bedroom 'creekhouses,' all with kitchens, living/dining rooms, fireplaces and decks – and some with lofts. Some units have creek-side views, others have hot tubs, and a few offer both. Two-bedroom units sleep up to four people, a great option for families ($25 for each additional person, children under 12 free). The on-site restaurant serves good food, so you don't need to brave the crowds to get a bite to eat.

Enchantment Resort *(☎ 928-282-2900, 800-826-4180; W www .enchantmentresort.com; 525 Boynton Canyon Rd; from $375)* This 1st-class, full-service resort is in Boynton Canyon, 5 miles off of Hwy 89A, northwest of Sedona. It's so exclusive, you can't even enter the driveway unless you're staying here or have reservations at one of the resort's three restaurants. Sprawled throughout the grounds, all rooms include patios and expansive views. But don't expect any little extras – nothing but the room is included in the exorbitant rate (there's even an additional fee for tennis rackets and golf clubs). The on-site spa, **Miiamo** *(☎ 888-749-2137; W www.miiamo.com)*, offers treatments, day packages ($215 to $362) and three-, four- or seven- night packages that leave you rested and rejuvenated (and your wallet much lighter).

PLACES TO EAT
Budget
Sedona Memories (☎ 928-282-0032; 321 Jordan Rd; entrées $5-7; open 10am-2pm Mon-Sat) This low-key sandwich spot a block off Hwy 89A features several vegetarian options, homemade bread and a quiet outdoor patio.

Thai Spices (☎ 928-282-0599; 2986 W Hwy 89A; entrées $6-14; open 5-9pm Mon-Sun, 11am-3pm Mon-Fri) Despite its unassuming exterior, this popular restaurant serves excellent spicy Thai food, including a wonderful coconut soup and a few macrobiotic dishes.

Coffeepot Restaurant (☎ 928-282-6626; 2050 W Hwy 89A; entrées $4-10; open 6am-2:15pm) This has been *the* place to go for breakfast or lunch for decades. It's always busy, and service can be slow, but it's friendly, the meals are reasonably priced and the selection is huge – it offers more types of omelets (101) than most restaurants have menu items.

New Frontier Natural Foods & Deli (☎ 928-282-6311; 1420 W Hwy 89A; open 8am-9pm Mon-Sat, 8am-8pm Sun) This natural-foods grocery store is a good place to stop for picnic supplies or to grab a sandwich from the deli.

Black Cow Café (☎ 928-203-9868; 229 N Hwy 89A; open 8am-9pm) Many claim the Black Cow has the best ice cream in town, and it certainly hits the spot on a hot, dusty day. You can also get sandwiches and soup.

Ravenheart (☎ 928-282-1070; 206 W Hwy 89A; open 6am-9pm) Offering a pleasant outdoor patio with good views, this coffee shop is the best spot for a jolt of caffeine and a pastry while you check your email ($2.75 for 15 minutes, $10 for 50 minutes). Despite being on the main drag, it's an oasis of tranquility.

Mid-range
Briar Patch Inn (buffet breakfast $12 Wed-Mon, $9 Tue) A wonderfully peaceful place, this inn (see Places to Stay) welcomes nonguests to its buffet breakfast. It's served on a long flagstone patio in the woods above the creek and is accompanied by a guitarist every day except Tuesday.

Heartline Café (☎ 928-282-0785; W www.heartlinecafe.com; 1610 W Hwy 89A; entrées $9-15; open 11am-3pm Thu-Tue, 5-10pm daily) This restaurant's name refers to a Zuni Indian symbol for good health and long life, and indeed the imaginative menu offers the kind of fresh, clean and tasty food you might expect. Lunch options include Thai-style vegetables, barbecued pork with apple-onion chutney, pecan-encrusted trout, a hot Cajun turkey sandwich and tea-smoked duck salad. Enclosed in a blue wall covered with flowering vines, the pleasant outdoor patio holds eight tables around a small clay fireplace.

Cowboy Club (☎ 928-282-4200; W www.cowboyclub.com; 241 N Hwy 89A; lunch/dinner entrées $8-12/$18-23; open 11am-4pm & 5-10pm) From the outside, it looks like a saloon; inside, the large and determinedly Southwestern **Grille Room** offers primarily steaks, though you'll also find chicken, fish and vegetarian options. Feeling venturesome? Consider trying rattlesnake. Pricier fine dining is offered in the **Silver Saddle Room**.

Pizza Picasso (☎ 928-282-4140; 1855 W Hwy 89A; entrées $8-14; open 11am-10pm) Offering creative toppings, delicious sauce and a lively atmosphere, this stylish, popular pizza joint has something for everyone.

Top End

Shugrue's Hillside Grill (☎ 928-282-5300; Hillside Plaza, 671 Hwy 179; entrées $20-30; open 11:30am-3pm & 5-9pm) Promising panoramic views, an outdoor deck from which to enjoy them and consistently excellent food, this restaurant is a great choice for an upscale meal. If it's too chilly to sit outside, don't fret – the walls are mostly glass, so you can still enjoy the scenery. The menu offers everything from steak to ravioli, but it is best known for its wide variety of well-prepared seafood. A jazz ensemble plays on the weekends.

Yavapai Dining Room (☎ 928-282-2900; Enchantment Resort; entrées $20-30; open 6:30am-9pm Mon-Sat, 11:30am-2:30pm Sun) Come here for the delicious and expansive Sunday champagne brunch ($29) amid peaceful red-rock surroundings. Dinners are good, if overpriced. You won't be allowed on the premises without advance reservations.

Dahl & DiLuca Ristorante (☎ 928-282-5219; W www.dahl-diluca.com; 2321 Hwy 89A; entrées $20-28; open 5-10pm) This café with red-check-ered tablecloths and wine-bottle candlesticks feels like the kind of place you'd find in a small Italian seaside town. It's a bustling, friendly spot with tasty food.

ENTERTAINMENT

Read the monthly *Red Rock Review* for local events. For information about symphony concerts, film festivals, Shakespearean plays and other events, contact the **Sedona Cultural Park** (☎ 928-282-0747, 800-780-2787).

On a dirt road off Hwy 89A, the laid-back **Oak Creek Brewery** (☎ 928-204-1300; W www.oakcreekpub.com; 2050 Yavapai Dr; open 4-9pm Mon-Thu, 11am-midnight Fri-Sun) serves handcrafted beers on an outdoor patio and features live music (rock, blues, reggae) most evenings. If you're looking for a place to practice your country two-step, head to **Rainbow's End** (☎ 928-282-1593; 3235 W Hwy 89A; open 11am-1am).

SHOPPING

Shopping is a big draw in Sedona, and visitors will find everything from expensive boutiques to T-shirt shops. Uptown along Hwy 89A is the place to go souvenir hunting. Just south of 89A on Hwy 179, **Tlaquepaque Village** (☎ 928-282-4838; W www.tlaq.com) is home to dozens of high-end art galleries. Across the street is **Crystal Castle** (☎ 928-282-5910; 313 Hwy 179), one of several stores hawking New Age books and gifts. Farther south, **Garland's Navajo Rugs** (☎ 928-282-4070; 411 Hwy 179) offers the area's best selection of rugs, as well as other Indian crafts.

GETTING THERE

Sedona-Phoenix Shuttle (☎ 928-282-2066, 800-448-7988; W www.sedona-phoenix-shuttle.com; one-way/round-trip $40/65) runs between Phoenix Sky Harbor and Sedona eight times daily; call to make reservations. For door-to-door shuttle service, call **Ace Express** (☎ 928-649-2720, 800-336-2239; one-way/round-trip $50/83). **Sedona Taxi Airporter & Tours** (☎ 928-282-5545) offers cab service to Flagstaff. While scenic flights depart from Sedona, the closest commercial airport is Phoenix (two hours) or Flagstaff (30 minutes).

Greyhound (☎ 800-229-9424; W www.greyhound.com) stops in Camp Verde, about 30 minutes south of Sedona, and in Flagstaff, about 40 minutes north. **Amtrak** (☎ 800-872-7245; W www.amtrak.com) stops in Flagstaff.

GETTING AROUND

Bob's Taxi (☎ 928-282-1234) offers local cab service. Rental cars are available through **Enterprise** (☎ 928-282-2052; W www.enterprise.com) and **Sedona Jeep & Car Rentals** (☎ 928-282-2227, 800-879-5337; W www.sedonajeeprentals.com).

Lake Mead & Hoover Dam
MAP 10

Even those who challenge, or at least question, America's commitment to damming the American West have to marvel at the engineering and architecture of the Hoover Dam. Set amid the almost unbearably dry Mohave Desert, the dam towers over Black Canyon and provides electricity for the entire region. Lake Mead is a popular boating, swimming and weekend-camping destination for Las Vegas residents.

ORIENTATION

Hoover Dam created Lake Mead, which boasts 700 miles of shoreline, while Davis Dam created the much smaller Lake Mohave. Black Canyon, the stretch of the Colorado just below Hoover Dam, links the two lakes. All three bodies of water are included in the recreation area, created in 1964. The Colorado feeds into Lake Mead from Grand Canyon National Park, and rafting trips through the canyon finish on the east end of the lake.

Heading north from I-40 at Kingman, Hwy 93 crosses Hoover Dam about 30 minutes southeast of Las Vegas. Traffic across the dam can be terrible; expect delays of at least 30 minutes. The main cities on the south tip of Lake Mead are Bullhead City and Laughlin (see Lonely Planet's *Arizona*). Visitors to the lake will find most services in Boulder City, a small town with a pleasant historic downtown about 7 miles west of the dam and 7 miles south of the visitors center.

INFORMATION

Alan Bible Visitor Center (☎ 702-293-8990; W www.nps.gov/lame; US 93, 5 miles west of Hoover Dam, 4 miles east of Boulder City; open 8:30am-4:30pm) is the National Park Service's main visitors center for the area. Here you'll find information on accommodations, boating and other recreational activities, as well as a small interactive display on desert life. The smaller **Katherine Landing Visitor Center** (☎ 928-754-3272; open 8:30am-4:30pm) is on Lake Mohave at the south tip of the recreation area. Admission is $5 per vehicle and is valid for five days. The **Boulder City Chamber of Commerce** (☎ 702-293-2034; 1305 Arizona St; open 9am-5pm Mon-Sat) is in Boulder Dam Hotel.

Nine marinas line these lakeshores. Due to droughts, **Las Vegas Bay** (☎ 702-565-9111; W www.drydockboatsales.com) is no longer a bay; you'll still find dry storage and campgrounds, but marina services have moved south to Hemenway Harbor, close to Hoover Dam and Boulder City. A few miles northwest is **Lake Mead** (☎ 702-293-3484; W www.lakemead marina.com). Along the west shore are **Echo Bay** (☎ 702-394-4066; W www .echobay7c.com), the well-appointed **Callville Bay** (☎ 702-565-8958; W www.callvillebay.com) and **Overton Beach** (☎ 702-394-4040; W www .overtonbeachmarina.com). On the Arizona shore is **Temple Bar** (☎ 928-767-3211; W www.sevencrown.com), one of the more remote spots on Lake Mead. **Willow Beach** (☎ 928-767-4747; W www.blackcanyonadventures .com) is on the east side of Black Canyon. The two marinas on Lake Mohave are **Cottonwood Cove** (☎ 702-297-1464; W www.cottonwoodcoveresort .com) and **Katherine Landing** (☎ 928-754-3245; W www.sevencrown.com). For emergency help, call ☎ 911, or the park dispatcher at ☎ 702-293-8932 (Nevada) or ☎ 800-680-5851 (Arizona).

SIGHTS & ACTIVITIES
Hoover Dam
A statue of bronze-winged figures stands atop Hoover Dam, memorializing those who built the massive concrete structure. An inscription reads, 'Inspired by a vision of lonely lands made fruitful' – a sentiment that epitomizes America's dam-building frenzy in the 20th century. At 726ft, Hoover Dam remains an engineering and architectural marvel and is one world's tallest dams.

Originally named Boulder Dam, Hoover was built between 1931 and 1936 and was the first major dam on the Colorado. Thousands of men and their families, eager for work in the height of the Depression, came to Black Canyon and worked in excruciating conditions – dangling hundreds of feet above the canyon in 120°F desert heat. Hundreds lost their lives. A 25-minute film at the visitors center features original footage of the construction and is an interesting look at the history of not just Hoover Dam, but the sentiments and values that motivated American dam building.

Hoover Dam Visitor Center (☎ 702-293-8321; W www.usbr.gov; US 93, east of Boulder City) is open daily from 9am to 5pm. Parking costs $5. Guided Discovery Tours (adult/child $10/4) are offered frequently between 9:30am and 4:45pm.

Boulder City/Hoover Dam Museum
In Boulder Dam Hotel in Boulder City, the **Boulder City/Hoover Dam Museum** (☎ 702-294-1988; admission $2) is worth a visit. It focuses primarily on construction of the dam, with exhibits on Depression-era America and the living conditions of the men and women who came to build the dam. Shot by the Bureau of Reclamation, a 20-minute film features historic footage of the project.

Boating
Rental boats include personal watercraft, 18ft runabouts for waterskiing and exploring, 24ft patio (pontoon) boats and houseboats (see Houseboating, under Places to Stay). At **Lake Mead Resort & Marina** (☎ 702-293-3484, 800-752-9669), 20ft ski boats cost $260 a day or $50 an hour, while patio

boats that seat 10 people and travel up to 10 mph cost $195 a day. Call the individual marinas for more information.

You can rent a kayak from **Desert River Outfitters** (☎ 928-763-3033, 800-529-2533; Ⓦ www.desertriveroutfitters.com). Kayak trips down the Black Canyon start at the base of Hoover Dam, cost $55 per person (four-person minimum) and require a $13 advance permit (☎ 702-293-8204).

Fishing

Fishing for striped largemouth bass is a popular sport on Lake Mead. While fly-fishing is possible, it's difficult and is only recommended at certain times of year. For current conditions, contact Michael Swartz of **Fish Vegas** (☎ 702-293-6294; Ⓦ www.fishvegas.com); he is an expert on Lake Mead fishing. He also offers guided trips for $250 for one or two people and can direct you to other guides.

You must carry a state fishing license, available from the marinas. If your license is from Nevada and you plan on fishing from a boat on Lake Mead or Lake Mohave, or from the Arizona shores, you must also have a use stamp from Arizona (and vice versa). A trout stamp is required if you intend to catch and keep trout. Licenses are not required for children under 14.

Cruises

If you want to see the lake but don't want to rent a boat, consider a sightseeing tour with **Lake Mead Cruises** (☎ 702-293-6180; Ⓦ www.lakemeadcruises .com). Its boat is a triple-decker, air-conditioned Mississippi-style paddle wheeler. Daily tours (adult/child $19/9) leave at noon, 2pm and 4pm from Hemenway, a couple miles north of the Alan Bible Visitor Center. The company offers a Sunday breakfast cruise (adult/child $28.50/15), dinner cruises ($34.50/21; 6:30pm Sun-Thu) and a Saturday dinner/dance cruise ($51). No meal-inclusive cruises are offered from mid-December through February.

Hiking

Though boating is the primary activity here, you'll find hiking trails throughout the recreation area. Stop by the Alan Bible Visitor Center or one of the ranger stations for information on trails and **ranger-led hikes**. Hiking in summer is discouraged, as temperatures can reach 120°F in the shade.

Swimming

Given the dry heat of the surrounding desert, swimming in Lake Mead is understandably popular. Because water levels vary, what was a beach one year may be a desert the next. Call or stop by the visitors center for a list of recommended beaches, and consider renting a boat to reach suitable water. Two miles north of the Alan Bible Visitor Center, the aptly named Boulder Beach (comprising pebbles and stone, not sand) is one good wading spot. Be sure to ask about pollution levels before swimming – houseboat owners sometimes dump raw sewage into the water rather than using pump-out stations.

PLACES TO STAY

In addition to the following options, Laughlin and Bullhead City, on the south tip of the recreation area, host several hotel-casinos (RVs can park overnight for free in casino parking lots), independent motels and chain hotels.

Camping

The National Park Service maintains eight campgrounds for tents and RVs (no hookups) in the recreation area ($10; first-come, first-served). All are in or near marinas and offer fire-grills and toilets. The nicest of the west side campgrounds is **Boulder Beach** (☎ *702-293-2340)*, overlooking the water and planted with cottonwoods and flowering trees. Set apart from the marina, it's quieter than other campgrounds. The other west-side campgrounds are at **Las Vegas Bay** (☎ *702-565-9111)*, **Callville Bay** (☎ *702-565-8958)* and **Echo Bay** (☎ *702-394-4066)*. Few sites at Echo Bay (beside the busy marina and hotel) and Las Vegas Bay (a quiet marina, thanks to low water levels) overlook the water.

If you're headed east to the Grand Canyon, your only option is **Temple Bar Campground**, beside Temple Bar Resort. On Lake Mohave you'll find two campgrounds at Cottonwood Cove and one at Katherine Landing.

Lake Mead RV Village (☎ *702-293-2540; on Lake Mead near Boulder Beach)*, **Callville Bay Resort** (☎ *702-565-8958)*, **Echo Bay Resort** (☎ *702-394-4000)*, **Overton Beach Resort** (☎ *720-394-4040)* and **Temple Bar Resort** (☎ *928-767-3211)* all offer full RV hookups ($18 to $25). On Lake Mohave, RV hookups are available at **Cottonwood Cove Resort** (☎ *702-297-1464; $26)* and **Lake Mohave Resort** (☎ *928-754-3245; $18)* at Katherine Landing.

Houseboating

One of the most popular ways to explore Lake Mead is to rent a houseboat, available through **Forever Resorts Houseboats** (☎ *800-255-5561;* W *www .foreverresorts.com)* and **Seven Crown Houseboats** (☎ *800-752-9669;* W *www.sevencrown.com)*. Rates vary widely depending on the season and size of boat. January 1 to June 15 and September 2 to December 31 are 'value seasons,' when rates are about $300 less than the rest of the year. Seven Crown rents the Grand Sierra (six nights for $3050), which has two bathrooms and officially sleeps 13 (though it's rather tight); the smaller, more basic Sierra (six nights for $2050) sleeps 10. Check the websites for complete information.

Hotels & Motels

Aside from campgrounds and houseboats, the only lodgings on Lake Mead are three properties owned by **Seven Crown Resorts** (☎ *800-752-9669;* W *www.sevencrown.com)*. You must call Seven Crown Resorts, rather than the motels themselves, to make reservations. Don't expect a *resort* in the classic sense of the word – these are more like motels. On the west side of the lake, with a pool overlooking the water, is the one-story **Lake Mead Lodge** (☎ *702-293-2074;* W *www.lakemeadmarina.com; double/suite $65-85/139)*. Despite its proximity to the marina, beach and campground, it is a quiet spot surrounded by grass and trees and is a five-minute drive from restaurants in Boulder City. Wake early to watch the sun rise over the lake, perhaps in the company of one of the resident roadrunners. Also on the west side, about an hour's drive from Boulder City, **Echo Bay Resort** (☎ *702-394-*

4000; double $90-115) is several stories high, has no pool and is rather loud and busy, as it sits amid a large marina. All rooms, even those with lake views, overlook a large parking lot.

The only lodging on the Arizona side of the lake is the pleasant and remote **Temple Bar Resort** *(☎ 928-767-3211; W www.templebarresort.com; cabin/double/suite $55-115)*, 47 miles east of Hoover Dam. Rooms vary widely; some are simple cabins with separate bathrooms and no lake views, while others are motel rooms with kitchenettes and lake views. If lake levels are high enough, a beach materializes. To get here, head 20 miles south of Hoover Dam on Hwy 93 and look for a marked, paved northbound road.

There are two motels on Lake Mohave. On the south side, at Katherine Landing, Seven Crown Resorts runs **Lake Mohave Resort** *(☎ 928-754-3245; double $85-115)*, offering basic motel rooms. **Cottonwood Cove Motel** *(☎ 702-297-1464; W www.cottonwoodcoveresort.com; 24 rooms; double $90-115)* features a swimming beach and rooms with sliding-glass doors that overlook the water.

Several basic motels line Hwy 93 west of Boulder City, the nicest of which is **El Rancho Boulder Motel** *(☎ 702-293-1085; 725 Nevada Way; single/double $65/85)*.

A couple miles west of the dam on Hwy 93, **Hacienda Resort** *(☎ 702-293-5000; W www.haciendaonline.com, double $50-80)* offers a taste of Las Vegas glitz, with more than 800 slot machines, gaming tables, several restaurants and live shows.

In 1933 **Boulder Dam Hotel** *(☎ 702-293-3510; W www.boulderdamhotel .com; 1305 Arizona; double/suite $89/159)* opened to accommodate tourists flocking to witness construction of the massive structure. John Wayne, Shirley Temple and President Roosevelt all stayed here. The simple rooms were remodeled in 2001 without regard to historic charm, but the colonial revival architecture and hint of old-world ambiance in the public spaces make this a nice alternative to a standard motel. Rates include breakfast.

On the north side of the lake, Overton offers several chain motels, including the **Best Western North Shore Inn at Lake Mead** *(☎ 702-397-6000; 520 N Moapa Valley Blvd; double/suite $57-110)*.

PLACES TO EAT

You'll find basic restaurants at the Temple Bar, Boulder Beach and Echo Bay marinas on Lake Mead, and at Cottonwood Cove and Katherine Landing on Lake Mohave. The other marinas provide small convenience stores with snacks and drinks.

In Boulder City, **Best Cellars** *(☎ 702-293-9540; 538 Nevada Way; open 11am-9pm Mon-Thu, 11am-midnight Fri-Sat)* feels like a California wine bar, with an extensive wine list and sidewalk seating. It serves sandwiches like the Grecian vegetarian (avocado, sprouts, roasted red pepper, baby greens and garlic mayonnaise served with terra chips, $7), cheese plates (Spanish Manchego, Italian Asiago, smoked Gouda and olives, for $11), baked Brie and fresh salads. On the other side of the gastronomic spectrum, try **Happy Days Diner** *(☎ 702-294-2653; 512 Nevada Way; open 7am-8pm)*, which features a soda fountain and diner classics like a corn dog ($3.39), grilled Reuben ($7) or a hot turkey sandwich ($7).

GETTING THERE & AROUND

There are no shuttles to or around the recreation area. The only way to travel is by car. You'll find major car rental agencies in nearby Las Vegas and Henderson, Nevada.

Kaibab National Forest (North Rim)
MAP 6

Arguably one of the region's most beautiful spots, the northern district of Kaibab National Forest mixes stands of tall graceful aspens, ponderosa pines and oaks with lush meadows of tall grass and wildflowers. Small sinkholes form natural ponds and wetlands that serve as watering holes for deer, coyotes and the occasional bear. Several excellent hiking and mountain biking trails wind through the forest, and while some make their way to canyon overlooks, the Kaibab is an idyllic setting on its own. Given an average elevation of about 8000ft, evenings are cool, even in midsummer.

ORIENTATION & INFORMATION

Adjacent to Jacob Lake Inn, the helpful USFS **Kaibab Plateau Visitor Center** (☎ 928-643-7298; open 8am-5pm May-Oct) features a small museum and is the best place for information on the many canyon viewpoints, drives, trails, campgrounds and historic sites along the North Rim. You can buy a *Kaibab National Forest, North Kaibab Ranger District* map, as well as books on outdoor activities in the region. The **Kaibab National Forest District Headquarters** (☎ 928-643-7395; 430 S Main; open 8am-5pm Mon-Fri) is in Fredonia.

✔ **TIP**

If you're here in September or October, stop by the Kaibab Plateau Visitor Center and ask for the *Fall Colors Tour* handout – it maps out the best Forest Service roads for foliage tours or bike rides.

SIGHTS
Grand Canyon Viewpoints

Several dirt Forest Service roads veer west off Hwy 67 at DeMotte Campground, offering secluded canyon views, as well as great hiking and biking (see Activities). Passenger cars can handle most of these roads in dry weather; check at the visitors center for road conditions. One of the better overlooks is **Fire Point** (about 45 minutes from the campground), which offers a panoramic view of the canyon. From Hwy 67 at DeMotte, drive west on FR 22 for 2 miles, head south 2 miles on FR 270, then take FR 223 another 13 miles to the rim. Other viewpoints include **Crazy Jug**, **Fence**, **Locust**, **Parissawampitts**, **North Timp** and **Timp**. There are no facilities or water at the viewpoints, but you can camp.

Fire Towers

Three steel towers, all on the National Register of Historic Places, are still used as fire lookouts: Built in 1934, **Big Springs** and **Jacob Lake** stand 100ft tall, while **Dry Park**, built in 1944, is 120ft tall. You can drive out to any of them and climb up for great views of the national forest. Though the lookout rooms at the top are locked, if someone is manning the tower, they'll usually let you in.

ACTIVITIES

Kaibab National Forest is an absolutely beautiful place to **hike** and **mountain bike**. You can bike along the canyon rim on FR 425 and FR 292 to **Crazy Jug** and **Monument Point** – a moderate-to-strenuous 25.5-mile round-trip. You'll likely have it all to yourself. To access the trailhead, pedal south 26.5 miles from the Kaibab Plateau Visitor Center on Hwy 67, then turn right on FR 22. Go another 10.5 miles to FR 206, turn left and pedal a mile to FR 425. Alternatively, you can drive to Crazy Jug and then bike (or hike) the 3 miles round-trip to Monument Point.

Another rim trail suitable for mountain biking or hiking is the **Rainbow Rim Trail**, an 18-mile one-way that connects five fingers of land overlooking the canyon – **Parissawampitts**, **Fence**, **Locust**, **North Timp** and **Timp**. The trail passes beneath ponderosa pines and drops into several steep-sided canyons filled with aspens and small meadows. You can tackle all or part of this trail, which is also accessible by car. To reach the viewpoints, head west from DeMotte on FR 22 to FR 206. From there, FR 271 heads to Timp and North Timp (via 271A, which veers off from FR 271), FR 294 heads to Locust, FR 293 heads to Fence and FR 214 heads to Parissawampitts.

For a hike or bike ride closer to Jacob Lake Campground & Lodge, try the easy trip to **Buck Ridge Viewpoint**, where views stretch north over the Arizona Strip all the way to Zion and Bryce National Parks in Utah. From the Kaibab Plateau Visitor Center follow Hwy 67 south just under a half mile to FR 461. Turn right on FR 461 and drive 4 miles to FR 264 (Buck Ridge Point Rd). From here it's 5 miles to the viewpoint. The road ends in a piñon-juniper stand near an abandoned mine, a nice place for a picnic.

In the winter, cross-country ski enthusiasts will find the stretch from Jacob Lake south to the park a tantalizing and rewarding adventure. Though the park is officially closed from mid-October through mid-May, strong cross-country skiers can make the 44-mile journey along Hwy 67 and camp at the North Rim Campground or anywhere else in the park, provided they have a backcountry permit. The backcountry office closes when the park closes, but rangers remain on the rim year-round and can sell you a permit.

PLACES TO STAY

Free dispersed camping is permitted throughout the national forest, opening up plenty of great spots to pitch a tent. For a site with superb canyon views, drive out to one of the viewpoints. USFS rangers ask that you refrain from camping right on the rim, as others seeking a view would have to walk through your campsite. Fire Point and Point Sublime lie within the national park; to camp at either, you must first obtain a backcountry permit.

See Places to Stay, North Rim (p165), for information about the DeMotte (particularly nice) and Jacob Lake Campgrounds.

Fredonia

As Fredonia lies 74 miles north of the rim, about the only reason you might visit is if you couldn't find lodgings closer to the park. In that case, you're better off staying in Kanab, 7 miles farther north. There's not much here beyond a few inexpensive motels, the **Kaibab National Forest District**

Headquarters (☎ *928-643-7395; 430 S Main; open 8am-5pm)*, a **post office** (☎ *928-643-7122; 85 N Main)* and a **police station** (☎ *928-643-7108; 130 N Main)*.

Stone cabins, many with kitchenettes, surround a pleasant grassy courtyard at **Grand Canyon Motel** (☎ *928-643-7646; 175 S Main; double $35-45)*. The courtyard holds a barbecue grill and a few picnic tables. The town's two other motels are the **Blue Sage Motel & RV Park** (☎ *928-643-7125; 330 S Main; single/double/RV $32/38/15)* and the **Crazy Jug** (☎ *928-643-7752; 465 S Main; single/double $38/49)*, with new rooms and the town's only restaurant.

Kanab

MAP 9 • **TEL 435** • **POPULATION 4492** • **ELEVATION 4925**

In 1874 Mormons settled remote Kanab, Utah. Drawn by the desert backdrop and stunning red-rock formations, Hollywood descended on the town in the 1920s. It has since served as a location for hundreds of movies and TV shows, including numerous Westerns and episodes of *The Lone Ranger* and *Gunsmoke*. Though the filmmaking craze here faded following spurts in the 1940s and '70s, the town still flaunts its silver-screen past with old movie sets and hotels where the stars once slept. A pedestrian-friendly downtown, peaceful surroundings and its proximity to several national parks make Kanab an excellent base from which to explore the Southwest. Paved roads lead to Grand Staircase-Escalante National Monument (20 miles), Zion (40 miles) and Bryce Canyon (80 miles). It's a 90-minute drive (80 miles) from here to the North Rim of the Grand Canyon.

ORIENTATION & INFORMATION

Lined by most of the businesses and lodgings, Hwy 89 snakes through town. Entering Kanab from the north, 89 turns into 300 West, veers sharply east as Center St for four blocks, turns south for a few blocks as 100 East, then continues as Hwy 89 east toward Lake Powell (64 miles). At the turn for Page, Alt 89 heads south toward the North Rim.

Kane County Travel Council (☎ *435-644-5033, 800-733-5263;* W *www .kaneutah.com; 78 S 100 East; open 9am-4pm Mon-Sat)* provides information on Kanab and the surrounding area. For more information on the region, contact the **Bureau of Land Management** (*BLM;* ☎ *435-644-4600; 318 N 100 East; open 7:45am-4pm Mon-Fri)* and **Grand Staircase-Escalante National Monument Visitor Center** (☎ *435-644-4680; 745 E Hwy 89; open 7:30am-5:30pm)*.

Other services include the **library** (☎ *435-644-2394; 374 N Main St)*, **post office** (☎ *435-644-2760; 39 S Main St)*; **hospital** (☎ *435-644-5811; 355 N Main St)* and **police station** (☎ *435-644-5854; 140 E South)*.

SIGHTS

Coral Pink Sand Dunes State Park

A visit to this 3700-acre **state park** (☎ *435-648-2800; admission $4)* is like a trip to the beach – minus the water, of course. Kids and adults alike can climb, slide and roll through pink dunes dotted with junipers and piñon pines and set against steep red cliffs. Hiking trails outside the park afford views of the dunes, Zion National Park and the Grand Canyon's North Rim. It's a fun place to play, particularly for children (bring spare clothes, as the dusty sand clings to everything). Camping is available (see Places to Stay). Ask about ranger programs. To reach the park, drive 13 miles north of Kanab on Hwy 89, then turn left on the 12-mile paved road.

Frontier Movie Town

A kitschy roadside attraction, **Frontier Movie Town** (☎ 435-644-5337, 800-551-1714; 297 W Center St; open 7:30am-11pm) is great fun for families. You can wander through old movie sets, brush up on such tricks of the trade as short doorways (to make movie stars seem taller) and relax with a beer on the small grassy courtyard. An on-site grill serves buffalo burgers. In summer the park stages a participatory Western spoof and Dutch-oven cowboy buffet dinner ($13), during which visitors sit in a semicircle of covered wagons (sans wheels) to boo the villains and cheer on the heroes.

Kanab Heritage Museum

For a glimpse into the region's popular history, this small **museum** (☎ 435-691-1852; 130 S East; open 2-9pm Tue-Fri) is worth a stop. While the few historical memorabilia aren't particularly riveting, you may enjoy browsing through the 30-plus spiral-bound notebooks filled with movie newspapers, magazine articles, written histories and photographs.

Powell Survey Monument

In a small park on the corner of 100 North and 100 West, this monument stands atop the established baseline from which the Grand Canyon was surveyed by Major John Wesley Powell in 1873.

Pipe Spring National Monument

Used by pioneers as a resting spot and cattle ranch, this literal oasis in the desert is both lovely and interesting. Visitors can experience the Old West amid cabins and corrals, an orchard, ponds and a garden. In summer, rangers and costumed volunteers reenact various pioneer tasks. Tours of the stone **Winsor Castle** (built by Mormons in 1869 for church tithing and for refuge from Indians) are offered every half-hour. A small museum examines the history of Kaibab Paiutes and Mormon settlement, while a pleasant half-mile ridge trail promises excellent views. The **visitors center** (☎ 928-643-7105; W www.nps.gov/pisp) sells backcountry permits for Grand Canyon National Park. The monument is off Hwy 389, 21 miles southwest of Kanab.

ACTIVITIES

Stop by the BLM office or visitors center for details on the many nearby **hiking** and **biking** opportunities, as well as **scenic drives**. For an easy, accessible hike in town, try the well-marked 1-mile **Squaw Trail**, which leaves from the north end of 100 East and leads 4000ft up to the Vermilion Cliffs. The folks at **Willow Canyon Outdoor Co** (see Shopping, p217) have lots of experience exploring the surrounding national parks and are happy to chat and share advice.

FESTIVALS & EVENTS

Held in late August, the annual **Western Legends Roundup** (W www
.westernlegendsroundup.com) celebrates the town's true pioneer and Hollywood past, kicking off with a wagon train, followed by a film festival, fid-
dle competition, cowboy poetry and music, Indian dances and wagon
rides. Folklore workshops cover such subjects as Western photography and
painting, and Dutch-oven cooking.

PLACES TO STAY

In addition to the lodgings listed below, Kanab hosts a few decent chain
hotels, including a Super 8, a Best Western and a Holiday Inn Express (the
most expensive option in town, with doubles starting at $90). You'll also find
a few no-frills motels along Hwy 89.

Camping

You can camp amid the dunes at **Coral Pink Sand Dunes State Park**
(☎ 435-648-2800, 800-322-3770; 22 sites; $14). RV hookups are only
offered at the five-site group spot ($70). Water, showers and restrooms
are available. Though it's beautiful and quiet campground, it can get very
windy, and the blown sand gets into everything.

The small and friendly **Hitch'n Post Campground** (☎ 435-644-
2142, 800-458-3516; 196 E 300 South; 14 sites, 3 cabins; site/cabin $18/20-26)
provides shaded grassy spots for tents and hookups. Cabins include TVs and
air conditioners. With a small pool, playground and shade trees, **Crazy
Horse Campark** (☎ 435-644-2782, 866-830-7316; 625 E 300 South; 74 sites;
tent/RV $14/19) attracts families. On the south side of town, **Kanab RV
Corral** (☎ 435-644-5330; 483 S 100 East; 40 sites; $20) is a tidy, quiet RV park
with a pleasant pool and a coin laundry.

Hostels

USA Hostels Grand Canyon (☎ 435-644-5554; W www.usahostels.com;
143 E 100 South; dorm/room $15/32) This small, friendly, privately run hos-
tel offers two private rooms and four dorm rooms with 24 beds. Though it
looks a bit rundown from the outside (picture an abandoned roadside
motel), the rooms are clean and quiet, and there's a small common area with
a TV, kitchen and useful information about area attractions.

Hotels & Motels

Parry Lodge (☎ 435-644-2601, 888-289-1722; W www.parrylodge.com;
89 E Center St; 89 rooms; double/suite $51-68/78-86) Rooms at this one-
story 1929 motel (some rooms are in a newer, two-story annex) are set
back from the road amid a large, tree-covered parking lot. It's a quiet,
pleasant spot, with a pool and formal dining room. Some rooms bear the
names of movie stars who stayed here while filming in southern Utah.
Each room includes a TV and phone and offers a touch more character
than standard motel rooms. Suites include kitchenettes, and two-room
doubles are available. This motel is a wonderful slice of Americana that
successfully combines modern convenience with 1940s charm. Rates
include breakfast.

Utah Trails Resort *(☎ 435-644-3311, 800-871-6811;* **W** *www.utahtrails resort.com; Hwy 89, 2 miles east of Kanab; teepee $80-150; open May-Oct)* Set against red-rock cliffs and surrounded by sage and piñon pines, this 257-acre resort offers guests the chance to sleep in one of 19 teepees. Sure, they're air-conditioned and decorated with Navajo rugs, Pendleton blankets and wooden chests, but with a little imagination you can pretend you're in the 19th-century West. The resort gives travelers a nudge in that direction, with campfire programs and cookouts, as well as archery and tomahawk-throwing lessons. You can even dress up in period costumes and watch movies and documentaries about the Old West. It may sound a little crazy, but it's a beautiful spot and a fun place for kids. An on-site bathhouse provides restrooms and showers.

Treasure Trail Motel *(☎ 435-644-2687, 800-603-2687;* **W** *www.treasure trailmotel.net; 150 W Center St; 29 rooms; single/double $38-58/50-78)* This friendly, family-run motel has spacious rooms, a small lawn and a pool. Some rooms have a refrigerator and microwave, and there is a coin laundry.

National 9 Inn/Aikens Lodge *(☎ 435-644-2625, 800-524-9999; 79 W Center St; 31 rooms; $43-76)* Another good option for families, this motel offers two-bedroom suites that sleep four and three-bedroom suites that sleep six. You'll find basic, clean rooms and a small pool.

Victorian Charm Inn *(☎ 435-644-8660, 800-738-9643;* **W** *www .victoriancharminn.com; 190 N 300 West; 20 rooms; $89 159)* Rooms in this bed-and-breakfast include fireplaces and Jacuzzis. While hardwood floors, a grand staircase, quilts and four-poster beds lend the place an old-time feel, the building is modern and rooms are fitted with Ethan Allen furnishings. Rates include a hot breakfast.

> ✔ **TIP**
>
> Featuring a playground, a big lawn and red rock surroundings, City Park is a great spot for a picnic with the kids.

PLACES TO EAT

Escobar's *(☎ 435-644-3739; 373 E 300 South; entrées $7-11; open 10am-9:30pm Sun-Fri)* Though it doesn't look like much on the outside, this is the best bet in town for Mexican food and a cold beer. It's Utah Mexican, so don't expect much of a kick, but the dishes are tasty, and the service is fast.

Rocking V Café *(☎ 435-644-8001;* **W** *www.rockingvcafe.com; 97 W Center St; entrées $8-20; open 11:30am-9:30pm)* Housed in an 1892 storefront and owned by Dallas transplants, this brightly painted café offers a welcome change from basic, uninspired roadside fare. The food is fresh and delicious, and the eclectic lunch menu includes buffalo burgers, deep-dish vegetarian enchiladas, Asian chicken salad and a grilled portobello sandwich.

Vermilion Espresso Bar & Café *(☎ 435-644-3886; 4 E Center St; entrées $4-7; open 7am-2:30pm Mon-Fri, 8am-1:30pm Sat)* Featuring Internet access, strong java, delicious pastries, deep-cushioned lounge chairs, a table full of books to peruse and Bob Dylan on the CD player, Vermilion is the closest thing to a big-city coffee shop you'll find around here. Try the huge breakfast sandwich of ham, cheese and egg on homemade bread. Lunch includes a New York deli–style veggie burger, hot tamales and a turkey sandwich à la Vermilion (smoked turkey, Swiss cheese, ranch dressing, tomato, lettuce, onions, herbs and spices, oven-baked on wheat bread with cranberry sauce). If you're planning a picnic or want something for the road, this is the place. Hours may be shortened during the winter.

Houston's Trails End Restaurant (☎ 435-644-2488; W www.houstons .net; 132 E Center St; entrées $6-20; open 6am-10pm) Playing on the city's real and make-believe Western heritage, servers at this dependable family-style restaurant dress in cowboy/cowgirl regalia, and the radio plays country music. Don't expect anything trendy or low-cal here, but regulars swear by the diner breakfast fare and carnivore classics like chicken-fried steak, burgers and ribs.

ENTERTAINMENT

To really dig into the whole cowpoke experience, take in a Western music and comedy show at the **Crescent Moon Theater** (☎ 435-644-2350; 150 S 100 East; adult/child under 12 $13/6.50; 8pm Mon-Sat). The more casual outdoor show at **Frontier Movie Town** (see Sights, p214) engages the audience in slapstick Western humor.

SHOPPING

If you plan on tackling any outdoor activities, **Willow Canyon Outdoor Co** (☎ 435-644-8884; W www.willowcanyon.com; 263 S 100 East; open 7:30am-9pm) offers a good selection of Grand Canyon guides, hiking and field guides, camping and backpacking gear, USGS maps, boots, sandals and clothes. Stop for a coffee and pastry, and grill the experienced staff for hiking tips and suggested trails.

For all kinds of cowboy gear, as well as Native American pottery, jewelry and rugs, stop by **Denny's Wigwam** (☎ 435-644-2452, 888-954-9544; W www .dennyswigwam.com; 78 E Center St; open 9am-6pm). If you find yourself en route to the North Rim with a broken camera, stop by **Terry's Camera Trading Co** (☎ 435-644-5981; 19 W Center St; W www.utahcameras.com; 8am-6pm Mon-Sat). Terry specializes in camera repair and has been leading photo tours of the region for 25 years. If he's not in, a sign on his door will list a number where you can phone him, or just ask around town.

GETTING THERE & AROUND

There's no bus or train service to Kanab, nor are there any taxis. **Greenhound Shuttle** (☎ 877-765-6840) is a quirky, personalized shuttle service that will take you practically anywhere you want to go for $0.95 a mile (for example, a trip to the North Rim runs $80). If you're hauling lots of gear, you'll be charged $20 for each additional passenger. The shuttle can drop you at a hiking trail and pick you up at a prearranged time or even come to your rescue should you run into car trouble.

Lees Ferry & Marble Canyon

To call **Marble Canyon** a town would be a slight exaggeration – it's not much more than three motels (each with a restaurant, fishing guides and a few other services) spread out over several desert miles. Along the river, just north off Hwy 89, is **Lees Ferry**, with a pleasant campground and easy trails to several interesting historic buildings. The town was named after John D Lee, who started the Lonely Dell Ranch and a primitive ferry service here in 1872 (see Ferryman of the Colorado, p236). The ferry ran until 1929, when the Navajo Bridge opened. Five thousand people were on hand to celebrate the event, as the bridge eased access to the remote North Rim, boosting tourism. This is the jumping-off point for most raft trips through the canyon, and anglers say it's the best spot in the area for fly-fishing.

ORIENTATION & INFORMATION

Twenty-five miles south of Page, Alt 89 spurs north off Hwy 89 and then west toward Jacob Lake and the North Rim. Fourteen miles after the split, Alt 89 crosses the Colorado on the new Navajo Bridge, the only road bridge on the river between Glen Canyon and Hoover Dams. Built in 1994, it takes over for the original Navajo Bridge (now a visitor attraction) and marks the southwestern end of Glen Canyon National Recreation Area. Beside the bridge is the **Navajo Bridge Interpretive Center** (☎ 928-355-2319; open 9am-5pm Apr-Oct). At this windswept outpost, you'll find outdoor exhibits, an NPS ranger and a small but well-stocked bookstore.

Almost immediately after the bridge, a marked side road heads 6 miles north to Lees Ferry. Just past the turnoff, you must pay a $10 entrance fee to the recreation area. A **ranger** (☎ 928-355-2234; irregular hours) is based in Lees Ferry.

SIGHTS & ACTIVITIES
Navajo Bridge

Pedestrians are free to walk across the Colorado on the old Navajo Bridge (834ft across, 467ft high), which offers great views south down Marble Canyon to the northeast lip of the Grand Canyon.

Historic Buildings

Two historic walking tours, one of **Lees Ferry** and one of **Lonely Dell Ranch**, are described in detail in the *Walking Tour Guide*, available for purchase at the Rainbow Bridge Interpretive Center or the Carl Hayden Visitor Center, in Page. Historic buildings at Lees Ferry include **Lees Ferry Fort** (1874), the **stone post office**, and the stone remains of the **ferrymen's homes** at the ferry-launching site (see Ferryman of the Colorado, p236), about a mile up the Colorado.

Lonely Dell Ranch provided for families who worked at the crossing in the 1880s and 1890s. The log cabins, a stone ranch house and a pioneer cemetery remain. Though the main ranch buildings lie only about 700ft up a dirt road from the parking area, a walking tour of the entire ranch is 1 mile round-trip. You'll find picnic tables and shade trees at the ranch. From Alt 89 take the paved road north toward Lees Ferry for 5.1 miles, then turn left and drive 0.2 mile.

Fishing

One local guide estimates that the calm waters and teeming rainbow trout draw 100,000 anglers a year to the 15 miles of river and 30 miles of shoreline around Lees Ferry. He insists that despite the numbers, you can always find a quiet spot to throw out a fly, and the fishing is consistently good. Though the river is fished year-round, the best seasons are spring and fall. In cooler months you'll be nymph fishing (ie, from the bottom of the river), while the summer heat draws trout to the surface for flies.

Each of the three lodges north of the bridge offer fishing guides and services. Bill McBurney of **Ambassador Guide Services** (☎ 800-256-7596; W www.ambassadorguides.com), adjacent to Lees Ferry Lodge (see Places to Stay & Eat), has been guiding fishing trips for more than 20 years. Rates range from $300 for one or two people to $500 for six.

Hiking

Day hikers have a few options at Lees Ferry. The **River Trail** follows the old wagon road to the ferry launch (see Historic Buildings), and an angler's trail leads about a half-mile farther upstream. Threading a narrow slot canyon, the 2-mile round-trip **Cathedral Canyon** trail is not defined. You must find your own way down the streambed to the Colorado. Parking for this hike is at the second pullout north along Lees Ferry Rd, just past the fee station.

Behind Lees Ferry Fort is the unmaintained **Spencer Trail**, which takes hikers 1700ft up a cliff to views of Marble Canyon. More adventurous hikers begin the 45-mile **Pariah Canyon Trail** here. This trail starts at the Lonely Dell Ranch parking area and ends at Alt 89 in Utah. This is a serious backpackers' trail – all hikers should contact a ranger about current conditions and let someone know their plans before heading out.

PLACES TO STAY & EAT

A few miles apart, three lodges stand amid the desert in the shadow of the Vermilion Cliffs. The 54-site USFS **Lees Ferry Campground** ($10; toilets but no showers or services) sits just before the launch ramp beside the river.

Marble Canyon Lodge (☎ 928-355-2225, 800-726-1789; single/double $58/68-75; open 6am-9pm) Simple motel rooms are available at this lodge on Alt 89, a half-mile west of the Navajo Bridge. Apartments and cottages that sleep up to six cost $92 to $143. You'll find a restaurant, small bookstore, coin laundry and a bar.

Lees Ferry Lodge/Vermilion Cliffs Bar & Grill (☎ 928-355-2231; W www.leesferrylodge.com; single/double $50/57-79) This stone building with a stone-walled courtyard is for those looking for something more than just a roadside motel. The cozy rooms are decorated in different themes. The cowboy room, for example, boasts a Western motif, with animal skins and horseshoes on the wall, horse-print bed covers and shower curtains, and a wood-burning stove. You can sit outside in the courtyard with a cold beer and enjoy the lovely Vermilion Cliffs. Despite the silent hum of the air conditioner and the occasional passing car, it's a peaceful spot. Two-bedroom suites cost $82, there are no phones, and only one room has a TV.

Occupying a long room with about 10 wooden tables and a rough-hewn beamed ceiling, the restaurant/bar serves hearty food and 135 types of beer. Lunch options include fish and chips ($9), burgers ($5.25), tuna melts ($8.50) and the most expensive peanut butter and jelly sandwich you'll find outside of New York City ($5.50). It serves breakfast and dinner as well.

Cliff Dwellers Lodge & Restaurant *(☎ 928-355-2261, 800-962-9755; 21 rooms; single/double $60/70)* About 8.5 miles west of the Navajo Bridge, this is the last place to stay until Jacob Lake for those headed west toward the North Rim. Expect standard motel rooms, some with private patios. A three-bedroom house, with a kitchen, two bathrooms and cable TV, costs $175 per night. You'll also find a restaurant (open 5:30am to 10pm), a bar, a gas station, a convenience store and a liquor store.

Page & Glen Canyon

Despite a hard fight by conservationists, work on Glen Canyon Dam began in 1956 and was completed seven years later. Glen Canyon slowly filled to become Lake Powell, the country's second-largest artificial reservoir. Most of the lake lies in Utah; only the south tip dips into Arizona. In 1972 the lake and more than a million acres of surrounding desert were established as Glen Canyon National Recreation Area. Set amid striking red-rock formations, sharply cut canyons and dramatic desert scenery, it attracts water rats year-round. The only paved roads to Lake Powell are at the marinas – thus the best way to explore its 1,960-mile shoreline is by boat.

ORIENTATION & INFORMATION

The region's central town is Page, on the southern tip of the recreation area. Once a drab construction town, Page is now a drab tourist town. Hwy 89 (called N Lake Powell Blvd in town) forms the main strip. Services include the **chamber of commerce** *(Map 8; ☎ 928-645-2741; 644 N Navajo Dam Plaza; open 9am-5pm)*, the **post office** *(Map 8; ☎ 928-645-2571; 44 6th Ave; open 8:30am-5pm Mon-Fri)*, the **library** *(Map 8; ☎ 928-645-4270; 479 S Lake Powell Blvd; open 10am-5pm Mon-Thu, 10am-5pm Fri-Sat)*, the **hospital** *(☎ 928-645-2424; Vista Ave at N Navajo Dr)* and the **police station** *(Map 8; ☎ 928-645-2463; 808 Coppermine Rd)*.

Five marinas serve the lake. The largest, and the only one in Arizona, is **Wahweap Marina** *(Map 7; ☎ 928-645-2433; 6 miles north of Page)*. A 30-minute ferry ride links **Bullfrog Marina** *(Map 7; ☎ 435-684-3000; west shore, 290 miles from Page)* and **Halls Crossing** *(Map 7; ☎ 435-684-7000; east shore, 238 miles from Page)*. On the lake's north end is **Hite Marina** *(Map 7; ☎ 435-684-2278; 230 miles from Page)*. The smallest marina is **Dangling Rope** *(Map 7)*, accessible only by boat. Of course, all distances are much shorter by boat. Marinas host rangers and small supply stores; all but Dangling Rope rent boats.

As the recreation area's only licensed concessionaire, **Aramark** *(☎ 800-528-6154; W www.lakepowell.com)* runs the marinas. You can call or visit its website to book rooms at one of two hotels on the lake, reserve a houseboat, rent other boats and arrange rafting trips and boat tours. Its website is an excellent resource for Lake Powell.

Carl Hayden Visitor Center *(☎ 928-608-6404; open 8am-7pm Memorial Day–Labor Day, 8am-5pm the rest of the year)* sits beside the dam, 2 miles north of Page. **John Wesley Powell Memorial Museum** (see Sights) offers information and can arrange tours. On the lake's north shore in Utah, the **Bullfrog Visitor Center** *(☎ 435-684-7400; open 8am to 5pm)* closes from

November through March; when it's closed, seek information from the **Bullfrog Ranger Station** (☎ 435-684-7400).

The recreation area entrance fee is $10 per vehicle or $3 per individual entering on foot or by bicycle. For general park information, contact the recreation area and **Rainbow Bridge National Monument** (☎ 928-608-6404; W www.nps.gov/glca; PO Box 1507, Page, AZ 86040-1507).

SIGHTS

Antelope Canyon

Everywhere you look in Page, there seems to be another photo of **Antelope Canyon** *(Map 7)*, a scenic slot canyon (much higher than it is wide) on the Navajo Indian Reservation, a few miles east of Page. There are actually two canyons – an upper and a lower Antelope Canyon. The only way to visit the more famous upper canyon is through an organized tour (about $28, including the permit to enter Navajo land). Unfortunately, these tours can be more about the process of taking a photo (where to take it, how to take it, when to take it) than about appreciating the canyon itself, so it becomes a strange tourist attraction, in which the act of recording the experience becomes the experience. Every day, particularly in summer, crowds of people pile into shuttles and schlep their tripods, cameras and film into the narrow canyon. Four tour companies offer trips into upper Antelope Canyon; **Roger Ekis's Antelope Canyon Tours** (☎ 928-645-9102; 22 S Lake Powell Blvd; W www .antelopecanyon.com) and **Overland Canyon Tours** (☎ 928-608-4072) are recommended.

Though not as deep or spectacular, the lower canyon is open to the public, though you still have to pay for shuttle service and a $5 tribal entry permit. To get there, take Coppermine Rd (Hwy 98) about 3 miles south of Page, then turn left on paved Antelope Point Rd.

John Wesley Powell Museum

In 1869 the one-armed John Wesley Powell led the first expedition through the Grand Canyon on the Colorado River (see History, p239). Two years later he went down the river again. This **museum** *(Map 8;* ☎ *928-645-9496, 888-597-6873; 64 N Lake Powell Blvd;* W *www.powellmuseum.org; open 9am-5pm, closed mid-Dec–mid-Feb)* displays memorabilia of early river runners, including a model of Powell's boat and photos and illustrations of Powell and his excursions. The small museum is worth a peek, as anyone visiting the canyon should know a little something about this amazing explorer. The museum can also arrange boat, road and helicopter tours (including scenic flights over the canyon).

Glen Canyon Dam

At 710ft tall, **Glen Canyon Dam** *(Map 7)* is the nation's second-highest concrete arch dam – Hoover Dam (p207) is 16ft taller. From April through October, free guided tours depart from the **Carl Hayden Visitor Center** *(*☎ *928-608-6404; open 8am-7pm Memorial Day–Labor Day, 8am-5pm the rest of the year)*. The tours last 60 to 90 minutes and leave every half-hour in summer, less frequently the rest of the year; the last tour leaves 90 minutes before the center closes. Tours take you across and then deep inside the dam in elevators. Construction lasted from 1956 through 1964. A display in the visitors center tells the story of the project and offers technical facts on water flow, generator output etc. Three videos – one on Glen Canyon, one offering footage of the construction project and one on operations at the dam – alternate every half-hour on the quarter-hour from 8:15am to 4:45pm.

Rainbow Bridge National Monument

On the south shore of Lake Powell, **Rainbow Bridge** *(Map 7)* is the largest natural bridge in the world, measuring 290ft high by 275ft wide. Most visitors arrive by boat and then hike a short trail, though recent droughts have suspended guided tours to the monument. It's about 50 miles by water (at least four hours round-trip) from Wahweap, Halls Crossing or Bullfrog. Serious backpackers can drive along dirt roads to access two unmaintained trails to the monument (each 28 miles round-trip). Both trailheads lie on the Navajo Indian Reservation; obtain a tribal permit from the **Navajo Parks & Recreation Department** *(☎ 928-871-6647; PO Box 90000, Window Rock, AZ 86515)*. Contact the department or the Carl Hayden Visitor Center for directions and more details.

ACTIVITIES
Boating

You can rent kayaks ($52), 18ft runabouts ($270) and 14ft fishing boats ($138), as well as water skis ($25) and other 'toys' at the marinas. Not all marinas offer all types of boats, so check the Aramark website (**W** www .lakepowell.com) or call each marina for details (see Orientation & Information, p220).

Fishing

An Arizona fishing license costs $12.50 for one day and $26 for five days. A Utah license costs $8 for one day and $16 for seven days (children under 14 don't need one). You can also get a stamp to fish in Arizona if you have a Utah license, and vice versa. All marinas sell licenses and provide information on bait, size and possession limits (for example, no live bait is allowed on the Colorado River).

Cruises

From Wahweap Marina, Aramark offers half-/full-day boat tours to Rainbow Bridge ($81/108), one-hour cruises on Wahweap Bay ($11), dinner cruises ($61) and other cruises on Lake Powell. For reservations contact **Aramark** *(☎ 800-528-6154; **W** www.lakepowell.com)*, **John Wesley Powell Memorial Museum** *(☎ 928-645-9496, 888-597-6873)* or Wahweap Lodge (see Places to Stay, p224).

ARA Wilderness Adventures *(☎ 928-645-3279)* offers a half-day float trip on the Colorado (no white water) from Glen Canyon through Marble Canyon to Lees Ferry.

Hiking & Biking

Ask at the visitors center for information and maps of the area's many **hiking** and **biking** trails.

If you just want to stretch your legs a bit while in Page, a few easy day hikes venture into the scenic red-rock country.

A popular photograph around town is the incredible view from a ridge overlooking the Colorado at **Horseshoe Bend**. As the name implies, the river bends around a stone outcrop, forming a perfect horseshoe. The hike to the overlook is about 1.5 miles round-trip. Though it's short and relatively flat, the mostly sand trail can be a slog. You might want to tote toddlers in a backpack, as there are no guardrails at the viewpoint. The trailhead is south of Page off Hwy 89, just across from mile marker 541.

The 8-mile **Rimview Trail**, a mix of sand, slickrock and other terrain, bypasses the town and offers views of the surrounding desert and Lake Powell. While there are several access points (pick up a brochure from the museum or chamber of commerce), a popular starting point is behind Lake View School, at the end of N Navajo Dr. From here you can also take a short nature trail loop.

Air Tours

Westwind Aviation (☎ 800-245-8668; W www.westwindaviation.com) offers aerial tours from Page Municipal Airport that take in Rainbow Bridge, the Grand Canyon, Lake Powell, Monument Valley, Sedona and Bryce Canyon. Prices vary widely by itinerary.

PLACES TO STAY

Clean, basic and overpriced chain hotels, including Best Western, Quality Inn, Days Inn and Holiday Inn Express, line N Lake Powell Boulevard in Page. Expect rates to drop at least $25 dollars in winter.

Camping

Lake Powell Campground (☎ 928-645-3374; 849 S Coppermine Rd; tent/ RV $17-26) offers RV sites with hookups ($26), a few tent sites ($17), an indoor pool and hot tub, laundry facilities and showers.

You can camp anywhere along the Lake Powell shoreline for free as long as you have a portable toilet or toilet facilities on your boat. Developed NPS campgrounds with sites for tents ($10 to $16) and RVs ($22 to $26) are available at **Wahweap**, **Bullfrog** and **Halls Crossing Marinas**. Call the marinas to make reservations (see Orientation & Information, p220). You'll find primitive campsites ($10; toilets only) at **Hite Marina**, on the north end of Lake Powell, and **Lees Ferry**, on the river just north of the Navajo Bridge Interpretive Center (see Lees Ferry & Marble Canyon, p217). Closer to Page is **Lone Rock Beach** ($6; showers and toilets), where you can camp on the waterfront (depending on water levels) and where there are showers and toilets. Call the **Carl Hayden Visitor Center** (☎ 928-608-6404) for information.

Houseboating

Despite hosting hundreds of houseboats, the lake is big enough that you could boat for several days and rarely see anyone else. If you're trying to decide whether to rent a houseboat here or on Lake Mead, Lake Powell offers much more dramatic scenery and plenty of secluded inlets, bays and coves. Summer rates range from $1106 to $3354 for three days to $1854 to

$6450 for a week, in boats ranging from 36ft to 59ft. Contact **Aramark** (☎ 800-528-6154; W www.lakepowell.com) for details and reservations.

Budget

Private rooms at the clean and quiet **Lake Powell International Hostel** (Map 8; ☎ 928-645-3898; 141 S 8th Ave; dorm/room $13/18-24) share a kitchen and living room (with a TV) with two other private rooms, so it's akin to staying at a three-bedroom apartment.

Several clean, well-run independent lodgings line 8th Ave. Housed in what was once worker housing during construction of the dam, they offer a low-key alternative to accommodations on the strip. Try **Uncle Bill's** (Map 8; ☎ 928-645-1224; W www.canyon-country.com/unclebill; 117 8th Ave). The note on the door of this welcoming motel reads, '1) open door, 2) go thru house, 3) we are out there somewhere; make a little noise and we will find you.' The owners encourage you to feel right at home – throw a steak on the grill, leaf through one of several hundred books that line bookshelves throughout the property, or just hang out. Uncle Bill, the self-professed 'mayor of 8th Avenue,' and his wife, an accomplished artist, are well connected in Page and are happy to suggest places to go and things to do. Well-appointed *chambre d'hotes* (small apartments with a living room, bathroom and kitchen) provide several options, from a room with shared facilities ($36 to $45) to a one-bedroom suite with a sofa bed in the living room ($79) or a three-bedroom suite ($119 to $149).

Other good lodgings on 8th Ave include **KC's Motel** (Map 8; ☎ 928-645-2947; 126 8th Ave; double/suite $36-59/79), **Lulu's Sleep Ezze Motel** (Map 8; ☎ 928-608-0273, 800-553-6211; 105 8th Ave; double $43-72) and **Red Rock Motel** (☎ 928-645-0062; W www.redrockmotel.com; 114 8th Ave; single/double $39/49, 2-/3-bedroom suites $65/80).

Hotels

The only hotel in or around Page with a direct view of the lake is **Wahweap Lodge** (Map 7; ☎ 928-645-2433, 800-528-6154; W www.lakepowell.com; 100 Lake Shore Dr; double $140-160). The small pool perches on red rocks and overlooks the water, and huge windows in the dining room offer panoramic views. The rooms are all basic; rates for lake-view rooms with tiny patios are about $15 more and are worth it. In the lobby you can book boat tours and arrange boat rental.

Surrounded by a golf course, away from the traffic and noise of the strip, **Courtyard by Marriott** (Map 8; ☎ 928-645-5000, 800-321-2211; 600 Clubhouse Dr; double $80-120) offers a peaceful alternative to other chain hotels in town. A landscaped courtyard with a large pool makes this a good spot for families.

On the north end of the lake, 96 miles upstream from the dam and 72 miles from the nearest town (tiny Hanksville, Utah), **Defiance House Lodge at Bullfrog Marina** (Map 7; ☎ 435-684-3000, 800-528-6154; W www.lakepowell.com; $118-182) offers remote lakeside accommodations. You're paying for the views, as the rooms are nothing fancy. Three-bedroom, two-bathroom family units ($182) sleep six.

PLACES TO EAT

The best place in town for breakfast is **Ranch House Grille** *(Map 8; ☎ 928-645-1420; 819 N Navajo Dr; entrées $4-9; open 5am-3pm)*. The big, white room offers little in terms of ambiance, but the food is good, the portions huge and the service fast. After a three-egg omelet and two huge pancakes ($5.65), you won't need to stop for lunch. Options like a breakfast burrito and spicy tortillas offer a bit of a Mexican twist, but basically this is a chicken-fried-steak, burger, tuna-melt, liver-and-onions kind of place.

Stromboli's *(Map 8; ☎ 928-645-2605; 711 N Navajo Dr; entrées $7-13; open 10:30am-9:30pm)* serves pizza and other Italian specialties and is popular for its low prices and large outdoor deck. More upscale Italian dining is offered at **Bella Napoli** *(Map 8; ☎ 928-645-2706; 810 N Navajo Dr; entrées $8-18; open 5-10pm)*.

Raft guides recommend **Dam Bar & Grille** *(Map 8; ☎ 928-645-2161; 644 N Navajo Dr; entrées $6-12; open 11:30am-10pm)*, a good spot for pub fare with a nod to the salad crowd, including such items such as nachos ($7) or a Caesar salad with smoked turkey ($11). If you're really hungry, try the 1lb burger with fries ($12). There's a microbrew-pub feel to the place, and the patio is pleasant on summer evenings, despite the strip mall view.

Next door the cavernous **Gunsmoke Saloon** *(Map 8; ☎ 928-645-2161; 644 N Navajo Dr; entrées $6-19; open 5-9pm)* serves barbecue dinners. Options range from a barbecue sandwich to a rack of ribs with salad, baked beans, corn, fries and bread. Steakhouse aficionados head to **Ken's Old West** *(Map 8; ☎ 928-645-5160; 718 Vista Ave; entrées $10-20; open 4-10pm)*. For Mexican try **Zapata's** *(Map 8; ☎ 928-645-9006; 615 N Navajo Dr; entrées $7-11; open 11am-10pm)*, a colorful café serving basic food with few surprises.

Though Wahweap Lodge's **Rainbow Room** *(Map 7; ☎ 928-645-2433; entrées $9-18; open 6-10am, 11am-2pm, 4-11pm)* is sometimes packed with tour-bus crowds, and the food is nothing special, there's something to be said for a meal with a view. The lodge overlooks the lake, and picture windows frame dramatic views of red rock against blue water. Try the breakfast or lunch buffet ($8 to $12) rather than the more expensive continental dinner. If nothing else, the adjoining bar is a good place to come for a sunset drink.

In the morning, swing by **Bean's Gourmet Coffeehouse** *(Map 8; ☎ 928-645-6858; 644F N Navajo Dr; entrées $2-5; 6am-5pm Mon-Thu, 7am-5pm Fri & Sat, 8am-noon Sun)* to grab an egg sandwich and coffee. If you'd like Internet access with your java, head to **Sit 'n' Bull Espresso** *(Map 8; ☎ 928-660-0918; 18 N Lake Powell Blvd; pastries $2-3; 7am-2pm Mon-Sat, 5-8pm Fri-Sat, 8am-1pm Sun)*, which serves coffee and pastries (think Hostess rather than gourmet) but no meals.

ENTERTAINMENT

For live country music and a big-barn feel, head to **Ken's Old West** *(Map 8; ☎ 928-645-5160; 718 Vista Ave; open 4-10pm Mon-Thu, 4-11pm Sat-Sun)*. It serves steak dinners and offers live music and dancing Thursday to Saturday. The kitchen stops serving at 11pm, but the music lasts till whenever.

If your taste leans more toward alternative rock, head to the popular **Gunsmoke Saloon** *(Map 8; ☎ 928-645-2161; 644 N Navajo Dr; open 5pm-1am).*

SHOPPING

If you're looking for Navajo crafts, including, pottery, basketry and kachina figurines, browse through **Blair's Dinnebito Trading Post** *(Map 8; ☎ 928-645-3008; 626 N Navajo Dr; open 8am-8pm).*

GETTING THERE & AROUND

Great Lakes Airline *(☎ 928-645-1355, 800-554-5111)* offers flights between Page Municipal Airport and Phoenix, Denver and Moab, Utah. Avis and Enterprise rent cars at the airport. There are no scheduled buses, though shuttles sometimes run in the summer; contact the chamber of commerce for current information. **Greenhound Shuttle** *(☎ 877-765-6840)* will take you wherever you want to go (including the North Rim) for $0.95 a mile.

Human history at the Grand Canyon began more than 10,000 years ago, when Paleo-Indian hunters passed through the canyon in search of big game.

HISTORY

From about 500 BC, various bands of Native Americans occupied the region, hunting in the forests that surround the canyon, farming on its alluvial terraces, constructing cliff dwellings in the canyon walls and building communities. Spanish treasure-seekers stumbled upon the canyon in 1540, but the land and its indigenous people were left relatively undisturbed by Europeans until trappers, traders and US government surveyors explored the region in the early 19th century. John Wesley Powell's much publicized trip down the Colorado River in 1869 and the completion of the transcontinental railroad that same year marked the beginning of the Grand Canyon's transformation from an obstacle to a destination. The Atchison, Topeka and Santa Fe Railroad arrived at the South Rim in 1901, and through the combined efforts of the railroad, the Fred Harvey Company and artists like Thomas Moran, the canyon took hold of America's imagination. In 1919, only 60 years after Army First Lieutenant Joseph Christmas Ives predicted that the canyon would be 'forever unvisited and undisturbed,' President Woodrow Wilson created Grand Canyon National Park, and a visit to the Grand Canyon was well on its way to becoming the quintessential American Experience.

Ancient Cultures of the Grand Canyon

Folsom, Humboldt, Jay, Mohave Lake and Pinto stone points and blades found across the uplands of the Grand Canyon suggest that the earliest inhabitants were the nomadic **Paleo-Indian** people of the Ice Age. Though there is no evidence to suggest that they occupied the canyon, they passed through the region more than 10,000 years ago in their search for Pleistocene megafauna such as mammoths, camels and giant sloths. They had few material possessions, and most of what they did have has been washed away, so the only record of their existence is the stone remains of their weapons. Archeologists believe that the size of these projectile points, and those that followed, reveal something about the cultures that produced them. Clovis points, from about 12,000 to 13,000 years ago, are twice as long as Folsom points (11,000 to 12,000 years ago), suggesting that later Paleo-Indians hunted smaller game. Scientists

T I M E L I N E

8000 BC	Paleo-Indian hunters pass through the Grand Canyon.
7000 BC– **1000 BC**	Archaic cultures occupy the canyon.
1000 BC– **1300 AD**	Basketmaker and ancient Puebloan cultures develop farming communities in and around the canyon.
1250	The Cerbat/Pai, ancestors of today's Hualapai and Havasupai, and Southern Paiute migrate to the canyon region.
1540	Spanish explorer Garcia Lopez de Cardeñas and his party of 12 arrive at the south side of the Grand Canyon.
1820s	Trappers and traders hunt for beaver and other furs in the canyon, exploring the Colorado River and its tributaries.
1848	Treaty of Guadalupe ends Mexican–American War; the USA gets Mexico's Northern Territory, including Arizona.
1851	Military men begin exploring and mapping the country's new territory.
1858–59	First Lieutenant Joseph Christmas Ives and his expedition become the first European Americans to reach the river within the canyon.
1863	President Lincoln creates Arizona Territory.
1865	Civil War ends.
1869	Transcontinental railroad completed; Hualapais surrender to US military and are confined to a reservation; John Wesley Powell becomes the first to successfully run the Colorado.
1870–90	Ranchers and settlers arrive in the Grand Canyon region. By 1890, the non-Indian population of the Arizona Territory reaches more than 88,000.
1871	John S Lee starts the first commercial ferry service across the Colorado River at today's Lee's Ferry.
1880	President Rutherford Hayes establishes the Havasupai Reservation.
1883	President Chester A Arthur confirms the Hualapai Reservation.
1884	JH Farlee builds the South Rim's first wagon-train from Peach Springs to Diamond Creek, two miles from the Colorado River, and builds the canyon's first hotel.
1890s	A stage line runs from Flagstaff to the South Rim.
1892–3	Peter Barry builds the four-mile Grandview Trail from Grandview Point.
1893	President Benjamin Harris proclaims the Grand Canyon a forest preserve.
1896	Bright Angel Hotel is established.
1897	John Hance becomes the first postmaster on the rim.
1899	Over 900 people visit the Grand Canyon.

T I M E L I N E

1901 The Santa Fe Railroad begins running from Williams to the South Rim.

1902 Winfield Hogaboom drives the first car to the Grand Canyon; photographers Ellsworth and Emory Kolb set up their studio on the South Rim.

1903 President Teddy Rosevelt visits the Grand Canyon; the Kaibab Trail is constructed from the Colorado River up Bright Angel Canyon to the North Rim; prospector turned tourist-entrepreneur Ralph Cameron imposes a $1 toll on his Bright Angel Trail.

1905 Fred Harvey Company opens El Tovar.

1906 Grand Canyon Game Preserve is set aside on the North Rim.

1907 Tourists cross the Colorado River to the north side in a cage strung on a cable.

1908 President Teddy Roosevelt creates Grand Canyon National Monument.

1910 Floods sweep away most of the homes in the village of Supai, on the Havasupai Reservation.

1912 Arizona Territory becomes a state.

1917 Tourists begin staying at Wylie's Way Camp, on the North Rim.

1919 The Grand Canyon becomes the United States' 15th national park; over 44,000 people visit.

1922 Fred Harvey Company builds Phantom Ranch, designed by Mary Colter, along the Colorado River.

1926 Automobiles overtake the railroad as the most popular form of transportation to the canyon.

1928 Grand Canyon Lodge is built on the North Rim; construction of a rigid suspension bridge to replace the old swinging bridge completes the cross-canyon Kaibab Trail; US government takes over Bright Angel Trail.

1929 Marble Canyon Bridge is dedicated near Lee's Ferry, replacing the ferry and making rim-to-rim travel possible.

1936 Hoover Dam is built on the Colorado River west of the canyon, creating Lake Mead.

1956 Two airplanes on eastward flights from Los Angeles collide over the canyon, resulting in the establishment of a national air-traffic control system.

1963 Controversial Glen Canyon Dam is built on the Colorado River east of the canyon, creating Lake Powell and destroying Glen Canyon.

1968 Train service to the park is discontinued.

1979 Grand Canyon National Park is designated a UNESCO World Heritage Site.

1989 Grand Canyon Railway offers a historic train ride to the South Rim from Flagstaff; more than four million people visit the Grand Canyon.

generally agree this is because large game herds had thinned, and nomadic hunters were forced to adapt to these changes.

THE ARCHAIC PERIODS

By 9000 years ago, Archaic cultures entered the Grand Canyon region from the Basin and Range Province to the northwest and replaced paleoculture. Archaic cultures, divided into Early, Middle and Late Archaic, span from 7000 BC to 1000 BC.

The **Early Archaic period**, characterized by seasonal habitation, atlatl weapons, weave sandals and groundstone tools, saw an increase in population on the plateaus despite the drier climate and the loss of large Pleistocene game.

About 6000 years ago, a drought that would last on and off for almost 2000 years defined the **Middle Archaic period**. Conditions became even tougher, and many peoples migrated to more amenable lands. Those who stayed moved between canyons and plateaus, sometimes camping in the caves and leaving evidence of their culture. Though the erosive nature of the sedimentary deposits means that most of these records have disappeared, Middle Archaic sites have been found in Bowns Canyon, located upstream from Lees Ferry.

Split-twig figurine found in the Grand Canyon

As the drought waned, about 4000 years ago (2000 BC), people returned to the region, and the 1000 year **Late Archaic** period began. Late Archaic evidence at the Grand Canyon includes gypsum points found north of the river and Shamans Gallery, a detailed pictograph panel on the North Rim. In Stantons Cave, perched in the Redwall Limestone of Marble Canyon, 50ft above the Colorado River, dozens of elaborate **split-twig animal figurines** depicting common prey, like mountain sheep, pronghorn antelope and deer reveal something about Late Archaic culture. Most are about palm-sized, and many are pierced by small twig or cactus thorn, representing arrows. Some were found in shrine like arrangements, with feathers and human hair attached. Radiocarbon dating tells us that these figures are 3200 to 5000 years old. Archeologists believe that nomadic groups used the caves for religious rituals, perhaps as a place to offer gifts to the gods in hopes of luring prey. Similar stick figures found in northern Arizona, Utah, the Mohave Desert and Nevada, as well as chipped stone tools such as those found close to the South Rim, link these early canyon inhabitants to the widespread desert culture. Stick figures found in the Grand Canyon are on display at Tusayan Museum (see p89).

The Late Archaic peoples had become more sophisticated than their predecessors. They moved seasonally from the canyon's depths to its rims, hunting bighorn sheep and searching for mineral pigments and medicinal plants in the side canyons, and tracking deer and harvesting pinyon nuts in the high country. Few archeological records remain to hint at their lives and culture. Scientists believe that they made fire, wore buckskin clothing and woven sandals, wove baskets (but did not make pottery) and traded with other cultures.

GRAND CANYON NATIONAL PARK

Cliff-side granaries built by ancestral Puebloans

BASKETMAKERS & ANCESTRAL PUEBLOANS

Corn (maize), squash and beans, cultivated in Mexico for at least 9000 years, arrived at the Grand Canyon around 500 BC. The **Basketmakers**, the canyon's earliest corn-growing people, are named after the intricate coiled and watertight baskets that they made. They lived in rock shelters and pithouses, cultivated cotton, hunted game and gathered wild plants.

In many ways, the Basketmakers were a transitional people who combined the hunting–gathering tradition of the Archaic culture with what would become a decidedly farming pueblo culture. They adorned themselves with stone, shell, bone, seed and feather jewelry; wore deerskins and square-toed sandals; and domesticated dogs and turkeys. Trade with other groups contributed to their development, and about 1700 years ago (300 AD), they began to make pottery, and the bow and arrow began replacing the atlatl and dart.

A complex religious life is evident through petroglyphs and clay figurines; they smoked ceremonial tobacco, played music on six-hole

HOPI INDIANS & THE GRAND CANYON

The canyon plays an integral part in the religion of 23 Hopi clans. According to oral traditions, Hopi ancestors emerged from Sipapuni, an elevated, circular hot spring in the canyon of the Little Colorado River about 4.5 miles above the confluence with the Colorado. They believe that their people will return to this sacred canyon spot upon their death. Hopis also traveled to the canyon to collect ceremonial salt from deposits just below the mouth of the Little Colorado, and ceremonial pilgrimages to the canyon continue today. Trade routes to the Havasupai and below-the-rim trails further link the Hopi to the Grand Canyon – clan symbols on canyon rocks and ceramic shards found in the area suggest that the Hopi visited the canyon regularly to collect blue-copper ore for use in paints.

flutes and made prayer sticks. By about 1100 years ago, pithouses had been replaced with stone structures.

Puebloan culture blurs with the Basketmaker culture, and the gradual shift from one period to the other is a result of complicated migrations and developments. (Anasazi, the term traditionally used to describe the early Puebloan culture, translates roughly as 'Enemy Ancestors.' Because Hopi and Zuni find this term offensive, contemporary scholars refer to the Anasazi as 'ancestral Puebloans,' or 'prehistoric Puebloans.') Puebloan culture, as defined and explained by archeologists, includes corn-growing cultures that inhabited the southern Colorado Plateau and the Four Corners Region. The word 'pueblo' means 'town' and refers to the above-ground adobe or stone structures in which these people lived. Religious ceremonies took place in *kivas*, circular below-ground buildings reminiscent of pithouses. Ancestral Puebloan culture is a general term that includes several distinct traditions based on pottery style, geographic location, architecture and social structure; it includes the Chacoan, Mesa Verde, Kayenta, Virgin River, Little Colorado River, Cohonina and Singua cultures. By about 700 AD, Basketmaker culture had been completely replaced by Puebloan culture.

From 700 AD to 1000 AD, various strains of early Puebloan culture lived in and around the canyon. On the South Rim, the Cohonina inhabited the canyon west of Desert View (including Havasu Canyon and the Coconino Plateau) and mingled with the Kayenta. They grew corn, squash and cotton, eking out a life as best they could in the dry desert country, and lived seasonally in the uplands and along the river. They made pottery, stone and bone tools, and they spun cotton for blankets and clothing. Pottery shards found in Chuar Canyon and unearthed during a flash flood suggest that, despite difficult conditions, a farming community thrived in the in the canyon 1200 years ago.

Paleoclimate research indicates that about 1000 years ago, precipitation increased slightly. For the next 150 years, the Grand Canyon experienced a heyday of farming activities. Various bands of ancestral Puebloans occupied side canyons, the rim and the river corridor, developing complex systems of irrigation to grow squash, beans and corn on alluvial

GHOST DANCE

Perhaps one of the saddest and most disturbing Indian records is a Paiute pictograph panel excavated in the Grand Canyon. It illustrates a Ghost Dance held along the river in the 1880s. Indians across the country believed that if they danced the ceremonial Ghost Dance again and again, the white man who had stolen their lands, massacred their people and destroyed their culture would disappear. Their lands would be returned to them; the dead deer, antelope, and other creatures that had lived there before would reappear; and they could continue life as they had known it before the white man arrived. Inspired by a Paiute named Wovoka, the Ghost Dance movement spread throughout the West.

But the Paiute and others danced and danced to no avail. By the late 19th century, the white man had arrived for good. Pioneers, miners, railroad men and the federal government were not going to let Indians get in the way of American progress and development, and the Paiute were forced to abandon their canyon home.

terraces and any arable land they could find, and controling erosion by building low rock walls. Taking advantage of the subtle shift in climate, they spread out, strengthened and flourished. The canyon during this period did not look like it does today. While it was by no means lush, the high water table, increased precipitation and wide alluvial terraces made it more amenable to agrarian communities than it would be today. Walhalla Glades, Kwagunt Delta, Deer Creek, Pinenut and Havasu Canyon are examples of canyon features that, through slight manipulation to take advantage of water and thwart erosion, ancestral Puebloans adapted for farming.

These cultures also used plants, animals and other natural resources for food, medicine, clothing, utensils, tools and religious ceremonies. An intricate trail system allowed access to nooks and crannies, as well as to the river, and spurs in all directions linked canyon communities and facilitated trade with cultures throughout the Southwest. Remnants of these paths can still be seen today; some were modified by prospectors, early tourist entrepreneurs and the National Park Service and are still in use. The Tanner Trail, for example, is an old Hopi route that descended into the canyon from the South Rim. One of the most striking of these ancestral Puebloan trails is a stick footbridge across a gap in the cliffs called the Anasazi Bridge, which can be seen on the north side of the river, upstream from President Harding Rapid.

Between 1150 and 1200, Puebloan Indians abandoned the Grand Canyon. Other centers of Puebloan culture, like Chaco Canyon in northwest New Mexico and Mesa Verde in Southern Colorado, were also abandoned during this period, and scientists cannot agree on exactly why such elaborate and thriving communities would so suddenly leave their homes. Analyses of tree rings, stalagmites and lake pollen suggest that a severe drought descended upon the region at about 1150. This drought affected precarious canyon conditions, dropping the table, drying up springs, halting sediment-rich flooding that helped minimize erosion, and reducing the number of acres that could be successfully farmed. After just a few years of drought, corn reserves dwindled, and canyon people were faced with malnutrition and starvation. Though there was no single mass exodus from the canyon, Puebloan peoples drifted away. Cohonina migrated towards Flagstaff; others drifted to and blended with Hopi mesas to the east. The Kayenta villagers stayed a bit longer than their contemporaries to construct fortlike buildings along the South Rim. According to archeologists, these defensive structures suggest that hostile invasions from migrating tribes further weakened the already vulnerable Puebloan communities and contributed to their withdrawal from the canyon. The Tusayan Ruin, on the east side of the South Rim, may have been the last Puebloan community in the Grand Canyon region. Archeological records show that it was not built until 1185 and was inhabited by a community of about 30 people for a mere 25 years.

Whatever the reason – drought, invasion or a combination of the two – by 1300 the Grand Canyon became merely an echo of the once-thriving agrarian Pueblo culture. Though the evidence suggests that they would return periodically, Pueblo Indians never returned permanently.

FROM 1250 TO TODAY

As the farming cultures of the Pueblo people exited the canyon, other cultures moved in. The **Cerbat/Pai**, ancestors of today's **Hualapai** and **Havasupai**, arrived from the Mojave Desert to inhabit the western side of the canyon south of the river. It's not clear when they took up permanent residence – some scholars believe that they came to the region about 100 years after the ancestral Puebloans left; while others believe that it was their arrival that contributed to the Puebloan's departure. Hualapai trace their origins to Kathat Kanave, an old man who sometimes took the form of a coyote and lived in Mada Widita Canyon (also known as Meriwitica), on the canyon's westernmost edge. He taught the Pai how to live in the canyon, explaining what herbs cured which ailments and how and what to plant. From this sacred mountain, the Pai people were separated: a frog led the Havasupai east to his lush home in Havasu canyon, while the Hualapai remained close to Meriwitica.

On the other side of the canyon, arriving at about the same time as the Pai (but unrelated), the hunter–gatherer **Paiute** migrated southward from the Great Basin of Nevada and Utah to inhabit the high plateau country once sparsely populated by the Virgin Puebloans. The few remaining Puebloans likely taught them how to squeeze water from the dust and rock to grow corn and squash in the canyon deltas, and they descended into the canyon to collect salt and other natural resources. Paiute rock art, or *tumpituxwinap*, tells us something about their lives and culture. They wore loin cloths, lived in branch and brush shelters, made baskets and reddish-brown pottery, used grinding stones for seeds, hunted with bows and arrows and crossed the river to trade with the Havasupai. Paiute bands who occupied the Grand Canyon about 800 years ago include the Kaibabits, Uinkarets and Shivwits.

Spanish Explorers & Missionaries

Europeans saw the canyon for the first time in September of 1540. Spanish explorer Francisco Vasquez de Coronado believed that seven cities of gold lay in the northern interior of New Spain, and though several efforts had proved fruitless (he instead found Native pueblos of stone and mud), he continued to traverse the region in search of gold. Natives told him about a great river that would reach riches at the Gulf of California, so he sent Garcia Lopez de Cardeñas and his party of 12 to investigate.

It is not clear where Cardeñas and his men stood when they first saw the Grand Canyon, but based on his written record, historians believe it was somewhere between Moran Point and Desert View, on the South Rim. Though Hopi guides knew of relatively easy paths into the canyon, they didn't share them, and Cardeñas' men managed to descend only about one-third before turning back. The canyon was too much of an obstacle, and the rewards were too little.

Finding no gold or riches of any sort, Spanish explorers left the canyon country to the natives. They were not, however, left alone and in peace. The Catholic church of Spain, more interested in converting the natives to Christianity than finding gold, spent the next several hundred years building missionaries in the Southwest and severely punishing resistors.

Despite the unwelcoming conditions, Spanish missionaries traversed the inhospitable terrain of Northern Arizona in search of both converts and routes to Santa Fe. Inevitably, some stumbled upon the canyon. In 1776, about 200 years after Cardeñas tried to reach the river, Francisco Thomas Garces reached the canyon in an effort to find a path to Santa Fe from what is now Yuma, Arizona. A kind and gentle man who is widely attributed as the second European visitor to the canyon, Garces named the river 'Rio Colorado,' meaning 'Red River.' He spent several days with the hospitable Havasupai. Because they had been sheltered in their canyon home, the Havasupai had not yet developed a fear and hatred of Spanish missionaries, and they showered him with feasts and celebration. He marveled at their intricate system of irrigation and treated them with courtesy and respect. He continued east into Hopi country, but they refused to give him shelter or food. Later that year, Silvestre Velez de Escalante, Francisco Atanasio Dominquez and Captain Bernardo Miera y Pacheco came upon the canyon while trying to find a route from Monterey, California to Santa Fe.

Historians believe that no more than a handful of Europeans visited the canyon from 1540 until the early 19th century. Their influence on the people and land of the region was minimal, for the canyon held nothing of interest for them. For Spanish explorers, it was a barrier to be overcome in their search for gold, and because there was nothing but dry, barren country, the indigenous peoples were left in relative peace. They had no way of knowing that what would begin as a trickle of American traders, trappers and government surveyors in the mid-19th century would end in a tumult of pioneers, prospectors and tourists that would transform their lives forever.

Trappers, Traders & Surveyors

In 1803, the Louisiana Purchase made the young United States the northeastern neighbor of New Spain, and in 1821 the Mexican Revolution secured Mexican independence from Spain. These two events opened up northern Arizona for trappers and traders, who took advantage of Mexico's lax control of the region.

Hundreds of fur trappers, employed by trading companies like William Henry Ashley's Rocky Mountain Fur Company, explored the rivers and tributaries of what would become Wyoming, Utah, Colorado, Arizona and New Mexico in search of pelts. Though none of them rafted the entire Colorado River through the canyon, French trapper Denis Julien scratched his name and the year (1836) along the cliffs as far downstream as Cataract Canyon. Ashley himself etched his name in rocks at Red Canyon in 1825 – when John Wesley Powell (see p239) came upon it in 1869, he named the rapids Ashley Falls.

James Ohio Pattie, an Iowa native who began trapping and mining in New Mexico in 1824, told his trapping stories to Timothy Flint, who published them as a personal narrative in 1831. Traveling without guides, Pattie related his frustration with the sheer cliffs of the canyon. Rather than beautiful and inspiring, Pattie described them as nothing but a hurdle that kept him from the river. Because so few trappers left written records, it is difficult to know exactly who came to the canyon and where they went, but historians speculate visitors include Christopher 'Kit' Carson, Pauline Weather and William Sherley Williams.

In the mid-19th century, several events occurred over the course of a few years that would transform the American Southwest within a half-century. With the Treaty of Guadalupe Hidalgo in 1848, the Mexican–American War ended, and the United States acquired Mexico's northern territory, which would eventually become Arizona, California, Nevada, Utah, Colorado and New Mexico. This, along with the territories acquired with the Louisiana Purchase only 40 years earlier, more than doubled the United States and forced the federal government to grapple with the problem of maintaining a Jeffersonian system of representative government and maintaining a national identity despite great geographical and cultural distances. That same year, gold was discovered at Sutter's Mill in California. In 1850, the territory of New Mexico, including Arizona and the Grand Canyon, was created.

Forty-niners headed to gold in California, and pioneers hoping to build homes in the new West needed wagon roads. Moreover, if the United States was to retain control over the vast wilderness that they had just acquired, they needed to know exactly what it was. And so the United States sent military men to identify and map its new territory. Expeditions led by Lieutenant James Simpson (1849) and Captain Lorenzo Sitgreaves (1851), both accompanied by artist Richard Kern, resulted in official reports of the region, but did not include the canyon itself. In 1856 and 1857, Edward Fitzgerald Beale was convinced that camels were best suited to the travel in the Great American Desert and used 76 of them to create a wagon trail along the 35th parallel. The road passed what is now Flagstaff and

FERRYMAN OF THE COLORADO

Believing that stories of good homesteading and plenty of water in Arizona were true, Utah Mormons moved south to the desolate desert land north and east of the Grand Canyon. They built Winsor Castle (now in Pipe Springs National Monument), a cattle ranch and a refuge from Indians, in 1870. That same year, Mormon leaders ordered John D Lee, exiled because of his participation in a massacre of non-Mormon emigrants in Mountain Meadow, to run a ferryboat across the Colorado to service the influx of Mormons to the region. His ferry would be the only river crossing on the upper Colorado, and he spent several years preaching his faith while shuttling prospectors and settlers – along with their mules, wagons and whatever else they needed – across the river. A wanted man, he occasionally had to leave his post to hide from the law. In 1874 they found him and tried him, and in 1879 he was executed for murder. The ferry crossing was used until 1929, when a bridge was built a few miles downstream. Today, river runners put in at Lees Ferry, and visitors can tour historic buildings at the site of his ferry launch.

Williams to connect to Captain Lorenzo Sitgreave's 1851 road to the Colorado River, between today's Lake Mead and Needles. Though camels never caught on like he had hoped, Beale made improvements on his road in 1858, and it was used by pioneers for several decades. Over the course of the next 80 years, it would be incorporated into the National Old Trails Highway, which then became Route 66 in 1926, which then became I-40 in the '70s.

In 1858, Army First Lieutenant Joseph Christmas Ives was appointed to explore the still mysterious 'big canyon' region. Directed to find an inland waterway, Ives set off on the steamboat *The Explorer* on December 31, 1858 from the Gulf of Mexico. He traveled upriver for two months but crashed into a boulder in Black Canyon (near today's Hoover Dam) before ever making it into the canyon. He abandoned his river efforts and set off on Beale's road, along with artists Heinrich Baldwin Mollhausen and Baron Friedrich W Von Egloffstein, geologist John Strong Newberry, various Indian guides, soldiers, packers, trail builders and about 150 mules. After about a month, they scrambled down a side canyon north of Peach Springs and became what historians believe to be the first European Americans known to reach the river within the canyon. Mollhausen and von Egloffstein are credited with creating the first visual representations of the Grand Canyon.

Frustrated with the difficulty of the terrain and the lack of water, Ives cut south to Beale's road west of Havasu Falls, and eventually returned east to organize the expedition's maps, landscape etchings and lithographs into a cohesive report on the 'big canyon'. While acknowledging its sublime beauty (perhaps the first to do so), Ives concluded that the region was 'altogether valueless. ... Ours has been the first and will doubtless be the last party of whites to visit this profitless locality. ... It seems intended by nature that the Colorado River, along with the greater portion of its lonely and majestic way, shall be forever unvisited and undisturbed.'

The idea of nature as a destination in itself, as something to be preserved as an American treasure, did not become a popular notion until the late 19th century. Until that point, Americans were interested in nature only in as much as it could be exploited for material gain. Within a quarter-century, this would change. But it would take the hand of artists, who would show the public the splendor and grandeur of the canyon, combined with a national need for an American identity and unity in the wake of Civil War, to shift American attitudes.

Removal of Native Americans

Since the early 19th century, US military forces had been pushing west across the continent, protecting settlers and wresting land from the Indians, who had little use for European concepts of land ownership. With the 1848 Treaty of Guadalupe and the discovery of gold at Sutter's Mill in California, Americans crossed the continent in unprecedented numbers. It wasn't long before they intruded into and permanently transformed the lives and homes of Native Americans who had lived in and around the Grand Canyon for centuries.

After the murder of Hualapai Chief Wauba Yuman in 1866, Hualapai chief Sherum engaged American troops in a three-year war. The US Army destroyed their homes, crops and food supplies until the Hualapai surrendered in 1869. They were forced onto a reservation on the lower Colorado, and, deprived of rations and unused to the heat of the lower elevations, many died from starvation or illness. The Hualapai escaped the reservation, only to be confined again when President Chester Arthur set aside the current 1,000,000-acre reservation on the south side of the Grand Canyon.

Like the Hualapai, the Navajo suffered intolerable cruelty in the name of American progress. During the winter of 1864–65, US Cavalry troops led by Colonel Kit Carson destroyed fields and property, killed anyone they found and drove the Indians up into Canyon de Chelly until starvation forced their surrender. Thousands of Indians were rounded up and forced to march to Fort Sumner in the plains of eastern New Mexico in an episode remembered in tribal history as 'The Long Walk.' Hundreds of Navajo died on the march or on the inhospitable new reservation. Despite this, the Navajo were one of the luckier tribes. A treaty in 1868 gave them a reservation of about 5500 sq miles in the heart of their ancient lands, and 8000 inhabitants of Fort Sumner, along with about another 8000 scattered Navajo, were allowed to settle on the new reservation. This grew over the years to its present 27,000 sq miles to the east of the Grand Canyon, making it the largest reservation in the United States.

While the Navajo were rounded up for the Long Walk, the Hopi, perceived as peaceful and less of a threat to US expansion, were left on their mesas. After the Navajo were allowed to return from exile, they came back to the lands surrounding the Hopi mesas. Historically, the Hopi have distrusted the Navajo, and it is ironic therefore that the Hopi Reservation is completely surrounded by the Navajo Reservation. Three mesas form the heart of the 2410-sq-mile Hopi Reservation. On top of the third mesa is Old Araibi, which the Hopi say has been continuously inhabited since the early 12th century.

Though the Havasupai escaped the brutality of the Indian Wars, they too were eventually forced to give up their lands and were confined to a reservation as Americans settled in the Grand Canyon region. In 1880, President Rutherford Hayes established an area 5 miles wide and 12 miles long as the Havasupai Reservation, which eventually was expanded to its present-day boundaries. A few years later, the Bureau of Indian Affairs established schools for the Hualapai and Havasupai children to teach them the ways of the white man. Their canyon home was increasingly disturbed by Anglo explorers, prospectors and intrepid tourists as the 19th century drew to a close and the Grand Canyon became a destination for European Americans.

Native Americans on the North Rim did not fare any better. Several bands of Paiutes had migrated southeast from the Great Basin to the high plateau country north of the Grand Canyon after AD 1000; there, they remained relatively undisturbed for more than 900 years. US westward expansion brought disease to the Paiute, settlers stole the Paiute's best lands, and by the late 1860s conflict with Anglo pioneers had become common. In the early

20th century, only about 100 Kaibab Paiute lived north of the canyon in Moccasin Spring. They were moved onto a reservation in 1907. Today, the Kaibab Reservation surrounds Pipe Springs National Monument, in the desert about 80 miles north of the North Rim.

John Wesley Powell

The onset of the Civil War postponed American explorations of the West, but soon after its conclusion in 1865, the federal government financed four major surveys. From 1867 to 1879, teams of geologists, naturalists, artists and others were sent to investigate western land and to determine its tourist, settlement and commerce potentials, as well as possibilities for exploiting its natural resources. Though John Wesley Powell was not part of these more prominent surveys, he scrambled together a makeshift team of volunteers and private funding (he would receive federal funding by the Department of the Interior in 1870) to finance his expedition to the Colorado River. A one-armed Civil War veteran and professor of geology, Powell had read Ives' report and was fascinated with the geology of the Colorado River. His work would set the stage for the canyon's transformation from a hurdle to a destination.

Tau-Gu, chief of the Paiute, overlooking the Virgin River with JW Powell (ca 1873)

In May of 1869, Powell and his crew of nine launched four wooden boats, laden with thousands of pounds of scientific equipment and supplies, from Green River, Wyoming. They floated peacefully until one of the boats, the *No Name*, smashed into rocks at rapids that Powell named Disaster Falls. Despite this mishap and the loss of supplies, they continued down the Green River, joined the Colorado River on July 17 and floated through Glen Canyon with relatively smooth sailing. The waters of the Colorado in the 'big canyon,' however, were not so kind. They pillaged their heavy boats around rapids and ran others, baked under the hot sun, repaired leaky boats and sustained themselves on dwindling rations of flour, coffee and dried apples. Powell took notes on the geology and natural history, and they spent a great deal of time scrambling over cliffs, taking measurements and examining rocks, canyons and streams in what Powell called their 'granite prison.'

On August 27th, they came to a particularly wild rapid that Powell named Separation Rapid. Here, three men – Bill Dunn and brothers Seneca and Oramel Howland, who were exhausted, fed up with their wilderness conditions and convinced that they would never make it through alive – abandoned Powell and hiked north out of the canyon in hopes of finding civilization. Instead, they were attacked and killed by Shivwits Paiute

Indians who mistook them for prospectors who had murdered a Paiute woman. The Powell expedition made it through the wild water, as well as through several other rough rapids, and emerged three days later close to what is now Lake Mead. After 14 weeks on the river, Powell and his crew became the first known people to explore the Colorado River through what Powell named the Grand Canyon.

Powell returned to the Colorado River in 1871 for a second expedition, this time with photographer EO Beaman, who produced about 350 images of the Grand Canyon, and artist Frederick Samuel Dellenbaugh. In 1873, Thomas Moran, the landscaper painter who would become the artist most associated with the Grand Canyon, and photographer John Hiller visited the rim country with Powell. Powell's 1875 report, entitled 'The Exploration of the Colorado River of the West,' as well as newspaper and magazine articles – and in particular the Moran and Hiller's visual representations that accompanied these written accounts – planted the seeds for the canyon as a tourist destination. Moran's painting *Grand Chasm of the Colorado*, purchased by Congress for $10,000, hung in the National Capitol building and would be influential in concurring national-park status to the Grand Canyon. For the first time, the general public saw images of the sublime and spectacular Grand Canyon. The images and tales piqued their interest, and within a quarter of a century, through the combined forces of the prospectors-turned-tourist guides, the railroad and the Fred Harvey Company, the Grand Canyon would become an iconographic American treasure.

Tourists Arrive

In the years after the Civil War, the United States accelerated efforts to build a transcontinental railroad in an effort to unite the country and promote western settlement. Surveyors were sent to find the most advantageous route, and in 1869 the line was completed.

GRAND CANYON NATIONAL PARK

John Hance (left) and others preparing to head down the Bright Angel Trail (ca 1902)

With the arrival of the Atlantic and Pacific Railroad to Flagstaff and Williams in the early 1880s, tourists trickled to the canyon's South Rim. In 1883, a total of 67 hardy tourists made the 20-mile trek from Peach Springs (the nearest train line to the Grand Canyon) to Diamond Creek. From there, they descended another two miles along Diamond Creek Wash to the Colorado River. In 1884, JH Farlee eked out the Grand Canyon's first wagon trail to Diamond Creek and built a hotel at the end of the line.

PROSPECTORS TURNED CANYON GUIDES

Though hundreds of mineral claims for copper, asbestos, silver and lead were located in the Grand Canyon after 1880, most of them did not pan out. Many prospectors discovered that they'd have better luck making money through tourism than mining. Farlee's makeshift hotel, eclipsed by their services, closed down in 1889, and tourism at the turn-of-the-20th-century revolved around prospectors who developed their trails, guided travelers into the canyon and built the South Rim's earliest lodges.

Hance Ranch

Prospector John Hance, who lives on in canyon lore as one of its most colorful characters, is credited with guiding the first canyon tourists, Edward Everett Ayer and his family and friends. Hance moved to the canyon rim three miles east of today's Grandview Point in 1883. In 1884, deciding that he would never make it rich on asbestos or copper, he filed for a 160-acre homesteading claim and built a cabin on the rim. He advertised in Flagstaff newspapers, charged guests $1 for dinner and lodging in his tents and guided visitors into the canyon on his mining trails.

In 1895, he sold Hance Ranch to James Thurber and JH Tolfree for $1500, and when the rim's first post office opened in his cabin in 1897, he became its first postmaster. Though he sold his asbestos claim by the river in 1901, Hance remained on the canyon rim, living in Bright Angel Hotel and working as a canyon raconteur for the Fred Harvey Company, until illness forced him to move to the Weatherford Hotel in 1918. He died in January 1919, a few weeks before the park was granted national-park status, and was the first to be buried in the Grand Canyon Cemetery.

THE HERMIT

Nicknamed the Hermit because of his quiet ways, his remote inner-canyon home and his refusal to engage in the squabbles with the park service, French-Canadian prospector Louis D Boucher arrived at the canyon sometime around 1890 and lived there for about 20 years. With a long white beard and laden with tools of his trade, he wandered throughout the canyon and tributaries on his white mule, looking for mineral claims. He sometimes guided tourists on his Silver Bell Trail from the rim to the springs, now called Dripping Springs Trail, or on his Boucher Trail to the Colorado. He built stone cabins by his copper claim next to the river; grew oranges, peaches, figs and other fruits and vegetables year-round; nurtured an orchard of more than 50 trees; and welcomed guests to his home at Dripping Springs. In 1912, after selling the upper portions of his trail to the railroad, the Hermit moved to Mohrland, Utah, where he worked in a coal mine.

Bass Camp

William Wallace Bass, a contemporary of Hance, set up a dude ranch 25 miles west of today's Grand Canyon Village in 1890. He drove to Williams to pick up guests, brought them to his camp over a two-day wagon ride and entertained them along the rim and, by 1901, on over 50 miles of inner canyon trails. He continued to run his lodge while tourist facilities developed around him, and it wasn't until 1923 that he finally closed it down.

MARY COLTER'S GRAND VISION

Mary Colter's buildings blend so seamlessly into the landscape that, were it not for the tourists strolling around them, you could conceivably not even notice the structures. Indeed, Colter's buildings add to Grand Canyon National Park because they succeed so magnificently in adding nothing at all.

Mary Colter (1869–1958) graduated from high school in St Paul, Minnesota in 1883 (at the age of 14), studied art in San Francisco and spent her entire career designing hotels, shops, restaurants and train stations for the Fred Harvey Company and the Santa Fe Railway. Beginning in the late 1870s, these two companies worked as a team to transform the American West into a tourist destination.

With the Indians confined to reservations and the completion of the transcontinental railroad in 1869, the western landscape and culture came to define America. It gave form to American ideals of independence and progress, and offered Civil War–weary citizens the chance to celebrate uniquely American traditions. Mary Colter's Grand Canyon buildings played upon these sentiments by offering travelers the opportunity to walk into an authentic, albeit romanticized, American West experience.

GRAND CANYON NATIONAL PARK

Artist Fred Kabotie explains the snake-legend painting in the Colter-designed Watchtower (ca 1932)

Her work follows the sensibility of the Arts & Crafts movement. In keeping with the nationalist spirit of the late 19th century, and in reaction against industrialized society, the Arts & Crafts aesthetic looked toward American models, rather than European traditions, for inspiration. The movement revered handcrafted objects, clean and simple lines and the incorporation of indigenous material (for an excellent example of classic Arts & Crafts design, stop by the Riordan Mansion in Flagstaff; see p188).

Colter spent a great deal of time researching all her buildings, exploring ancient Hopi villages, studying Native American culture and taking careful notes. The Colter buildings in Grand Canyon National Park use local material such as Kaibab limestone and pine, and incorporate stone, wood, iron, glass and brick. They embrace Native American crafts like woven textile and geometric design, and echo Indian architecture with kiva fireplaces and vigas on the ceiling.

The conundrum of preserving expanses of western land as sacred American wilderness while at the same time developing them for tourists was solved in part by Colter's brilliant designs. Her buildings, known as 'National Park Service rustic,' stand in harmony with their natural environment and served as models and inspiration for subsequent tourist services in national parks throughout the country.

Arnold Berke's *Mary Colter: Architect of the Southwest* is a beautifully illustrated and well-written examination of the life and work of Mary Colter.

Grand Canyon Stage Line

Realizing that passengers departing the train in Williams and Flagstaff were making their way up to the Grand Canyon, the Atlantic and Pacific hired James Thurber to run a regular Grand Canyon Stage Line from Flagstaff to the rim. By 1898, Thurber owned the stage line and shuttled about 300 visitors a week from the Bank Hotel in Flagstaff to his Hance Ranch. The stagecoach left three times a week, stopped at three rest spots along the bumpy and dusty 73-mile route and took about 12 hours. In 1896, Thurber built the Bright Angel Hotel, 14 miles west of today's Bright Angel Lodge, and extended the stagecoach line. He sold his line to Martin Buggeln in 1901 and his ranch to Buggeln in 1907. Though Buggeln expanded the ranch, building a 17-room, two-story hotel beside the existing structure, he never opened it to guests. He held onto his private holdings until his death in 1939. The park service bought the property in 1948, and in 1957 rangers razed what remained of Hance's original structures and Buggeln's never-used hotel.

Grand View Hotel

Prospector Peter Berry, among others, mined copper, gold and silver (including a 700-pound nugget of over 70% copper, which was displayed at the Chicago World's Columbian Exposition in 1893) at Horseshoe Mesa, 2500 vertical feet below Grandview Point. Berry and company built a rim-side cabin in 1888 and constructed the Grandview Toll Trail to their mines in 1893. Though the mining was relatively successful, Berry decided to augment his copper-mining with a tourist facility, and so in 1897 he built the Grand View Hotel.

GRAND CANYON NATIONAL PARK

Unlike Hance's rustic tents, Berry's accommodations boasted Hopi crafts, Navajo blankets, beamed ceilings, hardwood floors and comfortable furnishings. The hotel and trail became hugely popular with the mule-trekking set.

When Harry Smith's Canyon Copper Company bought him out, Berry built the Summit Hotel on his adjacent 160-acre homestead claim. Smith and Perry combined their structures to run the new Grandview Hotel from 1903 to 1907. In 1913, William Randolph Hearst bought the property, and though he threatened to build luxurious hotel accommodations (much to the chagrin of the Fred Harvey Company and the Santa Fe Railroad, which had

Artist Thomas Moran and his two daughters (ca 1905)

by that point developed Grand Canyon Village), he only used the land for cattle grazing. It wasn't until 1939 that the park service gained control of the hotels, land, trails and mining remnants. They destroyed the buildings, but today visitors can still hike along Berry's Grandview Trail and see the remains of his mine.

Ralph Cameron

Ralph Cameron bought out mining claims at Indian Garden and opened the inner-canyon Indian Garden Camp at the turn-of-the-century. In 1903, he acquired what was originally the Red Horse stage station and opened Cameron's Hotel next to Buggeln's Bright Angel Hotel. He retained control of Bright Angel Trail Rd as the park service, and the Fred Harvey Company developed services around him, forcing the construction of trails and facilities elsewhere (see History of Bright Angel Trail, p91).

TOURISM ON THE NORTH RIM

Because of its isolation, tourism on the North Rim developed more slowly, and even today it only receives 10% of the park's visitors. The Arizona Strip, the remote desert country north of the rim, was originally settled in the mid-19th century by Mormons, who were trying to escape increasingly strict laws against polygamy.

Most visitors to the Kaibab Plateau went for sport hunting. In June 1906, Teddy Roosevelt created Grand Canyon Game Preserve. The United States Forest Service prohibited deer hunting in the preserve and set about eliminating all of the animal's predators. James T 'Uncle Jim' Owens, in his capacity as the reserve's first game warden, guided hunting trips and oversaw the killing of hundreds upon hundreds of badgers, coyotes, wolverines, cougars and grizzly bears.

Following the first car to the North Rim in 1909 (it took three days from Kanab), the forest service began advertising scenic attractions in the Kaibab Plateau. In 1913, they built the 56-mile Grand Canyon Highway to the Bright Angel Ranger Station, at Harvey Meadow. Aldus Jensen and his wife ran a small tourist service with tent accommodation. They led guests along the Rust Trail to the river, where they would connect with Fred Harvey wranglers. In 1917, Wylie's Way Camp opened near the fire tower at Bright Angel Point, and Jensen closed down his services. A step above tents, but nothing like the elegance of El Tovar, Wylie's Way Camp could accommodate up to 25 guests and offered tent cabins; guided tours to Cape Royal, Point Sublime and other destinations; mule trips; and a central dining room.

GRAND CANYON NATIONAL PARK

Interior of a Bright Angel cabin (ca 1907)

Visitors arriving to the North Rim from the north had to take the 135-mile stagecoach from Marysvale, Utah to Kanab and then travel the 80 miles or so to the rim by whatever means they could find. Alternatively, beginning in 1907, they could hike into the canyon from the South Rim, cross the Colorado River in a cage strung on a cable, and hike up to the North Rim on the North Kaibab Trail (constructed in 1903). On the canyon's bottom, visitors stayed in a tourist camp at the mouth of Bright Angel Creek, the predecessor to Colter's 1922 Phantom Ranch.

Also in 1922, Gronway and Chauncey Parry began automobile tours to the North Rim, and Will S Rust opened a tourist camp outside the park's northern boundary. In 1919, a rough dirt road from Kanab to the Grand Canyon's North Rim was completed, and by 1925 more than 7000 visitors arrived at Bright Angel Point. In 1928, Union Pacific architect GS Underwood designed the original Grand Canyon Lodge, and a suspension bridge was built across the river to connect the South and North Kaibab Trails. Though a fire on September 1, 1932 destroyed the main lodge on the North Rim, it was rebuilt in 1937, and the guest cabins, still used today, were left unharmed.

THE RAILROAD, CARS & CROWDS ARRIVE

With the arrival of the railroad to the South Rim in 1901 (it never did make it to the North Rim), tourism at the canyon accelerated. Instead of paying $20 and enduring a teeth-rattling 12-hour stagecoach ride, visitors could pay $3.95 and reach the rim from Williams in three hours.

In 1902, brothers Ellsworth and Emery Kolb arrived, and within a few years they set up a photography studio (see Kolb Studio, p93) on the rim. Tourists could ride a mule into the canyon in the morning and have a photo of their journey by the next day.

GRAND CANYON NATIONAL PARK

Fred Harvey, who joined the Santa Fe Railroad in 1876 to provide hotels and services to its passengers, earned a reputation for luxurious track-side accommodation, fine dining and impeccable service. In 1905, only four years after the train's arrival at the rim, his Fred Harvey Company built El Tovar, an elegant hotel, and Hopi House, built by Hopi Indians. Hopis entertained tourists with dance and craft demonstrations and sold their crafts at Hopi House.

Now that the Native Americans had been confined to reservations and the wilderness had been tamed, Americans began to see an innocence and authenticity in Native American culture and in

Emery, Blanche and Ellsworth Kolb standing on the back porch of the original Kolb Studio (ca 1904)

the natural landscape that was lacking in industrialized life. No longer a threat, Native Americans and their crafts and lifestyle became a subject for the tourist gaze.

The Grand Canyon, with its proximity to the Indians of the Southwest and its spectacular wilderness scenery that could be enjoyed from the comfort of rim-side hotels, offered Americans a safe opportunity to return to a romanticized past. Furthermore, the landscape of the American West, unique in its geologic features and sublime magnificence, gave a young country looking for a history and a unifying identity something to claim. The US may not have had the churches, writers and artists of Europe, but it had a western landscape more awesome than the Swiss Alps and older than its the Old World's historic cities. The American West gave the country a unique identity, and tourists flocked to the Grand Canyon.

RIVER RUNNERS IN THE CANYON

While tourism on the rims and on inner-canyon trails developed feverishly at the beginning of the 20th century, the idea of rafting on the 277 miles of the Colorado River through the canyon attracted only a few intrepid adventurers. One of the earliest of these was Robert Brewster Stanton, who went down the river in 1889 to survey it for a rail line. He lost several men, and the idea of a rail line along the river was abandoned. After 1900, several prospectors survived the trip, and in 1911 the Kolb brothers filmed their river expedition and began screening it to tourists.

Of the many early tourists who tried to raft the river but never finished, honeymooners Glen and Bessie Hyde would become the most famous. They set out in 1928, without life-jackets, to be the first man and woman pair to run the Colorado through the canyon. They ran the 424 miles from Green River, Utah to Bright Angel Creek (including the rapids at Cataract Canyon) in 26 days and hiked up to Bright Angel Lodge for a rest, publicity photographs and interviews. Though witnesses say Glen seemed excited to continue, and loved the media attention, Bessie hinted at being less than thrilled to return to the river. As Emory Kolb and his daughter Edith walked them to the trailhead, Bessie noticed Edith's shoes and, looking at her own hiking boots, commented rather sadly 'I wonder if I shall ever wear pretty shoes again.' As fate would have it, she never would. The honeymooners never emerged from the canyon, and their disappearance remains one of the park's greatest mysteries.

In 1938, Norman Nevills started the first commercial river-running business, but by 1949 still only 100 people had run the Colorado through the Grand Canyon.

The Fred Harvey Company hired architect Mary Colter (see the boxed text, p242) to build tourist facilities from indigenous materials that would echo the architecture of Pueblo Indians and blend into the natural surroundings. Her buildings include the Hopi House (1905), Lookout Studio (1914), Hermits Rest (1914), Phantom Ranch (1922), the Watchtower (1932) and Bright Angel Lodge (designed in 1916 but built in 1935).

A year after the arrival of the railroad, journalist Winfield Hogaboom and three friends made the first automobile trip from Flagstaff to the South Rim on a steam-driven Toledo-8. The car broke down, and Hogaboom walked 18 miles to Berry's Grand View Hotel for help, but they finally made it after a five-day journey. After a few days' visit at the canyon, everyone but the driver, Oliver Lippincott, returned to Flagstaff by train. By 1929, most of the canyon's 200,000 visitors arrived by car.

The Grand Canyon as a National Park

In 1908, President Theodore Roosevelt created the Grand Canyon National Monument, and in 1919 President Woodrow Wilson made Grand Canyon the 15th national park in the US. Over 44,000 people visited the park that year. By 1956, more than one million people would visit the Grand Canyon.

In 1974, the traffic congestion had gotten so bad that the park service started shuttle services, and in 1976 the park saw more than three million visitors. Even the sky became overcrowded; in 1987 a federal regulation required sightseeing planes and helicopters to fly higher over the canyon and banned them from certain areas.

In 1993, only 130 years after Ives had predicted that the canyon would be 'forever left unvisited and undisturbed,' almost five million people visited Grand Canyon National Park.

The Grand Canyon Today

While the North Rim has not developed much beyond what it was in 1930, the Grand Canyon's South Rim has changed dramatically since the park's pioneer period. The National Park Service centralized tourist facilities at Grand Canyon Village, a decision that, while resulting in an ever more congested 40-mile stretch along the South Rim, has allowed for vast areas of undeveloped wilderness. Ironically, considering the efforts that are made today to minimize automobile travel to the park, superintendents in the canyon's early days as a national park worked to attract visitors traveling by automobile.

The Great Depression slowed the frenzy of park development, and from 1933 to 1942, the Civilian Corps Conservation, the Public Works Administration and the Works Progress Administration did everything from touching up buildings to creating trails and cleaning ditches. Fewer

DAMNING THE GRAND CANYON?

In January 1964, the Pacific Southwest Water Plan proposed that two gigantic dams be built on the Colorado River in the Grand Canyon. Dams at Marble Gorge and Bridge Canyon, on opposite ends of the park, would use the thousand feet of elevation loss between Glen Canyon Dam (to the east) and Hoover Dam (to the west) to generate 2.1 kilowatts of hydroelectric power. Seven southwestern states supported the plan, believing that the dams would raise money to support water projects to their benefit. The Bureau of Reclamation claimed that the dams would result in only minor flooding of Grand Canyon National Park itself, including Havasu Creek and Lava Falls.

David Brower, who in 1952 had become the first paid executive director of the Sierra Club and had since been a thorn in the side of the Bureau's dam-loving Floyd Dominy, spearheaded a publicity campaign against the dams. Full-page ads in the *Washington Post*, the *New York Times*, the *San Francisco Chronicle* and the *Los Angeles Times* attacked the Bureau's argument that tourists would better appreciate the Grand Canyon from motorboats. 'Shall we also flood the Sistine Chapel,' an ad asked, 'so tourists can get nearer the ceiling?' Dump trucks of letters, 95% of them outraged at the thought of a dam in the Grand Canyon, flooded the Bureau of Reclamation, and by 1967 the plan was dead.

For more on the damming of the Colorado River, America's dam-building frenzy and the battles of the conservation movement, pick up Marc Reisner's compelling and altogether readable *Cadillac Desert: The American West and Its Disappearing Water*.

tourists visited during this period, giving rangers breathing room to develop interpretive programs – the predecessors of today's ranger talks.

The dearth of visitors from the Depression through the end of WWII resulted in a quieter, more relaxed Grand Canyon National Park. However, as soon as the war ended, Americans – in love with their cars and eager to explore and celebrate their country – inundated the national parks. The flood prompted another flurry of construction, and from 1953 to 1968 the park built more trails, enhanced existing trails, improved roads and built Maswik, Kachina and Thunderbird Lodges. Steel and concrete buildings joined the classic rustic style of El Tovar and Mary Colter's architecture.

Despite the problems and political battles that have surfaced as the park becomes more and more popular, including debates over automobile restrictions, regulations for scenic flights and limits on motorized boats on the Colorado River, the National Park Service's vision of a centralized South Rim has prevented sprawling development. It is still possible to take a short hike and feel as if the entire park is your own.

In 1979, Grand Canyon National Park was designated a World Heritage Site by the members of UNESCO. One hundred years after the first train of tourists arrived at the South Rim, the National Park Service continues to grapple with the dilemma of how to ensure access to one of America's greatest natural treasures while at the same time preserving the wilderness that everyone comes to experience.

GRAND CANYON NATIONAL PARK

While neither the longest nor the deepest canyon in the world, the Grand Canyon is certainly one of the most awe-inspiring.

GEOLOGY

Geologists are particularly captivated, as the canyon showcases a remarkably well preserved, two-billion-year-old slice of geologic history. Half of Earth's life span is revealed in its exposed layers, serving as a window into our planet's past.

The Story in the Rocks

The story starts down in the canyon's innermost recesses, where the Colorado River continues to carve a deep channel into progressively older rock. The bottommost layer, **Vishnu schist**, is dark and fine-grained, with vertical or diagonal bands that contrast with the canyon's horizontal upper layers. Look carefully to spot intruding bands of pinkish **Zoroaster granite**. Together, these are among the oldest exposed rocks on Earth's surface.

The schist offers evidence that 2 billion years ago the canyon region lay beneath an ancient sea. For tens of millions of years, silt and clay eroded into the water from adjacent landmasses, settling to the seafloor. These sediments, along with occasional dustings of lava and ash, accumulated to a thickness of 5 miles and were later buried beneath another 10 miles of additional sediment. By 1.7 billion years ago these layers had buckled and uplifted into a mighty mountain range that rose above the water. In the process, intense heat and pressure transformed the sedimentary layers into the metamorphic rocks schist and gneiss.

At the time, the region lay near the equator, but the uplifted landmass soon began a northward migration while undergoing a long spell of erosion. So much of the uplifted material eroded away that it left a significant gap (or unconformity) in the geologic record – from 1.7 billion to 1.2 billion years ago. Lost with hardly a trace was the mountain range itself, which finally wore down into a low coastal plain. Gradually the landmass sank back into the sea, providing a platform for marine algae, which secreted the Bass limestone that now sits atop the Vishnu schist. Marine fossils in the Bass limestone include such primitive life forms as cabbage-like **stromatolites**.

In the late **Precambrian** era (1.2 billion to 570 million years ago) the region alternated between marine and coastal environments as the ocean repeatedly advanced and retreated, each time leaving distinctive layers of sediment and structural features. Pockmarks from raindrops, cracks in drying mud and ripple marks in sand have all been preserved in one form or another, alongside countless other clues. Much of this evidence was lost as erosional forces scraped the land back down to Vishnu schist. The resulting gap in the geologic record is called the **Great Unconformity**, where older rocks abut against much newer rocks with no intervening layers. Fortunately, pockets of ancient rock that once perched atop the Vishnu schist still remain and lie exposed along the North and South Kaibab Trails, among other places.

The Precambrian era came to an end about 570 million years ago. The subsequent **Paleozoic** era (570 to 245 million years ago) spawned nearly all of the rock formations visitors see today. The Paleozoic also ushered in the dramatic transition from primitive organisms to an explosion of complex life forms that spread into every available aquatic and terrestrial niche – the beginning of life as we know it. The canyon walls contain an abundant fossil record of these ancient animals, including shells like cephalopods and brachiopods, trilobites and the tracks of reptiles and amphibians.

The Paleozoic record is particularly well preserved in the layers cut by the Colorado, as the region has been little altered by geologic events such as earthquakes, faulting or volcanic activity. Every advance and retreat of the ancient ocean laid down a characteristic layer that documents whether it was a time of deep oceans, shallow bays, active coastline, mudflats or elevated landscape. Geologists have learned to read these strata and to estimate climatic conditions during each episode. In fact, the science of stratigraphy, the reading of rock layers, stemmed from work at the canyon, at a time when American geology was in its infancy and considered vastly inferior by European geologists.

Considering the detailed Paleozoic record, it's puzzling that evidence of the following **Mesozoic** period (245 to 70 million years ago) is entirely absent at the canyon, even though its elaborate layers are well represented just miles away on the Colorado Plateau and in nearby Zion, Bryce and Arches National Parks. Towering over the landscape just south of the South Rim, Red Butte is a dramatic reminder of how many thousands of feet of Mesozoic sediments once covered the canyon 70 million years ago. So what happened to all of this rock, which vanished before the river even started shaping the canyon? About 70 million years ago the same events that gave rise to the Rocky Mountains created a buckle in the earth known as the **Kaibab Uplift**, a broad dome that rose several thousand feet above the surrounding region. Higher and more exposed, the upper layers of this dome eroded quickly and completely.

Evidence from the past 70 million years is equally scarce at the canyon, as the movement of materials has been *away* from the canyon rather than into it. Volcanism has added a few layers of rock in parts of the west canyon, where lava flows created temporary dams across the canyon or simply flowed over the rim in spectacular lava waterfalls, the latter now frozen in time. The stretching of Earth's crust also tilted the region to the southwest, shifting drainage patterns accordingly.

But the story that interests visitors most, namely how the canyon has changed in the past 5 million years, is perhaps the most ambiguous chapter of all. Geologists have several competing theories but few clues. One intriguing characteristic is that the canyon's east end is much older than the western portion, suggesting that two separate rivers carved the canyon. This fits into the oft-repeated 'stream piracy' theory that the Kaibab Uplift initially served as a barrier between two major river drainage systems. The theory assumes that the western drainage system eroded quickly into the soft sediments and carved eastward into the uplift, eventually breaking through the barrier and 'capturing' the flow of the ancient Colorado River, which then shifted course down this newly opened route.

GEOLOGIC WONDERS

- ✔ **Vulcans Throne** (p113) – The park's most impressive cinder cone
- ✔ **Bright Angel Canyon** (pp99, 114, 119) – An excellent example of how creeks follow fault lines across the landscape
- ✔ **Havasu Creek** (p139) – Stupendous travertine formations and beautiful waterfalls
- ✔ **Toroweap Overlook** (p113) – The canyon's most dramatic viewpoint
- ✔ **Vishnu Temple** (p118 – One of the canyon's most prominent temples

Alternate theories assume other river routes or different timing of the erosion, placing it either before or after the uplift. Until more evidence is uncovered, visitors will have to simply marvel at the canyon and formulate their own theories about how this mighty river cut through a giant bulge in Earth's crust millions of years ago.

Reading the Formations

After their initial awe has worn off, many visitors are eager to learn how to identify the formations that so neatly layer the canyon. The distinctive sequence of color and texture is worth learning, as it repeats itself over and over again on each rim, from each viewpoint and along each trail. Simply memorize the catchphrase, 'Know The Canyon's History, See Rocks Made By Time,' in which the capital letters (KTCHSRMBT) represent the formations from rim to canyon floor.

Starting at the top, a layer of creamy white **Kaibab limestone** caps the rim on both sides of the canyon. This formation is about 300ft thick and erodes to form blocky cliffs. Limestone surfaces are pitted and pockmarked, while rainwater quickly seeps into the rock to form sinkholes and underground passages. Fossils include brachiopods, sponges and corals.

The **Toroweap Formation** is the vegetated slope between the cliffs of Kaibab limestone above and massive Coconino cliffs below. Similar in composition to the Kaibab, the Toroweap is a pale yellow to gray crumbly limestone that also contains marine fossils.

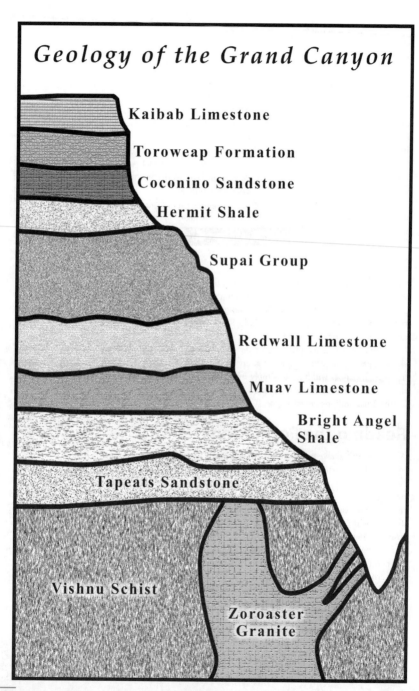

Geology of the Grand Canyon

Kaibab Limestone

Toroweap Formation

Coconino Sandstone

Hermit Shale

Supai Group

Redwall Limestone

Muav Limestone

Bright Angel Shale

Tapeats Sandstone

Vishnu Schist

Zoroaster Granite

It's quickly evident how sandstone erodes differently than limestone when you descend past **Coconino sandstone** along the Bright Angel Trail, one of the few places a trail can negotiate these sheer 350ft cliffs. Inspect the rock face closely to spot fine crosshatches, evidence of wind-blown ripples that once crisscrossed huge sand dunes. Even more fascinating is the wealth of fossilized millipede, spider, scorpion and lizard tracks found in this formation.

Below these mighty cliffs lies a slope of crumbly red **Hermit shale**. This fine-grained shale formed under shallow tidal conditions and contains fossilized mud cracks, ripple marks and the footprints of reptiles and amphibians. Today it supports a distinctive band of shrubs and trees including oak, hop tree and serviceberry. Hermit shale is so soft that in the western canyon it has eroded completely, leaving a broad terrace of Esplanade sandstone.

A ROCK PRIMER

Rocks are divided into three large classes – sedimentary, igneous and metamorphic – each well represented in the Grand Canyon.

Sedimentary rock originates as accumulations of sediments and particles that cement together over time. Borne by water or the wind, the sediments generally settle in horizontal layers that preserve many features, suggesting how they formed. Three types of sedimentary rock are present in the canyon. **Limestone** comprises little more than calcium carbonate, a strong cement that softens and easily erodes when wet. **Sandstone** consists of sand particles that stack poorly, leaving lots of room for the calcium carbonate cement to penetrate, making this a very hard and durable rock. At the opposite end of the spectrum from limestone, **mudstone** (including shale) consists of flaky particles that stack so closely together, there's little room for the binding cement. Thus mudstone is often very soft and breakable.

Igneous rock originates as molten magma, which cools either deep underground or after erupting to the surface as lava or volcanic ash. Volcanic rocks are common west of Toroweap Valley, where they form such prominent features as Vulcans Throne and Lava Falls. Granite that cooled deep inside the earth lies exposed along the inner gorge – in fact, canyon explorer John Wesley Powell originally named the river corridor Granite Gorge.

Metamorphic rock starts out as either sedimentary or igneous, then transforms into other kinds of rock following exposure to intense heat or pressure, especially where the Earth's crust buckles and folds into mountain ranges. Metamorphic rock usually remains hidden deep underground. Two types of metamorphic rock are common in the canyon. Deriving from shale, sandstone or volcanic rock, **schist** lines the inner gorge and is distinguished by narrow, wavy bands of shiny mica flakes. Forming light-colored intrusions within the schist, **gneiss** is characterized by its coarse texture and the presence of quartz and feldspar.

Just below the Hermit shale are the red cliffs and ledges of the **Supai Group**, similar in composition and color but differing in hardness. This is a set of shale, limestone and sandstone layers, and each dominates different portions of the canyon. All formed under similar swampy coastal conditions, where shallow waters mingled with sand dunes. Deposited some 300 million years ago when amphibians first evolved, these formations preserve early footprints of these new animals. Supai cliffs can be stained red by iron oxides or black from iron or manganese.

Next is the famous **Redwall limestone**, one of the canyon's most prominent features. Viewed from the rim, the Redwall is a huge red cliff that towers 500 to 800ft over the broad Tonto Platform. The Redwall also forms a dividing line between forest habitats above and desert habitats below. The rock is actually light gray limestone that has been stained red by iron oxides washed down from layers above. This formation is pitted with many caves and alcoves and contains abundant marine fossils, including trilobites, snails, clams and fish.

Muav limestone is a small slope of varying thickness that marks the junction of Redwall sandstone and the Tonto Platform. This marine formation contains few fossils but features many eroded cavities and passages.

Perched just above the dark inner gorge, the broad, gently sloping Tonto Platform is the only break in a long jumble of cliffs and ledges. The platform is not a formation at all but rather the absence of one, where soft greenish **Bright Angel shale** has been largely stripped away to reveal the hard Tapeats sandstone beneath.

The last and oldest Paleozoic sedimentary layer is the **Tapeats sandstone**, below which lies the huge gap (the Great Unconformity) that separates the sedimentary layers of the canyon from the ancient Vishnu schist of the inner gorge. Collectively referred to as the Tonto Group, Tapeats, Bright Angel and Muav all formed along the same ocean shoreline. Tapeats originated with coarse cobbles along an ancient beach, Bright Angel shale comprises fine mud deposits that collected just offshore from the beach, and Muav limestone consists of calcium carbonate that fused in deep water.

Forces at Work

What's truly remarkable about the Grand Canyon is not how big it is, but how small it is. In terms of sheer volume, much more material has been removed from the Grand Wash Trough just below the canyon or other stretches where the river meanders across vast floodplains. But the canyon's narrow scale continues to concentrate erosive forces in dramatic fashion. As the canyon widens with age, it may no longer be as impressive a sight.

Obviously foremost among the erosive forces is water, which chisels virtually every inch of the landscape. From the smallest raindrop to the mightiest flash flood, water is an immensely powerful erosive force. Its differing effect on various rock types is readily apparent in the canyon's stair-step profile – the softer rock formations crumbling into gentle slopes at the foot of sheer hard cliffs.

On a subtle level, water may simply seep deeply into the rock, dissolving some minerals and converting others to slippery clay. The water gradually weakens the rock matrix, causing large or small bits of rock to break free. In Surprise Canyon a massive landslide totaling 1 cubic mile slid 1500ft, though most landslides are much smaller.

A weathering effect known as frost riving occurs when water works down into cracks and freezes. Freezing water exerts a tremendous outward force (20,000 pounds per square inch), which wedges into these crevices, prying loose blocks of rock from the canyon cliffs.

Streams have gradually eroded defined side canyons on both rims, cutting back ever deeper into their headwalls. This effect is especially pronounced on the higher-altitude North Rim, as it catches more runoff from passing storm systems. This rim also angles to the south, pouring its runoff *into* the canyon. While the South Rim also slopes to the south, that means its waters flow *away* from the canyon, slowing the pace of erosion.

As parallel side canyons cut back toward their headwalls, they create the canyon's distinctive temples and amphitheaters. Neighboring streams erode either side of a long promontory or finger of rock, then carve the base of the promontory, leaving the tip stranded in open space. Over time these isolated islands of elevated rock weather into rugged spires called temples, while the headwalls of the side canyons become amphitheaters.

Water is not always as patient and imperceptible. Late-summer thunderstorms cause flash floods that sculpt the landscape over the course of minutes. A tiny trickling brook carrying grains of sand can quickly explode into a torrent that tosses house-sized boulders with ease.

Although the Colorado cut through the soft sedimentary layers at lightning speed, the river has now reached extremely hard Vishnu schist, and erosion has slowed dramatically. As the river approaches sea level, downward erosion will cease altogether, even as the canyon continues to widen. This lateral (sideways) erosion proceeds 10 times faster than downward cutting. Thus, far in the future, the Grand Canyon may be referred to as the Grand Valley.

Hollowed out like a massive inverted mountain range, the Grand Canyon wields a profound influence across hundreds of miles of northern Arizona, dramatically altering the local environment and the lives of the region's plants and animals.

ECOSYSTEM

For some species it presents an insurmountable obstacle, while for others it's a life-sustaining corridor through a forbidding desert – humans have experienced both perspectives.

Sprawling across 1.2 million acres, Grand Canyon National Park protects a sizable portion of the vast Colorado Plateau, an elevated tableland that spans the Four Corners states – Arizona, Utah, Colorado and New Mexico. The park also protects 227 free-flowing miles of the Colorado River, among the greatest of all North American rivers. The region encompasses a rich mix of species and ecosystems, where Rocky Mountain forests and meadows abut components of three great American deserts – the Mojave, Sonoran and Great Basin. Altogether the park is home to 1500 plant species, 305 bird species, 76 mammal species, 41 reptile and amphibian species, and 26 fish species.

Life Zones

After studying the region's wide cross section of ecosystems, biologist C Hart Merriam developed the concept of life zones. On an 1889 expedition for the United States Department of Agriculture, Merriam conducted a field study of the canyon and nearby San Francisco Peaks. He found that as he climbed to altitude, the distinct bands of vegetation he crossed correlated to a journey northward in latitude to Canada. Similarly a trip down into the canyon correlated to a journey south into Mexico. Merriam concluded that each upward climb of a thousand feet is roughly equivalent to traveling north 300 miles, with corresponding changes in temperature, solar exposure, moisture and other environmental factors. Although his life zones concept has been replaced by more sophisticated ecological models, the concept has profoundly shaped biological thought to this day.

On the highest peaks of the North Rim perches the **boreal forest**, an offshoot of the Rocky Mountains that includes many of the same plants and animals. Unlike other canyon habitats, this is a land of cool, moist forests and lush meadows. Snowfall may exceed 150 inches and persist for six to seven months of the year, conditions that favor trees like the Engelmann spruce, Douglas fir and quaking aspen and animals like red squirrels, blue grouse and broad-tailed hummingbirds.

Broad, flat plateaus on both rims are dominated by **ponderosa pine forest**. Around 7000ft this species forms nearly pure stands of stately, fragrant trees. Temperatures are moderate, and rainfall averages about 20 inches a year. Characteristic species include the unique Abert's and Kaibab squirrels, as well as a variety of bird species, ranging from American robins to northern flickers.

Sharing the rim with ponderosa pines and cloaking the canyon walls down to about 4000ft are **piñon-juniper woodlands**. These forests of piñon pines and Utah junipers signal desert-like conditions, where snow scarcely ever falls and annual rainfall hardly exceeds 10 inches. Shrubs such as cliff rose, sagebrush and Mormon tea thrive here. Animals include rock squirrels, cliff chipmunks, and scrub and piñon jays.

Ponderosa pine

Between the canyon's inner gorge and the great cliffs that line its rims lies a broad apron known as the Tonto Platform. Here at 3000 to 4000ft clings the **desert scrub community**, a zone of blazing summer heat and little rain. Dominating the platform is low-growing blackbrush, along with a handful of other hardy species such as prickly pear cacti. Visitors will spot few birds and only the occasional black-tailed jackrabbit or white-tailed antelope squirrel.

From springs along the canyon rim, down permanent streams to the Colorado is a separate and distinct habitat known as the **riparian zone**. The presence of precious water draws many plants and animals to this zone. Crimson monkeyflowers and maidenhair ferns mark the scattered seeps and springs, while stream banks near the river are choked by tamarisk, an aggressive introduced plant. Red-spotted toads and beavers share these waters with ducks, herons and other birds that come to drink.

Life Through the Seasons

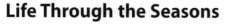

The canyon encompasses a wide variety of climatic extremes in which seasons are as complex as the landscape. While one rim celebrates spring, the other rim may still languish in the grip of winter, and in the depths of winter the canyon floor can experience hotter temperatures than in summer elsewhere in the country.

April ushers in the first long spells of fair weather, interrupted by lingering wet winter storms. Even as golden eagles and peregrine falcons nest along the river, the North Rim may remain under many feet of snow. Migrant birds arrive in numbers through May. Along the South Rim and within the canyon itself, wrens, phoebes and warblers fill the air with song and activity. Mammals likewise take advantage of the short season between winter cold and summer heat. Chipmunks and squirrels lead the charge, bounding energetically amid the rocks and trees.

By June, however, temperatures begin to soar, and animal activity slows to a trickle. Daytime temperatures in excess of 100°F are the norm through August. Torrential afternoon thunderstorms alleviate the agony for a few hours each day. June through August is usually the best time to observe wildflowers along the North Rim, while the best time on the South Rim is from August into October.

Clear, cool days make autumn the ideal time for visits to the park, though wildflowers have gone to seed and many birds have already made the journey south. Remaining behind are the resident animals – mammals fattening up for hibernation and a handful of birds that feast on the plentiful seeds. Other animals remain active through winter, especially on the canyon floor, where temperatures remain moderate and snow rarely falls.

Animals Great & Small

Wildlife in the park ranges from secretive bighorn sheep and prehistoric condors to scampering lizards and nosy ringtail cats, all scattered across a vast region. In only a few places do animals congregate in conspicuous numbers. Remain patient and alert and you'll take home lifelong memories.

Bird-watching is a particularly rewarding exercise, as the park hosts more than 300 recorded species. The canyon shelters one particular species that draws bird watchers from around the world – the endangered California condor, sometimes in flocks of a dozen or more.

In many areas of the park, visitors will encounter a wide variety of reptiles, birds and mammals. Pack or purchase a few field guides to help you identify what you find.

LARGE MAMMALS

While bighorn sheep do stand guard on high cliff faces, elk and deer wander through mountain meadows and mountain lions lurk in forest nooks, your chances of finding many large mammals are relatively slim. They'll likely show up when you least expect them, so keep your eyes open.

Mountain lion

Mountain Lions

Even veteran biologists rarely see the **mountain lion**. But a large population does live here, and the canyon rates among the best places in North America to spot this elusive cat. While mountain lions roam throughout the park, they gravitate to forests along the North Rim in pursuit of their favorite food, mule deer. Reaching up to 8ft in length and weighing as much as 160 pounds, this solitary animal is a formidable predator that rarely bothers humans.

Mule Deer

Rim forests and meadows are the favored haunts of **mule deer**, which commonly graze at dusk in groups of a dozen or more. After their predators were systematically hunted out of the park in the early 1900s (even Teddy Roosevelt came to the canyon to hunt mountain lions), the deer experienced a massive

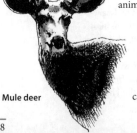

Mule deer

population explosion. Less common on the South Rim and within the canyon, deer move seasonally to find water and avoid deep snows.

Bighorn Sheep

Like solemn statues, **bighorn sheep** often stand motionless on inaccessible cliff faces or ridgelines and are readily identified by their distinctive curled horns. During breeding season, males charge each other at 20mph and ram horns so loudly the sound travels for miles. Look for bighorns in side canyons along the Tonto Platform beneath the South Rim. Bring binoculars, as hikers seldom encounter this animal at close range, and never for more than a moment.

Coyotes & Foxes

Wild members of the dog family include the ubiquitous **coyote** and its much smaller cousin, the **gray fox**. Both share the same grayish-brown coat, and each has adapted to human activity, growing increasingly comfortable around roads, buildings and (of course) any unattended food. You stand a good chance of seeing coyotes in daytime, especially around meadows, where they hunt for rodents. Foxes often emerge at night, when you might spy one crossing a trail or road.

Coyote

SMALL MAMMALS

Small mammals are much more abundant than their larger cousins, including many types of common squirrels, chipmunks and small carnivores. Look for these around campsites and picnic grounds and beside trails or roadside pullouts.

Chipmunks & Squirrels

While similar in appearance, the region's three chipmunk species do bear subtle differences. The South Rim is the exclusive domain of the gray **cliff chipmunk**, an extremely vocal species that can bark an estimated 5800 times in a half hour, twitching its tail with each call. This species shares the North Rim with **least chipmunks** and **Uinta chipmunks**, although cliff chipmunks are relegated to rocky ledges and cliffs. Least chipmunks inhabit open areas and carry their tails erect when they run, while Uinta chipmunks live in forests and are abundant around North Rim campgrounds and picnic sites.

Chipmunk

The most conspicuous members of the squirrel family are speckled gray **rock squirrels**, which scoot fearlessly amid visitors' feet along rim trails and viewpoints. Hoping for handouts (strictly forbidden), these large squirrels will boldly explore unattended gear or sidle up to resting hikers. True to its name, this species nearly always inhabits rocky areas.

Living on opposite rims, **Abert's** and **Kaibab squirrels** present a classic evolutionary test case, demonstrating how the canyon divides populations into distinct species. These long-eared squirrels were a single population only 20,000 years ago, when forests grew in the canyon. The squirrels split into two populations when the climate warmed and dried and the canyon transformed into desert habitat. Today the two remain so closely related that scientists can't agree whether to rank them as separate species, despite obvious color differences. Both the light-bellied Abert's squirrel of the South Rim and the dark-bellied Kaibab squirrel of the North Rim depend on ponderosa pine forests for their livelihood, rarely wandering more than 20 yards from these trees. Each species is common on its respective rim.

Wood Rats

Although they bear a superficial resemblance to city rats, **wood rats** are extraordinary, gentle creatures with many interesting attributes. The canyon's four species share a maddening propensity for stealing small shiny objects like watches or rings and leaving bones, seeds or other objects in exchange – hence the animal's common nickname, the trade rat. Wood rats are also famous for building massive stick nests that are used by countless generations. Upon dismantling these nests and examining their contents, biologists have been able to document more than 50,000 years of environmental prehistory in the region.

Ringtail

One of the area's most intriguing creatures is the nocturnal **ringtail**, which looks like a wide-eyed housecat with a raccoon tail. Once common around park campsites, where they would emerge at night to raid camper's food supplies, ringtails have been discouraged by modern food storage techniques, though they are still observed along the rims and river corridors.

BIRDS

Whether you enjoy the aerial acrobatics of swifts and swallows atop rimside cliffs or the bright songs of warblers among riverside thickets, there's no question that the canyon's 300-plus bird species are among the region's premier highlights.

Small Birds

A harbinger of spring, the **broad-tailed hummingbird** zips energetically about the park from May through August. Males bear a notch in their wing feathers that creates a distinctive whirring sound in flight, making this diminutive bird sound impressively big, thus attracting mates. They are common in wildflower-filled forest glades on both rims.

Forests and campgrounds on both rims host large numbers of the sparrow-sized **dark-eyed junco**. Hopping about the forest floor in search of seeds and insects, this bird is conspicuous for its black hood and its habit of nervously flicking its tail outward to flash white outer tail feathers. Similar in appearance but restricted to trees is the **mountain chickadee**, a perennial favorite with children because its merry song sounds like *cheese-bur-ger*. Both species are hardy and among the handful of birds that remain in the park year-round.

The first birds many visitors encounter are **white-throated swifts**, which swoop and dive over towering cliff faces at rim viewpoints. Designed like sleek bullets, these sporty 'tuxedoed' birds seem to delight in riding every wind current and chasing each other in playful pursuit. Flying alongside the swifts are slightly less agile **violet-green swallows**, which are a familiar sight around campgrounds and park buildings.

Only hikers that descend to the sparsely vegetated Tonto Platform will spot the beautiful **black-throated sparrow**, one of the few species able to survive in this scorching desert habitat. Sporting a jaunty black bib and crisp white facial stripes, this bird brightens scrubby slopes with its sweet *chit-chit-cheee* song.

The stirring song of the **canyon wren** is for many people the most evocative sound in the park. So haunting is this song, it hardly seems possible that this tiny reddish rock-dweller could produce such music. Starting out as a fast series of sweet tinkling notes, the song fades gracefully into a rhythmic cadence that leaves you full of longing.

Underscoring the importance of water in this desert landscape, it comes as a shock to find **American dippers** (formerly known as water ouzels) beside streams deep within the canyon. These lovable and energetic bundles of gray feathers rarely leave the cascading streams, where they dive beneath the cold water to capture insects and larvae. Look closely to spot the flash of this bird's whitish, translucent eyelids, which allow it to see underwater.

Birds of Prey

Of the six owl species occurring regularly in the park, none is as familiar as the common and highly vocal **great horned owl**, which regularly fills the echoing canyons with its booming hoots. This is among the largest and most fearsome of all raptors, and when one moves into the neighborhood, other owls and hawks hurry on to more favorable hunting grounds or run the risk of being hunted down as prey themselves. Hikers may be startled to glance up and spot this bird's huge glaring face and prominent 'horns' (actually long erect feathers) as it peers down at them from a crevice along the rim.

Great horned owl

Commanding vast hunting territories of some 50 sq miles, powerful **golden eagles** are typically observed in passing, as they travel widely in search of jackrabbits and other prey. Boasting 7ft wingspans, they are among the canyon's largest birds, second in size only to recently arrived **California condors**. Watch for the characteristic golden tint on the eagle's shoulders and neck.

Given their endangered status in recent decades, **peregrine falcons** are surprisingly common throughout the park. Here they find plenty of secluded, cliff-side nesting sites, as well as one of their favorite food items, white-throated swifts, which they seize in midair. Look for the falcon's long, slender wings and dark 'moustache.'

AMPHIBIANS & REPTILES

Peregrine falcon

Amphibians and reptiles seldom garner the attention they deserve, but a surprising range of beautiful and unique species call the canyon home. Lizards and snakes are especially well represented here. Other resident species

CONDORS

When critically endangered **California condors** were released at the nearby Vermilion Cliffs in 1996, the canyon experience was profoundly altered. As was the case when wolves were reintroduced to Yellowstone National Park, visitors seem utterly fascinated by the condors. With 9ft wingspans and horridly wrinkled featherless heads, these birds are an unforgettable sight.

It's a miracle condors are around at all, seeing as their world population declined to less than two dozen birds in the 1980s. Many assumed these gigantic prehistoric holdovers were on the brink of extinction. Following a concerted captive breeding effort, however, there are now 35 condors in the canyon region, including one fledgling in the summer of 2003.

Fortunately, for the birds and park visitors alike, condors have a decided attraction to large crowds of people. This is an evolutionary trait, as condors are carrion feeders, and crowds of large mammals like humans are more likely to produce potential food. As a result, condors often hang around popular rim viewpoints like Grand Canyon Lodge on the North Rim and Grand Canyon Village on the South Rim. Visitors are granted world-class, close-up views – sometimes too close, as condors seem to delight in swooping up from behind obstacles and gliding mere feet over visitors' heads. Makes you wonder if they're trying to startle someone into falling – dropping in for lunch, you might say!

Condor populations are far from secure, however, even in the park, where they seem to be have plenty of food and room to roam. The true test will be whether the species can successfully reproduce. Pairs laid one egg in 2001 and two eggs in 2002. These efforts failed, but of two nesting attempts in 2003, one nest appears to be successful at the time of this writing. The canyon birds are all still young and inexperienced, so biologists hope that as the birds mature, more pairs will form and try to breed. Given that condors live about 50 years, there's plenty of time for these birds to settle down in their new home.

include geckos and iguanas, the rare (and venomous) Gila monster, blind snakes and pink rattlesnakes, to name just a few.

Frogs & Toads

Bleating choruses of common **canyon tree frogs** float up from boulder-strewn canyon streams each night. Gray-brown and speckled like stone, these tiny frogs dwell in damp crevices by day, emerging at night beside rocky pools.

Occupying similar habitat (because water occurs in limited patches) is the aptly named **red-spotted toad**, a small species with (you guessed it) red-tipped warts covering its body. Its nighttime song around breeding pools is a high musical trill.

Lizards

Perhaps the most abundant and widespread reptile in the park is the **eastern fence lizard**, a 5- to 6-inch-long creature you'll likely see perched atop rocks and logs or scampering across the trail. During breeding season, males bob enthusiastically while conspicuously displaying their shiny blue throats and bellies. Females have dark, wavy crossbars on their backs and only a pale bluish wash underneath.

As delicate in appearance as a fragile alabaster vase, the **banded gecko** has thin, practically translucent velvety skin. Emerging at night to hunt small insects, this lizard is not readily found unless you're hiking the desert slopes at night with a flashlight.

Easily the strangest reptile in the park is the rarely seen **Gila monster**, which looks like a 2ft long orange-and-black sequined sausage. Though often placid, it is capable of quick lunges and powerful bites with its massive black-rimmed jaws. The lizard holds on tenaciously as its venomous saliva enters bite wounds. While no human deaths have been attributed to this species, the venom is a potent neurotoxin, and victims should seek immediate medical care. Though encounters are rare, this lizard is best left alone.

Snakes

Home to some 20 snake species, the park is a great place to learn about these misunderstood animals. Commonly encountered in a range of habitats is the **gopher snake**, often mistaken for a rattlesnake, as it vibrates its tail in dry leaves when cornered or upset. Sporting an attractive tan body with dark brown saddles, this lithe constrictor preys upon rodents and small birds.

But the snakes that elicit the most interest are the three resident species of **rattlesnake** – speckled, black-tailed and western. Nothing quite approaches the jolt of terror and adrenaline prompted by the angry buzz of a rattlesnake. Both humans and wild animals react with instinctive fear, even though rattlesnakes rarely strike unless provoked. In another show of evolutionary adaptation, the pink rattlesnake resides solely within the canyon depths. Tinted to blend in with the canyon walls, this is a subspecies of the common western rattlesnake.

Rattlesnake

INSECTS

Summer visitors will likely hear **desert cicadas**, whose ceaseless rasping and clicking is produced by vibrating membranes stretched over resonating sound chambers. Finding one of these inch-long insects is another matter altogether, as they are masters of camouflage – one reason they're able to screech all day and still avoid predators.

Also notable are inch-long, shiny metallic blue **carpenter bees**, which tunnel through dead wood in dry forested areas. Unlike colonial hive-making bees, carpenter bees lead solitary lives and spend much of their time chasing away interlopers who might move into their hard-earned tunnels.

The canyon's many butterfly species are highlighted by the distinctive orange-and-black **monarch butterfly**, which flutters through the park in large numbers in late summer, en route to Mexican wintering grounds. This large, showy butterfly avoids predation because as a larva it feeds on milkweed plants that contain noxious alkaloids – animals that try to eat monarchs suffer a severe reaction to these plant compounds.

Plant Life

The park supports a fantastic mix of plant communities and is home to more than 1400 species from four of North America's major biological provinces – the Rocky Mountains and the Mojave, Sonoran and Great Basin Deserts. Each province contributes unique species to the mix. Plants of the Rocky Mountain province are found on both rims, especially the North Rim, where Engelmann spruce and quaking aspen form distinctive moist forests. Desert provinces occupy the inner canyon, where the climate is much hotter and drier. Mojave plants are found from downriver up to Hundred and Fifty Mile Canyon, Sonoran plants (including ocotillo and mesquite) dominate the central canyon, while Great Basin plants (rabbitbrush, sagebrush, etc.) take over from lower Marble Canyon to Lees Ferry.

This complex assemblage of plants is a fascinating puzzle that patient visitors can piece together. See Planning, Suggested Reading (p63), for recommended field guides to the region.

HANGING GARDENS

Even though much of the Grand Canyon region appears arid, there is in fact a tremendous amount of water locked up inside the layers of porous sandstone – the byproduct of countless torrential rainstorms, which pour down onto the surface and percolate deep into the stone. Over time this water flows laterally and emerges from cliff faces as various seeps and springs. Flowing waters erode soft sandstone, causing the rock to collapse and form cool, shady overhangs. The constant water supply then fosters a rich community of algae on vertical surfaces and below that lush gardens of delicate flowering plants and ferns known as hanging gardens. These gardens of maidenhair ferns, columbines, orchids, monkeyflowers and primroses are a welcome sight to parched desert travelers. Botanists also treasure these alcoves, as many of the plants are unique to the Colorado Plateau, occurring nowhere else but in these hanging gardens.

TREES

Due to their prominence and longevity, trees serve as excellent indicators of different life zones and local environmental conditions. The stately **ponderosa pine**, for example, defines the distinctive forested belt between 6000 and 8000ft. In many places along the North Rim and on the highest points of the South Rim this species forms nearly pure stands that cover many acres. To identify this species, look for large spiny cones, needles in clusters of three and yellowish bark that smells like butterscotch.

At higher elevations ponderosa pines mingle with two other species that characterize the Rocky Mountain boreal forest. **Engelmann spruce** has a curious bluish tinge to its needles and inch-long cylindrical cones with paper-thin scales. To confirm its identity, grasp a branch and feel for sharp spiny-tipped needles that prick your hand. Young Engelmann spruce are a favorite choice for Christmas trees because they flaunt such perfect shapes. **Quaking aspen** is immediately recognizable for its smooth, white bark and circular leaves. Every gust of wind sets these leaves quivering on their flattened stems, an adaptation for shaking off late snowfalls that would otherwise damage fragile leaves. Aspen groves comprise genetically identical trunks sprouting from a common root system that may grow to more than a hundred acres in size. By budding repeatedly from these root systems, aspens have what has been called 'theoretical immortality' – some aspen roots are thought to be more than a million years old.

Habitats at the lower edge of the ponderosa pine belt are increasingly arid, but two trees do particularly well along this desert fringe. **Piñon pines** are well known for their highly nutritious and flavorful seeds, sold as 'pine nuts' in grocery stores. These same seeds have been a staple for Native Americans wherever the trees grow, and many animals feast on the seeds when they ripen in fall. Piñons have stout rounded cones and short paired needles. Together with **Utah junipers**, piñon pines form a distinctive community that covers millions of acres in the Southwest. Such 'PJ woodlands' dominate broad swathes of the South Rim and canyon walls down to 4000ft. Blue, berrylike cones and diminutive scale-like needles distinguish junipers from other trees. Birds feed extensively on juniper 'berries', prompting the seeds to sprout by removing their fleshy coverings.

Engelmann spruce

Consorting with piñons, junipers and ponderosas is the beautiful little **Gambel oak**, whose dark green leaves turn shades of yellow and red in autumn and add a classy palette of color to an already stunning landscape. Often occurring in dense thickets, oaks produce copious quantities of nutritious, tasty acorns long favored by Native Americans and used to make breads, pancakes, soups and ground meal.

Rivers and watercourses in this harsh desert landscape are lined with thin ribbons of water-loving plants that can't survive elsewhere. Towering prominently above all others is the showy **Fremont cottonwood**, whose large, vaguely heart-shaped leaves rustle wildly in any wind. Hikers in the canyon's scorching depths find welcome respite in the shade of this tree. In spring, cottonwoods produce vast quantities of cottony seed packets that fill the air and collect in every crack and crevice.

Since construction of upstream dams, aggressive weedy **tamarisk** has replaced ancestral communities of willows and other native plants. Though this delicately leaved plant from Eurasia sports a handsome coat of soft pink flowers through summer, its charms end there, for this plant robs water from the soil and completely overwhelms native plant communities. Producing a billion seeds per plant and spreading quickly, this species now dominates virtually every water source in the Southwest deserts.

SHRUBS

Despite the prevalence of tamarisk along stream banks, a few native plants manage to hold on. Easily recognized are **catclaw acacia** and **honey mesquite**, thorny members of the pea family that produce seeds in elongated, brown peapods. Each species features delicate leaflets arranged in feather-like sprays, though acacia has little rounded leaflets, while mesquite has long narrow leaflets. Acacia seeds are very hard and must be scratched up in tumbling floodwaters before they'll germinate. Mesquite was a staple among Southwest Indians, providing food, fuel, building materials and medicines. Charcoal of this tree is prized today for the unique flavor it lends to barbeques.

Stretching from the base of rim cliffs to the inner gorge, the broad, flat Tonto Platform is almost entirely covered by a single desert shrub known as **blackbrush**. Presenting a somber face on a barren, uniform habitat, this dark shrub reaches great ages and is only rarely replaced by young seedlings. Life is spare for this plant, its leaves little more than skinny needles and its flowers lacking petals. Scattered among the blackbrush are a few other shrubs, including **banana yucca**, a stout succulent related to agave and century plants. Growing in a dense rosette of thick leaves that reaches 2ft high, this plant sends up a 4ft flowering stalk in the spring followed by fleshy, banana-like fruit. So much energy goes into this reproductive effort that the plant waits years between blooming cycles.

Many shrub species cloak the canyon walls above the Tonto Platform. Here the steep slopes offer a variety of shaded niches and seeps or springs where shrubs form thickets. In spring and early summer these sweet-scented thickets fairly hum with bees, butterflies and birds at work among the abundant blossoms. While blooming, the white-flowered **fendlerbush** is a powerful magnet for such butterflies as admirals and painted ladies. This 9ft high shrub sports curious flowers with four widely separated, spoon-shaped petals.

Another shrub with widely spaced petals (though in fives) is the common **Utah serviceberry**. Well named, this member of the rose family has been used extensively by countless peoples in the Southwest for food, medicine and other utilitarian purposes. Shaped like tiny apples, the bluish-purple berries are not terribly tasty but have been a food staple for millennia.

Common throughout forested areas of the park are seven types of **currants** and **gooseberries**. All produce varyingly sweet and edible (though mainly spiny) berries that are an important food source for wildlife and occasionally consumed by humans. Some species bear sticky leaves that are pungent when lightly rubbed.

Abundant on both rims is the distinctive **big sagebrush**, a plant that dominates millions of acres of dry desert habitat from northern Arizona to Canada. Tolerant of cold and rain to a degree not found in other desert species, sagebrush ranges from valley floors to high desert peaks across the West. Three lobed leaves and an aromatic scent make identification of this species a cinch.

CRYPTOBIOTIC CRUSTS

One of the Grand Canyon's most fascinating features is also one of its least visible and most fragile. Only in recent years have **cryptobiotic crusts** begun to attract attention and concern. These living crusts cover and protect desert soils, literally gluing sand particles together so they don't blow away. Cyanobacteria, among Earth's oldest life forms, start the process by extending mucous-covered filaments that wind through the dry soil. Over time these filaments and the sand particles adhering to them form a thin crust that is colonized by microscopic algae, lichens, fungi and mosses. This crust absorbs tremendous amounts of rainwater, reducing runoff and minimizing erosion.

Unfortunately, this thin crust is quickly fragmented under the impact of heavy-soled boots, not to mention bicycle, motorcycle and car tires. Once broken, the crust takes 50 to 250 years to repair itself. In its absence, the wind and rains erode desert soils, and much of the water that would otherwise nourish desert plants is lost.

Visitors to the canyon and other sites in the Southwest bear the responsibility to protect cryptobiotic crusts by staying on established trails. Literally look before you leap – intact crusts form a glaze atop the soil, while fragmented crusts bear sharp edges.

WILDFLOWERS

The park's dazzling variety of wildflowers put on an extravagant show – and as habitats range from arid desert to snowy heights, there's always something blooming somewhere from early spring on. Even in midsummer, pockets of water foster lush wildflower gardens in shaded recesses within the canyon, while sudden thunderstorms trigger brief floral displays.

Raising eyebrows whenever encountered by hikers, the oddly inflated **desert trumpet** presents its loose arrangement of tiny yellow flowers anytime between March and October. Just below the flowers, the stem balloons out like a long slender lozenge. Old stems maintain this shape and are just as curious as the living plant. Sometimes wasps drill into the plant and fill its hollow stems with captured insects as food for developing larvae.

One of the more conspicuous desert flowers, especially along roadsides, is the abundant peachy-pink **globe mallow**. Shooting forth as many as 100 stems from a single root system, they can tint the desert with their distinctive color. At least 10 mallow species live within the park.

Seeps, springs and stream banks are fantastic places to search for some of the most dramatic flower displays. The brilliant flash of **crimson monkeyflowers** amid lush greenery comes as something of a shock for hikers who've trudged across miles of searing baked rock. Apparently, someone once saw enough of a monkey likeness to name this wildflower, but you're more likely to notice the 'lips' that extend above and below the flower.

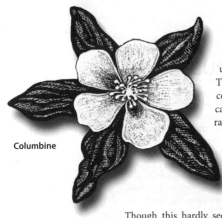

Columbine

Columbines are also common at these seeps and springs, though some species range upward into moist forested areas of the park. The gorgeous **golden columbine** is most common in wet, shaded recesses of the inner canyon. **Red columbine** is a rare find in a wide range of forests and shaded canyons, while the blue-and-white **Colorado columbine** is a resident of Rocky Mountain spruce-fir forests along the North Rim. The long spurs of columbine flowers hold pockets of nectar that attract large numbers of butterflies and hummingbirds.

Though this hardly seems the place to find orchids, the beautiful **giant helleborine** is in fact common at seeps and springs within the canyon. The distinctly orchidlike flowers are a medley of green and yellow petals with purple veins. Though it goes without saying you should never pick flowers in a national park, it's especially important that these precious orchids be admired and left undisturbed.

Scarcely noticeable among needle-blanketed forest floors, the intricate **lousewort** is nevertheless a common plant in the ponderosa pine and spruce-fir zones. Finely cut, fernlike leaves hide the plant's red-tipped white flowers, which grow close to the ground.

OTHER PLANTS

Prickly pear

Although they could be classified with wildflowers, the park's two dozen cacti are a group of plants unique unto themselves. Foremost among the cacti are the 11 members of the prickly pear group, familiar for their paddle-shaped pads that resemble beaver tails. In fact, one of the most common species is called **beavertail cacti**, while a rarer species is known as **pancake pear**. Both the pads and fruit are commonly eaten after proper preparation. Be aware that the spines (glochids) detach easily on contact and are highly irritating.

Often dubbed the classic beautiful cacti, stunning **claret cup hedgehog cacti** shine like iridescent jewels in the dusty desert landscape, where they are the first to bloom in spring. Their deep scarlet flowers burst forth from as many as 50 stems per clump, blooming simultaneously for a period of several days.

Of the park's 20-plus ferns the **maidenhair fern** deserves special mention because it forms dense sheets of bright green at countless desert oases. Lacy and delicate, this fern requires a continuous supply of water but otherwise does well in an imposing landscape. You'll recognize it by its fan-shaped leaflets and wiry black stems.

A close examination of the park's juniper trees reveals an extremely abundant but easily overlooked plant – yellow-green **juniper mistletoe**. Parasitic, but apparently not harming its host trees, mistletoe produces tiny fruits that birds like robins and bluebirds absolutely love. Carried in the birds' digestive tracts, the seeds adhere to new tree branches once excreted.

Stresses on the System

Locked in by dams at both ends of the canyon, the once mighty Colorado River has undergone profound changes, with significant impact on the many plants and animals that depend on the river and its natural cycles. Few species, either aquatic or terrestrial, escape the impact of these changes, although some species benefit while others are harmed.

No group of animals has suffered more than the handful of native fish that once thrived in the warm, sediment-laden waters of the *Rio Colorado* (Colored River) – originally named because it flowed like murky soup full of rusty brown sediments. Upstream from the canyon, Glen Canyon Dam now captures nearly all of the 380,000 tons of sediment that once flowed annually through the canyon. The dam instead releases clear cold water in a steady year-round flow that hardly mimics the ancestral seasonal flood cycle. Under this managed regime, unique fish like the Colorado squawfish, razorback sucker and prehistoric-looking humpback chub have been almost entirely displaced by introduced trout, carp and catfish that flourish in the current conditions.

Some changes are more dramatic, while others are so subtle that scientists are only beginning to understand them. On the obvious side has been the gradual loss of riverside beaches, as the river is no longer depositing sediments in backwater stretches. Beaches have also become overgrown, since the river no longer floods and sweeps away seedlings that root on open sand. Former sandbanks are now densely vegetated, many with impenetrable thickets of highly invasive tamarisk. On the more subtle side is the chain reaction that begins when sunlight penetrates clear water and nourishes algal growth (formerly limited in the murky river). The algae support a food chain that ascends to diatoms, then invertebrates and nonnative rainbow trout. Algae also soak up phosphorus, a critical nutrient that otherwise fuels aquatic diversity.

Harder to quantify is the daily swarm of helicopter and plane flights into the canyon. These may not directly harm plants and animals, aside from the noisy intrusion, but it's hard to argue that loud aircraft don't count as a form of pollution in this otherwise pristine wilderness. Another insidious consequence of planes, cars and factories is the pall of air pollution that frequently hovers over the canyon. It's a grim reminder of modern life to visit such a stupendous landscape and have to peer through smog as if you were still in the city. Perhaps it can serve as a gentle prod to reconsider choices we make in our everyday lives.

APPENDIX

General Grand Canyon Information

Grand Canyon National Park
☎ 928-638-7888
Ⓦ www.nps.gov/grca

Canyon View Visitor Center
☎ 928-638-7644

North Rim Visitor Center
☎ 928-638-7864

Grand Canyon North Rim
☎ 928-638-2612
Ⓦ www.grandcanyonnorthrim.com

Grand Canyon South Rim
☎ 928-638-2631
Ⓦ www.grandcanyonlodges.com

National Parks Pass Customer Support Center
☎ 888-467-2757
Ⓦ www.nps.gov

Medical Clinic
☎ 928-638-2552

Accommodations

Xanterra
☎ 303-297-2757, 888-297-2757
Ⓦ www.xanterra.com

Grand Canyon Lodge
☎ 928-638-2612
Ⓦ www.grandcanyonnorthrim.com

Grand Canyon Lodges, South Rim
☎ 928-638-2631
🅆 www.grandcanyonlodges.com

Havasupai Campground
☎ 928-448-2121

Havasupai Lodge
☎ 928-448-2111

National Park Service Campgrounds
☎ 800-365-2267
🅆 www.reservations.nps.gov

North Rim Backcountry Office
☎ 928-638-7868

South Rim Backcountry Office
☎ 928-638-7875

South Rim Kennels
☎ 928-638-0534

Transportation

Fred Harvey's 24-Hour Taxi
☎ 928-638-2822

Grand Canyon Coaches
☎ 928-638-0821

Grand Canyon Railway
☎ 800-843-8724
🅆 www.thetrain.com

Tour Operators

AirStar Helicopters
☎ 928-638-2623, 800-962-3869
🅆 www.airstar.com

American Dream Tours
☎ 928-527-3369
🅆 www.americandreamtours.com

Apache Stables
☎ 928-638-2891
🅆 www.apachestables.com

Air Grand Canyon
☎ 928-638-2686, 800-247-4726
🅆 www.airgrandcanyon.com

Grand Canyon Airlines
☎ 928-638-2407, 800-638-2407
🅆 www.grandcanyonairlines.com

Grand Canyon Field Institute
☎ 928-638-2485
Ⓦ www.grandcanyon.org/fieldinstitute

Grand Canyon Helicopters
☎ 928-638-2764, 800-541-4537
Ⓦ www.grandcanyonhelicoptersaz.com

Grand Canyon Tour Company
☎ 800-222-6966
Ⓦ www.grandcanyontourcompany.com

Grand Canyon Tours of Splendor
☎ 866-525-2675
Ⓦ www.grandcanyonsplendor.com

Havasupai Tourist Enterprise
☎ 928-448-2141
Ⓦ www.havasupaitribe.com

Hualapai Tribal Enterprises
☎ 928-769-2419
Ⓦ www.hualapaitours.com

Marvelous Marv's
☎ 928-635-1935, 800-655-4948
Ⓦ www.marvelousmarv.com

Museum of Northern Arizona
☎ 928-774-5211
Ⓦ www.musnaz.org

Open Road Tours
☎ 928-226-8060, 800-766-7117
Ⓦ www.openroadtours.com

Papillon Grand Canyon Helicopters
☎ 928-638-2419, 800-528-2418
Ⓦ www.papillon.com

Terry's Camera Trading Co
☎ 435-644-5981
Ⓦ www.utahcameras.com

Westwind Aviation
☎ 800-245-8668
Ⓦ www.westwindaviation.com

Activities

Ambassador Guide Services
☎ 800-256-7596
Ⓦ www.ambassadorguides.com

Apache Stables
☎ 928-638-2891
Ⓦ www.apachestables.com

Arizona River Runners
☎ 602-867-4866, 800-477-7238
Ⓦ www.raftarizona.com

Backroads
☎ 800-462-2848
Ⓦ www.backroads.com

Canyon Rim Adventures
☎ 800-897-9633
Ⓦ www.canyonrimadventures.com

Canyon Trail Rides
☎ 435-679-8665
Ⓦ www.canyonrides.com

Discovery Treks
☎ 888-256-8731
Ⓦ www.discoverytreks.com

Grand Canyon Dories
☎ 209-736-0805, 800-877-3679
Ⓦ www.oars.com/gcdories

Grand Canyon River Trip Information Center
☎ 928-638-7843, 800-959-9164
Ⓦ www.nps.gov/grca/river

High Sonoran Adventures
☎ 480-614-3331
Ⓦ www.hikethecanyon.com

Hualapai River Runners
☎ 928-769-2219, 888-255-9550
Ⓦ www.river-runners.com

Lees Ferry Anglers
☎ 928-355-2261, 800-962-9755
Ⓦ www.leesferry.com

Marble Canyon Outfitters
☎ 928-355-2245, 800-533-7330
Ⓦ www.mcg-leesferry.com

Mule Desk, North Rim
☎ 928-638-9875

Northern Arizona University Grand Canyon Semester
Ⓦ www.grandcanyonsemester.nau.edu

OARS
☎ 209-736-2924, 800-346-6277
Ⓦ www.oars.com

Outdoors Unlimited River Trips
☎ 928-526-4546, 800-637-7238
Ⓦ www.outdoorsunlimited.com

Sky Island Treks
☎ 520-622-6966
Ⓦ www.skyislandtreks.com

Useful Organizations

Environmental Education
Ⓦ www.nps.gov/grca/education

Grand Canyon Association
☎ 800-858-2828
Ⓦ www.grandcanyon.org

Grand Canyon National Park Foundation
☎ 928-774-1760
Ⓦ www.grandcanyonfoundation.org

Grand Canyon Trust
☎ 928-774-7488
Ⓦ www.grandcanyontrust.org

Beyond the Grand Canyon

Alan Bible Visitor Center (Lake Mead NRA)
☎ 702-293-8990
Ⓦ www.nps.gov/lame

Aramark
☎ 800-528-6154
Ⓦ www.lakepowell.com

Boulder City Chamber of Commerce
☎ 702-293-2034

Carl Hayden Visitor Center (Glen Canyon NRA)
☎ 928-608-6404
Ⓦ www.nps.gov/glca

Flagstaff Visitor Center
☎ 928-774-9541, 800-842-7293
Ⓦ www.flagstaff.az.us

Hoover Dam Visitor Center
☎ 702-293-8321
Ⓦ hooverdam.usbr.gov

Kaibab National Forest District Headquarters
☎ 928-643-7395

Kaibab Plateau Visitor Center
☎ 928-643-7298

Katherine Landing Visitor Center
☎ 928-754-3272

Navajo Bridge Interpretive Center
☎ 928-355-2319

Rainbow Bridge Monument
☎ 928-608-6404
Ⓦ www.nps.gov/glca

Sunset Crater National Monument
☎ 928-526-0502
Ⓦ www.nps.gov/sucr

Tusayan Ranger Station
☎ 928-638-2443
Ⓦ www.fs.fed.us/r3kai

Walnut Canyon National Monument
☎ 928-526-3367
W www.nps.gov/waca

Williams Visitor Center
☎ 928-635-4061
W www.visitwilliams.com

Wupatki National Monument
☎ 928-679-2365
W www.nps.gov/wupa

Maps

United States Geological Survey
☎ 888-275-8747
W www.usgs.gov

Grand Canyon National Park, Trails Illustrated/National Geographic

Bright Angel Trail Hiking Map & Guide, Earthwalk Press

Indian Country Guide Map, AAA

Recreational Map of Arizona, GTR Mapping

Kaibab National Forest: North Kaibab Ranger District

Kaibab National Forest: Tusayan, Williams & Chalender Ranger Districts

Public Land Information Map Center, W www.publiclands.org/mapcenter

Books

Lonely Planet's *Arizona*,
  by Rob Rachowiecki and Jennifer Rasin Denniston

Lonely Planet's *Southwest*,
  by Jeff Campbell, Rob Rachowiecki and Jennifer Rasin Denniston

101 Questions about Desert Life, by Alice Jablonsky.
  Tucson, AZ: Southwest Parks & Monuments Association, 1999.

Along the Rim: A Guide to Grand Canyon's South Rim from Hermits Rest to Desert View, by Michael F Anderson and Nancy J Loving.
  Grand Canyon, AZ: Grand Canyon Association, 2001.

American Indians: Answers to Today's Questions, by Jack Utter.
  Norman, OK: University of Oklahoma Press, 2002.

Beyond the Hundredth Meridian: John Wesley Powell & the Second Opening of the West, by Wallace Stegner.
  New York: Penguin, 1992.

Bicycling America's National Parks: Arizona and New Mexico: The Best Road and Trail Rides from the Grand Canyon to Carlsbad Caverns, by Sarah Alley.
  Woodstock, VT: Countryman Press, 2001.

Brighty of the Grand Canyon, by Marguerite Henry.
  New York: Rand McNally Press, 1952.

Building the National Park: Historic Landscape Design & Construction,
by Linda Flint McClelland.
Baltimore, MD: Johns Hopkins University Press, 1998.

Cadillac Desert: The American West & Its Disappearing Water, by Marc Reisner.
New York: Penguin Group Publisher, 1993.

Canyon, by Michael P Ghiglieri.
Tucson, AZ: University of Arizona Press, 1992.

Canyon Hiking Guide to the Colorado Plateau, by Michael Kelsey.
Provo, UT: Kelsey Publishers, 1999.

Cowboys, Miners, Presidents & Kings: Story of the Grand Canyon Railway, by Al Richmond.
Williams, AZ: Grand Canyon Railway, 1995.

Day Hikes from the River: A Guide to 100 Hikes from Camps on the Colorado River in Grand Canyon National Park, by Tom Martin.
Flagstaff, AZ: Vishnu Temple Press, 2002.

Exploring the Grand Canyon: Adventures of Yesterday & Today, by Lynne Foster.
Grand Canyon, AZ: Grand Canyon Association, 2003.

A Field Guide to the Grand Canyon, by Stephen Whitney.
Seattle: Mountaineers Books, 1996.

A Field Guide to the Plants of Arizona, by Anne Epple.
Helena, MT: Falcon Press, 1997.

Fun Guide to Exploring the Grand Canyon, by Larry Lindahl.
Grand Canyon, AZ: Grand Canyon Association, 2002.

Grand Canyon-Flagstaff Stagecoach Line: A History & Exploration Guide,
by Richard and Sherry Mangum.
Flagstaff, AZ: Hexagon Press, 1999.

Grand Canyon Geology, edited by Stanley S Beus and Michael Morales.
New York: Oxford University Press, 2003.

Grand Canyon River Guide, by Buzz Belknap.
Boulder City, NV: Westwater Books, 1995.

The Harvey Girls: Women Who Opened the West, by Lesley Poling-Kempes.
New York: Marlowe & Co, 1994.

How the Canyon Became Grand: A Short History, by Stephen J Pyne.
New York: Penguin, 1999.

In the House of Stone & Light: Introduction to the Human History of the Grand Canyon, by J Donald Hughes.
Grand Canyon, AZ: Grand Canyon Association, 2003.

An Introduction to Grand Canyon Ecology, by Rose Houk.
Grand Canyon, AZ: Grand Canyon Association, 2003.

An Introduction to Grand Canyon Geology, by L Greer Price.
Grand Canyon, AZ: Grand Canyon Association, 2003.

An Introduction to Grand Canyon Prehistory, by Christopher M Coder.
Grand Canyon, AZ: Grand Canyon Association, 2000.

I See Something Grand, by Mitzi Chandler.
Grand Canyon, AZ: Grand Canyon Association, 2003.

The Kolb Brothers of Grand Canyon: Being a Collection of Tales of High Adventure, Memorable Incidents & Humorous Anecdotes, by William C Suran.
Grand Canyon, AZ: Grand Canyon Association, 2003.

Life in a Narrow Place, by Stephen Hirst.
New York: David McKay Co, 1976.

Living at the Edge: Explorers, Exploiters & Settlers of the Grand Canyon Region, by Michael F Anderson.
Grand Canyon, AZ: Grand Canyon Association, 1998.

Mary Colter: Architect of the Southwest, by Arnold Berke.
New York: Princeton Architectural Press, 2002.

Mountain Biking Arizona, by Sarah Bennett.
Guilford, CT: Falcon, 1995.

A Naturalist's Guide to Canyon Country, by David B Williams.
Helena, MT: Falcon Press, 2001.

Navajo Rugs: The Essential Guide, by Don Dedera.
Flagstaff, AZ: Northland Publishing, 1996.

Over the Edge: Death in Grand Canyon, by Michael P Ghiglieri and Thomas M Myers.
Flagstaff, AZ: Puma Press, 2001.

People of the Blue Water: A Record of Life among the Walapai & Havasupai Indians, by Flora Greg Iliff.
Tucson, AZ: University of Arizona Press, 1985.

The Place No One Knew: Glen Canyon on the Colorado, by Eliot Porter.
Layton, UT: Gibbs Smith Publisher, 2000.

Polishing the Jewel: An Administrative History of Grand Canyon National Park, by Michael F Anderson.
Grand Canyon, AZ: Grand Canyon Association, 2001.

Puzzler's Guide to the Grand Canyon, by Kristy McGowan and Karen Richards.
Boulder, CO: Puzzler's Guides, 2002.

A River Runner's Guide to the History of the Grand Canyon, by Kim Crumbo.
Boulder, CO: Johnson Books, 1994.

A Story That Stands Like a Dam: Glen Canyon & the Struggle for the Soul of the West, by Russell Martin.
Salt Lake City: University of Utah Press, 1999.

Sunk Without a Sound: The Tragic Colorado River Honeymoon of Glen & Bessie Hyde, by Brad Dimock.
Flagstaff, AZ: Fretwater Press, 2001.

There's This River: Grand Canyon Boatman Stories, edited by Christa Sadler.
Flagstaff, AZ: Red Lake Books, 1997.

Wild Plants & Native Peoples of the Four Corners, by William W Dunmire and Gail D Tierney.
Albuquerque, NM: Museum of New Mexico, 1997.

Bookstores

The park's primary bookstore is at Canyon View Plaza, on the South Rim.

Books & More Store
☎ 928-638-0199
Ⓦ www.grandcanyon.org

Northern Arizona University Bookstore
☎ 928-523-6673
Ⓦ www.bookstore@nau.edu

INDEX

PLACES TO STAY

PLACES TO STAY

PLACES TO EAT

PLACES TO EAT

ANNOUNCING
BANFF, JASPER &
GLACIER NATIONAL PARKS

NEW TITLE

Banff, Jasper & Glacier National Parks

1 74059 562 9
Available March 2004
296 pp, 8 pp color, 25 maps
US$19.99 | UK£12.99
Korina Miller, Susan Derby
& David Lukas

Paddle the turquoise waters of glacier-fed lakes, snowshoe through fresh powder and melt into soothing hot springs. Glimpse elk and bighorn sheep along the highest road in North America. Enjoy night stars from a backcountry campsite or the deck of a posh resort. Our comprehensive, inspiring guide to Banff, Jasper & Glacier will help you connect with this stunning region.

- GET BUSY – you're spoiled for choice with skiing, hiking, biking, mountain climbing, white-water rafting, horse-back riding and canoeing
- KID AROUND – recommended activities, restaurants, lodgings and cultural events for the whole family
- DELVE DEEPER – explore the less-touristed Waterton Lakes, Yoho and Kootenay National Parks
- ESCAPE THE CROWDS – insider tips on finding high-season solitude
- LEARN MORE – insightful chapters provide background on the history, geology and ecosystem of the Canadian Rocky Mountains